McKinley, Murder
and the Pan-American
Exposition

McKinley, Murder and the Pan-American Exposition

A History of the Presidential Assassination, September 6, 1901

ROGER PICKENPAUGH

McFarland & Company, Inc., Publishers

Jefferson, North Carolina

LIBRARY OF CONGRESS CATALOGUING-IN-PUBLICATION DATA

Names: Pickenpaugh, Roger, author.
Title: McKinley, murder and the Pan-American Exposition : a history of
the presidential assassination, September 6, 1901 / Roger Pickenpaugh.
Description: Jefferson, North Carolina : McFarland & Company, Inc.,
Publishers, 2016. | Includes bibliographical references and index.
Identifiers: LCCN 2016026694 | ISBN 9781476666303 (softcover : acid
free paper) ∞
Subjects: LCSH: McKinley, William, 1843–1901—Assassination. |
Czolgosz, Leon F., 1873?–1901. | Pan-American Exposition (1901 :
Buffalo, N.Y.)
Classification: LCC E711.9 .P53 2016 | DDC 973.8/8092—dc23
LC record available at https://lccn.loc.gov/2016026694

BRITISH LIBRARY CATALOGUING DATA ARE AVAILABLE

ISBN (print) 978-1-4766-6630-3
ISBN (ebook) 978-1-4766-2591-1

Front cover: William McKinley delivering his last address, Buffalo,
New York, September 5, 1901 (Library of Congress)

Printed in the United States of America

McFarland & Company, Inc., Publishers
Box 611, Jefferson, North Carolina 28640
www.mcfarlandpub.com

To Jill

Table of Contents

Acknowledgments

A project of this sort produces a number of debts. As with so many other projects, my greatest debt is to my wife, Marion. She accompanied me on a number of research trips, served as a skilled proofreader, and once again assumed the tedious task of preparing the index. Her only request was a simple one. After our first visit to Buffalo, in May, and encountering snow flurries, she informed me that my next book had better be set in the Virgin Islands.

My mother, Fern Pickenpaugh, again served as a proofreader and supporter.

Having two stepdaughters and sons-in-law in northern Virginia made research trips to Washington, D.C., a blessing. Thanks again to Mike and Anya Huie and Jocelyn and Patrick Brooks, as well as grandchildren Parker Dianne and Patrick Harrison Brooks.

Locally, members of the Noble County Authors' Guild acted as skilled proofreaders and much needed supporters. Thanks to Jim Leeper, Mary Lou Podlasiak, Gary Williams, and Ken Williams. Noble County, Ohio, prosecuting attorney Kelly Riddle read the entire manuscript. Her comments on the Czolgosz trial were especially helpful. Likewise, Dr. Rick Nelson of The Ohio State University Hospital offered incisive comments on medical aspects of the work. John Schockling provided numerous comments, particularly on the Exposition's agricultural displays. Professor Kim Fuller of Plains, Georgia, offered a number of incisive comments, as did Dr. Evan Kutzler, a recent Ph.D. graduate from the University of South Carolina.

Librarians and archivists, of course, make any work of history possible. First and foremost for this one was Cynthia Van Ness, director of library and archives at the Buffalo History Museum. Her patience, professionalism, and courtesy were most appreciated. Thanks to her, my eight trips to Buffalo were all productive. Early on, I also appreciated the skilled assistance of Sara Lawrence, who for some reason deserted Buffalo for the Pacific coast.

I also made a number of trips to the Buffalo and Erie County Public

Library. There I enjoyed the able help of Amy Pickard, Carol Pijacki, Rhonda Konig, and Franklin Clendening.

At the National Archives II in College Park, Maryland, Jason Staton helped me out with manuscript materials. Holly Reed and Carla Simms did the same in the photographic section.

Closer to home, Karl Ash and Mark G. Holland provided valuable assistance at the William McKinley Presidential Library & Museum in Canton. It is a wonderful facility, and I would urge anyone planning to visit the Pro Football Hall of Fame to work in a side trip a few blocks away.

Much of the time spent in writing this book took place in Houston. While there I enjoyed the help of Sandi Edwards, head of reference services at the Fondren Library at Rice University.

As they have so many times in the past, the staff of the Muskingum University Library made this book possible. During the research process, my main inter-library loan contact person, Zelda Patterson, retired. This made her nervous, but Zelda's successor, Connie Burke, proved to be a capable successor. Thanks also to Jamie Berilla and Nicole Robinson.

Preface

On the afternoon of September 6, 1901, President William McKinley entered the garish, multicolored Temple of Music at Buffalo's Pan-American Exposition. A veteran politician, he instinctively walked straight to the spot where he was to receive the public at a long planned reception. The popular chief executive, re-elected overwhelmingly ten months earlier, was looking forward to the event. He genuinely enjoyed meeting with his constituents, and he treasured the smiles he encountered as he shook their hands.

Among those not looking forward to the reception was George Cortelyou, McKinley's personal secretary. Loyal, efficient, and protective, Cortelyou was worried about the wide-open nature of the receiving line. A number of world leaders had recently been assassinated by members of a growing anarchist movement. Twice Cortelyou had attempted to remove the reception from the president's Buffalo schedule. Twice his boss had reinserted it.

McKinley would have been wise to have heeded his secretary's concerns. Among those waiting in line to enter the Temple was a troubled young man named Leon Czolgosz. A native of Michigan and son of immigrant parents, Czolgosz had worked at a variety of factory jobs. Over time he had become disillusioned with American capitalism and his Roman Catholic faith. A few months earlier he had attended a lecture by Emma Goldman, a prominent anarchist widely known as "Red Emma." Young Leon became infatuated with both her and her beliefs, although the proportions are difficult to determine.

Czolgosz came armed with a .32-caliber revolver he had recently purchased after arriving in Buffalo. He concealed it with a handkerchief; and since the day was very hot, the presence of the handkerchief did not raise any flags among the president's small protective detail. Indeed, an individual who appeared to be an Italian aroused more suspicion, simply because of his dark, "foreign" appearance.

For McKinley and Czolgosz, the paths to Buffalo were divergent. The president had enjoyed a life of opportunities, and with the help of personal ability, ambition, and hard work, he had taken advantage of them. For the immigrant Czolgosz, the opportunities had been less numerous, though not entirely non-existent. He had become deeply suspicious of the industrial America that McKinley embraced, and he had come to disdain the captains of industry who were the president's staunchest supporters.

Buffalo and its exposition were more in step with McKinley's views. The eighth largest city in America, Buffalo had emerged as a major industrial center, a factory town whose growth was supported by the protective tariffs the president famously espoused. The fair was accurately billed as a celebration of Western Hemisphere unity and friendship. Yet at the same time it was also celebrating American industrial might, specifically the potential that electrical transmission, pioneered at nearby Niagara Falls, held for America's manufacturing future. Over one hundred thousand low wattage bulbs outlined the Exposition's gaudy structures, giving evening visitors an overwhelming view of the potential of the new power source.

It was a diverse convergence that took place at Buffalo, and it presaged many of the triumphs and tensions that would mark the "American Century" then dawning. In McKinley was the personification of the marriage between industrialization and conservative politics. Czolgosz represented the doubts that would emerge about that marriage, particularly as they related to the treatment of the working men and women who became cogs in the industrial machine. Waiting in the wings was Vice President Theodore Roosevelt, who would eventually lend a certain respectability to Czolgosz's skeptical views of industrial society.

Even the Exposition, where the drama ultimately unfolded, reflected the paradoxical aspects of the developing Twentieth Century America. Its displays celebrated the country's burgeoning industrial output. Its buildings, starting with those "harshly" colored and leading to soft pastels, supposedly represented the triumph of "civilization" over "savagery." But the implication of this reflected the racism still prevalent at the time. Indeed, Buffalo's black leaders had to fight to have a "negro exhibit," showcasing the accomplishments of American blacks, included at the fair. And Buffalo's working men, flexing the muscles of America's nascent labor movement, struck for higher wages as they constructed the "Rainbow City" that was to become the Pan-American Exposition.

These contradictory stories play out in the pages that follow. So, too, does the story of Buffalo's growth. Also included is the War of the Standards, the sometimes savage battle between Thomas Edison, on one side, and George Westinghouse and Nikola Tesla, on the other, over whether direct current or alternating current should become America's accepted method of delivering electrical power.

All of these plots and personalities led to Buffalo on that fateful September day. The pages that follow detail them, the story of a beloved president, that of a would-be assassin, and that of a city eager to showcase the triumphs of industrial America and its role therein.

1

McKinley: A Career of Opportunities

For good or ill, war has shaped—and often defined—a number of generations of Americans. So it was with William McKinley and his contemporaries. Born in Niles, Ohio, on January 29, 1843, McKinley arrived at the younger end of what was to become the Civil War generation.

William was the seventh of nine children born to William and Nancy Allison McKinley. The families of both his parents had been in America since the early 1700s, and both of the boy's grandfathers had served in the American Revolution. Like so many thousands of others, the McKinleys and the Allisons had made their way westward from Pennsylvania to Ohio. William McKinley, Sr., owned or rented anywhere from two to four iron furnaces in the Mahoning Valley. The income kept his family fed and clothed, but provided little more. His wife devoted herself to her children, whom she raised with full measures of discipline and affection, and to the Niles Methodist Church, where she and her sister served as caretakers and faithful members.[1]

Although his education had been limited, William, Sr., enjoyed reading. He kept a small collection of books and subscribed to monthly magazines. Both parents stressed education, and, realizing the tiny hamlet of Niles could not provide it, they moved their family to nearby Poland, where there was a high school, in 1852. Young William fished, swam, became adept with a bow and arrow, and flew kites. But academics quickly became a priority. "He was always studying, studying, studying, studying all the time," a friend would later recall. As time went on he became especially skilled at public speaking, taking part in local debating societies. His mother, so devoted to the church, had charted for him a life in the ministry. He inherited her piety, making a public profession of faith at age ten, but his career path would follow a different course.[2]

As William grew, the slave controversy in the United States was pushing all other political issues to the side. According to one of his teachers, the youth had strong feelings on the subject. "Practically, the McKinleys were very strong abolitionists, and William early imbibed very radical views regarding the enslavement of the colored race," his mother recalled. He would visit a tannery, owned and largely operated by Democrats, and engage in "warm" but friendly discussions of the subject.[3]

In Washington, D.C., discussions on slavery and its expansion became much warmer and much less friendly as the 1850s ended. Dred Scott, John Brown, and Uncle Tom became household names as the country rushed toward civil war. The tipping point came in 1860 when the Republican Party elected its first president, Abraham Lincoln. Lincoln was not an abolitionist. He did not call for the outlawing of slavery in the states where it existed, but he did adamantly favor keeping the institution out of all federal territories in the West. The South did not appreciate the distinction, and in December 1860, its states began leaving the Union. For the next four months, as the country dissolved by pieces, Americans North and South, watched and wondered if the dissolution would be a peaceful one.

It would not. On April 12, 1861, as United States Navy ships attempted to provision Fort Sumter, a U.S. garrison in Charleston Harbor, the Confederates opened fire from the shore. Although a strong case could be made that Lincoln had maneuvered the South into war, none of that mattered at the time. The flag had been fired upon, and a wave of patriotism swept the North, replete with rallies that led tens of thousands of young men to enlist. One such meeting was held in Poland, and William McKinley, age eighteen, attended with his cousin, Will Osborne. Many of the young men there rushed to sign up. McKinley and Osborne did not, choosing instead to give the matter more rational deliberation. "It was done," Osborne later observed, "as McKinley has done the most things in his life, as the logical offspring of careful conclusion." The result, however, was the same. Enlistment, the pair determined, was their duty. On June 6, 1861, William McKinley left home, a private with the Poland Guards.[4]

Their destination was Camp Chase, a training camp located about four miles west of Columbus. It was there that the Poland Guards were mustered in, becoming part of the Twenty-Third Ohio Volunteer Infantry. The outfit was at first commanded by Col. William S. Rosecrans, with Rutherford B. Hayes serving as a major. (James A. Garfield was also at Camp Chase, the lieutenant colonel of the Forty-Second OVI.) It had to be a strange environment for the Poland teenager. However, one fellow recruit remembered that McKinley "took to soldiering naturally," learning military texts with "scarcely an effort." The pious youth also avoided the secular temptations of military life, or at least most of them. He did not drink, but he did develop an affinity for cigars. Following a Sunday worship service he wrote in his diary, "All day I felt the love of God in my heart and notwithstanding the surroundings there was an inward calmness and tranquility which belongs to the Christian alone."[5]

In late July the Twenty-Third departed Camp Chase for service in western Virginia. They traveled by rail to Clarksburg, followed by a two-day march to Weston, where the unit was first stationed. Guarding bridges and similar unexciting duties in various communities made up the men's days until September 10, when the outfit received its baptism of fire at the Battle of Carnifax Ferry. The Twenty-Third played little part in the fight, coming away with just two men wounded. After it was over McKinley encountered the Tenth Ohio, which had fared much worse. Describing the sounds of the wounded, he wrote, "The sighs and groans were pitiable."[6]

Despite limited action, McKinley's military demeanor was attracting the attention of his superiors, particularly Hayes, who would become a mentor and lifelong friend. Advancement quickly followed. After serving as clerk to the brigade quartermaster, he became commissary sergeant of the Twenty-Third in March 1862. The assignment made him responsible for the care and feeding of several hundred soldiers.

In the late summer of 1862, Gen. Robert E. Lee, buoyed by a series of victories while fighting on the defensive in Virginia, led his Confederate Army north. McKinley's regiment was assigned to the Army of the Potomac, charged with stopping Lee. On September 14 the Twenty-Third took part in the Battle of South Mountain, losing thirty-two killed and ninety-five wounded.

Three days later, along Antietam Creek and adjacent to Sharpsburg, Maryland, came a much bigger fight, the bloodiest day of the entire war. McKinley and his comrades were posted on the Union left, far from the initial action. During the mid-morning hours, as part of the Ninth Corps, they were ordered to put pressure on the Confederate right to prevent Lee from reinforcing his beleaguered left and center. The corps commander, Gen. Ambrose Burnside, foolishly focused on a stone bridge instead of the fordable creek, resulting in heavy casualties and no progress. After several wasted hours, his men finally established a beachhead on the other side of the bridge. They began an advance toward Sharpsburg but soon came under fire from Gen. A. P. Hill's Confederate division, the last of Lee's forces to reach the battlefield that day.

The supply train had not arrived before the battle began, and the men had taken their positions at 2:00 a.m. with no rations. Now it was 2:00 p.m. McKinley was the acting brigade commissary officer, and he was determined to get his regiment fed. On his own, the sergeant went two miles behind the lines, recruited stragglers to assist him, and loaded a wagon with food and coffee. Then, with a volunteer assistant in tow, McKinley headed the wagon toward the sounds of musketry and cannon. Two officers ordered him to turn the wagon around, orders the normally obedient soldier chose to ignore. They continued through several volleys of infantry fire and had the back end of the wagon removed by a small piece of shot, but they made it, to the cheers of the hungry men.[7]

After Antietam McKinley's division was ordered back to western Virginia. This spared both Hayes and McKinley the horrors of Fredericksburg, Chancellorsville, and Gettysburg, perhaps changing the course of history. The sergeant first returned to Ohio to recruit for the Twenty-Third, depleted by disease and battle. He also worked in a visit home. When he headed back to Virginia it was as a second lieutenant, a promotion recommended by his regimental commander and approved by Governor David Tod, for his bravery at Antietam. Although normally stoic, McKinley was, according to his sister, "bubbling with enthusiasm" over the promotion. Lieutenant McKinley had a new assignment as well. As brigade quartermaster he was responsible for all the unit's supplies—and a mountain of paperwork.[8]

A series of raids and skirmishes marked McKinley's next several months in the army. Returning from one such operation, the men were joined by a number of fugitive slaves. A comrade was impressed watching McKinley help a woman over several ditches and carrying one of the children for at least a mile. Although he did not again participate in a battle like Antietam, the young lieutenant saw action at Kernstown, Virginia, on July 24, 1864. At one point in the fight Hayes sent him to the front to order a regimental commander to withdraw. He did so under heavy infantry and artillery fire. On September 19, at the Battle of Opequon, McKinley was ordered to ride forward and determine if a force of cavalry was Union or Confederate. They were the latter, and on their hasty retreat, the lieutenant's orderly was killed.[9]

McKinley advanced to captain by the time the war ended. In July 1865, just before being mustered out, he learned that he had received a brevet promotion to major. He was proud of the title and held on to it for the rest of his life. After he was elected president a former comrade asked McKinley how he should address him, explaining that he had known him as a soldier, a congressman, a governor, and now president-elect. "Call me major," McKinley responded. "I earned that. I am not so sure of the rest."[10]

Indeed, he had become so enamored of the service that the major applied for an appointment as captain in the regular army. His superiors endorsed the application, and a board of examination approved him. His father, however, disapproved of the appointment. The son listened, likely saving himself a postwar career of remote assignments and slow promotions. McKinley was home, and he was twenty-two.[11]

The youthful veteran quickly decided on a career in law, although politics was likely in the back of his mind. McKinley began studying under a Poland attorney, who recognized his ability and encouraged him to further his legal education. In September 1866 he left for Albany Law School in New York. There he often attended the theater and parties but, as always, devoted himself to his studies. His time there was brief. In March 1867 McKinley returned home and was admitted to the bar in Warren, Ohio. Later that year he moved to Canton to begin his practice. George W. Belden, a prominent Canton attorney, noticed him and made him a partner. Belden was easing himself out of the profession, and McKinley enjoyed the fruits of a prosperous practice.

Gradually he worked his way into politics, first as a speaker supporting Republican candidates. In 1868 Gen. Ulysses S. Grant sought the presidency, and McKinley began organizing Grant Clubs in the Canton area. He also became chairman of Stark County's Republican Central Committee. The next year the ambitious attorney threw his hat into the ring, running for county prosecutor. Democrats generally won local elections, but not this one. Two years later, when the GOP renominated McKinley, the Democrats redoubled their efforts, anxious to defeat a potential rising Republican star. They succeeded. McKinley lost by 143 votes.[12]

Despite his ambition, McKinley did not live by politics alone. He joined the local Grand Army of the Republic post and several fraternal organizations and became Sunday school superintendent at the Methodist church. Soon friends noticed that McKinley was also frequenting a local bank much more than his finances required. The reason was personal, not financial. The cashier at the bank was Miss Ida Saxton, daughter of the bank's owner, James Saxton. Like McKinley's parents, Mr. Saxton was a firm believer in education, sending his daughter to a Pennsylvania seminary and, rare at the time, allowing her to enter the working world. The two were soon a couple, a friend noticing that, "Ida was tense when he was not with her." Their wedding took place on January 25, 1871, in Canton's Presbyterian Church. Mr. Saxton gave them a house on Market Street. The home would one day include the most famous front porch in America.[13]

On Christmas Day 1871 Ida gave birth to a daughter, Katherine, "Katie" to her father. Over time Ida became possessive of the child. She never let her go out alone, and she fretted when McKinley took her for a ride. A second daughter, Ida, was born on April 1, 1873, a date that proved cruelly ironic. She was "sickly" from birth and died on August 22. Her mother would never

During their honeymoon in January–February 1871, Ida and William McKinley had these portraits taken in New York (used by permission from McKinley Presidential Library & Museum, Canton, Ohio).

be the same. She "became short tempered" and "spent days in bed." Then, on June 25, 1875, Katie died of typhoid fever. The McKinleys' happiness, already made tenuous as a house of cards, came crashing down. From then on any strength Ida possessed came from her husband, and she clung tenaciously to him. He gave up walking and riding and limited his working hours to be by her side. Concern for his fragile wife would be his dominant emotion for the rest of his life. In the eyes of Julia Foraker, wife of Ohio politician Joseph Foraker, a friend and occasional rival of McKinley's, "Her husband [was] a shield between her and reality, [and it] made of her a pathetically spoiled and difficult woman."[14]

Next to Ida, the most important person in McKinley's life was Cleveland businessman Mark Hanna. It is not clear when the two men first met, likely during the early 1870s at one of the myriad social events mandatory for the man of business and the man of politics. They were thrust together in 1876 in the wake of a violent coal mine strike in Ohio's Tuscarawas Valley. At the request of local authorities, McKinley's former commanding officer, Gov.

Rutherford B. Hayes, reluctantly sent in the militia. The strike was broken, and a group of miners was arrested for disorderly conduct. After learning that no local lawyer would represent them in court, McKinley accepted their case *pro bono*. He presented their side of the matter thoroughly and unemotionally. In the end only one of his clients was convicted. Labor would never forget.

Neither would Mark Hanna. Although he was among the mine owners, Hanna was impressed with McKinley's dignified and efficient presentation. Unlike most Gilded Age entrepreneurs, Hanna had earned a reputation for fairness—and even sympathy—toward his workers, and it is likely that the outcome disturbed him far less than it did his fellow operators.

Whatever the reasons, a deep and lasting friendship emerged from the courtroom drama. Politically the two men were almost completely in synch. Both favored the benchmark Republican planks of economic protectionism, the gold standard, and, up to a point, support of business. In terms of personality, the two men complimented each other. Hanna brought to the table a talent for organization and a strong, driving temperament. McKinley had drive as well, but he tempered it with tact and a tendency toward careful deliberation. These traits led some to mischaracterize the relationship between the two men. Henry L. Stoddard once observed that McKinley "had the conservatism of his Scotch-Irish ancestry, overlaid with a deep veneer of kindness which many took for weakness." Indeed, in later years political opponents would paint Hanna as a Machiavellian puppet master, with McKinley naively jumping at the other end of the string. Gradually the stereotype stuck in many quarters. Subsequent historians have determined otherwise, as did contemporaries who knew both men well. Although McKinley recognized and appreciated Hanna's talents and left many organizational details to his friend, there was no doubt as to who was the senior partner. The journalist H. H. Kohlsaat would recall, "There is an impression that Mark Hanna controlled William McKinley. That is not so. [Hanna's] attitude was always that of a big, bashful boy toward a girl he loves."[15]

In 1876 Rutherford B. Hayes was the Republican candidate for president. The election was razor close—his opponent, Charles Tilden, took the popular vote—but when a federal commission awarded the contested electoral votes of three Southern states to Hayes, he prevailed by one vote. Although the victory was controversial, Hayes entered the White House knowing he would have at least one staunch ally on Capitol Hill. McKinley had decided to run for Congress. In August the thirty-four-year old defeated three challengers at the district convention to take his party's nomination. In the general election he stressed the tariff issue, insisting that high duties protected jobs as well as aiding business interests. Apparently a majority of voters agreed with the Canton lawyer. He won by 3,300 votes.[16]

McKinley's views on protection were both strongly and sincerely held. They went back to his childhood days, when he heard his father complain of cheap foreign iron competing unfairly with his business. As an adult he grew to believe that American industry could not yet challenge foreign competitors. Still, he asserted, "It is labor I would protect." There is little reason to doubt his sincerity. As a member of Congress his first act was to present a petition from steelworkers in his district opposing any reduction of the tariff, the first of many he would offer.[17]

In 1878 McKinley faced a tough campaign for re-election, thanks to Democrats in the state legislature, who, weary of the popular upstart, gerrymandered his district. Despite the opposition's machinations, he prevailed by just over 1,200 votes. Two years later his majority was 3,572. As he solidified his position with the voters, McKinley was also strengthening his role in the House. In 1880 fellow Ohioan James Garfield left the body to run for president. This opened a vacancy on the important Ways and Means Committee. Garfield recommended McKinley, and he received the coveted spot.[18]

When in the capital, the McKinleys lived at the Ebbitt House in a suite of two rooms. One served as the representative's office, the other as a bedroom. Virtually all of their time in the city was spent there, Ida's illness keeping them away from most social affairs. Headaches and what were apparently epileptic attacks, along with severe colds, became the pattern of her life. Although the degree of severity varied, she was never totally well. During his time in the House, McKinley employed a personal maid, who never left her side during his working hours.[19]

Although he was always solicitous of his wife's needs, McKinley did not put aside his ambitions and return to the less strenuous life of a Canton barrister. When he sought re-election in 1884, he easily achieved it, despite the fact that Democrat Grover Cleveland was elected president, the first member of his party to win the office since 1856. In December 1887 Cleveland devoted his entire annual message to tariff reform, citing a treasury surplus he felt was unfair to taxpayers. Congressional Democrats followed his lead by introducing a bill that would sharply reduce rates. This was heresy to McKinley and most of his fellow Republicans. On May 18, 1888, the Ohio representative delivered a strong speech against the measure. He criticized the bill's potential to destroy American firms, for including nothing for farmers, and for lowering wages of workingmen. All of this reasoning went for naught when the bill passed the Democratic House. It later died in the Senate.

McKinley's peroration on the tariff only enhanced his prestige, particularly among members of the GOP. At the 1888 Republican Convention in Chicago he was briefly considered as a compromise candidate for president. He and Hanna had pledged their support to Ohio senator John Sherman, and McKinley promptly squelched the movement. "I do not request—I demand, that no delegate who would not cast reflection upon me shall cast a ballot for me," he told the assembly. His forthright statement brought forth an enthusiastic outburst of applause. Benjamin Harrison ended up being the nominee, and in November he defeated Cleveland. The Republicans also regained control of the House. McKinley was considered for speaker of the house, but he lost to the able, irascible, and sarcastic Thomas B. Reed of Maine. However, he ended up with a significant consolation prize, the chairmanship of the Ways and Means Committee, making him the key player in any tariff legislation. In the position, he worked well with Reed, calming members the speaker had offended with his sharp tongue.[20]

In 1890 Congress, by strict party line votes, passed a measure that came to be known as the McKinley Tariff, his crowning legislative achievement. McKinley had risen, and by the standards of the nineteenth century congress, risen quickly. His future in politics seemed bright, but then, two years after winning his sixth term in Congress, he failed to win a seventh.

There were two main reasons for his defeat. One was his landmark tariff bill. Its high duties on tin imports were unpopular with consumers. Democrats drove home the point during the campaign by paying peddlers to sell household goods at inflated prices and put the blame on the law. A more significant factor was Ohio's Democratic state legislature, which had again gerrymandered McKinley's district. The redistricting forced the veteran congressman to face a Democratic majority of three thousand in the general election. He entered the contest with his usual determination and a generally hopeful attitude. But it was not enough. The Election of 1890 was a Democratic landslide, producing a House majority of 236 to 88. McKinley was among those swept away—though just barely. He lost by 300 votes.[21]

In defeat McKinley's friends and advisors saw opportunity. Ohio would elect a governor in 1891, and they believed the office would be his for the asking. On a practical level, the post was barely worth having. Ohio's constitution at the time guaranteed a weak chief executive, one who could not even veto bills. Yet on a political level, there were few better places to be than in the Buckeye State's governor's office. The office brought with it a high level of prominence, making its occupant an automatic leader of not just the state but the national party as well.

Ohio politics of the late 1800s were fractious and complicated. Before McKinley made up his mind, he wanted to make sure that he had the support of rival Republican Joseph Foraker and his followers. When Foraker agreed to place his name in nomination at the state party convention, McKinley went forward. He secured the nomination unopposed and waged an intensive campaign, speaking all around the state. The effort paid off. McKinley defeated his opponent, incumbent governor James Campbell, by twenty thousand votes. A substantial Republican majority in Ohio's General Assembly promised harmony.[22]

The new governor delivered his inaugural address on January 11, 1892. It included such diverse topics as Ohio's exhibit at the upcoming World's Colombian Exposition in Chicago and a report on the Buckeye State's canal system. As governor the man most closely associated with high tariffs pushed through the state legislature a series of new laws to aid labor. It became illegal for employers to prevent their workers from joining a union. Other measures required automatic couplers and other safety devices to protect railroad and streetcar workers. McKinley also guided an arbitration bill through the general assembly, making Ohio just the second state to establish a board to settle labor-management disputes. Behind the scenes the governor aided the board by wringing concessions from union and business leaders, both of whom trusted him.[23]

In January 1895 a delegation of union officials from the Hocking Valley coal fields appeared at McKinley's office with a shocking report. Miners in the region, out of work for months, were facing destitution. Many were on the verge of starvation. The governor alerted the Columbus Board of Trade, and a carload of provisions was soon on its way to Nelsonville. One at a time, McKinley called on Ohio's other major cities for assistance, and the relief effort continued for the remainder of the winter. State officials made monetary contributions, topped by a one hundred dollar donation from the chief executive. McKinley would report that Ohioans had donated over thirty-five thousand dollars in money and provisions and aided 2,722 families.[24]

Ohio had no governor's mansion at the time, so, as was the case in the nation's capital, the McKinleys lived in a suite of rooms at the Chittendon House, a downtown Columbus hotel. When the hostelry burned, they relocated to the Neil House. Ida remained his priority, her condition his main concern. As first lady of Ohio her health improved somewhat. She turned to crocheting, reportedly producing several thousand pairs of bedroom slippers. She gave most of them to children, whose company she cherished. Every afternoon at three the governor opened a window in his office and waved a handkerchief in the direction of the Neil House. Shortly an answering flutter would reply. The other lady in the governor's life, Mother McKinley, occasionally traveled to Columbus by train to see her son. Despite his prominence, she retained her unwavering stoicism. Asked once by a fellow passenger if she had relatives in Columbus, she replied simply, "Yes, I have a son there."[25]

In 1892 there was a McKinley presidential boomlet at the GOP convention. The governor neither encouraged it nor acted to quell it. Hanna pushed the effort behind the scenes, but the Republicans ended up renominating Harrison, who went on to lose his rematch with Grover Cleveland. The Democratic victory, combined with McKinley's strong, albeit dark horse, showing at the Republican convention appeared to set up the Ohioan as the party front-runner for 1896. Even geography favored him. In the fourteen presidential elections spanning 1868 and 1920, the Republicans nominated Ohioans ten times. Eight of them won, Harrison in 1892 and Taft in 1912 being the exceptions. And while none were spectacular and few were even competent—Grant and Harding, after all, bracketed the Buckeye contingent in the White House—Republicans kept handing the nomination to Ohioans. McKinley certainly appeared to be next in line.

Then came 1893, the year a depression struck the country, and an event that threatened to obliterate whatever hopes McKinley may have harbored for the presidency. It was February, and the governor was on a train bound for New York. At Buffalo, sadly ironic as future events would prove, the train stopped, and McKinley received a telegram. Robert Walker, an old friend, had failed in business in Youngstown. His notes, many countersigned by McKinley, were being called in.

McKinley had signed the paper naively. When Walker gave him new notes to sign, he had accepted his friend's word that they were renewals and not new notes. What McKinley believed amounted to only a few thousand dollars turned out to be a debt exceeding $100,000. The governor returned to Ohio, where friends had gathered at the Cleveland home of Myron Herrick, an Ohio politician and close friend. Hanna, away on business, rushed home. The men quickly agreed on a plan. Hanna, Herrick, and a few other confidants became trustees of McKinley's property, assuming the responsibility for payment of the notes. Surreptitiously, the men solicited funds from wealthy friends, who gave generously and lifted the governor from his obligations.

The main threat was not financial but political. After all, could a man who had so bungled his personal finances really be qualified for the presidency? To that question the people gave a surprising answer. Rather than being critical, the public responded with sympathy and understanding. They respected McKinley's forthright statements accepting responsibility. Rather than viewing him as a fool, they saw him as a man who had aided a friend only to become, like so many others, the victim of a severe depression. "I am receiving an excessive mail and so full of comfort," the governor wrote to

Herrick. The crises, both financial and political, had passed, and McKinley's path to the presidency again seemed clear.[26]

In 1893 Ohioans returned their governor to office with an eighty thousand-vote majority. The next year McKinley introduced himself to voters outside the state with an extensive speaking tour. The country had fallen into a severe depression, and President Cleveland was being blamed. Republicans saw an opportunity to return to power, and their candidates believed the popular governor could help. He did his best, delivering 371 speeches in sixteen states, speaking to an estimated two million people. Along the way he impressed party leaders at the state and local levels, forging important connections as he looked ahead two years. The election results were overwhelming, producing the largest transfer of congressional power in American political history. The Democrats lost 113 House seats, and the Republicans gained 117. GOP fortunes, so gloomy just two years before, now shone brightly.

In January 1896 McKinley's second term as governor ended, and he returned home to Canton. For the first time in two decades, excepting the year following his congressional loss, he did not hold political office. In welcoming the ex-governor home, the *Canton Repository* observed, "It is just plain Mr. McKinley of Canton, now; but wait a little while."[27]

2

Czolgosz: "A dreamer,
always a dreamer"

In 1872 Paul Czolgosz left Prussia for the United States, arriving on New Year's Day 1873. He was one of many Polish Catholics fleeing persecution at the hands of Chancellor Otto von Bismarck. Paul's destination was Detroit. A brother had preceded him to the Michigan city, writing that jobs were plentiful there. Paul quickly secured both work and lodgings and soon sent for his wife, Mary, and their three children. She arrived in May, and the couple's fourth child, Leon, was born just one month later.[1]

Leon Czolgosz was not destined to have the same opportunities that William McKinley did. For one thing, the arrangement of letters in his last name ruled out the presidency—or virtually any other elected office above the municipal level—in nineteenth century America. He did, however, arrive in a land of opportunity, where his chances for success were greater than they would have been in the homeland he never saw.

After the assassination of McKinley, Dr. Walter Channing, a respected Boston area psychologist, determined to investigate Czolgosz's background in a search for answers. He sent an underling, Dr. Lloyd Vernon Briggs, whose notes, located at the Massachusetts Historical Society, are invaluable in researching the life of the assassin. Neighbors told Briggs that they remembered Paul Czolgosz as "foxy," a talented story-teller, a card player who gambled on occasion, and a moderate drinker. They also agreed that he was a hard working laborer, indeed that all the Czolgoszes were "a hard working family of farmers." He worked at a variety of jobs, including stints in the city's sewers and its loading docks. Mary supplemented the family income by taking in laundry. Their labors allowed the Czolgoszes to occupy the first floor of a three-story house on Benton Street.

Anxious to achieve the American dream, Paul was soon packing up his family for a series of moves. They successively relocated to the Michigan communities of Rogers City, Alpena, and Posen, before heading back to

Alpena. Later they lived near Pittsburgh, in Cleveland, and on a farm close to Warrensville, Ohio. Czolgosz worked at a lumberyard and at a Lake Huron dockyard, among other jobs. Meanwhile the family continued to grow, a new Czolgosz arriving about every other year. In 1883, living in Posen, Mary gave birth to a daughter, the family's tenth child. The baby arrived healthy, but complications from the delivery led Paul to rush his wife to a doctor in nearby Alpena. She lingered for six weeks before dying.[2]

It is not clear how his mother's death affected young Leon. Even before the loss, he was, in his father's words, "always quiet and retiring." He could not get acquainted with other children and would refuse to play with them. Paul described him as "fairly obedient." When he did get punished for some misdeed, Leon would say nothing, but his father related that he "could tell by his looks that he was thinking more than most children could say." As he grew older he remained extremely bashful. His family did not recall him ever dating; nor did he form any close friendships with anybody of either sex.[3]

During the family's second period of residency in Alpena, Leon received about four years of education at both a parochial school and the village's public school. His brother Waldeck later insisted that Leon was "considered the best scholar" of all the students. His education ended when the family moved to Natrona, Pennsylvania, about twenty miles from Pittsburgh. There Leon, then sixteen, entered the working world. He got a job in a bottle works, carrying red-hot bottles from the ovens to cooling racks. He at first received seventy-five cents for what was likely a twelve-hour day. Later his daily wage was increased to a dollar. At the same time, Paul was working at the Philadelphia Diamond Factory, a chemical works.[4]

In 1891 Paul took his family to Newburg, Ohio, a suburb of Cleveland. He built a saloon, which he ran for five months before renting it to a brewing company. Leon found work at the Newburg Wire Mills, remaining there for seven years. His schedule was arranged so he worked ten hours a day for a week or two then twelve hours of night work for one or two weeks. He earned about eight dollars a week for the day work and about twelve dollars a week when on the night shift. Although the manager of the wire mill termed Leon "rather of an agitator" who "talked too much to his men," his colleagues considered him to be "a very steady worker." They insisted that he "never gave any trouble; never quarreled or got into any disputes with other workmen, but was quiet and cheerful." They also noted, however, that he "never had much to say" but "sat around and kept to himself." They termed him "a dreamer, always a dreamer." He worked as a wire winder, which was considered a skilled position, and before he left he was "a sort of assistant superin-

Bertillon card (mug shot) of Leon Czolgosz taken September 6, 1901 (collection of the Buffalo History Museum, used by permission).

tendent of some machines." His foreman said Czolgosz received far fewer fines than most of his colleagues, and they were mainly for minor infractions, such as letting the wire run slack.[5]

Czolgosz's fellow workers thought enough of him that they accepted the Polish Catholic into the Golden Eagle Society, a fraternal organization. This was despite the fact that "the [other] members were Americans and socially above him." Characteristically, Leon attended few meetings, but he always paid his dues. Shortly before he quit working at the mill, he paid up six months ahead.[6]

During his years at the wire mill, Czolgosz frequently turned up at his father's former saloon, which had been purchased by a couple named Dryer. According to Mr. and Mrs. Dryer, he would arrive after the day shift, wash up, and sit down to read the newspaper, which he was always anxious to see. Although he generally sat in a corner by himself, Leon would occasionally get into a card game if urged to complete a foursome. If gambling was involved and he lost, that generally ended his participation. The Dryers never heard him use foul language, nor did he ever lose his temper. Sometimes he fell asleep at his table. Mr. Dryer considered him to be "rather stupid and dull-like." To Mrs. Dryer, Czolgosz was "kind of broke-down like." She also remembered that he would never fight but would leave if there was any trouble at the bar. Indeed, he would not even kill a fly but would brush them off or would catch them and let them go.[7]

In 1893 or 1894 there was a strike at the wire mill when management attempted to cut wages. Scabs were hired, and the strikers were blacklisted. Leon was out of work for six months before the mill hired a new foreman. He was armed with a list of the strikers' names, but he did not know them personally. Czolgosz applied for work under the name of Fred C. Nieman, "Nieman" meaning "nobody" in Polish.[8]

Leon had work, but he also had a changed attitude. As Waldeck recalled, his brother "got quiet and not so happy." Both men's views on faith shifted in the wake of the strike. Until then both Waldeck and Leon had been faithful members of the Catholic Church. They believed their priests' teachings that if they were in trouble or need and prayed about the matter, their prayers would be answered. During the strike they prayed for work but received no answer. The brothers went to their parish priest and asked for proof of the church's teachings. The cleric only repeated the advice that they pray, but again no relief was forthcoming. Confused, they purchased a Polish language Bible and read it together four or five times. Somehow this led them to the conclusion that the priests "told it their own way," leaving out vast sections of the Scriptures.[9]

As they formed these new opinions, Leon and Waldeck met others who had arrived at the same conclusions. Waldeck later recalled his brother telling one of these acquaintances that "the priest's trade was the same as the shoemaker's or any other." The two Czolgoszes branched out, securing books on religion and other topics, leading them to conclude that they "knew how it was." They became voracious students, securing books in Cleveland or sending away for them. For about a year and a half they read together. Then Leon became more withdrawn, preferring to read alone, and Waldeck gradually lost interest.[10]

In 1897 the family had saved up enough money to purchase a fifty-five-acre farm in Orange Township, four miles from Warrensville, Ohio. The boys put in their savings, including fifty dollars Leon had deposited in a Cleveland bank. It had taken more than two decades, but Paul Czolgosz, an immigrant who had arrived with virtually nothing, was now a landowner. It was an impressive achievement, one that was indicative of what was possible in America. If his son Leon was impressed, he does not appear to have mentioned it. Indeed, his views of what was possible in America were turning in a very different direction.[11]

In 1897 Leon came down with an apparent respiratory disease. Family members later noted that he visited at least four doctors. One of them put down his symptoms as "Short breath (catarrh). Palpitation. Some wheezing." He became a frequent customer at the local pharmacy, one relative estimating that he spent two hundred dollars on various drugs. At one point he sent away for some sort of "inhaling machine." Nothing seemed to help, and Leon rejected Waldeck's suggestion that he go to a hospital. "There is no place in the hospital for poor people," he replied. "If you have lots of money you get well taken care of." On August 29, 1898, Czolgosz approached his foreman at the wire mill and informed him that he was quitting work, that, as the boss recalled it, "he was going out into the country for his health."[12]

Retiring to the family farm, Leon became more and more withdrawn. Perhaps it was the battery of pills he was taking, or perhaps it was his growing disillusionment with his faith and industrial America. In any event, his sister-in-law, the wife of his brother Jake, believed he "acted queerly." Paul's brother Michael, who lived in Cleveland, said of the family, "They have looked upon [Leon] as a sort of 'old woman' or 'grandmother,' and they seem to have called him such because of his habit of falling asleep and being at times rather stupid." The kindest words that Briggs heard from the family came from Leon's sister, Victoria, who termed him "rather lazy but a nice boy."[13]

One member of the family who had nothing good to say about Leon was his step-mother. Paul had married Katren Metzfaltr about a year and a half after Mary died. Although their relationship seemed to be good for several years, by the time the family relocated to the Warrensville farm, it certainly was not. Katren was convinced that there was nothing wrong with her lethargic stepson except for a desire to avoid the hard work of the farm. When she would ask him to perform a chore, Leon would answer with a simple, "Yes," then either fail to do the task or wait for some time before beginning. This led to arguments between the two. Indeed, Czolgosz's sister Victoria recalled, her brother never swore, but "he came pretty near it in talking with her." Leon's antipathy for her was such that he would not eat with the family when Katren was around. If she was away, he would often catch and fry fish for himself and his siblings. However, if his stepmother suddenly appeared, he would flee to his room, leaving his brothers or sisters to watch the skillet. If nobody was around, he would simply leave it on the stove to burn. Eventually he would not eat with his family at all. Instead he took all of his meals, mainly consisting of bread, milk, and cake, to his room.[14]

Whether or not his stepmother's theory about Leon's apparent state of oscitancy was correct, it is clear that he contributed very little labor to the farm. He slept late and often fell asleep in a chair with virtually no warning. In good weather he would often be found asleep beneath a tree. According to Victoria, reading and sleeping occupied the bulk of his time. Waldeck added that he would walk every afternoon to the nearest store to secure the daily newspaper and "would read all the papers he could get in English or Polish." Stories "pertaining to strikes [or] working-men" especially interested him. Paul agreed that his son was frequently reading or sleeping. However, the father insisted to Briggs that Leon "was not a hard worker because he was ill."[15]

Czolgosz was not entirely inactive, but any activity was always on his terms. If something did not interest him, he wanted no part of it. One thing that did attract his interest was fixing things around the farm. He repaired wagons and other machinery and also mended fences from time to time. Indeed, his brother Joseph insisted that Leon could "could do anything in the way of fixing up around." He once took apart a broken clock, and after he reassembled it, it worked fine. Another time he mended a pitcher that had been "broken all to pieces" by "putting wires about it." His work was so good that the vessel again held milk.[16]

Czolgosz's favorite activity appeared to be hunting. His sister-in-law claimed it was virtually all he did besides sleep. Sometimes he would go in pursuit of squirrels, but rabbits were his favorite quarry. Leon would go armed with a shotgun, a revolver, and a stick. Sometimes he also took a bag. If the rabbit was some distance away, he would use his shotgun. If it was near, Czolgosz employed the handgun, with which, Waldeck said, he was quite adept. Sometimes he used his bag to cover one end of a rabbit hole, then either prodded the other end with his stick or built a fire to drive the animal into the bag. Although he generally killed them with the stick, on at least one occasion, he brought three home alive.[17]

Although his family was able to inform Briggs of Czolgosz's day-to-day activities—or lack thereof—throughout the late 1890s, they were unable to share his thoughts. The reason was simple: Leon had not shared any thoughts with them. More and more he kept to himself, alone with his reading or alone in sleep, turning in early in the evening. His sister-in-law considered him always "cranky." Waldeck believed he became increasingly restless. Joseph described him as "always awful bashful," a view with which Paul Czolgosz concurred.[18]

Perhaps the only insight into Czolgosz's thoughts was his choice of reading material, which was becoming increasingly radical. Indeed, in Gilded Age America, Leon needed to do no more than read the newspapers he craved to become imbued with radical notions. Violent clashes between striking workers, strikebreakers, and either police or militia were common at a time when growing corporate interests were squeezing every penny of profits they could as labor fought for what it believed to be its fair share. Management's often brutal response to strikers, sometimes backed by the full strength of the national government, led many in that direction. Eventually they would lead Leon Czolgosz to seek the company of anarchist meetings and then to inform one of the acquaintances he formed that he "was looking for something more active."[19]

3

Buffalo: Growth of an Industrial City

Journals of early white explorers indicate that there were three Native American cultural groups in the Niagara region in the early 1600s. The Kahquah Nation resided mainly in Ontario, although there were a few east of the Niagara River Buffalo until the late 1630s. The Erie than arrived and dominated during the 1640s.

In the early 1650s the Senecas, part of the Five-Nations Confederation, defeated or drove away all three tribes. The Senecas did not occupy the region but used it as a hunting and trapping grounds. This remained the pattern for the next century.[1]

The first white settler in what would become Buffalo was Daniel de Joncaire, a French trader who arrived during the 1750s. Although white settlement in meaningful numbers was still a half century away, a number of Seneca Indians arrived in 1780. They came from the Genesee Valley, where Gen. John Sullivan, acting under orders from George Washington, conducted a punitive raid against tribes supporting the British. Sullivan's band burned villages as well as crops and orchards. The Senecas, many on the verge of starvation, sought refuge at British-held Fort Niagara. They remained there during what was, even by Buffalo standards, a brutal winter. When it abated, at the urging of the Redcoats, they established a settlement on Buffalo Creek later known as West Seneca.[2]

Fort Niagara had been built by the French during the early 1720s. Over the following decades it expanded into an impressive fortification, encompassing nearly an acre. The British captured the fort, which had not been designed to stop artillery, during the French and Indian War. They retained it throughout the American Revolution, and, because the fledgling American government was too weak to do anything about it, for several years beyond. As a result, the first wave of white settlement was New York Loyalists, individuals who had supported the British during the war and now found them-

24

selves unwanted by their patriot neighbors. Over two decades some 10,000 headed to Fort Niagara, where they were sent on to available lands in Ontario.[3]

In 1796, under the terms of the Jay Treaty, the British gave up Fort Niagara. At the same time the native tribes were ceding lands outside of their reservations. Although these developments seemed to clear the way for white settlement, it came at first in a trickle. A pioneer resident later recalled that the settlement consisted of seven log cabins in 1798. One served as a tavern, and another was an "Indian store." A blacksmith also arrived that year.[4]

The Seneca lands were part of 3.3 million acres that, in 1797, became the property of the Holland Land Company, a consortium of six Amsterdam banking houses. The company engaged Joseph Ellicott to survey their holdings. Ellicott immediately determined that the site which was to become Buffalo should be the main settlement. However, he first occupied himself with opening a road through the purchase area and laying out townships. It was not until 1803 that Ellicott got around to mapping out village lots.[5]

Ellicott planned to name his settlement New Amsterdam. It was not to be. From the outset American settlers trumped Dutch proprietors, and by the early 1800s the name "Buffalo" had come into common usage. Even Ellicott quickly yielded to the inevitable, referring to the community as "Buffalo, alias New Amsterdam," in an 1801 diary entry. There are many theories as to the origin of the name. One says it came from nearby Buffalo Creek; and Buffalo Creek, according to old timers among the Senecas, earned its name from the fact that great herds of bison had roamed the area at least into the 1720s.[6]

In 1804 settlements based on Ellicott's survey began. Mail service reached Buffalo the same year. Still, visitors were less than impressed by the nascent city. One wrote, "There were perhaps twenty houses, of which only three or four were frame.... Some streets were partially laid out, but the whole place was full of stumps and there were no fences." Another 1804 visitor, Dr. Timothy Dwight, president of Yale College, believed "the spot is unhealthy," considered the inhabitants "a casual collection of adventurers," and observed that there were "about as many Indians in the village as white people."[7]

Dr. Dwight's impressions notwithstanding, Buffalo continued to grow. A courthouse and a jail went up in 1810, and the village boasted a population of nearly five hundred. On February 10, 1810, the town of Buffalo was formally established by law. By then there were three taverns and one church, the latter shared by all the town's congregations. In 1811 brothers Smith and Hezekiah Salisbury launched the *Buffalo Gazette*, the community's first newspaper. That same year one John Melish paid a visit to Buffalo. Contradicting Dr. Dwight's earlier observations, he noted, "Buffalo is handsomely situated at the east end of Lake Erie, where it commands a beautiful view of the Lake." The number of taverns had increased to four, and the village also boasted eight stores. Melish concluded, "Upon the whole I think this is likely to become a great settlement."[8]

Then came the War of 1812, and with it a major setback to Buffalo's aspirations. Things remained relatively peaceful on the Niagara frontier until July 11, 1813, when a British raiding party, 250 in number, landed below Black Rock and captured a small navy yard on Scajaquada Creek.

The enemy returned in December, eager for revenge. Early that month American general George McClure abandoned Fort George, an installation on the Canadian side of the Niagara River. A British force was approaching, and the men's terms of enlistment were expiring, so the action was prudent. What was not prudent was McClure's decision to burn the nearby community of Newark. When the flames subsided 150 houses were destroyed and some 400 people were left homeless as winter approached. From a tactical standpoint the destruction accomplished nothing.

One thing Americans should have learned during the War of 1812 was that burning down communities was a very stupid decision. After the Yankees thus destroyed York (now Toronto) the British occupied and burned much of Washington, D.C. Following the sack of Newark they headed first to Fort Niagara, which fell easily, and then to Buffalo. Some two thousand men guarded the settlement. Many were undisciplined militia, and when the English arrived during the night of December 29–30, about eight hundred of them disappeared.

In fact most Buffalo residents stuck around longer than many of their guardians. They methodically packed what provisions they could and headed out into the bitterly cold night. The attackers were also methodical. They remained three days, burning 143 buildings, every structure except the jail, a blacksmith shop, and one residence. Nearly forty residents were dead, tomahawked and scalped by the Indian allies of the British. According to one account nothing was left living but a cat, "which wandered disconsolately about the smoldering ruins of its late home."[9]

Despite the thoroughness of the destruction, Buffalo's recovery was rapid. A relief committee of western New York communities raised thirteen thousand dollars. The state legislature added fifty thousand, and additional funds came from New York City, Albany, and the Holland Land Company. By May 1814 the *Gazette* reported that Buffalo boasted twenty stores, taverns, and shops. Fourteen months later the paper announced that there were as many houses built or being built as had been burned by the invaders. In 1816 a new courthouse went up.[10]

The following year workmen began building the Erie Canal. Buffalo's leading citizens immediately realized the benefits to be gained if their community became its western terminus. So, too, did the citizens of Black Rock, a short distance north. At first Black Rock seemed to hold all the cards. It possessed an outstanding natural harbor, along with a shipyard and warehouses. Buffalo, however, was not about to concede. Civic leaders began work on their own harbor and pointed out to canal commissioners that their city, unlike Black Rock, was safely beyond the range of British guns in Canada. A more convincing argument was Buffalo's location on Lake Erie. This fact carried the day for Buffalo. As the commissioners noted, "The waters of Lake Erie are higher at the mouth of Buffalo Creek than they are at ... any point down the Niagara, and every inch gained in elevation will produce a large saving in the expense of excavation throughout the Lake Erie level."[11]

On October 26, 1825, the canal was opened to Lake Erie. New York Governor De Witt Clinton was among the dignitaries who boarded the *Seneca Chief* at Buffalo to make the first voyage to Albany. As the boat began its journey a cannon fired. It was the first of a series of artillery pieces that carried word of the departure all the way to Albany then south down the Hudson to New York City. There the process was reversed, Buffalo eventually gaining confirmation that the news had been received across the state.[12]

It had cost a hundred dollars and taken six weeks to transport a ton of wheat by wagon from western New York to Eastern markets. The canal cut the cost to ten dollars and the time to just over a week. For Buffalo the canal brought docks, warehouses, boat repair facilities, and a demand for labor to operate them. It also made the city a stopping point for a flood of Americans and Europeans bound for Midwestern states. So great were their numbers that accommodating them became Buffalo's "principal and most profitable business" during the early canal years. Solicitors were on hand to greet the emigrants, hoping to direct them to the packet boats they represented. They were not deterred by any sense of honesty. One assured nervous potential passengers that the ship he represented had a "low pressure engine" that ran on cold water, water that was never allowed "to come to the boil." Competition between the solicitors was so intense that the police sometimes had to be called.[13]

Many of the people passing through Buffalo were destined to become Midwestern farmers. Soon their grain products were headed for Buffalo and the canal. At first all was unloaded by hand. Then, in 1842, Joseph Dart, a Buffalo merchant, built a grain elevator with a steam-powered conveyor to unload the grain. By 1855 there were ten elevators in operation, a number that would grow to 27 after the Civil War and 43 by 1887.[14]

View of the industrial city of Buffalo ca. 1900 with the Erie County Jail in the right foreground (collection of the Buffalo History Museum, used by permission).

Prosperity brought growth. In 1832, with an estimated population of ten thousand, Buffalo became a chartered city. At the first meeting of the board of aldermen, held on June 4, the main order of business was to establish a fire department. Gas lights arrived in 1848, and the next year the Buffalo City Water Works Company received its charter. Meanwhile the population grew rapidly. The 1850 census showed that Buffalo had 42,261 residents. Ten years later the number reached 81,126.[15]

The growing city did not have room for its native inhabitants. Beginning in 1838 an outfit known as the Ogden Company made an effort to purchase all tribal lands in western New York. In 1838 the company held a council of chiefs. At the meeting they obtained what one Buffalo historian termed "a doubtful conveyance" and later secured from Congress "an equally doubtful ratification" of the treaty. Under its terms the company acquired the remaining reservation land for $202,000. Subsequent investigations into the negotiations "disclosed a scandalous condition of bribery and corruption, shameful methods of … intoxication." The public outcry against the company was so great and many Indians so reluctant to leave for promised lands in

Kansas that the Ogden Company began to renegotiate. It took four years, but in 1842 the Natives began to depart. Three years after that virtually all were gone.[16]

There were occasional setbacks to Buffalo's progress. One of the most disastrous occurred on the night of October 18–19, 1844. What was described as "a most remarkable and destructive gale" blew the entire night. Its winds sent lake water into the city two feet deeper than had ever been known. The storm claimed numerous wharves and one-third of the city's stone pier. Ships garnished a number of streets. Small homes near the lake were washed away, and several chimneys came down. The damage was placed at $200,000. Between 30 and 40 people lost their lives, most of them drowning victims.[17]

A different type of killer—cholera—struck Buffalo in 1832, 1834, and again in 1849. The 1832 outbreak seemed to begin with an English immigrant, who brought the disease to Quebec. It continued up the St. Lawrence, reaching Buffalo in early summer. The city quickly established a board of health and set up a special hospital. Steamboats entering the harbor were stopped, and no one could disembark until they had passed a medical inspection. The same applied to canal boats and stage coaches. Despite the precautions there were between 180 and 250 cases, resulting in between 80 and 120 deaths. The 1834 outbreak was less serious, although one of the victims was Major A. Andrews, the city's mayor.

The 1849 outbreak began with a single case on May 30. By July 12 there had been 356 reported cases, and the death toll had reached 103. The overwhelming majority of the fatalities occurred on the east side of the city among foreign residents and laborers who had come to Buffalo to work on an enlargement of the Erie Canal. Most of the blame was placed on another canal, dug for manufacturing purposes, the water of which had become stagnant. The deadliest single day was July 24, when the disease claimed 32 victims. Before it abated in early September there were some 3,000 reported cases and some 900 deaths.[18]

In 1822 a young Millard Fillmore located in Buffalo. He taught school at first but soon began practicing law. In 1828 he was elected to the state assembly. Four years later, at age 32, he won a seat in Congress. In 1848 Fillmore was elected vice president on the Whig ticket. When President Zachary Taylor died two years later, Fillmore succeeded to the presidency. The Whigs did not renominate him in 1852, but in 1856 the American Party, which was opposed to immigration, did. He lost that campaign and retired to Buffalo.[19]

Buffalo's other president, Grover Cleveland, was elected mayor in 1881. He ran on a reform platform in a city that one local newspaper had termed "the worst ring-ridden community in the state." Cleveland delivered on his promise, vetoing numerous spending measures for projects that would have lined the pockets of local politicians and their friends. After he left to serve as governor of New York the reform effort went on in the form of a civil service commission. Cleveland was elected president in 1884, lost to Benjamin Harrison in 1888, then defeated Harrison four years later. Historians consider him to be the 22nd and the 24th president.[20]

Not all corruption was entirely political. Prostitution was big business along a section of Canal Street known as "Two tough and torrid blocks of trouble." At one time the area was home to fifteen dance halls and a hundred saloons. On May 21, 1872, the *Buffalo Express* reported,

> Our city was ablaze with brilliantly-lighted gambling halls, boisterous "concert saloons," and other riotous places of debauchery and crime. Respectable people were jostled on every corner of the streets by "cappers" for the faro bank, or interceppimps and runners for houses of ill-fame, or shocked by the unearthly screeches from the hideous "free and easies," which kept up their hideous yells from evening until early morning.[21]

Despite the corruption and "debauchery," Buffalo was not without cultural attainments. The first schoolhouse in the settlement was built in 1806 but was destroyed by the British torches. In 1812 New York State set up a system of common schools. Buffalo opened a district school under that system in 1818. In 1847 the University of Buffalo opened with 72 medical students in a rented church building. Two years later its own facility opened. The school added a pharmacy college in 1886 and schools of law and dentistry in the early 1890s.[22]

In 1857 Seth Grosvenor, a wealthy New Yorker who had lived briefly in Buffalo during his childhood, left the city ten thousand dollars to establish a public library. At a time when free public libraries were rare, the city council was reluctant to accept the bequest. They finally did in 1859, but the library was not opened until 1871, as the library's board of trustees searched for a building and watched Grosvenor's gift grow. Its first home was a group of rooms above the Buffalo Savings Bank. In 1895 it moved to a new building on the corner of Franklin and Edwards Streets.

Buffalo also worked to preserve its past. The Buffalo Historical Society was founded in May 1862, with Millard Fillmore serving as the first president. Later the historical society moved into a new headquarters, erected as the New York Building for the Pan-American Exposition. New York State paid $100,000, the city of Buffalo $30,000, and the historical society $45,000. It remains the home of the Buffalo History Museum.[23]

In 1868 Frederick Law Olmsted, the designer of New York's Central Park, surveyed the city to plan a park system. His firm created a design for a series of parks connected by tree-lined boulevards. As was the case with the library, the city council was less than enthusiastic at first, but by the mid-1880s they were on board. By 1901 Buffalo had five major parks and numerous smaller green spaces. The city zoo opened in 1892 with a collection of elk and—appropriately enough—buffalo.[24]

As the nineteenth century drew to a close Buffalo had a lot going for it. A manufacturing and transportation center, it was also a city that gave attention to culture and heritage. The 1900 census would place Buffalo eighth among American cities with a population of 352,387. Add the proximity of Niagara Falls, and Buffalo seemed well positioned to host one of the expositions that were becoming almost annual events in America. The falls also offered another advantage, electrical power in seemingly limitless supply. It would not only provide energy for an exposition; it would, in the end, supply that exposition with a major theme.

4

McKinley: From the Front Porch to the White House

For William McKinley, "retirement" was a refreshing period. After over twenty years in public life, the lack of responsibility was a tonic. He and Ida were home at Canton, able to relax and visit with friends. Still, everybody, the ex-governor included, knew this was not so much retirement as intermission. In January 1895 Mark Hanna retired from the business world, and the embryonic McKinley campaign became his full-time occupation. He started with a Southern strategy, renting a house in Thomasville, Georgia. In March McKinley came down for a three-week visit. It was a given that no Republican candidate would carry the Democratic "Solid South." Having no chance at elected office, Southern Republicans cared only about patronage. Hanna, therefore, had to convince them that McKinley's election was inevitable and that they should get on the bandwagon early and deliver a large bloc of convention delegates.[1]

In February 1896 Benjamin Harrison announced that he would not be a candidate. After he withdrew, Senator William B. Allison of Iowa emerged as a potential candidate but quickly fizzled. The same was true of Speaker of the House Thomas B. Reed, whose caustic personality hurt his chances. Meanwhile, Hanna's Southern strategy had paid off. When the 1896 Republican National Convention opened in St. Louis on June 16, McKinley had nearly two hundred delegates from the region.

Except for a dust up over the money issue—gold vs. silver—in the party platform, which would turn out to be a prelude to the general election campaign, the convention was anticlimactic. McKinley gained his party's nomination on the first ballot with 661½ votes. His nearest competitor was Reed, who managed only 84½. Political etiquette dictated that a candidate not appear at the convention, so McKinley remained in Canton, listening by telephone as the Ohio delegation put him over the top. Canton went wild on news of the nomination. Horns, whistles, and firecrackers punctuated the night to the somewhat more mellow accompaniment of band music. As an enthusiastic outpouring of humanity descended upon McKinley's Market Street home, a supporter dashed out the back door, shouting, "You have my sympathy." It was the beginning of a long night that saw the newly christened nominee speak to fifty thousand well-wishers.[2]

For vice president, the convention nominated New Jersey corporate attorney Garrett A. Hobart, who added strength to the ticket in the East. The McKinleys and the Hobarts would become close socially, and the vice president would become an involved member of the administration. It is likely that no succeeding vice president held such influence until Jimmy Carter and Walter Mondale redefined the office some eight decades later.[3]

The ticket appeared unstoppable in what everybody assumed would be a strongly Republican year. Then the Democrats met in Chicago and a 36-year-old politician electrified the convention and changed the dynamics of the campaign. William Jennings Bryan was a native of Salem, Illinois, who later moved to Lincoln, Nebraska, became interested in politics, and served two terms in the U.S. House. Bryan was an advocate of the free coinage of silver, an issue that had caught on in the South and West and was quickly gaining momentum. Advocates called for the nation's mints to coin silver at a ratio of sixteen-to-one compared with gold. The rationale was that this would inject more currency into the economy, helping to end the depression. A growing third party, the Populists, had emerged from the movement. Farmers, laborers, and miners largely composed the party, and an intense distrust of Democrats, Republicans, and Wall Street drove it.

At the convention, Bryan blatantly, but sincerely, co-opted the issue. A gifted orator, he addressed the gathering and delivered an impassioned plea on behalf of silver. The Nebraska politician leapt into political immortality when he concluded, "You shall not press down upon the brow of labor this crown of thorns; you shall not crucify mankind upon a cross of gold!" The convention devolved into pandemonium. The next day Bryan became the presidential candidate of a suddenly revitalized Democratic Party.[4]

Informed by phone of Bryan's nomination, McKinley reportedly said, "That is rot," and hung up the receiver. If the Major reacted with disdain, Hanna responded with panic. Bryan had announced a marathon speaking tour that would eventually take the candidate over 18,000 miles, delivering nearly six hundred speeches in twenty-seven states. Hanna and other party leaders urged their candidate to match the Democratic nominee's effort. McKinley, characteristically, remained calm, politely but firmly informing them that he would not try to equal Bryan's performance. "Don't you remember that I announced that I would not under any circumstances go on a speech-making tour?" he reminded one of them. "If I should go now it would be an acknowledgment of weakness. Moreover, I might just as well put up a trapeze on my front lawn and compete with some professional athlete as go out speaking against Bryan. I have to *think* when I speak."[5]

There would be no trapeze, but McKinley's front lawn was about to become the centerpiece of his campaign. In 1888 Benjamin Harrison had chosen to remain home and let the voters come to him. McKinley would duplicate that strategy, albeit on a much larger scale. The decision was sound. While Bryan exhausted himself on his grueling tour, McKinley would sleep in his own bed every night; and thanks to a generally friendly press, his words would reach as many voters. Also, as historian Lewis L. Gould has noted, "McKinley ... seemed to be more stable and statesmanlike [than Bryan] in his home setting."[6]

The candidate worked hard to reinforce that view and to make sure that nothing go wrong. McKinley was a creature of careful discipline, but there was no guarantee that his visitors would be. To avoid potential embarrassment, delegations wishing to visit first needed to contact McKinley headquarters. The group's leader would soon receive an invitation from the campaign to come to Canton and meet with the Major. Upon arrival he would be asked what he planned to say. If the leader replied, "Anything that comes to me," McKinley would kindly but firmly ask him to write out his remarks and submit them to him for review. "With your permission I shall make some suggestions and return it to you," the nominee would add.[7]

Despite the careful behind-the-scenes preparations, the campaign projected a quaint, homey image. McKinley often stood on a chair to speak and frequently interrupted his own speech to glance toward his neighbors' fence and greet their daughter. If she had been away for a time, the Republican candidate for president would ask, "Where were you today, Mary? I was looking for your pink dress."[8]

McKinley stuck by his decision not to leave Canton. Between June and November he was away from town only three days, each time fulfilling a prior speaking engagement. His lack of travel did not prevent him from meeting the voters. Between June 19 and November 2, 750,000 people came to Canton in over 300 delegations that represented thirty states. The variety of the delegations was remarkable. Cleveland sent representatives from their Anglo-American community known as the British Isles American McKinley Club. There were also the Chicago Italian Club, the Swedish-American Club of Rockford, Illinois, and Cleveland's Bohemian-Slav Republican Club. Sometimes the timing of the groups' visits was ironic. One day saw a group of Confederate veterans in the morning and a contingent of black ministers in the afternoon.

The most frequent visitors were workingmen, who arrived in a near-constant stream. With sound currency and high tariffs the twin pillars of their campaign, the Republicans were eager to present a united front of supporters representing both labor and management. The latter, scared to death of Bryan, was likely more enthusiastic, and factory owners sent trainloads of employees to Canton to cheer for McKinley. While many of these workers actually did support him, others were Democrats eager for a day off. Such details did not matter to the Republicans, who cited their presence in large numbers as proof of labor's unwavering support. There were railroad employees and even groups of traveling salesmen, but industrial workers made up the bulk of the delegations. They came from such establishments as the White Sewing Machine factory in Cleveland, the American Tin Plate factory of Elmwood, Indiana, and the Oil Well Supply Company of Pittsburgh. Another Pittsburgh firm, the Jones and Laughlin steel mill, reportedly sent eighty percent of its five thousand employees, a contingent that required forty-four train cars.[9]

Thanks to Hanna and his main deputy, Charles G. Dawes, there was much more to the McKinley effort than the fabled front porch. Dawes devoted much of his attention to fund raising, a task made considerably easier by the terror with which the business community beheld Bryan. Their fear and Dawes's skills resulted in nearly $3,600,000 in campaign cash, double what the GOP had spent in 1892. A number of corporate interests contributed in six figures. The funds allowed them to launch a "campaign of education," eschewing the traditional parades and bonfire blazing rallies. The McKinley forces printed over 200 million pamphlets in a dozen languages, employing a hundred workers in the Chicago mailroom alone. They targeted a variety of groups, including "colored voters," women (who could vote in three states), traveling salesmen, and bicyclists.[10]

If Bryan and McKinley chose different campaign styles, they also selected different issues to emphasize during the canvass. As he traveled the country, Bryan spoke mostly about free silver, the subject that had propelled him to his party's nomination. At first McKinley countered with arguments in favor of gold. However, in September, on orders from the candidate himself, Republicans switched their emphasis to the tariff. "McKinley, Protection, and Prosperity" became the theme of party pamphlets and speakers.[11]

On October 31 McKinley brought his campaign to a close, not on his front porch but at the Canton Tabernacle. After making one last pitch on behalf of sound currency and high tariffs, the candidate turned personal. "I have been accustomed to receive from your hands so many kindnesses for so many years that I was prepared for almost any demonstration," he told the

Ida and William McKinley at a dinner party at the Mark Hanna residence in Cleveland (used by permission from McKinley Presidential Library & Museum, Canton, Ohio).

cheering crowd. "But this latest one fills me with gratitude and thankfulness quite inexpressible, and brings to me an honor the appreciation of which I could not conceal if I would."[12]

Three days later Canton, along with the rest of the country, cast its votes. The city was up early, with bands and other groups in the streets as early as six o'clock. By 8:30 a.m., according to one estimate, over half the city's voters had cast their ballots. Indeed, when McKinley arrived at his precinct to vote at nine that morning, his ballot number was 230 out of 382 registered voters. "Major McKinley looked serene and happy," the *Canton Repository* observed, "and greeted everyone with a pleasant 'Good morning,' shaking by the hand many who had gathered about."[13]

That evening, just after sunset, crowds began to accumulate again in the streets. Thousands gathered opposite the Clark Building, where returns were projected "by means of an excellent stereopticon." Telegraph connections and the *Repository*'s special long-distance telephone line helped assure that Canton's citizens would receive the most up-to-the-minute results available. At the McKinley home, where the candidate spent the evening in his library, several telegraph and telephone connections kept those who had gathered there abreast of the returns. The Major generally remained standing, chatting with his guests when he was not receiving reports. At six o'clock he retired for a brief nap, awaking to the news that New York was safely in the Republican column. More significant, New York City had for the first time voted for a GOP presidential candidate. The news continued positive. "Before 9 o'clock," the *Repository* noted, "it became apparent that the result would be a landslide for Republicanism."[14]

Although not quite a landslide, McKinley had scored a significant victory. He received 7,105,144 votes to Bryan's 6,307,897. His margin in the electoral college was 271–176. McKinley even managed to carry four border states, Maryland, Delaware, Kentucky, and West Virginia, states that were typically part of the Democrats' "Solid South."[15]

On the morning after the election a crowd filled the sidewalks and streets around the home of the president-elect. Messenger boys from Canton's two telegraph companies arrived constantly, delivering congratulatory messages by the dozens. At about 10:00 a.m. McKinley appeared in his library, where his brother, Abner, posted him on the latest returns. He told a group of reporters that naps he had been able to snatch during the night had kept him refreshed.

Canton, too, paused for a few days of rest. Then, on Saturday, the city "ratified the election of her illustrious citizen in a manner befitting the great honor that had been conferred upon her." Once again, delegations poured into town. Some 25,000 people made up the crowd. They witnessed a parade replete with brass bands, area politicians, and marchers from such groups as the Honest Dollar Marching Club and the Sound Money Drum Corps. McKinley watched from a platform that had been erected in his yard late in the campaign. He clapped and waved to the passing delegations but, likely to his relief, did no speaking on this occasion. Even Canton's Democratic newspaper was gracious. The *Stark County Democrat* congratulated McKinley, adding, "The people have decreed that the Presidency shall go to a Republican this year and we know of no Republican that we would rather see the honor conferred upon than Major McKinley, our fellow townsman."[16]

President McKinley took the oath of office on March 4, 1897. Mother McKinley, a few months from her death, made the trip. Her priorities remained unchanged. Shortly before the ceremony, Abner was overheard—in a pleading style—telling her, "Mother, this is better than a bishopric."[17]

Before taking the oath of office, the president-elect met with his predecessor. An adherent of the gold standard, whose views had been repudiated by his own party, Cleveland was likely pleased with the results of the election. He concluded with an apology. "I am deeply sorry, Mr. President, to pass on to you a war with Spain," Cleveland said. "It will come within two years. Nothing can stop it." McKinley's response is not known, but Cleveland's apology would prove prescient.[18]

The new president began his inaugural address by "invoking the guidance of Almighty God." He then turned to the currency issue. "It should all be put on an enduring basis," he suggested, "not subject to easy attack, nor its stability to doubt or dispute." McKinley warned against increasing government debt and called for "an adequate income secured by a system of taxation" to avoid it. At the same time, he asserted, "The strictest economy must be observed in all public expenditures, and extravagance stopped wherever it is found."[19]

In discussing tariff revision, McKinley called for trade reciprocity with other countries. The idea had been first put forward by James G. Blaine, the Maine politician who served as secretary of state during James Garfield's abbreviated presidency and again under Benjamin Harrison. In 1889, during his second tenure in office, Blaine's state department hosted representatives from seventeen Latin American countries at the first Pan-American Congress. For twenty weeks the delegates covered a variety of issues, a contemporary journalist reported, "in a spirit of mutual respect and consideration." One thing that was clear was the overwhelming desire of most of our neighbors to enter into reciprocal commercial relations. The McKinley Tariff Bill was introduced in Congress a few weeks later, and Blaine lobbied hard to get a reciprocity clause included. He succeeded, although the language was weaker than the secretary desired. Still, his department negotiated nearly twenty agreements. But the victory—and the policy—proved to be short lived. After retaking control of Congress in 1892, the Democrats pushed through new tariff legislation that strictly curtailed the president's ability to conclude such arrangements. Now the Republicans were back in power, led by a newly inaugurated president who realized that America "had outgrown the defensive confines of the tariff wall." His views, however, had advanced beyond those of a majority of his party, and McKinley would have to proceed with caution on the issue.[20]

McKinley called for further civil service reform, new laws to curb trusts, and "the restoration of our American merchant marine," which had fewer vessels than it did before the Civil War. The president also announced that he was calling a special session of Congress. He did so reluctantly, but, "The condition of the public Treasury … demands the immediate consideration of Congress." Repeating the words of the presidential oath, he concluded, "This is the obligation I have reverently taken before the Lord Most High. To keep it will be my single purpose, my constant prayer; and I shall confidently rely upon the forbearance and assistance of all the people in the discharge of my solemn responsibilities."[21]

5

McKinley: Domestic Priorities and Foreign Challenges

One of the first tasks for the new president was dealing with a deluge of office seekers, the bane of every Gilded Age Chief Executive. Civil Service reforms, passed in the wake of the Garfield assassination, had reduced the number of jobs the president was responsible for filling. That, however, only increased the competition for those remaining. It was a situation that taxed even McKinley's legendary patience, and on at least one occasion it proved too much. When one individual demanded to know why he would not make a certain appointment, an irritated McKinley snapped back, "Did it ever occur to you that in matters of this kind the President does not have to give his reasons?"[1]

McKinley wanted Mark Hanna in his cabinet, preferably as postmaster general, a position that included a vast patronage network. Hanna was dubious. He feared the appointment would come across as a political payoff. Besides, he had a different office in mind. He had long desired a seat in the U.S. Senate. When the president named Sen. John Sherman, a revered Ohio politician, secretary of state, there was suddenly a vacancy in Hanna's home state.

Critics would later charge that McKinley made the appointment solely to make a place in the Senate for his friend, in effect shoving Sherman out of the way. This was denied by Capt. J. C. Donaldson, Sherman's longtime aide, who later recalled that his boss was anxious to accept the position. The senator was facing a tough re-election campaign in 1898, and the State Department offered a fitting capstone to a dignified career. The potential threat to Hanna's goal of a senate seat was Gov. Asa Bushnell, an ally of the prickly Senator Foraker, and as such not a great fan of either McKinley or Hanna. The appointment was his to make. Bushnell tried to play it coy about his plans, but following intense political pressure, some emanating from the White House, both Bushnell and Foraker fell in line.[2]

The president forged an especially close working relationship with his vice president. Julia Foraker remembered Garret Hobart as being "so kind it was a sort of genius," so the two men's personalities certainly meshed. McKinley quickly brought Hobart into his inner circle, seeking his counsel and often using him as a congressional liaison. The journalist Arthur Wallace Dunn later termed the relationship "a singularly interesting development," explaining, "For the first time in my recollection ... the Vice President was recognized as somebody, as part of the Administration, and as a part of the body over which he presided."[3]

The relationship went far beyond official business. Along with Myron Herrick, an old McKinley friend, Hobart invested the president's $50,000 annual salary. The McKinleys and the Hobarts vacationed together, one trip taking them to Lake Champlain, and the two couples' "Washington season" opened with Thanksgiving dinner at the White House. The vice president and his wife occupied a home diagonally across from the executive mansion, and members of each household frequently dropped in unannounced on the other. Indeed, Jennie Hobart later recalled, "The attitude of the two families toward each other was more personal than official." Over time the president came to depend on Mrs. Hobart to stand beside Ida at White House receptions. Her presence seemed to calm the first lady, and that, in turn, calmed the president. "The President constantly turned to me to help her wherever I could," she later recalled, "not because I was Second Lady, but because I was their good friend."[4]

As time wore on, the president also came to rely upon George Cortelyou. A holdover from the previous administration—he had served as Cleveland's stenographer—Cortelyou was soon promoted to assistant secretary. J. Addison Porter, McKinley's secretary, was demonstrating that he was not up to the job. He also possessed a pompous attitude, the type that McKinley did not appreciate. Soon the efficient and urbane Cortelyou was secretary in everything but name. The president, always wishing to avoid controversy, did not fire Porter, but when his secretary requested numerous leaves of absence, the president cheerfully approved them.[5]

The transition from the fussy Porter to the more soothing Cortelyou was a metaphor for the new administration. To the extent possible in Victorian-era America, McKinley tried to dispense with pomp and formality. He frequently slipped past White House security to enjoy walks around the neighborhood. Local children, anticipating their president's schedule, were often waiting for him, encounters he enjoyed. The contrast with the Cleveland

and Harrison Administrations was stark. As one reporter observed, "Everybody seems to feel that a cloud has been lifted from over the White House. The feeling that the executive mansion was a place, exclusive, reserved, and guarded has disappeared."[6]

Under McKinley the White House also became much more open to reporters. After they repeated GOP charges of an illegitimate son, Cleveland, somewhat understandably, came into office with a distaste for newspapermen. His attitude hardened when, in Cleveland's opinion, they "sensationalized" his 1886 marriage to 21-year old Francis Folsom. During his first month as president, McKinley signaled a softening of this point of view by attending a reception of the Gridiron Club, a fraternity of top capital reporters. Cleveland had never gone. Three months later, as he journeyed to Nashville on his first presidential tour, McKinley entered the scribes' car for an informal conversation, staying over an hour. As his first year in office came to a close, the president curried more favor when he invited reporters and their wives to a holiday reception at the White House, a gesture unheard of under Cleveland.[7]

More important were the practical measures taken to aid the fourth estate. A table was set aside in the East Wing, and representatives of Democratic papers were equally welcome to share the space. Porter briefed them twice daily. Later, as Cortelyou assumed more of the secretarial duties, he began issuing statements, assuming the role of press secretary, a position that would not be formalized for another three decades. Although all of this was in keeping with McKinley's personality, there were practical political benefits as well. Obviously it would tend to make press coverage more friendly; but it also helped bring about a shift in the *locus* of the press's attention. Since the impeachment of Andrew Johnson, Congress had been the center of attention in Washington—and the center of attention in the press. McKinley's policies—and eventually the war with Spain—helped make the White House relevant again.[8]

McKinley was what would later be termed an "activist president." An individual who genuinely loved to travel and meet the people, he would make over forty trips outside Washington during his presidency, establishing what his successor later termed the "bully pulpit." It was part of a process which, notes historian R. Hal Williams, "in some sense began the modern presidency."[9]

McKinley first addressed the economy, the issue most responsible for his election. He called a special session of Congress just a few days after being inaugurated to consider a tariff bill. In fact, Nelson Dingley, chairman of the House Ways and Means Committee, had been at work on the legislation since

December. McKinley lobbied behind the scenes to make reciprocity a part of the bill, but realizing the conservative nature of old guard Republicans, he treaded carefully. He also did some public lobbying, telling the Cincinnati Commercial Club, "Good trade insures good will." As passed, the law, which the president signed on July 24, contained few changes. Among them was a doubling of the duty on sugar, which raised enough revenue to end nearly a decade of trade deficits. Its reciprocity provisions were less than McKinley had hoped for. He gained authority to negotiate treaties that could lower rates up to twenty percent, but only for a five-year period. Still, the president made the most of what he got. He named John Kasson, an Iowa politician and diplomat, to the post of negotiator. Over the course of two years Kasson secured seventeen pacts. And McKinley kept lobbying. In 1899 he told the Boston Commercial Club, "We have quit discussing the tariff and have turned our attention to getting trade wherever it can be found," adding that the U.S. was "seeking our share of the world's markets." By then an upturn in the economy and success in war allowed the chief executive to talk from a position of political strength.[10]

Although a shrewd politician, Christian good will remained a centerpiece of McKinley's political character. Lyman Gage, his treasury secretary, recalled an incident at a cabinet meeting. The war with Spain was just under way, and Secretary of War Russell A. Alger was facing blistering criticism for his direction of the American effort. The governor of the Alaska Territory, a presidential appointee, had issued a proclamation stating, "The American people owe thanks to God for having brought to our knowledge the weakness of our Department of War." Alger was incensed, and he wanted McKinley to fire the offending executive. The president read the proclamation and pointed out that the governor did not mention Alger by name. "You see, I am the Commander-in-Chief of the Army and Navy," McKinley explained. "Perhaps he means me." That would be worse, Alger retorted, still demanding his removal. "I'll find out whether he means you or me," the president promised. "If I find out he means me, shall I tell you what I'll do?" The secretary tried to respond, but McKinley interrupted, "Well, if I find out he means me, I'll forgive him." Even the disgruntled Alger joined in the laughter that followed.[11]

Although Ida had been a staunch temperance advocate, McKinley drank moderately, often enjoying a glass of wine with his dinner. He smoked ten or more cigars a day but would not allow himself to be photographed while puffing. As he told a friend, "We must not let the young men of this country see their president smoking."[12]

Of course McKinley remained solicitous of his invalid wife. He would often leave his office to check in on her, and most days the couple had lunch together. She was usually in a chair or in bed, suffering from frequent headaches or fainting spells. P. M. Rixey, a Navy doctor who became her personal physician, showered her with attention and soon became a favorite of both Ida and the president. With his assistance and that of Jennie Hobart, she steeled herself for White House social events. Still, as Julia Foraker observed, the first lady was "physically unequal to the thing she was attempting to do," putting all the guests "under a certain strain." H. H. Kohlsaat recalled that Ida often fainted at dinners, adding, "She did not fall out of her chair, but became rigid. The President would throw a handkerchief or napkin over her face and proceed with the conversation as though nothing had happened."[13]

Although the new president had assumed that domestic issues would dominate his agenda, foreign affairs soon intruded. In his inaugural address McKinley had promised to work toward agreement on an international bimetallic standard. He dispatched a three-man commission to Paris and London, but the effort failed. Plummeting silver prices and gold discoveries in Alaska and South Africa blunted the appeal of the issue, as did lukewarm support overseas.

McKinley also came up short in trying to resolve outstanding issues with Great Britain. One was the border with Alaska, long in dispute and suddenly of greater importance because of the Yukon gold strike. Another was the 1850 Clayton-Bulwer Treaty, which pledged that neither country would have exclusive control over a future Isthmusian canal. In 1897 the president sent a commission to Central America to survey a route for such a canal. Interest in the project made the treaty suddenly appear to be a bad deal, so much that some in Congress favored abrogating the pact. In the end the Alaska border proved too vexing for the two sides to reach an agreement. The administration did secure from Britain a treaty giving the U.S. exclusive right to construct a canal but not to defend it militarily. It went nowhere in the Senate, and both issues would be left for the Roosevelt Administration to address.[14]

McKinley had more success with the annexation of Hawaii. The issue went back to 1893, when pineapple growers and sons of missionaries deposed Queen Liliuokalani in a bloodless revolution, set up a provisional government, and sought American annexation. The Harrison Administration was in favor, but when Grover Cleveland again assumed the presidency he withdrew the treaty. The Democrat was concerned about the support the American minister and the warship *Boston* had provided the rebels, support Cleveland considered inappropriate.[15]

The election of a Republican gave Hawaiians seeking annexation reason to hope. They dispatched a delegation to Washington to meet with the president-elect. McKinley received them but said he would make no statement of policy until he was inaugurated. Once that day passed he focused his attention on the tariff. However, events soon brought the Hawaiian issue to the forefront. By 1897 Japanese made up nearly one-fourth of the islands' population. This concerned Hawaii's Caucasian leaders, and in March they began sending back workers arriving from Japan.

The Japanese government responded by filing a formal protest, not with Hawaii but with the United States. It also dispatched the cruiser *Naniwa* to the islands. This produced some bluster from Theodore Roosevelt, an assistant secretary of the navy. Teddy called for the construction of a dozen new battleships and said the U.S. should "hoist our flag over the island, leaving all details for after action." His boss, John Long, was more measured in his response, but he did order the commander of the *Oregon*, anchored in San Francisco, to be "prepared in all respects, to proceed, at short notice to the Hawaiian Islands." Meanwhile McKinley was acting, seeing to it that an annexation treaty was drawn up. "We need Hawaii just as much and a good deal more than we did California," he told Cortelyou. "It is manifest destiny." When the treaty was submitted to the Senate Japan protested but at the time was not powerful enough to do much more. Instead it was southern Democratic senators, queasy about Hawaii's racial makeup, and sugar beet interests, leery of competition, who scuttled the treaty. It failed in June and again in December, despite strenuous lobbying by Roosevelt.[16]

It was war that eventually tipped the balance. When the Senate again took up annexation in June 1898 it was against a backdrop of patriotic fervor and concerns for national security. Opponents mounted a filibuster and introduced a number of crippling amendments. Neither succeeded, and on July 6 the Senate approved the measure 42–21, with 26 not voting.[17]

Noticeably absent in these critical foreign policy discussions was the secretary of state. It soon became painfully obvious that Sherman was not up to the job. Virtually deaf and often confused and forgetful, the secretary frequently embarrassed the administration when he gave interviews. Had McKinley been able to focus on domestic policy, as was his desire, this would not have mattered so much. But with a number of foreign issues confronting him—and a big one on the horizon—the president needed someone upon whom he could rely.

That person ended up being William R. Day, a Canton attorney whom McKinley had named assistant secretary. Day had no background in diplomacy and no political ambitions. His only motive in coming to Washington was a desire to help an old friend. That he did, and to a degree neither man could have anticipated when he accepted the post. The president first put him in charge of the Hawaiian issue, altogether bypassing Sherman, who opposed annexation. Very quickly Day assumed the duties of secretary of state. In 1898 he would also assume the office.[18]

Events would soon demonstrate that the president needed the most capable advisors he could secure. The situation in Cuba was making Grover Cleveland's prediction of a war with Spain more and more likely. Cuba had long bristled under its mother country's authoritarian rule. In 1868 the Caribbean island had revolted against Spain. That first revolution lasted a decade before Madrid promised reforms. Many Cubans were dubious, and many relocated to the United States, continuing the revolution as a propaganda effort. In the late 1880s the cold war again turned hot under patriot and poet José Martí. By then more than sixty pro-revolution *juntas* were in operation in Florida.

Martí and such military leaders as Maximo Gómez and Antonio Maceo adopted a "scorched earth" policy aimed at Cuba's lucrative sugar industry. They could not afford to engage in set piece battles—Spain would eventually send over 200,000 soldiers to deal with them—so the rebels, numbering 40,000 or less, engaged in hit-and-run operations.[19]

As all this went on President Cleveland announced and pursued a policy of neutrality. At the same time Spain was making it difficult to remain neutral. In early 1896 Madrid sent Gen. Valeriano Weyler y Nocilau, who would later become known as "Butcher," to Cuba. Weyler immediately instituted a policy known as "reconcentration." Under it he ordered some 400,000 rural residents, who were suspected of supplying the insurgents, into Spanish-controlled cities. Food shortages, combined with inadequate housing and sanitary facilities, made the reconcentration centers into death traps. Soon the policy was responsible for over 100,000 deaths.[20]

The *juntas* made sure the American people were kept informed of the atrocities. In New York the Cuban Revolutionary Party formed, soon becoming a powerful lobbying and public relations concern. Two of the city's newspapers did all they could to help spread the word. William Randolph Hearst's *New York Journal* and Joseph Pulitzer's *New York World* became the most prominent purveyors of what would come to be called "yellow journalism." Their accounts of the suffering in Cuba, splashed across the front page under banner headlines, were always lurid and often inaccurate. It is unclear to what extent the papers shaped public opinion and to what extent they simply reflected it. What is beyond doubt is that the *Journal* and the *World* kept Cuba in the public eye.[21]

As William McKinley entered the presidency he told a friend, "We want no wars of conquest, [and] we must avoid the temptation of territorial aggression. War should never be entered upon until every agency for peace has failed; peace is preferable to war in almost every contingency." A devout Christan, McKinley was likely sincere in his desire for peace; but there were also practical reasons for avoiding conflict. Showing a prescience some of his successors would lack, and perhaps realizing the American military would not necessarily be greeted as liberators, he worried about post-war strife. "What I have in mind is what will come after war," he told Henry Stoddard, "the problems we do not see now but that are sure to come in some way." There were also economic considerations. McKinley had been elected as the "advance agent of prosperity." The possibility of war and its effects on trade were making Wall Street, where the president had numerous allies, nervous. The economy improved steadily during 1897, and the shrewd politician in the White House was leery of anything that might set back the recovery.[22]

The president needed reliable first-hand information about the crisis in Cuba. He got it from William J. Calhoun of Chicago, an old friend and former congressman, who left in early May and spent nearly a month touring the island. His report, delivered to the president on June 22, described a countryside "wrapped in the stillness of death and the silence of desolation." The territory beyond the military lines had been denuded of all signs of life "except an occasional vulture." Homes and fields had been burned "and everything in the shape of food destroyed." The suffering at the camps growing out of the reconcentration policy made his "heart bleed for the poor creatures." Calhoun reported that, "All classes of Cubans backed the revolution," and he predicted that if the war continued it would lead to "the complete destruction of property and the almost total elimination of the island's population."[23]

McKinley knew he had to act. On June 26 he sent a strongly worded note to Madrid. He accused Weyler of "wanton destruction" of property and of intentionally causing human suffering. "[I]n the name of the American people and ... common humanity," he protested against Spain's "uncivilized and inhumane" war and demanded that they abide by the "military codes of civilization." McKinley instructed his newly appointed ambassador to Spain, Stewart L. Woodford, to give the Spanish three months to end the uncivilized warfare in Cuba. If they did not, American intervention was likely. Meanwhile feelers from the State Department went out to Great Britain, France, Germany, and Russia, seeking their reaction to possible American recognition of the Cuban rebels. None of the countries objected.[24]

Premier Antonio Cánovas del Castillo waited until August 4 to reply to McKinley's note. The response was as sharply worded as the president's message. The devastation of Cuba, he asserted, had begun with the rebels, although he did concede—apparently with a straight face—that there had been some early "unintentional neglect" of the *reconcentrados*. He reminded the Americans that civil wars often had led to destruction, citing Gen. William T. Sherman's Georgia campaign as an example. The way to prevent further death and destruction, Cánovas suggested, was for the U.S. to end the "public and organized direction" that the rebels received from the American *juntas*.[25]

Four days after sending his reply, Cánovas was dead, the victim of an Italian anarchist assassin. The death, which was not deeply mourned at the American State Department, brought to power former premier Práxedes Sagasta, a harsh critic of Weyler's tactics, who had suggested that Cuba be granted political autonomy. Upon assuming office on October 14, Sagasta recalled the hated Weyler. His replacement, Rámon Blanco y Arenas, continued the war but rejected Weyler's harsher policies. Autonomy for both Cuba and Puerto Rico was announced on November 15. Residents gained the right to vote for an assembly that would run the islands' domestic affairs. Sagasta was trying, but close examination revealed reforms that were more apparent than real. Although Cubans gained the right to vote, the policy was arranged in a manner that would guarantee that either Spain or Spanish Cubans would control the legislature. In addition the governor general, appointed by Madrid, held an absolute veto. Blanco labored sincerely to improve the lot of the *reconcentrados*, but he was elderly and infirm, and the scope of the challenge was too much for him.[26]

Although the reforms amounted to very little, they won McKinley some favorable publicity and bought him some time to see what developed. In his first annual message to Congress, delivered on December 6, he pleaded for patience. The president put the Spanish reforms in the most positive light possible. Speaking of the Sagasta government, he wrote, "I shall not impugn its sincerity, nor should impatience be suffered to embarrass it in the task it has undertaken." Still, he left Spain with a thinly veiled warning. The "near future," McKinley insisted would determine whether or not "the indispensable condition of a righteous peace" was likely to be achieved. "If not, the exigency of further and other action by the United States will remain to be taken. When that time comes that action will be determined in the line of indisputable right and duty."[27]

Just before Christmas Spain agreed to an American request to provide relief for the starving *reconcentrados* via the Red Cross. McKinley appealed to the public to support the effort. He also made an anonymous donation of five thousand dollars. Only after his death did the public learn of the president's contribution.[28]

Cuban autonomy went into effect on January 1, 1898. Virtually everybody opposed the new policy, rebels because they felt it did not go nearly far enough, conservative Spanish Cubans because they believed it gave away too much. On January 12 the latter group rioted. Joining them were disenchanted army officers shouting, "Viva Weyler!" Twelve days later McKinley made the decision to dispatch the second-class battleship *Maine* to Cuba in case any subsequent outbursts posed a threat to Americans. Both Spain and the American public were told that the vessel was simply resuming the practice of friendly naval visits that had been suspended under President Cleveland.[29]

The ship arrived without incident on January 25. Her captain, Charles D. Sigsbee, visited local officials and even attended a bullfight. At the same time security on board was tight. The captain posted additional sentries, especially at night, and ammunition was kept at hand near the ship's six-inch guns.[30]

On the evening of February 15 Sigsbee was in his cabin, catching up on paperwork and personal correspondence, when he heard a sound like a rifle shot followed by "bursting, rending, and crashing." Then came "ominous metallic sounds, as if the ship were rending itself into pieces." The ship's forward magazines had exploded, claiming the lives of two officers and 264 sailors. There were only 96 survivors. Sigsbee believed an external mine to be the cause of the explosion, but well aware that the wrong choice of words could lead to war, his initial dispatch to Washington was measured. "Public opinion should be suspended until further report," he advised.[31]

Sigsbee's counsel was wise but pointless. Hearst's *Journal* ran a headline charging, "The Warship Maine Was Split in Two by an Enemy's Infernal Machine." To drive home the point, the paper ran a drawing that showed the ship with a mine underneath wired directly to a Spanish fort. Several newspapers followed the *Journal*'s lead, but others were more responsible. The *Washington Evening Star* polled a group of naval officers, most of whom believed the explosion had been an accident. They had good reason for their opinions. Since 1895 there had been thirteen fires connected with spontaneous combustion aboard Navy ships. Shortly before the *Maine* explosion disasters had been narrowly averted when bunker fires broke out aboard the battleship *New York* and the cruiser *Cincinnati*.[32]

McKinley and Secretary of the Navy John D. Long moved quickly to call a court of inquiry to investigate the explosion. Navy Department regulations required this, but it was also good politics. The public was reassured that something was being done, and it helped prevent a congressional inquiry likely to result in posturing and bluster. Capt. William T. Sampson, a respected officer, was in charge of the five-member panel, which on February 20 sailed from Key West to Havana. Spain proposed a joint investigation, which Washington wanted no part of. As the two countries conducted their separate inquiries they did coordinate diving operations and work cooperatively to preserve evidence.[33]

As the court of inquiry sat, the U. S. discovered that Spain was attempting to purchase two cruisers being built in England for Brazil's navy. Further intelligence reports indicated that Madrid was planning to send torpedo boats, small fast vessels designed to attack larger ships, to Cuba. McKinley responded by summoning Rep. Joseph Cannon, chairman of the House Appropriations Committee, to the White House. The president asked for a $50 million defense bill with no strings attached. On March 7 Joseph "Fighting Joe" Wheeler, a former Confederate cavalry commander turned Alabama congressman, introduced the measure and punctuated it with a "rebel yell." It passed both the House and the Senate unanimously. Although touted as a war measure, it is likely that McKinley intended it more as a deterrent aimed at Spain. Secretary Long termed it a "peace measure." In one stroke the president demonstrated congressional unity and showed that the United States could appropriate such a sum without the need to borrow or raise taxes. Reporting from Madrid, Woodford observed, "It has not excited the Spaniards—it has stunned them."[34]

Thirty of the fifty million went to the Navy, where an ambitious assistant secretary was eager to spend it. Shortly after the election Senator Henry Cabot Lodge went to Canton to visit the president-elect. During their conversation the Massachusetts lawmaker lobbied to secure the position for his friend Theodore Roosevelt. McKinley spoke well of the New Yorker but added, "I hope he [has] no preconceived plans which he would hope to drive through the moment he got in." Lodge assured McKinley that "he need not give himself the slightest uneasiness on that score," somehow keeping a straight face.[35]

Once in office Roosevelt encouraged the sedate Long to take off as many days as he pleased and to extend his 1897 summer vacation, warning him of Washington's excessive heat. During these absences the acting secretary kept busy. Many of his actions could have been viewed as insubordination, but most helped prepare the Navy for the wartime challenges that lay ahead. When he learned that Commodore John Howell was being considered for command of the Asiatic Squadron, Roosevelt urged George Dewey to take advantage of his political connections to win the appointment instead. Later he ordered Dewey to sail from Japan to Hong Kong, keep his ships full of coal, and in the event of war, be prepared to launch offensive operations in the Philippines. Put in charge of purchasing, Roosevelt added 131 new vessels, tripling the fleet. Included were the two cruisers destined for Brazil that Spain had coveted. The Navy bought or leased some one hundred merchant ships, all the way from ocean liners to private yachts. Four lighthouse tenders were pressed into service, as were two vessels belonging to the U.S. Fish Commission.[36]

On March 16 Roosevelt confided to his sister, "What the Administration will ultimately do I don't know. McKinley is bent on peace, I fear."[37]

McKinley was bent on peace, but events were headed the other way—and they were becoming irresistible. On March 11 Senator Redfield Proctor of Vermont rose to deliver a speech concerning his recent trip to Cuba. Proctor was a respected conservative, and at a time when impassioned oratory over Cuba was the norm, his reasoned, almost flat delivery made his words all the more effective. At a Havana hospital he reported seeing "400 women and children ... lying on the floors in an indescribable state of emaciation and disease, many with the scantiest covering of rags—and such rags!" He continued, "Outside Havana all is changed. It is not peace, nor is it war. It is desolation and distress, misery and starvation." Proctor concluded that the *Maine* was not the issue. Instead the matter was "the entire native population of Cuba struggling for freedom and deliverance from the worst misgovernment of which I ever had knowledge."[38]

Proctor's measured appeal was a blow to the administration. Senator Proctor hailed from the McKinley wing of the party, and his words caused many key constituencies that were supportive of the president to change their minds. Religious leaders who had cried for peace now viewed intervention as the Lord's work. Conservative newspapers suddenly clamored for war. Perhaps most significant, business leaders began to change their minds. As the *Wall Street Journal* observed, "Senator Proctor's speech converted a great many people in Wall Street who had heretofore taken the ground that the United States had no business to interfere in a revolution on Spanish soil."[39]

Three days later McKinley's hopes for peace received another blow. Word arrived from Havana that the court of inquiry had unanimously determined that an external explosion was responsible for the loss of the *Maine*. The court did not directly implicate Spain, but the yellow press and the American people were not likely to dwell on that detail. The president spent the next four days huddled with members of Congress. On the 25th, a Friday, he received word of the court's report, devoting the rest of the day to a cabinet meeting. The group decided to wait until Monday to send the report to Congress, hoping against hope for a diplomatic miracle during the interim.[40]

On Monday, March 28, the report arrived on Capitol Hill, accompanied by a presidential letter. The purpose of the letter was to cool heated passions, but because of its very timidity it had the opposite effect. The commander-in-chief expected Spain's "sense of justice" to triumph, adding somewhat piously, "In the meantime deliberate consideration is invoked." The Democrats responded by calling for recognition of the "Cuban Republic," and a substantial number of Republicans threatened to join them. Speaker Reed in the House and Vice President Hobart in the Senate labored valiantly to quash war resolutions, but both men knew they could not hold out much longer. Following an acrimonious session Hobart went directly to the White House and invited the president to take a ride with him. "Mr. President," he warned, "I can no longer hold back the Senate. They will act without you if you do not act at once." McKinley asked, "Do you mean that the Senate will declare war on its own motion?" The loyal vice president said it would, adding, "I can restrain them no longer," to which McKinley replied, "Say no more."[41]

Still the president resisted. Unlike many of those clamoring for war, he had witnessed one conflict and witnessed it up close. One evening McKinley was enjoying a walk with his personal physician, Army Captain Leonard Wood, a close friend of Roosevelt's. "Well, have you and Theodore declared war yet?" the president asked. Wood responded, "No, Mr. President, but I think you will, sir." To that McKinley shook his head, asserting, "I shall never get into a war until I am sure that God and man approve. I have been through one war; I have seen the dead piled up, and I do not want to see another."[42]

But the pressure was becoming unbearable, and the strain was showing. Secretary Long confided to his diary, "He has been robbed of sleep, overworked; and I fancy that I can see his mind does not work as clearly and directly and as self-reliantly as it otherwise would." Added the ever faithful Cortelyou, the president was "bearing up under the great strain, but his haggard face and anxious inquiry of any news which has in it a token of peace tell of the sense of tremendous responsibility and of his devotion to the welfare of the people of this country."[43]

On March 26, as he prepared to submit the *Maine* report to Congress, McKinley had Day send a message to Ambassador Woodford. It summarized the American position and offered a final proposal. It repeated the country's desire for peace and disclaimed any designs to possess Cuba. Then the message got down to business: "The President suggests that if Spain will revoke the reconcentration order and maintain the people until they can support themselves and offer to the Cubans full self-government, with reasonable indemnity, the President will gladly assist in its consummation." He further agreed to help mediate if both parties so desired. When Woodford asked for clarification on the phrase "full self-government," Day responded unequivocally that it "would mean Cuban independence."[44]

McKinley followed up with three proposals for Woodford to submit to Spanish authorities. The first was an armistice until October 1 with the president conducting negotiations between Spain and the insurgents. The second was the revocation of the reconcentration order. Finally, if terms for peace could not be agreed upon by October 1, McKinley would step in and act as the "final arbiter" between the two parties. In presenting these demands, Woodford failed to make it clear that McKinley had definitely made Cuban independence a condition of any agreement. It may not have mattered because Spain only agreed to ending reconcentration. Madrid would only accept an armistice if the rebels asked first and if Blanco approved the terms. Hobart, Day, Mark Hanna, and other leading Republicans were at the White House when McKinley received the reply on March 31. None were rabid war men, but all agreed that the response fell far short of what was acceptable. On April Fool's Day the president began work on his war message.[45]

The president, it was announced, would send his message to Congress on April 4. That was soon delayed two days to give the president more time to get his thoughts down on paper. On April 6 both houses of Congress assembled at the Capitol, along with a crowd of some ten thousand. At about noon McKinley heard from Fitzhugh Lee, a Confederate cavalry commander and the nephew of the Confederacy's most revered general. Lee was serving as the American consul in Havana, and he prayed for time to get all Americans safely off the island if war was to come. Delay the message until Monday, the 11th, he pleaded. McKinley summoned a delegation of congressional leaders to the White House and told them he was going to do as Lee had asked. The politicians were indignant, pleading and threatening, and finally the harassed president snapped. Handing the paper to Cortelyou, he pounded his desk with his fist and said, "That message shall not go to Congress as long as there is a single American life in danger in Cuba. Here [McKinley instructed Cortelyou], put that in the safe until I call for it."[46]

McKinley called for his seven thousand-word message on April 11 and sent it to Congress, where it promptly fell flat. The president asked the legislators to authorize "armed intervention," but did not ask for a declaration of war. There was also no call to recognize the Cuban government. Indeed he spoke against recognition of "the so-called Cuban republic." This was, in reality, a wise move. Recognition could have placed invading U.S. armies under Cuban law and under the leadership of Cuban generals. Congress did not grasp this, and the legislators attempted to add amendments recognizing a Cuban government as Speaker Reed labored to tamp them down. Finally Senator Henry Moore Teller of Colorado proposed a compromise. The Teller Amendment asserted that "the people of the island of Cuba are, and of the right to be, free and independent," adding, "The United States hereby disclaims any disposition or intention to exercise sovereignty, jurisdiction, or control over said Island." The measure broke the impasse and made Teller a bit of a hero. However, his true motive was likely to keep tariffs on Cuban sugar, thus protecting domestic sugar beet growers, including those in Colorado.[47]

Congress passed the resolution April 19, and the president signed it the next day. Spain severed diplomatic relations on the 21st. Woodford left Madrid on the Paris express, brandishing a pistol as the train passed rock-throwing mobs. McKinley ordered a naval blockade of Cuba, an act of war, on the 22nd, and Spain declared war two days later. On the 25th McKinley asked Congress to declare war. Two resignations followed. One came from John Sherman, a staunch opponent of war. Day took his place at the State Department. The other came from the assistant secretary of the navy, who in the view of Secretary Long deserted his post "to ride a horse and, probably, brush mosquitoes from his neck on the Florida sands."[48]

6

McKinley: Commander-in-Chief and Beyond

When war began William McKinley was commander-in-chief of an army of 28,000 officers and men. No unit larger than a regiment existed. There were ten bureaus, most burdened with so much red tape and paperwork that virtually nothing could get done. Two men were responsible for untangling this mess, and neither was quite up to the job. One was Maj. Gen. Nelson A. Miles, the commanding general. A Civil War veteran and Indian fighter, he had grown old and grumpy, and his political ambitions would soon get the best of him. The other was Russell A. Alger, the secretary of war. Also a Civil War veteran, Alger had become a successful businessman and GOP politician. When McKinley named him to the post, Mark Hanna had joked that the War Department was the only cabinet office "for which a busy man could spare the time from his own affairs." This was true enough in the peacetime army, but the *Brooklyn Eagle* was prescient when it observed, "We certainly tremble to contemplate a war conducted under his direction." Alger was soon in above his head, and the clash of egos that just as quickly occurred between him and Miles only made matters worse.[1]

On April 22 President McKinley called for 125,000 volunteers for two years of service. He would ask for 75,000 more on May 25. The Army established major training camps near Chattanooga and at Falls Church, Virginia, with smaller facilities at San Francisco, San Antonio, New Orleans, Tampa, and Mobile. Some of the militia outfits arrived at the sites well equipped, but many showed up unarmed and in civilian clothing. The shortages overwhelmed the 57 officers composing the Quartermaster's Department. There were only enough modern Krag-Jorgenson rifles and carbines (themselves not particularly efficient weapons) to supply the regulars and a handful of volunteers. The rest were issued single-shot Springfields that fired a .45-caliber black powder slug. Worse, Alger discovered that no American factory was capable of turning out light khaki cloth for tropical uniforms. The Army did acquire some canvas fatigues, but most of the men headed to Cuba wore blue woolen shirts and trousers.[2]

Trusting neither Alger nor Miles, McKinley, who had once considered making the Army his career, became commander-in-chief in fact as well as in name. He had a room next to his office equipped with twenty telegraph lines and garnished with maps from the Office of the Coast and Geodetic Survey. Kept secret from the public, it was soon christened the "War Room." The Civil War veteran attempted to appoint officers on the basis of merit, undoubtedly remembering the decidedly mixed record of "political generals" three decades earlier. Desirous of sectional harmony, McKinley asked Fitzhugh Lee and "Fighting Joe" Wheeler to don blue uniforms as major generals. Both agreed, and Wheeler served conspicuously.[3]

Not everyone approved of the president's course, and the number of threatening letters arriving at the White House increased dramatically. The process actually began shortly after the sinking of the *Maine*. Those missives generally threatened to seek revenge if war was not declared. Once the conflict began the would-be assailants demanded that it be ended. They came from, among others, "A Republican," "A Vet," and "A True American," the last of which threatened to blow up the White House. At the time the Secret Service was still largely devoted to apprehending counterfeiters, although they did post extra agents to the White House. The letters were referred to the superintendent of the Washington, D.C., police.[4]

The first good news of the war came from far away. As he waited in Hong Kong Commodore Dewey stocked up on coal, even purchasing a pair of British colliers and their cargoes. On April 25 he received word from Secretary Long that war had begun and orders to head for the Philippines to capture the Spanish fleet. Dewey's flotilla arrived at Manila Bay during the early morning hours of May 1, slowing so as to reach the city at first light. Dewey held all the cards. Four of his six ships had armored decks. None of the enemy vessels did, and the largest, *Castilla*, was made entirely of wood. The American fleet was faster and better armed. Although the Spanish shore batteries boasted 226 guns, 164 were muzzle loaders, centuries out of date. Like his Civil War commander, David G. Farragut, Dewey's idol, the commodore was about to earn glory after decades of loyal service. He was aboard his flagship, *Olympia*, Capt. Charles V. Gridley commanding.[5]

At about 5:30 a.m. *Olympia* was two and a half miles from the Spanish ships, and Dewey said, "You may fire when you are ready, Gridley." The flagship passed the Spanish fleet, firing from port, then turned 180 degrees and steamed past them again, opening up with her starboard guns. The other ships followed, repeating the process over and over. As the fourth pass began the Spanish flagship, *Reina Cristina*, charged into the bay to attack *Olympia*. The action was more valiant than prudent. The Spanish ship was sunk, half her crew casualties. At that point Gridley informed Dewey that the American flagship was short on ammunition. The squadron retreated into the bay to check on the situation, determining the report was erroneous and that there was plenty of ordnance to complete the task. After improving upon the lull to enjoy breakfast, the Americans steamed back toward the Spanish fleet, which surrendered 75 minutes later.[6]

Sketchy accounts of the victory arrived in America May 2 from Madrid via London. Confirmation, in the form of Dewey's official report, followed five days later. The news gave America its first hero of the war. Congress voted ten thousand dollars to award Dewey a Tiffany sword, and there was a brief "Dewey for President" boomlet. But the victory also produced difficulties of the type McKinley had predicted. Soon after the battle Emilio Aguinaldo y Famy, exiled leader of a Philippine revolution, returned from Hong Kong and met with Dewey. As Aguinaldo remembered it, the commodore promised independence. Dewey's recollection was different. The complications growing out of the situation would later prompt the president to observe, "If old Dewey had just sailed away when he smashed that Spanish fleet, what a lot of trouble he would have saved us."[7]

On April 29 another Spanish fleet, consisting of four armored cruisers and three torpedo-boat destroyers, left the Cape Verde Islands. They were bound for Puerto Rico, which Spain had assumed would be America's first target in the Caribbean. Adm. Pascual Cervera y Topete was in command. For a variety of reasons he later changed the destination to Santiago de Cuba on the island's southern coast. The U.S. had learned of the fleet's location, and Commodore Winfield Scott Schley was dispatched to bottle it up. Schley did not believe the intelligence, and he wasted several days chasing phantoms. Once he arrived off Santiago de Cuba he almost immediately departed, not returning for nearly 24 hours. Then he announced plans to go back to Key West for coal, which he did not need. Desperate messages from the Navy Department urged Schley to do his duty. They eventually took, and on May 28 Cervera's fleet was trapped in the harbor.[8]

McKinley had originally leaned toward a direct attack against Havana. Now he shifted the objective to Santiago de Cuba. On May 29 orders went to Maj. Gen. William Rufus Shafter, commanding the Fifth Corps at Tampa, to ready his men to board transports for the voyage to Cuba.[9]

Shafter's force at Tampa had been growing during the month of May.

Before they could depart to fight the Spanish, however, they had to battle logistical challenges that were daunting. Only two railroads served Tampa, and just a single track connected the city to the port, several miles south. Complicating the situation was the fact that over a thousand freight cars had arrived, all of them lacking bills of lading. This forced men to search from box to box and car to car to find items they needed, whether clothing, grain, or siege guns.[10]

Among the outfits arriving was the First U.S. Volunteer Cavalry, destined to be known as the Rough Riders. They reached Tampa on June 5, and after a hungry 24 hours their officers, including Col. Leonard Wood and Lt. Col. Theodore Roosevelt, reached into their own pockets to provision the men. A worse blow came on June 7, after Shafter had been ordered to set sail. Roosevelt feared his unit would be left behind when no train arrived to deliver them to the port. He and Wood solved the problem by commandeering a coal train and making it backtrack to Tampa. They then bluffed their way around two regiments to secure places on the transport *Yucatan*. The Rough Riders, Teddy in tow, were going to Cuba.[11]

After a number of postponements, as the men sweltered aboard the transports, the fleet sailed on June 14, reaching Santiago six days later. Although he could likely have taken the city easily, Shafter disembarked eighteen miles east at Daiquirí. Two black soldiers, members of the famed "Buffalo Soldiers," drowned in the landing, the first casualties of the war. Among the first general officers going ashore was "Fighting Joe" Wheeler, who improved upon his opportunity to draw first blood and gain a bit of glory. He ordered his forces forward and attacked the Spanish at Las Guásimas. The move was successful, and as the enemy retreated, Wheeler, forgetting what war he was in, reportedly shouted, "We've got the damn Yankees on the run!"[12]

On July 1 Shafter ordered attacks on El Caney, Kettle Hill, and San Juan Hill. This was the day that Theodore Roosevelt galloped into immortality—and deservedly so—although his gallantry showed more on Kettle Hill than on San Juan Hill. He was not alone, however. Brig. Gen Henry Lawton had 81 killed and 360 wounded taking the stone fort at El Caney. Total casualties for the day were 205 killed and 1,180 wounded. Among those making signal contributions were the various black units. Lt. John J. Pershing, whose nickname "Black Jack" would grow from his service with the "colored" Tenth Cavalry, later wrote, "We officers of the Tenth Cavalry could have taken our black heroes in our arms. They had again fought their way into our affections."[13]

The Americans now commanded the heights overlooking Santiago de Cuba. Rear Adm. William Sampson, Commodore Schley's superior, had the Spanish fleet trapped in the bay. Despite these advantages, Shafter considered withdrawing some five miles, claiming the move would make it easier to get supplies. McKinley and Alger left the final decision to their general but warned him of "the effect upon the country" a retreat would have. Shafter stayed put.[14]

The situation improved on July 3 when Cervera attempted to escape with his fleet. It was Manila Bay all over again as the superior American ships pummeled the Spanish vessels. Indeed, the Americans soon turned from attackers to rescuers, bringing aboard survivors from the battered enemy fleet. Both victors and vanquished were gracious. When Cervera was taken aboard the *Iowa*, the American crew broke out in cheers, and the admiral bowed to his captors. The butcher bill for the day was one American killed and one wounded and 323 Spanish killed, 151 wounded, and 1,813 captured.[15]

By then whatever fight Shafter might have had in him was gone. He first insisted that the Navy must force its way into the harbor, not appreciating the fact that said harbor was mined. On July 9 Gen. José Toral, commanding at Santiago, proposed that his force, still bearing arms, be permitted to march unmolested to Holguín, 75 miles to the northwest. Shafter urged Washington to agree, and General Miles, who had been dispatched to Cuba supposedly to stiffen Shafter's backbone, agreed. William McKinley did not. The reluctant commander-in-chief understood better than his generals what war was about. "What you went to Santiago for was the Spanish Army," he wrote. "If you allow it to evacuate with its arms you must meet it somewhere else. This is not war." Toral surrendered on July 16.[16]

Meanwhile a new enemy, not unanticipated, was threatening the American soldiers in Cuba. In early July the first cases of yellow fever appeared. Within a week there were 150. At the same time malaria and dysentery plagued about half of the Fifth Corps. The sick list went from 3,370 on July 27 to 4,290 on August 2. (Eventually the corps would lose 243 men killed in action, while disease claimed 771.) At this point Lieutenant Colonel Roosevelt, never one to worry about such details as insubordination, stepped in, composing a "round robin" letter, signed by most of the unit's top commanders. It, and a subsequent missive addressed to Shafter, accused the War Department of letting the corps die "like rotten sheep" while doing nothing to avert the disaster. The letter was leaked to the press, which annoyed the president, who had received peace feelers from Spain. It was also unnecessary; Alger had already ordered the Fifth Corps home. The first troops left on August 7, the last on the 25th.[17]

They returned to Montauk Point, Long Island, a site named Camp Wikoff in honor of one of the fallen on San Juan Heights. As at Tampa, the facility was never able fully to handle the deluge of soldiers. Private charity combined with the government to alleviate the worst of the suffering. On September 3 the president and Vice President Hobart paid a visit. "I am glad to meet you," McKinley said. "You have come home after two months of severe campaigning, which has embraced assault and siege and battle, so brilliant in achievement, so far-reaching in results as to command the unstinted praise of all your countrymen."[18]

The last action in the Caribbean was a campaign Miles launched against Puerto Rico. Although the people of the island had not been caught up in the revolutionary spirit of Cuba, they suspected they might fare better under the United States, which did not (yet) have a record of colonialism. In any event, the welcome was warm when Miles captured the coastal city of Ponce on July 27. His forces were advancing in southern Puerto Rico when, on August 12, word of the armistice arrived. The campaign had cost the Americans seven killed and 36 wounded, about one-tenth the Spanish casualties.[19]

The armistice also brought an end to fighting in the Pacific. After Dewey defeated the Spanish fleet in Manila, Maj. Gen. Wesley Merritt was put in command of an expeditionary force of about 11,000 officers and men sent from San Francisco to capture the Philippine capital. On the way they were instructed to take the Spanish island of Guam. That proved quite easy. On June 20 the first contingent of the force reached the island, and the cruiser *Charleston* lobbed a few shells at Agaña, the capital city. Two Spanish officials came out in a small boat. Guam had not received any news in two months, and the officials apologized for not being able to return what they believed was a salute. The formal surrender took place the next day.[20]

General Merritt's force reached the Philippines in late July. The general's twin orders from the president were to force a Spanish surrender and to provide security and order to the islands. Individual rights were to be protected, but the inhabitants had to accept American authority. The Spanish were not anxious to carry on the fight. They knew they were about to lose Manila, and their main concern was that it fall to the Americans and not to the 14,000 rebels Aguinaldo had surrounding the city. Still, there was the matter of honor, so important to the Spanish. Governor-General Don Fermin Jáudenes y Alvarez agreed to surrender but only if the Americans launched an attack and if the insurgents were kept out of the city. "So I had to fire," Dewey later recounted, "to kill a few people." The sham battle took place on August 13, one day after the armistice. All went according to the script, the Spanish surrendering on schedule.[21]

The insurgents were less cooperative. In reality, American policy left them little room to be. "There must be no joint occupation with the insurgents," McKinley instructed Dewey and Merritt. Meanwhile the rebels began stockpiling arms and consolidating their hold on positions outside Manila. Boredom and drinking among the American soldiers did not help, and there was a number of incidents and occasional gunfire. Serious fighting began on February 4, 1899, when an American patrol encountered a group of insurgents. It is not clear who fired first, but the skirmish quickly escalated. The next day the U.S. launched general offensive operations. The rebellion went on until March 1901, when American forces captured Aguinaldo. Sporadic resistance continued for more than a decade. Philippine independence came in 1946.[22]

On June 3, with Cervera bottled up in Santiago's harbor, McKinley decided to send out peace feelers through third parties. Day submitted four demands. First Spain must evacuate Cuba and turn the island over to the United States. Next Spain must also cede Puerto Rico. Third the U.S. would retain a port in the Philippines. Finally, Madrid must give up one of the Marianas Islands, likely Guam. Day warned that further resistance would result in harsher terms. Spain did not respond.

By mid–July Guam had been taken, Puerto Rico seemed about to be, and the United States had an even stronger hand in Cuba. On the 18th, through the French, Spain offered Cuban independence for peace. Eight days later Jules Cambon, France's ambassador to the U.S., gave McKinley a letter from the Queen Regent seeking terms. Cambon did a little lobbying, reminding the president and the secretary of state that America had gone to war over Cuba alone, and Spain's offer should be sufficient to end it. Day reminded him that fighting was occurring elsewhere, adding that the United States could not yet talk with certainty on all points. Cambon returned on July 28 and again on August 4 to plead Spain's case, only to be told by the president that Cuba, Puerto Rico, and Guam "do not admit of discussion." Members of McKinley's own party would have been surprised to learn that Cambon termed the chief executive "inflexible."[23]

The Philippines did admit of discussion, mainly because the cabinet was sharply divided on the issue. Three favored annexing the entire archipelago. Three others, including Day and Long, desired only a naval base. Alger was not sure what he wanted.

Cambon informed Spain that the American position was fixed and that further delays would only lead to stiffer terms. Madrid understood, and on August 12 Cambon and McKinley signed an armistice. It contained the American demands, left the fate of the Philippines to future negotiations, and stopped the shooting. Secretary Day headed the five-man delegation bound for Paris and the formal peace talks. On September 16, just before they departed, McKinley instructed the group that they should insist on not just Manila for the United States but the entire island of Luzon.[24]

Although he may not have fully realized it himself, McKinley was inching toward support for annexation of the Philippines. There were several reasons arguing in favor of it. The islands would be valuable as a Far East naval base. Business saw the possibility of new resources and markets. The Filipinos, Americans on the scene believed, were not capable of self-government. Abandoning the islands would create a vacuum that Germany or some other power would likely be quick to fill.

Ever the savvy but cautious politician, McKinley was anxious to divine the verdict of the people. Congressional elections were approaching, and starting October 11, the president went on a week-and-a-half speaking tour of the Midwest and plains states. Among his stops was the Trans-Mississippi Exposition in Omaha. Duty and responsibility were constant themes, and they struck a responsive chord with his audiences. Later humanitarianism and Christian obligation were added to the mix. Five days after returning to Washington, McKinley instructed the peace commission to insist upon the annexation of the Philippines. This produced back-and-forth discussions in Paris, but the Americans held the upper hand. Spain's last hope died when the voters returned a Republican congress to power, demonstrating that the people supported the president and his policies. On November 21 Day put forward what was basically an ultimatum: the U.S. would pay $20 million for the Philippines. Spain had one week to think it over. It only took them four days. On December 10 both parties affixed their signatures to the Treaty of Paris.[25]

Now it was up to the United States Senate, a body that could be just as stubborn as the Spanish negotiators. The debate produced strange bedfellows. Vocal anti-imperialists included former presidents Harrison and Cleveland, along with Andrew Carnegie and Mark Twain. William Jennings Bryan quietly and cynically urged Democrats to support the pact, believing it would supply him with a campaign issue in 1900. What likely tipped the scales in favor of ratification was the Filipino uprising. With American forces under fire, McKinley realized the people would insist on approval. So did the Senate, and on February 6, 1899, they ratified the agreement. The vote was 57–27, two more than the required two-thirds.[26]

The war was over, but there were still pesky details with which to deal. One was the Philippine rebellion. Another was Cuba. The Teller Amendment had promised that the United States would only control Cuba until "pacification." Yet, as in the Philippines, American political and military leaders doubted if the rebels were ready for self-government. Gen. Leonard Wood, Teddy's friend and commander, became the military governor. He built roads, schools, and hospitals. He also horsewhipped Cubans who violated sanitary rules. His reign, however, was relatively brief. Cuba gained independence in May 1902.[27]

Another problem lay much closer to home. Alger's mismanagement of the War Department had become too much for even the normally patient McKinley. The breaking point came when reports leaked of "appalling conditions" aboard transports returning Americans from Cuba. McKinley gave the secretary a two-day chewing out as he demanded information about arrangements to bring the men home. As "Algerism" entered the language as a synonym for incompetence, Republican congressional candidates beseeched McKinley to sack the unpopular secretary. Peace eased the situation until the Philippine uprising brought the promise of more military action—and more potential mismanagement. Finally McKinley had had enough, although he could not bring himself to wield the axe. Instead the loyal Hobart did the president's dirty work, securing Alger's resignation on July 18, 1899.[28]

With the war over, McKinley was able to return to the economic issues so important to him. Prosperity, he believed, demonstrated that protection should no longer be the centerpiece of American economic policy. The war had made the United States a player in world affairs. Now it must assert its economic leadership, capturing world markets in the process. Unfortunately, many of McKinley's fellow Republicans remained devoted to protectionism, while Democrats felt reciprocity was no more than protectionism in sheep's clothing. As a result many of the administration's reciprocity treaties disappeared in the labyrinth that was the Senate Finance Committee. In September 1899 a hurricane hit Puerto Rico, killing three thousand and destroying the island's main crop, coffee. McKinley and Elihu Root, Alger's successor, proposed ending all tariffs between Puerto Rico and the contiguous states. Congress was aghast, concerned not just for the policy but also for sugar beet farmers, tobacco farmers, and cigar manufacturers. The best the administration could get was a lower tariff, with the revenues to be used to benefit the new possession.[29]

On other issues the president talked a good line but did little more. In his 1898 and 1900 annual messages he called for an eight-hour day for government workers. In 1899 he asserted, "Combinations of capital organized into trusts to control the conditions of trade among our citizens, to stifle competition, limit production, and determine the prices of products used and consumed by the people are justly provoking public discussion, and should early claim the attention of Congress." He added that state legislation was inadequate, insisting there must be "a complete system of laws throughout the United States." Ironically, as events would turn out, Theodore Roosevelt at about the same time termed talk against trusts "aimless and baseless."[30]

In his inaugural address, McKinley asserted that "lynchings must not be tolerated in a great and civilized country like the United States." No action followed. He did instruct the War Department to raise additional black regiments and to commission a handful of black officers above the rank of lieutenant. McKinley also appointed a number of African-American customs collectors and filled what were considered traditional "black offices," such as superintendent of postage stamps. These modest actions were disappointing to the president's numerous black supporters, who had reason to expect more. He may have wanted to do more, but the Civil War veteran in the White House staunchly desired sectional unity. That desire and civil rights were mutually incompatible, and McKinley leaned much further toward the former, which also happened to be politically safer.[31]

As the 1900 Republican convention got under way in Philadelphia, McKinley's renomination was a certainty. Who would claim the second spot on the ticket was uncertain. Vice President Hobart had died on November 21, 1899. Root was the president's first choice for the office, but with the uprising in the Philippines, both men came to agree that the secretary would be more useful at the War Department.

To many in the party the hero of San Juan Hill seemed the obvious choice. Roosevelt, who had been elected governor of New York in 1898, denied any interest. To friends he complained that the job would be boring. Yet in his public denials he never shut the door entirely, perhaps because he was aware of the increased prestige the office had enjoyed during the McKinley-Hobart years. When he showed up at the convention in a wide-brimmed army hat, some delegates began to refer to the conspicuous headgear as an "acceptance hat." Senator Foraker placed McKinley's name in nomination, and Roosevelt seconded it. Then the Rough Rider sat back as the convention unanimously nominated him for vice president. Not everyone was enthusiastic about the choice. Annoyed by McKinley's refusal to step in, Hanna howled, "Don't any of you realize there's only one life between that madman and the Presidency?"[32]

Roosevelt charged into the 1900 campaign the way he had charged up Kettle Hill—all out. Bryan was again the Democratic candidate, and he again took his show on the road. His speeches were a strange amalgam of anti-imperialism, anti-trust, and pro silver. McKinley returned to Canton but refused to campaign, even from his front porch, feeling it would be undignified for a sitting president to solicit votes. His running mate took up the slack, delivering some six hundred speeches. The effect is hard to determine, but the presence of a genuine war hero likely stirred up enthusiasm for the ticket, and Roosevelt's conversion to an anti-trust position may have blunted Bryan's populist appeal.[33]

Prosperity at home and triumph overseas proved a winning combination. On November 6 voters returned McKinley to office. He won the popular vote 7,218,491–6,356,734, even carrying Bryan's hometown precinct. The electoral vote was 292–155. Both margins were greater than in 1896. The Republicans retained control of both houses of Congress. It was an impressive mandate, and it gave the president reason to look forward with confidence to a successful second term.[34]

7

The War of the Standards

Just after midnight on November 16, 1896, William Rankine, secretary of the Niagara Falls Power Company, pulled down three switches at Power House 1. Twenty-six miles away three more switches went down at the power house of the Buffalo Railway Company. "For a minute or two," wrote a reporter present at the railway company, "there was a humming, then a heavy buzzing and then there was heard a steady roaring whirr." Sparks flew, transformer coils began to turn, and the roar grew louder. At first engineers and company officials stood transfixed. "Then," the reporter gushed, "the triumph of man over matter and natural forces burst upon them with overwhelming force and every man in the transformer [room] gave vent to his joy and his gratitude by cheering the big machines."[1]

Although cannons, steam whistles, and bells announced the news to the city, the first transmission was only a test of the system. There still remained, in the words of the railway company's manager, "a few little technical things" to be hammered out before the streetcars began running on Niagara power. Apparently they were dealt with quickly. On November 19 the company ran trains on three lines with current generated at the falls. "In every respect the test was satisfactory," reported the *Buffalo Commercial*. "The cars ran on time, steadily and smoothly." The successful test suggested a bright future for Buffalo, powered by current from the falls. It also, for all practical purposes, marked the end of what had come to be called "the war of the standards." It had been a vicious—even deadly—fight, culminating at Buffalo with a final triumph for alternating current and its champions.[2]

It should not come as a surprise that the idea for the first mass commercial distribution of electricity rested with Thomas Edison. In 1878 the inventor, still perfecting his incandescent bulb, announced plans to light up all of lower Manhattan. Two years later the Edison Electric Illuminating Company of New York was incorporated. In 1881 the company began installing 18 miles of copper mains under the city's streets, as well as fuses, switches, and the other accouterments necessary to bring Edison's plans to fruition. Meanwhile

66

the Wizard of Menlo Park had established his headquarters in a four-story building on Pearl Street. The frugal Edison had selected the site carefully. Its proximity to the city's business district, he believed, would assure a steady supply of paying customers, while the building's actual location in a slum area would keep his rent low. Time would prove Edison right about the former and wrong about the latter.

The effort encountered stiff opposition from arc lighting firms and gas companies, whose pipes ran under the same streets where Edison planned to lay his conduits. The commissioner of public works required that Edison pay five dollars a day to each of five "inspectors." None, the inventor ruefully noted, ever showed up to inspect anything, but the entire quintet arrived each Saturday for their pay.[3]

Edison overcame this and all other obstacles, and on September 4, 1882, he threw the switch that inaugurated the service. Some 400 bulbs came on, a number that would grow to 2,500 within a month and five thousand in four months. Consumers were delighted with the bulbs' steady light, the lack of any "nauseous smell," and the ease of operation. Soon Manhattan's gas consumers were requesting in overwhelming numbers that their service be cut off so they could switch to Edison power.[4]

There was only one problem with Edison's system. Its electrical tentacles could only reach out about half a mile. That was because his plant worked on direct current, which, as its name implies, could only send electricity in one direction, directly to the customers' lamps. There was, however, another power standard, alternating current, lurking on the horizon. AC flowed from generator to bulb and then back again several times a second. More important, alternating current could be stepped up to extremely high voltages, which could be transmitted several miles, then stepped down again for domestic use. Edison seems to have never grasped the concept of AC. "How do they make the current go the other direction?" he reportedly asked. Over time, as the strange current emerged as a challenge to his electrical empire, his confusion grew into hostility.[5]

As Thomas Edison began advancing toward DC obstinacy, Nikola Tesla was arriving in America. Tesla, the son of a Serbian Orthodox priest, was born in 1856 in what was then the Austro-Hungarian Empire and today is Croatia. While a young boy, stroking the family's black cat, he was amazed when his action produced a "shower of sparks." He asked his father what caused the phenomenon, and the elder Tesla replied that it was electricity, the same as lightning. At that point, an obsession was born.

In 1875 Tesla entered the Joanneum Polytechnic School at Graz, Austria, enrolling in mathematics and physics. He was soon inspired by Jacob Poschl, a physics professor, whose demonstrations, utilizing the most modern inventions, led him to change his field of study to engineering. In 1880, following a period of carousing and gambling that may have been brought on by his father's death, Tesla enrolled at the Karl-Ferdinand University in Prague. He remained only a year before moving to Budapest, where he first worked in a government telegraph office before quitting to focus on inventing. Later he helped install a new telephone exchange in the city. His work attracted the attention of Edison representatives, who invited him to join them in the Paris office. While there Tesla often discussed plans he had mentally conceived for an AC motor, but his Edison colleagues were uninterested in the idea.[6]

In 1884 Charles Batchelor, Edison's chief lieutenant, came back to America from a trip to France. He suggested that the talented young scientist be brought across the Atlantic. Tesla arrived on June 6, but his time with Edison was brief and unhappy. Upon meeting the great American inventor, he began discussing his ideas concerning alternating current. Edison immediately cut him off with a curt, "Hold up! Spare me that nonsense. It's dangerous. We're set up for direct current in America." Later Edison offered his new employee a fifty-thousand-dollar bonus if Tesla could make good on his claim that he could improve the company's DC dynamos, resulting in a tremendous cost savings. When Tesla came through and asked for his promised bonus, Edison responded, "Tesla, you don't understand our American humor." Tesla didn't, and after six months with Edison, he left.[7]

Tesla's next experience with American entrepreneurs was even worse. In December 1884 New Jersey businessmen Benjamin A. Vail and Robert Lane hired the gifted Serb to organize the Tesla Electric Light and Manufacturing Company. He patented a number of inventions for the arc lighting firm, turning them over to the company in return for shares of stock. Then, when everything was in place, Vail and Lane abandoned Tesla, forming a new company and leaving Tesla with no patents and worthless stock. Work proved hard to get, and for a time he toiled as a day laborer, digging ditches for two dollars a day.[8]

It did not take long for one of Tesla's foremen to realize that his talents went far beyond a pick and shovel. Eventually this led to an introduction to Alfred S. Brown, an engineer with Western Union Telegraph Company, and Charles F. Peck, a New Jersey lawyer with an interest in electrical inventions. The two offered to sponsor Tesla in his work, forming the Tesla Electric Company in April 1887. Finally the gifted inventor could work to make his AC dreams a reality.[9]

Meanwhile, a more practical inventor was embracing AC as a potential power source. In 1867, at the age of 21, George Westinghouse had invented a mechanical device for returning derailed railroad cars to the tracks. He followed that up with a reversible railroad frog, a switching device that allowed a train to cross from one track to another. Just over a year later Westinghouse patented his railway air brake. A revolutionary breakthrough in safety, the device significantly reduced stopping times and meant brakemen would no longer have to operate hand brakes in all sorts of weather from the roofs of cars. Westinghouse then went to England, establishing both factories and markets for his inventions. While there he became interested in the use of electricity to operate railroad signals. He began buying up patents, adding to them inventions of his own design. Upon returning to America in 1881, he established the Union Switch and Signal Company in Pittsburgh.[10]

Westinghouse quickly became enamored of electricity and its commercial possibilities. At the same time he was painfully aware of the distance limitations of Edison's DC dynamos. As Westinghouse pondered the problem, French inventor Lucien Gaulard and his British business partner, John D. Gibbs, were working on a solution. In 1881 the pair obtained a British patent for an alternating current system that utilized a "secondary generator" (transformer) to reduce voltage to levels safe for domestic consumption at the point of delivery. Current therefore could be sent several miles at high voltage then stepped down for use in homes or businesses. Gaulard and Gibbs demonstrated their system in London in 1883, and the following year at the Turin Exhibition. The pair ran a line from Turin to Lanzo, a community in the Alps 25 miles away, and safely delivered power to both places, as well as points in between.

In 1885 Westinghouse read about the Gaulard-Gibbs system in the British journal *Engineering.* At the time one of his employees was in Italy to attend his father's funeral. Westinghouse contacted the young man and asked him to check out the European pair's work. After viewing a fifty-mile circuit and discussing the system with European scientists, the Westinghouse employee forwarded a positive report to his boss. The Pittsburgh entrepreneur purchased the U.S. patent from Gaulard and Gibbs for $50,000.[11]

Westinghouse put William Stanley, an electrical engineer in his employ, in charge of improving the Gaulard-Gibbs transformer and making it commercially feasible. Because his health was poor, Westinghouse allowed Stanley to set up shop in his hometown, Great Barrington, Massachusetts. Another Westinghouse employee, Reginald Belfield, was dispatched to western Massachusetts to assist. Meanwhile, on January 8, 1886, the Westinghouse Electric Company was incorporated. It was the inventor's fifth corporation. As Westinghouse engineers in Pittsburgh worked to make better generators and transformers, Stanley labored to create a working AC system, and Belfield strung

4,000 feet of copper wire. Finally, on March 20, Stanley put his system to practical use, transmitting power from a plant two miles away and lighting up some 150 lamps in thirteen stores and seven other buildings. The plant operated several months before someone accidentally dropped a screwdriver into the generator. Despite that setback, the age of AC power had arrived.[12]

Westinghouse conducted further successful tests in the Pittsburgh area before deciding to launch his AC business competitively. His first customer was Adam, Meldrum, & Anderson, a four-story department store in Buffalo. The service was inaugurated the day before Thanksgiving, 1888. The following Monday the store held an open house, not to sell merchandise, but to show off its 498 AC-powered lamps. In a short time Westinghouse had 27 more orders for his new system of power delivery.[13]

Within two years Westinghouse AC was serving 130 cities and towns, and Edison salesmen were beginning to worry. The sudden competition jolted Edison (so to speak), who had enjoyed a monopoly of the incandescent lighting business. In late 1887 he launched his attack on Westinghouse and AC with a series of patent infringement lawsuits. The Wizard also lobbied in support of bills before the New York and Virginia legislatures that would have limited currents to 300 volts, putting AC systems out of business. Edison even ventured to Richmond to testify personally before a committee of the state senate. His foray into politics failed, as did his legal maneuvers.

Edison then took his case directly to the public, issuing a pamphlet entitled, "A Warning From the Edison Electric Company." It began with a threat of legal action. The Edison company, the missive asserted, held patents on "all practical incandescent lamps." Those using his competitors' systems, therefore, faced the possibility of lawsuits. Edison then turned to a different kind of threat—the threat that alternating current supposedly posed to life and limb. The pamphlet recounted, in gruesome detail, cases of individuals who had been fatally shocked at the hands of AC power. Still more frightening were the potential dangers. What if a transformer failed, Edison ominously asked, sending high tension current through a home or office to claim its unsuspecting occupants? By contrast, the pamphlet concluded, "There is no danger to life, health, or person, in the current generated by any of the Edison dynamos."[14]

Edison was fighting a losing battle, and he soon acquired a questionable ally. Harold Brown had been a salesman for various electrical firms and was an inventor who had never been quite able to secure a patent. In 1888 he was promoting himself as an "electrical engineer" and operating a business in New York City which produced equipment to make arc light dynamos somewhat safer. On June 5 he entered the AC vs. DC fray when a letter he had written attacking the "damnable" current appeared in the *New York Post*. The letter was couched in terms of public safety, with populist undertones. "The public must submit to *constant danger from sudden death*," Brown asserted, "in order that a corporation may pay a *little larger dividend*." While making his case for putting public safety ahead of corporate greed, Brown did not ignore his own profit motives. Most of his business was based on DC power, and like Edison before him, he called for limiting AC transmission to 300 volts. Other "safety" measures he recommended dovetailed nicely with services his firm provided.[15]

Brown quickly found himself a celebrity, at least in the world of electricity. He approached Edison, who, to Brown's claimed surprise, offered him the use of his New Jersey laboratory. Soon the Edison lab was offering a quarter apiece for stray dogs. Brown considered taking cats but rejected the idea, in part because "they ... have claws."[16]

On July 30, 1888, Brown took his macabre dog show public, inviting the electrical community to a demonstration at Columbia College. Some 800 showed up. "Gentlemen, it is only by my sense of right that I have been drawn into this controversy," he began. Inaccuracy followed sanctimony. "I represent no company and have no financial or commercial interest." He then killed a dog with a single AC jolt, but only after subjecting it to numerous excruciating DC shocks. At that point, as Brown made ready to electrocute a second canine, a representative of the SPCA stepped onto the stage and ordered him to knock it off. Then an AC proponent stood up and offered to take a shock of one thousand volts AC if Brown would take the same amount of DC. He demurred. As his skeptical audience began to depart, Brown shouted, "I wish this experiment had not been interrupted. I have enough dogs to satisfy the most skeptical. The only places where alternating current should be used are the dog pound, the slaughterhouse, and the state prison!"[17]

The last statement was telling—and likely calculated—because Brown and Edison had been working to make sure that the "Westinghouse current" became the instrument of death in the New York prison system. It started with Dr. Alfred P. Southwick, a Buffalo dentist, who, in 1881 was watching when a drunk stumbled onto a live wire and was instantly, and apparently painlessly, killed. This started the good doctor to thinking that electrocution might be a more humane method of capital punishment than hanging. Southwick began collecting dogs from the Buffalo pound for experiments similar to those Brown would later conduct. He also got himself appointed to a state commission that would recommend to the legislature a new means of execution.

That committee considered 34 methods of inflicting death, including the guillotine, crucifixion, stoning, and shooting the condemned out of a cannon. From the outset, however, they leaned toward electrocution, and in December 1887 Dr. Southwick decided to solicit some expert advice in the field. He wrote to Edison, and the Menlo Park inventor, two months before issuing his "Warning" pamphlet, sensed an opportunity. How better to cement AC's reputation as a deadly current than to make it the official instrument of executions? Summoning his most avuncular tone, the Wizard responded, recommending "'alternating machines,' manufactured principally in the country by George Westinghouse.... The passage of current from these machines through the human body, even by the slightest contacts, produces instantaneous death."[18]

It was an endorsement in reverse but an effective one. Edison's observations likely cemented the committee's inclination toward electrocution, and they may have played a role when the legislature voted overwhelmingly to adopt its recommendation.

In passing the law the politicians also established a panel to make recommendations as to how best to put the measure into effect, offering Edison and Brown another opportunity. The two DC advocates invited the panel's members, along with press representatives, to a December 5, 1888, demonstration at Edison's West Orange lab. Brown conducted the gathering, but Edison leant it a certain amount of credibility simply by showing up. This time Brown began his performance by dispatching two small calves with AC jolts. The first went down in about thirty seconds, the other in fewer than ten. Then Brown strapped his electrodes to a 1,230-pound horse, far larger than any likely convict. It took three tries to kill the equine victim, but after about thirty seconds of 700 AC volts, the animal fell dead. Brown and Edison had to be pleased when the *New York Times* observed the next day that "alternating current will undoubtedly drive the hangmen out of business in this state." The state committee agreed, recommending alternating current for executions.[19]

Questionable though his experiments may have been, they established Brown as the apparent expert in the field of killing living beings by means of electricity. His credentials were such that the State of New York assigned him the task of acquiring and installing dynamos and electric chairs at three New York prisons. Brown, of course, wanted to secure Westinghouse generators to deliver the deadly currents, but Westinghouse, of course, would not sell. Through back-channel maneuverings, he located used machines, making sure the voltage matched that of the dynamos the company used to provide household current. There was only one catch, but it was a substantial one. The state would not pay Brown for his services until the system produced a successful execution. Strapped for cash, Brown wrote Edison seeking an advance of $5,000. "Do you not think it worth doing," Brown pleaded, "as it will enable me … to shut off the alternating current circuits in the State?"[20]

The Wizard did think it was worth doing, and soon the whole world knew that he did. On August 25, 1889, under the less-than-subtle headline, "FOR SHAME, BROWN!" the *New York Sun* published a cache of letters that had been pilfered from Brown's office. They revealed that Edison had long supported Brown, both technically and financially, and they strongly suggested that the pair's motivation was not the safety of the public but the destruction of a commercial rival. Brown found himself inundated by a wave of public criticism, but it extended no further. The man behind the curtain, pulling the strings all along, was also the individual who had first brought light into American homes, and Edison escaped the controversy virtually unscathed.[21]

Undaunted by the adverse publicity, Brown continued to bluster. In November 1889 the widely read *North American Review* ran an article he had written titled, "The New Instrument of Execution." The piece was a thinly veiled attack on AC as an agent of instant death. An article penned by Edison, appearing in the same issue, "The Dangers of Electric Lighting," further drove home the point.[22]

By the time the articles were published, Brown had a genuine human being for the ultimate experiment on the killing powers of alternating current. William Kemmler was a native of Philadelphia, a fruit and vegetable peddler, and a man possessed of a "fondness for alcohol." During one of his frequent drunken binges he married a woman who had seduced him, but upon learning that she had not bothered to divorce her previous husband, Kemmler abandoned her. He then became involved with another married woman, Matilda "Tillie" Ziegler. In late 1887, soon after becoming acquainted, William and Tillie relocated to Buffalo, passing themselves off as a married couple under the aliases John and Matilda Hort.[23]

The relationship was a rocky one, punctuated by arguments over William's boozing and Tillie's alleged infidelity. It all came to a head at about 8:00 a.m. on March 29, 1889. Kemmler had spent most of the previous night at one of Buffalo's waterfront saloons, although accounts vary as to his sobriety at the time. Drunk or sober, he picked up a hatchet and delivered 26 blows to Tillie's head, neck, and chest, as her daughter from the previous marriage looked on in horror. Then Kemmler walked to his landlady's room and announced, "I killed her, and I'll take the rope for it."[24]

But Harold Brown and the State of New York had, they believed, a better idea. On May 10, following a four-day trial, a jury found Kemmler guilty of murder. Three days later Judge Henry Childs sentenced him to "the death punishment by being executed by electricity." At that point W. Bourke Cockran, a pricey lawyer, as well as a former and future congressman, stepped in, launching a series of appeals. He claimed his motives were purely altruistic, but behind the scenes Westinghouse was paying Cockran's fees, which approached six figures. The entrepreneur was willing to pay any price to try to prevent an execution powered by his company's generators. It was all for naught. The eloquent and persistent Cockran went all the way to the United States Supreme Court, but in the end judges at every level ruled that electrocution did not constitute cruel and unusual punishment. Kemmler's execution was set for August 6, 1890, at the state prison in Auburn, New York.[25]

During his time at Auburn Kemmler dried out, came to God, and grew close with warden Charles Durston and his other keepers. Mrs. Durston read Scripture to him and taught him to read. On the eve of his execution the warden joined Kemmler as he received the sacrament of Holy Communion. The convicted man assured Durston, "I am not afraid, Warden, so long as you are in charge of the job. I won't break down if you don't."[26]

Early the next morning Kemmler had his last breakfast. He shared the meal with Joseph Veiling, an Erie County deputy, who had been his jailer in Buffalo. Kemmler seemed genuinely glad to see Veiling. "Joe, I want you to stick by me through this thing," he told his former keeper. "Don't let them experiment on me more than they ought to." Following breakfast, Kemmler's head was shaved, and he, Warden Durston, and Deputy Veiling went to the basement death chamber. Twenty-six witnesses, including two reporters, were waiting. As they entered the room, Durston announced, "Gentlemen, this is Mr. Kemmler." The condemned man was given the opportunity to speak, responding, "Well, I think I am going to a good place, and the papers has been saying a lot of stuff about me that wasn't true. That's all I have to say." Then he sat in the chair as Veiling, his hands trembling, attempted to strap him in. "Don't get too excited, Joe," Kemmler said. "I want you to make a good job of this."[27]

The executioners did not, as things turned out, make a good job of it. For one thing, the dynamo and engine were located in a prison shop, several hundred feet away. The switch and other instruments were in a separate room adjoining the death chamber. This made proper communication extremely difficult. At 6:40, after the last electrode was applied, Durston said, "Goodbye, William," then knocked on the door of the switchroom. This was the signal to throw the switch and start 1,700 volts of Westinghouse generated AC surging through Kemmler's body. But for how long? Dr. Carlos F. MacDonald, president of the State Commission on Lunacy, and Dr. E. C. Spitzka, a New

York neurologist, had been appointed supervising physicians for the execution. Before he gave the order to start the current flowing, Durston asked the pair how long it should remain on. Neither was quite sure, but they finally settled upon fifteen seconds.[28]

When the warden gave the signal, the witnesses heard a click and watched as Kemmler stiffened and groaned. After several seconds his complexion turned ashen, and after seventeen seconds, Dr. Spitzka announced, "That will do. Turn off the current. He is dead." So it appeared. However, as the current did its work Kemmler's right index finger had curled, and the nail had impaled the first joint, causing it to bleed. Now that the power was off, blood continued to ooze from the wound, meaning his heart still had to be beating. This, along with twitches that indicated breathing, shocked the witnesses. Cries of, "Great God! He is alive!" "Turn on the current," and "For God's sake, kill him and have it over," erupted. Dr. Spitzka agreed, shouting, "Turn on the current instantly. This man is not dead." Once again the dynamo lumbered into operation, and once again Kemmler's body stiffened. This time the power remained on about four minutes. Capillaries burst, and blood dotted the condemned man's face. A blue flame arose behind his neck. The smell of burning flesh permeated the room. "The stench was terrible," reported the *New York Times*.[29]

Dr. MacDonald later dismissed Kemmler's signs of life as "a series of slight spasmodic movements by the chest." He added, "There were no evidences of a return of consciousness or of sensory function." Most of the other witnesses did not see it that way. A few fainted. Others became ill. Some left the room. "I'd rather see ten hangings," New York's deputy coroner later said. O. A. Jenkins, sheriff of Erie County, who left the scene in tears, remarked simply, "Electrical executions will never do." Added Dr. Spitzka, "I believe this will be the first and last execution of the kind."[30]

Alternating current had killed, but it had done so far less efficiently than Edison and Harold Brown had predicted. Whatever adverse publicity the Kemmler execution may have produced, it paled in comparison with Westinghouse AC's record of efficiency. In just four years the company's annual sales had risen from $150,000 to over $4 million.

Meanwhile Westinghouse formed an important alliance. His AC system lacked a reliable motor, exactly what Nikola Tesla had been working on. To power it the brilliant Serb had developed the "Tesla polyphase system." It used multiple currents to increase efficiency, and it was a major breakthrough. The inventor introduced his new system on May 16, 1888, delivering a lecture to the American Institute of Electrical Engineers at Columbia College. The talk made Tesla's reputation. It also forced a number of established electrical engineers to realize that this newcomer had suddenly made much of their work obsolete. Westinghouse quickly got in touch with Tesla, purchasing his patents for $70,000 and bringing him to Pittsburgh to try to devise a means of matching his polyphase motors with Westinghouse's single phase stations. This proved difficult, and the final results, while useful, fell short of expectations. In the end, Tesla remained in Pittsburgh only a year. Despite the disappointment, his admiration for Westinghouse, formed at their first meeting, did not waver.[31]

In early 1892 the Thomson-Houston Company merged with Edison General Electric. Thomson-Houston was the larger company, and its executives largely ran the new firm, simply named General Electric. Edison received a seat on the board, but his influence, like his name, was gone. One thing that did not change was the rivalry with Westinghouse. The next battlefield in the war of the standards was Chicago, where the World's Columbian Exposition was to be held in 1893. Realizing the value of the publicity the fair could provide, the Pittsburgher undercut GE with a bid of $399,000 to light the event. The bid was $80,000 less than that of the company's new rival.[32]

Although Edison's influence at GE was not what it had been before the merger, he still had plenty of fight left in him. The Wizard launched a patent infringement suit, claiming Westinghouse's one-piece incandescent bulb design was basically his design. The courts agreed. Undaunted, Westinghouse had his engineers modify a two-piece bulb he had already patented. His "stopper lamp" held a filament that could be replaced without replacing the globe. The Chicago fair would boast 180,000 of these bulbs, and since they did not last as long as the Edison lights, Westinghouse shipped 70,000 extra. Meanwhile Westinghouse engineers were at work on an AC station to light that many bulbs at a time, a daunting task considering the fact that, until then, the maximum capacity of an AC plant was 10,000.[33]

The engineers were up to the challenge, and when the fair opened on May 1, 1893, they had everything in place. In addition to the quarter of a million lamps, Westinghouse workers had installed 385 transformers, generators, switchboards, and wiring for all the exposition buildings and other features, including numerous fountains. Incandescent lighting had never been attempted on such a scale, and, as Westinghouse had anticipated, the public was impressed. At night they were overwhelmed by building exteriors and illuminated fountains that turned the grounds, in the words of one historian, into "a veritable fairyland." Yet equally impressive was the sight of the Westinghouse plant, located in the Hall of Machinery. It included twelve one-thousand-horsepower dynamos, each ten feet high, and a forty-circuit switchboard. Most remarkable, a single imperturbable young operator ran the entire system. Although AC had long been on the ascendancy, the fair locked in its dominant position. After the exposition opened, over 80 percent of the electrical devices ordered in the United States were powered by alternating current.[34]

Westinghouse's success in Chicago came as the company was setting its sights on the greatest electrical challenge—and opportunity—yet to be presented in America. Its results would prove to be numerous. For Westinghouse it would represent the final, decisive battle in the war of the standards. For Buffalo it would prove to be an opportunity for further economic growth, as well as domestic illumination. And it would provide the city's leaders with the chance to showcase their city before the world in a unique and dramatic way.

8

Buffalo: Niagara and the Triumph of AC

For years scientists and dreamers had been looking to Niagara Falls as a potential source of power. Indeed, harnessing its beautiful green waters had been a boyhood dream of Nikola Tesla. In 1875 local entrepreneur Charles B. Gaskill had diverted Niagara River water at the top of the falls into a vertical canal. This drove the wheel which operated his flouring mill. Within a few years a paper mill, a brewery, a barrel factory, and a fork and spoon factory had sprung up at the same location. In 1881 Buffalo businessman Jacob Schoellkopf used the river to generate DC power to light the streets of the community of Niagara Falls.[1]

The Niagara capitalists received a setback with the formation of the Free Niagara Movement. Early day conservationists, they protested the presence of the factories at the falls and their canals, which diminished the volume of water. In 1878 the governor-general of Canada proposed an international park. New York responded five years later, setting up a park on the American side of the falls and shutting down the mills. Industry could relocate a mile or more above the falls, but the challenge of diverting water around the public lands and depositing it below guaranteed that waterpower on the Niagara would be complicated and costly.[2]

The challenge attracted the attention of Thomas Evershed, a division engineer on the Erie Canal. In early 1886 Evershed proposed construction of a canal well above the parkland. It would lead to a series of wheel pits eighty to a hundred feet deep, each of which would supply power to an individual mill. A drainage tunnel would return the water to the Niagara at a point below the falls. Evershed said his system would accommodate 238 mills of 500 horsepower each. The proposal attracted the interest of businessmen in Niagara Falls and Buffalo, the latter hoping to generate electricity at the site to send the 22 miles to their city. They incorporated the Niagara Tunnel, Power and Sewer Company and enthusiastically made plans to move forward with the project. Unfortunately Evershed estimated the cost of his scheme at $9 million to $10 million, and the large banking houses the company approached, wary of the risks, did not share the directors' enthusiasm.[3]

Undeterred, the Niagara interests enlisted the aid of William B. Rankine, a local boy who had made good as a New York attorney. Rankine put the group in touch with potential deep pocket investors from the Big Apple and personally went to see J. P. Morgan. The powerful financier expressed general approval of the plan, but he was less than thrilled with its leadership. When Rankine asked for suggestions, Morgan replied, "Well, there is Adams. If you can get him, I'll join you." With that, Edward Dean Adams, an investment banker with Winslow, Lanier, & Company in New York, became involved with the Niagara Falls Power project. He would stay involved until 1926. With Morgan on board, other investors followed. In 1889 the Cataract Construction Company was founded. It purchased the entire capital stock of the recently renamed Niagara Falls Power Company. Adams became president of the Cataract Company. "As good business policy," the local board members were invited to remain.[4]

In early 1890 Adams and Coleman Sellers, a respected Philadelphia engineer, ventured to Europe to study the continent's hydropower projects. Meanwhile the Cataract Company announced a competition to solicit ideas on how to proceed. The top prize was three thousand dollars, with invitations to participate going out to 23 Europeans and only five Americans. Among those invited to take part was Westinghouse, but he declined. When an employee urged him to participate, the businessman replied, "These people are trying to secure $100,000 worth of information by offering prizes, the largest of which is $3,000. When they are ready to do business, we will show them how to do it."[5]

That would eventually be exactly what happened, but at the time the project was still grounded in Evershed's concept of separate water wheels. One of Adams's fears was that manufacturers would not accept power emanating from a central station. In the past, he explained, factories had generated their own power, and he feared owners would be reluctant to give up "personal supervision of [their] own supply of power, however crudely and inefficiently applied." That was still the thinking on October 4, 1890, when construction began on the tunnel. Four months later Swiss electrician Charles E. L. Brown announced that he had transmitted a hundred horsepower of electricity some one hundred miles. Adams and Sellers became convinced that an electrical project was the way to go, and in December 1891 the board of directors made it official. Instead of a series of water wheels, power would come from a pair of central stations, each containing ten 5,000-horsepower turbines.[6]

Shortly after the company committed itself to hydroelectricity, Sellers issued invitations to six companies which had "a scientific staff competent to design such novel machines as [were] required, and of ample facilities for their construction." Three went to Swiss firms, three to American. Two of the latter were Thomson-Houston and Edison General Electric, the merger still being a while away. The third was addressed to Westinghouse, proof that the Cataract Company was indeed "ready to do business."[7]

Meanwhile 1,300 workers had been laboring since October 4, 1890, on the Niagara River tunnel. The decision to go with electrical power had reduced its length from nearly three miles to just one, but the work was still dirty and dangerous. When exposed to air the shale at the tunnel site quickly crumbled, posing a serious threat of cave-ins. Officials first shored up the tunnel with timbers. Finally, following numerous accidents, the company decided to line the entire tunnel with four layers of bricks laid in Portland cement. The action cost the company $416,000 but likely saved numerous lives. Still, 28 men were killed before the tunnel was completed in December 1892.[8]

Construction work on the Niagara Falls power plant (collection of the Buffalo History Museum, used by permission).

As the workmen toiled and died, officials of the Cataract Construction Company confronted their final major decision. Having settled on an electrical power project, they now had to decide whether it would operate on direct or alternating current. From the outset, Sellers leaned in the direction of AC. Following a visit to Pittsburgh in the spring of 1892, he was also impressed with both the Westinghouse facility and its engineers. Adams and Sellers gave a strong indication of their proclivity toward AC in April 1892 when they engaged the Scotsman George Forbes as a consultant. A Fellow of the Royal Society and a former president of the British Electric Light Company, Forbes was a strong advocate of alternating current. After studying the six corporate proposals, Forbes recommended rejecting out of hand the DC submissions of Edison GE and Thomson-Houston. On May 19 he wrote, "I do not consider that these designs have sufficient merit to induce you to accept any delay in the hopes of getting something more perfect in this direction."[9]

There was only one argument against alternating current, but it was a potent one. The lack of a workable AC motor would be a serious impediment for a project at least as interested in supplying power for industrial concerns as it was in providing lighting for residences and offices. As serious as the concern was, it was largely overcome at a most unlikely place, the Gold King Mine, located near Telluride, Colorado. The mine owners, facing tough times, needed a cheap, reliable source of power. In early 1891 they asked the Westinghouse Company if it could provide one. Soon an AC generator, three miles of copper wire, and a one-hundred-horsepower Tesla motor were following Horace Greeley's advice. The system delivered power at an efficiency of 83.5% at full load, and the motor operated the mine's stamping mill effectively. As Adams later noted, "The successful transmission of power at so high a voltage, to so great a distance, for the operation of so large a motor by alternating current ... was a notable advance in electrical power development." On May 6, 1893, the directors of the Niagara Falls Power Company formally adopted alternating current. This decision, along with Westinghouse's success in Chicago, for all practical purposes, marked the end of the war of the standards.[10]

At first Westinghouse's triumph appeared to be short lived. Five days after adopting AC for their project, the Cataract Company informed its bidders that none would receive the prized contract. Instead, after milking information from all of the competitors, the firm hired Forbes to design its generators, leaving Westinghouse and the others out in the cold. The results were less than ideal. In August the company invited Westinghouse to produce and install generating equipment based on the Forbes design. Despite the earlier rebuff, the Pittsburgh industrialist sent a pair of engineers to the falls. They reported back that they could not work with Forbes's system.

The problem centered on frequencies. Forbes proposed 16⅔ cycles, a frequency Westinghouse argued was far too low, especially for efficient incandescent lighting. He proposed a frequency of 33⅓ cycles and flatly asserted that his firm could not guarantee any dynamo of less than 30 cycles. Eventually Adams persuaded Westinghouse to compromise at 25 cycles, which became the standard for electrical power for a number of years.

Westinghouse had one other demand, about which he was adamant. Both he and his engineers had come to dislike and distrust George Forbes. The Scotsman was condescending, and Westinghouse viewed him as a potential commercial rival. The entrepreneur bluntly informed Sellers that his firm would not work with Forbes. He further asserted that Forbes be shown no plans or specifications for equipment. The Cataract Company needed Westinghouse more than it did Forbes, and its leaders knew it. From that point on he was effectively isolated. Forbes appealed to William Rankine, but to no avail. Meanwhile the company's association with Westinghouse paid off as the Pittsburgher's engineers turned out improved meters, switches, circuitry, and insulation.[11]

Still, there were many challenges. The Westinghouse generators at the Chicago fair were one thousand horsepower. Those at Niagara would be five thousand. The water wheels and switching equipment had to be of an entirely new design. It would also be the first large power project intended more for industrial power than for lighting. As with daunting projects in the past, Westinghouse and his engineers proved that they were up to the task. They installed and successfully tested their first turbo-generator in April 1895.[12]

As the Westinghouse men designed and built, the Cataract Company bought up more than a square mile of land adjacent to the power house. If they could not deliver power all the way to Buffalo, they would at least have an early day industrial park full of customers. On August 26 the company began supplying electricity to their first one, the Pittsburgh Reduction Company, later ALCOA, an aluminum manufacturer with a large appetite for current. Soon the location was attracting carborundum, steel, and electroplating firms. Also dotting the Niagara plain were chemical plants producing sodium, silicon, magnesium, potassium, graphite, and chlorine. As the wires reached out toward Buffalo, new factories went into operation along the route. Among them was the Tonawanda Iron & Steel Company's Niagara Furnace, located in North Tonawanda, a northern suburb of Buffalo. On November 5, 1896, from his home in Canton, President-elect McKinley pressed the button which transmitted by wire the power to light the fires of the new furnace.[13]

When Buffalo received power eleven days later, it marked the culmination of a long process. Rankine had first sought a franchise from city officials in October 1894. They did not grant it until December 16, 1895, and the lines were not begun until several months later. Unlike the design of the Niagara power plant, which utilized the most up-to-date technology available, the power lines made use of telegraph technology, woefully inferior for the needs of the Niagara project. Lightning disrupted service and blew out transformers. Inferior insulation added to the problems. So, too, did mischievous boys, who tied stones to strings and threw them over power lines, bringing them into contact with telegraph and telephone wires. The pink lightning flashes that resulted amused the youths. The power failures that followed amused neither the Cataract Company nor its customers.[14]

Appreciating the damage of adverse publicity in an infant industry, the Cataract Company worked hard to correct the defects. As 1897 dawned the manager of the Buffalo Railway Company told a reporter there had been "no interruptions worth speaking of." He added, "Any interruption that we have had in the even flow of the current has been of a trifling nature and it is growing less every day." Meanwhile Buffalo was enjoying the benefits of ready lighting. The parks commission voted to erect lights around Park Lake for nocturnal skating, and electrical lighting quickly became a standard feature of new Buffalo homes and businesses. In 1902, the first year the government conducted a census on power production, the Niagara power stations were generating about one-fifth of all the electrical energy produced in the United States.[15]

In 1895 Atlanta played host to the Cotton States Exposition. It was there that representatives of South and Central American nations proposed a Pan-American Exposition involving all the countries of the Western Hemisphere. Leaders from western New York lobbied to play host, and the International Exhibitors' Association backed them up.[16]

The Pan-American Exposition Company was organized in New York City on June 25, 1897. J. M. Brinker of Buffalo was the chairman. Speaking to reporters, he said the goal of the event was to "fittingly illustrate the progress which has been made in public life during the nineteenth century in the New World." The directors selected Cayuga Island, less than two miles from the city of Niagara Falls, as the site for the exposition. Plans called for eight outer buildings, connected by eight octagonal rotundas, surrounding the main inner building. The themes for the outer buildings were to be Substance, Locomotion, Domicile, Education, Recreation, Invention, Industries, and Arts and Sciences. After the exposition ended, all were to be converted into factories. It is not clear to what extent the arrival of electricity influenced the directors' planning. However, as 1897 ended, they announced that both Nikola Tesla and Thomas Edison had agreed to serve as consultants. They further promised that the exposition would "show the wonders of electricity as they have never been shown before."[17]

On August 26, 1897, President McKinley came to the island and drove a ceremonial stake, officially launching construction for the fair. As 1898 began the board let the contracts for the main exposition buildings. Then everything changed. War with Spain was clearly on the horizon, making an event celebrating U.S. and Latin American harmony dubious at best. On March 24, 1898, the board met, and following a long discussion, voted to postpone the fair until such time as political conditions were more favorable. The Pan-American Exposition—and the Niagara Frontier—would have to wait.[18]

9

Exposition: Plans
and Problems

As 1898 ended, Buffalo, led by Conrad Diehl, the city's energetic mayor, decided to try again. On December 5 Diehl sent the city's common council a special message, calling for a revival of the Exposition project. It appealed both to civic pride and pecuniary possibilities. "Assuredly," the mayor proclaimed, "the event will afford an uncommon opportunity for acquainting a great number of visitors with the attractions and advantages of Buffalo, not only as a place of residence, but as the seat of innumerable industries, soon to be fostering the effect of cheap power and expanding commercial possibilities."[1]

On January 5, 1899, a delegation of prominent Buffalo businessmen and politicians, led by Mayor Diehl and accompanied by Senator Thomas Collier Platt, paid a visit to the White House. President McKinley received them in the Cabinet Room and told the visitors that he recalled driving the first stake on Cayuga Island for the abortive 1898 fair. After listening to a twenty-minute presentation from Diehl, the president said he "wished the proposed exposition the greatest measure of success."[2]

Good wishes were nice, but what the Buffalo delegates really craved was formal government recognition and the promise of participation. Two weeks following the White House visit, Rep. De Alva Stanwood Alexander, Buffalo's representative in the U.S. House, introduced a measure to provide half a million dollars for a Government Building and numerous displays at the exposition. It cleared the House 141–16, sailed quickly through the Senate, and was signed into law by the president. The federal government had made the Pan-American Exposition official. Meanwhile, the citizens of Buffalo were enthusiastically purchasing stock to support the effort. The original charter, passed by New York's state legislature and signed by Gov. Theodore Roosevelt on January 20, called for a million dollars in capital stock. That amount was realized in just six days. A second bill, increasing the figure to $2,500,000 and granting permission to float bonds in the same amount, was rushed through at Albany.[3]

On March 7 the 335 original incorporators gathered at Buffalo's city hall to elect a twenty-five-man board of directors for the exposition. A total of 118 men received at least one vote. Mayor Diehl topped the list with 242 votes. With few exceptions, lawyers and businessmen dominated the group. Two board members, William Hengerer and F. C. M. Lautz, were German immigrants. Hengrerer had started as a clerk in the dry goods house he now owned. Another, John G. Milburn, was a native of England. He was also considered to be "at the head of the bar in western New York." Harry Hamlin was the founder of "the largest trotting-horse breeding establishment in the world."[4]

Two days later, with the mayor presiding, the board met for the first time. They chose board member George L. Williams as treasurer and Edwin Fleming as secretary, directing the latter to begin communicating with governors to try to secure their states' participation. Milburn was put at the head of a five-man committee charged with drawing up a set of bylaws. The board met again on the 18th and elected Milburn president. They also accepted an offer from the Ellicott Square Company to rent rooms in their downtown building for headquarters until May 1, 1901, at a total cost of $18,000. Finally, the board approved a set of bylaws, establishing monthly meetings. They also set up a number of rules discouraging any conflict of interest. The exposition company could not enter into any contract with a director; and any director who accepted a position with the company would be required to resign. Perhaps most significantly, the bylaws called for the appointment of a director general, "who shall perform the duties of a general manager and exercise such supervision, direction and control of the details of the operations and affairs of the company as will tend to promote the efficiency of every agency employed."[5]

The most pressing decision facing the board was the location of their exposition. The fair was scheduled to open on May 1, 1901, giving them just two years—in a city whose weather could be capricious—to get everything in place. The directors had twenty potential sites to consider. (For reasons unclear, Cayuga Island was not among them.) These they quickly whittled down to three. One, termed the Front Site, was located close to downtown Buffalo, where the Niagara River meets Lake Erie on the city's waterfront. It contained about 340 acres. The Rumsey Site was much farther north. It comprised some 300 acres between Elmwood and Delaware Avenues near the community of Kenmore. Most of it was farmland owned by brothers Bronson and Dexter Rumsey. The Riverside Site consisted of 350 acres along the Niagara River adjacent to Strawberry Island.[6]

The question of site selection quickly became the first major controversy faced by the directors. The Front Site had some powerful—and vocal—supporters. Among them were Charles W. Goodyear, a member of the Exposition board of directors, and the *Buffalo Express*, which termed the Front "The People's Site." The paper may have been right. According to the *Buffalo Courier*, a public meeting held May 17 resulted in "a stampede of sentimentality in favor of the Front." The *Express* reported that the matter was put to a vote and the Front carried the day 200–5, the dissenters favoring the Riverside Site. By then Buffalo's city council had also approved a resolution endorsing the Front.[7]

The Pan-American executive committee, established by the directors to deal with the nuts-and-bolts operations of the Exposition, was less enthusiastic about the site. The Front brought with it expensive logistical problems. A water area 6,000 feet long and 800 feet wide would have to be filled up to eight feet above water level, a project that would cost half a million dollars. The relocation of a railroad, which bisected the site, and the removal of a number of buildings would put the price tag in seven figures. With much to consider and much at stake, the directors decided to call in some expert umpires. They engaged Daniel H. Burnham, John C. Olmsted, and Warren H. Manning "to examine the 20 locations that have been suggested for the Pan-American Exposition and to recommend such as are suitable." All were eminently qualified for the task. Not only was Burnham a prominent Chicago architect, he had served as director of works at the World's Columbian Exposition. Olmsted's father, Frederick Law Olmsted, had designed New York's Central Park. Now the younger Olmsted was running the family business. Manning was a highly regarded landscape architect in Boston.[8]

The men visited all twenty sites. When they were done, the trio recommended the Front as their first choice, followed by the Rumsey Site and the Riverside Site. In selecting the Front, Burnham, Olmsted, and Manning cited both the practical and the aesthetic. In the former column was the location's easy access from the city's most populated districts, ample water and sewage facilities, and the proximity of electrical transmission lines. The latter included "possible Venetian effects" in the area to be filled, cool breezes from the lake and the river, and "the vast view of the lake, river, Canada and city of Buffalo."[9]

In the end, despite the views of the experts and apparent public sentiment, economics trumped aesthetics. On May 13, citing the high cost of developing the Front, the board of directors by a vote of 18–3, decided to go with the Rumsey Site. The total cost of the location was approximately $200,000, including a rent payment to the Rumsey Brothers of $91,520. Goodyear resigned from the board in protest. Otherwise the fallout was less than might have been expected.[10]

The board next turned its attention to the employment of a director general, as called for in the by-laws. There appears to have been little question over the most qualified person to seek. On June 9 a telegram arrived at the United States Legation in Buenos Aires, asking William I. Buchanan, the United States minister to Argentina, to accept the position. Buchanan replied that he would only agree if he had assurances that he would be director general "in fact, as well as in title." The enterprise could only be successful, he continued, if there was present "a high degree of efficiency in organization and rapidity and coherence in the execution of the work." Therefore, it was necessary that "the entire details connected with such work pass through the office of the Director-General." The board agreed, naming Buchanan to the post on November 8 and stating that all Exposition bureaus were subject to his direction except for the Bureau of Finance and the Bureau of Law and Insurance. He received a thirty-month contract with a total salary of $30,000.[11]

The board was wise to agree to Buchanan's terms. In employing their director general, they secured an individual whose entire adult life had prepared him for the task ahead. Born September 10, 1852, in rural Miami County, Ohio, William Inesco Buchanan spent his formative years on the family farm. Chores included milking cows, chopping wood, and helping with threshing and haying. For recreation there was hunting, swimming, and, in the winter, sleigh rides.

By 1875 Buchanan was living in Dayton, where he worked as a salesman for a tobacco and cigar firm, traveling frequently and extensively. He nevertheless found time for romance. In 1878 the youthful salesman married Lulu Williams. A daughter was born the next year, and soon after that, the Buchanans relocated to Iowa, where Lulu's brother-in-law wanted William to join him as a salesman in his growing china, glassware, and crockery business. When not on the road, Buchanan became active in local theater, directing and performing in several musical productions. In 1887 he became involved in a more ambitious venture. Sioux City had determined to host a harvest celebration at a specially constructed building termed the Corn Palace. The structure was decorated with a variety of grains and grasses and filled with agricultural displays. Parades and other events filled a five-day program. Buchanan was associated with the event for four years, eventually serving as general manager.[12]

In 1890 Buchanan was appointed as one of Iowa's two representatives on the National Commission for the World's Columbian Exposition. Soon he was named to the committee on fine arts and made chairman of the committee on agriculture. Subsequent appointments placed him in charge of the department of agriculture, the department of livestock and forestry, and the department of dairying. In those positions Buchanan fired off hundreds of letters, requesting participation from state boards of agriculture and associations of beekeepers, dairymen, and livestock raisers. He also fought for his departments, securing additional exhibit space and added acreage for livestock exhibits. A trip to a kennel club show in New York resulted in additional canine exhibits. His efforts led to more than 19,000 packages of materials representing thirty-four countries. They also left Buchanan with experience that would be invaluable when he ventured to Buffalo.[13]

From an early age, Buchanan had dabbled in Democratic Party politics. In 1893 the contacts he made paid off when, at the urging of prominent Iowa Democrats, President Cleveland named him U.S. minister to the Argentine Republic. The Senate confirmed him, and on May 7, 1894, the Buchanan family disembarked at Ensenada, followed by a rail trip to Buenos Aires. As with everything he undertook, Buchanan threw himself into his work, sending to the State Department almost daily reports on a variety of topics. He worked hard to learn Spanish, eventually becoming, in the words of his biographer, "relatively fluent." His efforts earned him the respect of Argentinean officials as well as prominent Americans residing in Buenos Aires. In 1896 the latter group petitioned President-elect McKinley to retain the Democratic diplomat. Meanwhile, Buchanan submitted his resignation, an action he considered proper. No response arrived from the State Department. Finally, in early 1897 Buchanan requested a leave of absence and made for home. He arrived in New York on March 2, 1897, and caught a train for Washington, where he planned to brief State Department officials on what he had learned in Argentina. Instead, he was diverted to the White House, where the new president shocked him by refusing to accept his resignation. Buchanan was heading back to South America, but this time he was going alone. Congress had declared war on Spain, and the dangers resulting from anti–American feelings meant Lulu and the couple's two children must remain behind. Sixteen lonely months lay ahead.[14]

The telegram from Buffalo ended those lonely months. Although the task before him, to produce an ambitious world's fair in just two years, would be daunting, Buchanan would be reunited with his family in his home country. He approached his new duties with relish. As the director general later wrote, his primary goal was to demonstrate "that the peoples of the Western hemisphere should know each other better than heretofore and be better informed than they have been with regard to the capabilities and needs not only of their own but of [the Americas] as a whole, and of the opportunities existing therein for commercial activity and energy."[15]

This goal made foreign participation at the Exposition imperative, a fact the directors realized even before Buchanan arrived on the scene. At their May 1899 board meeting the group had approved a recommendation from the executive committee that a ten thousand-dollar appropriation be made "for the purpose of carrying on the Exposition work in the South American countries." The following year missions were dispatched to Mexico, Central America, and the West Indies. From the outset, the State Department worked hand-in-hand with the Exposition to secure the involvement of Western Hemisphere countries and colonies. In June 1899 the department sent a circular note inviting all of them to participate, accompanied by an invitation from the Exposition directors.[16]

Because of the distances involved and the short amount of time available to make plans, Buchanan knew the Latin American countries would have to be quickly brought on board. As a result he focused first on securing their participation; the missions sent south were a factor of this concern. This attention paid to Latin America soon led to a minor international incident. In February 1900 Buchanan learned that the Canadians were feeling "a trifle piqued over our seeming purpose to pay more attention to the Republics to the southward than ... to the Dominion." The fact that Canada's formal invitation had been delayed through some oversight only exacerbated the situation. Buchanan took the dust-up seriously, dispatching a three-man delegation led by commissioner-general John Weber to soothe any hurt feelings north of the border. The group first met with the prime minister, Sir Wilfred Laurier, who rather stiffly noted that Canada had taken no action because it had not received a formal invitation. They then talked with the minister of agriculture. That official was more reassuring, saying the invitation mix-up was not a source of offense and reassuring the delegation that Canada would "make every effort to have a creditable exhibit." On March 27 Canada formally agreed to participate in the Exposition.[17]

By then other countries were sending their RSVP's, most of them positive. Guadeloupe, whose acceptance came either the last week of 1899 or the first of 1900, appears to have been the first. Peru, Chile, and Honduras soon followed. Spring saw the Dominican Republic added to the list. At the same time, a number of countries sent their regrets. Often, there was a certain poignancy in their reasons. Venezuela said its participation depended in part on "the establishment of peace in the country." They did not make it. Paraguay cited "material impossibility" in declining Buffalo's offer. The British governor of Barbados wired the State Department that he regretted "that the paucity of natural products of the colony renders it inexpedient that it should participate." Eventually twenty Western Hemisphere countries and colonies participated in the Exposition. Seven of them, Chile, Ecuador, Honduras, Mexico, Canada, Cuba, and San Domingo, erected their own buildings.[18]

Buchanan arrived with strongly held views concerning his vision for the Exposition. As he noted in a magazine article, all such events should be:

> a source of gladness and delight, and a pride as well.... [They should] bring together about these central salient points, those finishing, connecting links of fountains, of brilliant lighting effects, of music, of gardens, of entertainments, and of novelty, which go far toward making up the real life of a great Exposition.[19]

Color was to be an important part of that vision. Unlike Chicago's Columbian Exposition, which gave the world an antiseptic "White City," Buffalo would overwhelm with a gaudy "Rainbow City." And thanks to Buffalo's access to electrical power, the colors would glow well into the night, with prominent fountains and sculpture punctuating the panorama of color the director general had in mind. Nor would natural beauty be ignored. Buchanan had been on the job only a few days before word went out that trees were to dot the grounds; and greenhouses were ordered to nurture the thousands of flowers that would permeate the landscape.[20]

By the time Buchanan assumed his duties as director general, the Pan-American's board of architects had been at work for five months. Unlike previous expositions, which held competitions to select participating architects, the Pan-American board selected and invited members of the eight-member group to take part. There were three from Buffalo, George Cary, August Esenwein, and Edward B. Green; three from New York, John M. Carrere, Walter Cook, and John Galen Howard; and two from Boston, Robert S. Peabody and George Shepley. They held their first meeting on June 17, 1899, electing Carrere as chairman. They also approved a job description that made them responsible for "plans, elevations, and full-sized details of ornamentation, but not construction details, local supervision, or administration."[21]

By then the buildings and grounds committee had compiled a list of desired "major buildings," including Manufactures and Liberal Arts, Agriculture, Horticulture, Mining, Forestry, Electricity, Ethnology, Machinery and Transportation, Graphic Arts, and a Temple of Music. At their second meeting, held on July 12, the architectural board discussed how these structures would be incorporated into an overall design scheme for the Exposition. Nine days later they met again and refined the suggestions made on the 12th. The board also agreed on an architectural style it termed "a free Renaissance, with apparent roofs and overhanging eaves." Then the eight architects got down to the business of dividing the assignments for the various buildings. There appears to have been virtually no clash of egos. Each man was asked his personal preference, and most ended up with their first choice.[22]

The plum assignment for the architects was the Electric Tower. The tallest structure on the exposition grounds, it would be the focal point of the fair, playing the same role the Eiffel Tower had played at the 1889 Exposition Universelle in Paris. The executive committee had set aside $200,000 to construct it. Even here the board members kept their egos in check, arriving at a consensus decision in favor of Howard. Carrere was put in charge of the overall plan, making sure that his colleagues' designs harmonized into a coherent final product.[23]

Next to Buchanan, the man who would be most responsible for the ultimate success or failure of the Exposition was Newcomb Carleton. As director of works, he was in charge of all construction projects as well as gas and water lines, electrical transmission, plants, and groundskeeping. On September 26, 1899, Carleton and his crews got down to work, launching the task of transforming the Rumsey Brothers' farmland into a festive fairyland of light and color. Men and teams began removing the old topsoil, taking up fences, and digging holes for trees. By November 6 they had moved 14,400 feet of fence, planted 2,400 poplars, 1,190 willows, and 700 shrubs, and had begun excavation for the east lake. Two greenhouses were in place to raise perennials for planting during the fall of 1900 and spring of 1901. Meanwhile, an outside contractor finished the fence around the grounds on October 25.[24]

The landscape bureau devoted much of November to scraping and piling topsoil to make gardens the following spring. Its workers also prepared greenhouses and nurseries for winter, propagating 34,000 cuttings. In addition, they found time to plant an additional 8,887 trees, shrubs, and other plants. A hundred loads of leaves were gathered from the cemetery and public park to protect the trees and plants during the winter.[25]

Meanwhile Buchanan was making arrangements to achieve his goal of creating a harmonious Rainbow City. On March 7, 1900, armed with a unanimous endorsement from the National Society of Mural Painters, he asked the executive committee to name Charles Yardley Turner director of color for the Exposition. Turner would serve thirteen months at a yearly pay rate of five thousand dollars.[26]

A Baltimore native, born in 1850, Turner had attended the National Academy of Design in New York before making the obligatory artist's pilgrimage to Europe in 1878. In Paris he studied under Jean Paul Laurens, whose paintings were known for their "almost photographic realism." After three years in Europe, Turner returned to America, setting up a studio in New York and remaining financially afloat by teaching. His reputation was enhanced in 1882 when he exhibited three paintings at his *alma mater*. All received critical acclaim. Two years later Turner became president of the Art

Students League, where he had been teaching. His new responsibilities left Turner ample time to paint. In 1891 the artist had his first major auction-exhibition, where 156 of his works were sold.[27]

In 1892 Turner received an appointment that would provide valuable experience for his future duties in Buffalo. Francis D. Millet, director of decorations for the World's Columbian Exposition in Chicago, asked Turner to serve as his assistant. As his biographer notes, "Turner's involvement in the Fair was a uniquely edifying experience since he had the chance to participate in the greatest artistic experiment of such a large scale where the architect, sculptor, and painter would work together to insure the growth of the allied arts." The extent of his specific contributions has been largely lost to history. The one that is known is more a technical than artistic accomplishment. Turner devised a method of using "a spray pump" to apply paint to the White City's large buildings.[28]

After Chicago much of Turner's work involved painting murals, often for hotels and public buildings. It was in this role that he developed the reputation among his peers that led them to recommend him to the Pan-American officials.[29]

From the start Turner's goal was to use color to illustrate "the fierce struggle of man to overcome the elements." He planned to accomplish this by presenting "harsh" colors at the south entrance to the fair. These would gradually give way to more subtle hues, culminating with the Electric Tower, which was to be a pastel structure. "I will begin with crude, brilliant colors," he told one reporter, "and as you advance the colors will be more refined." To another he explained, "On the buildings in the southern end of the great court the primary colors are laid on in all the richness of the savage taste. They become gradually milder till they culminate in the soft harmonies of the Electric Tower." Implicit in all this was a subtle racism, an assumption that the white man was responsible for overcoming the "savage taste" of earlier eras. It is doubtful that this was Turner's overt intent; in any event, as will be seen, the racism of the Pan would become more obvious in other areas.[30]

Still, the coloration of the buildings was less than subtle. The Horticulture Building, one of the first that most visitors would encounter, was "an intense orange." The nearby Temple of Music, according to a historian of the fair, was "the gaudiest building of the lot." Its main color was a "quite pure" red, with a blue and green dome above. Opposite the Temple, the Ethnology Building sported a similarly colored dome. By the time one got to the Electricity Building and the Agriculture Building, man's triumph was asserting itself, and more subtle yellows were prevailing. This triumph reached its pinnacle at the Electric Tower, an ivory colored structure garnished with gold and green trim. Turner considered green to be "one of the more recent and refined colors." He also saw it as symbolic of Niagara Falls, the source of Buffalo's—and the Exposition's—power.[31]

Turner began by sketching the layout of the Exposition and coloring it. Deciding that this did not give him the necessary perspective, the artist had colored scale models of the major buildings made. However, he still relied on larger drawings to determine the colors of such details as doorways and pinnacles.[32]

As Turner planned his Rainbow City, much of the practical work of creating an exposition was going ahead. In early November 1899 the board of directors awarded the contract for the Service Building. The firm of William Heinrich's Sons submitted the low bid of $20,900. The first structure to go up on the Pan Am grounds, it was to serve as the headquarters for Exposition officials. The sons got right to work and in ten days had the roof beams of the three-story building in place. Carlton and his staff began to move in on December 13, and other officers soon followed. The Service Building housed thirty-eight offices on the ground floor, plus a kitchen and dining rooms. The second floor had sleeping apartments for officials who would remain on site. On the top level were dormitories, the photographer's studio, and printing offices. In March the board of directors voted to install "a switchboard of at least fifty drops" and employ an operator.[33]

On December 15, 1899, George K. Birge, of the buildings and grounds committee, formally announced that Galen Howard's design of the Electric Tower had been approved—with modifications. The committee wanted the architect to include a restaurant at the one hundred-foot level of the three hundred-foot structure. They also called for elevators to reach the restaurant and the observation platform at the top of the tower.[34]

Because of the complicated nature of its construction and the intricate steel framework necessary, Buchanan recommended that the construction of the tower be let under separate bids. One would be for the steelwork, the other for the wood construction of the two wings and the staff work of the entire tower. Ironically, it was the latter contract that ended up being a headache for Buchanan. The Passaic Steel Company submitted the low bid of $68,500 for both material and construction, a rate for steel of only ten dollars a ton. The low bid for staff work, submitted by the firm of Smith & Eastman, was $90,000, much higher than anticipated. With the foundation costing five thousand, the elevators ten thousand, and the statuary $22,000, plus "incidentals" that could reach over $30,000, the director general saw the tower's budget rising as high as the structure itself. He summoned architect Howard and director of color Turner to a meeting with a representative of

Smith & Eastman and members of the building and grounds committee. Howard reluctantly agreed that "certain eliminations [will] be made from the decorative treatment of the Tower which [will] simplify it and render it less expensive." Buchanan conceded that these changes, largely involving statuary, "would be injurious to the general attractive effect desired." They would also reduce the Smith & Eastman bid to $59,000.[35]

As bids for more of the Exposition's main buildings came in, Buchanan faced similar problems. On April 7 he and Carlton considered twelve bids for construction of the Horticulture Building, the Forestry Building, and the Graphic Arts Building. A. P. Kehr submitted the low bid of $155,000. However, the two officials learned that Kehr had never built any structures similar in design. In fact, he had no experience constructing any large buildings. Kehr insisted that he had "a thoroughly capable person who would take charge," but he refused to name him. At the recommendation of the director general, the next lowest bidder received the contract at an increased cost of fifteen thousand dollars.[36]

In early July the executive committee rejected all bids on both the Temple of Music and the Ethnology Building. In both cases the bids went over the estimated costs, by nearly twelve thousand dollars in the case of the Temple of Music. Eventually the contractors came around. Joseph Metz agreed to construct the Ethnology Building for $60,000, which was $17,464 below his original bid. John Feist submitted a new bid of $55,000 for the Temple of Music, a reduction of $16,588.[37]

All this mattered because the director general was becoming concerned over finances. On April 24, well before most of the major buildings had been bid, Buchanan informed the executive committee that approved contracts already obligated the Exposition Company to $1,600,000. Regular monthly expenses he placed at thirty thousand dollars. The committee responded by requesting that the board of directors make no further appropriations until it had "provided sufficient funds for the successful carrying out of the plans of this committee." Specifically, it called for "a scheme for raising on the bonds of the company the additional money required by the company to complete its buildings and open the Exposition."[38]

The board responded at a special meeting by approving the borrowing of $2,500,000 on the company's bonds. Despite the infusion, the director general urged caution—and for good reason. On July 19 he reported that the company's liabilities, including contracts already authorized as well as estimates for wages and "incidental expenses," amounted to $3,561,941. In addition, the Exposition had already paid out nearly $700,000 since its inception. Many expenditures, Buchanan noted, lay ahead. Some were big ticket items, such as the Exposition hospital and the "Triumphal Bridge" that was to serve as the Expo's main entrance. Also yet to come were expenses for police and fire protection, as well as costs of publicity and such necessary details as "ticket canceling machines and turnstiles." Altogether, Buchanan predicted, the Exposition's budget would total nearly five million dollars. On July 1 the amount of cash in the treasury was $496,692.[39]

Always in competition with his fiscal worries was the director general's desire to put on a first class show. Music had been an important part of Buchanan's life, and he wanted to make it a main feature of the Exposition. The centerpiece of the Temple of Music was a "magnificent four-manual organ of fifty-three speaking registers." The eighteen thousand-dollar instrument was built by Emmons Howard of Westfield, Massachusetts. Free recitals became a daily feature of the Exposition. Seventy-five organists, including seven from Buffalo, participated. Exposition officials eventually secured a number of bands to perform open-air concerts. Their engagements ranged from a few days to three months. Many were martial organizations, but the Carlisle Indian Band, the Puerto Rican String Band, and the Boston Ladies' Band also participated. So did two of the most famous musical organizations of the day. The Exposition later engaged Victor Herbert's Orchestra, sixty strong, for two weeks at a cost of $5,800. John Philip Sousa's fifty-piece band would receive a four-week, twenty thousand-dollar contract. It called for two daily concerts, plus "other special features," not to exceed four hours a day. The March King agreed, despite his desire for a longer engagement.[40]

If Buchanan wanted a festive exposition, he also wanted a safe one. Fire protection, the director general believed, was the city's responsibility. At a meeting with Mayor Diehl and other municipal officials, he asserted, "The exposition company is composed of the citizens of Buffalo, and citizens of Buffalo are entitled to Buffalo's fire protection." His Honor did not disagree. On August 25 hose Company No. 31 occupied its new headquarters on the Exposition grounds. A fire truck and a chemical engine were among the equipment in place. In addition Buchanan ordered that fire extinguishers be placed in all buildings. The larger structures also received reels of hose, all connected and ready to go.[41]

Although the Exposition could have likely also procured city police officers, the company decided to establish its own force. The board of directors voted to create the department at its February 6, 1900, meeting. They later ordered fifty signal boxes installed on the grounds, tied to a switchboard at the police station. The force was not organized until May 4. Four men reported for duty that day, a number that would eventually grow to 249, including an eighteen-man bicycle squad that patrolled outside the fence to "keep transgressors from getting over and under the fence and into the grounds." The entire force would eventually make 351 arrests, including one for murder.[42]

On May 15, 1900, Buchanan urged the executive committee to appoint a medical director. The director general did not make a specific recommendation, feeling the selection was "one which may be better left in your hands." Two weeks later he repeated that he would not recommend anyone for the position but added, "Many have personally expressed to me their hope that Doctor Park will be designated for the position." The committee took the hint and two days later named Dr. Roswell Park to the post. In announcing the appointment, the *Buffalo Commercial* quoted an unnamed Exposition official as saying, "Dr. Park made no attempt to get the position, which came to him entirely unsolicited, because it was felt that he was pre-eminently the best man we could secure."[43]

He likely was. A Connecticut native, born in 1852, Park received both a Bachelor's and a Master's Degree at Racine College in Wisconsin. In 1876 he earned his Medical Degree from Northwestern. Park interned at Chicago's Cook County Hospital, where, a biographer notes, "he became an expert in the treatment of gunshot wounds." The youthful physician remained in Chicago until 1883, when the University of Buffalo Medical School offered him its chairmanship. He accepted, soon becoming a surgeon at Buffalo General Hospital. There he pioneered surgical techniques for treating epilepsy and spina bifida. Dr. Park also urged his colleagues to adopt antiseptic surgery long before its acceptance by most doctors. Perhaps his greatest contributions to medicine lay in the area of cancer research and treatment. Believed to be contagious and venereal by the nineteenth century medical community, its victims were often shunned by hospitals. Realizing that the number of cancer cases was growing rapidly—he predicted that it would became a major cause of death in the twentieth century—Park secured a ten thousand-dollar appropriation from the state legislature in 1898. With the funds he established the New York State Pathological Laboratory of the University of Buffalo. The laboratory took an interdisciplinary approach, employing a variety of specialists to conduct research. It was soon considered "the gold standard" of cancer research, with the result that numerous similar institutions were set up both in the U.S. and abroad. Dr. Park's sterling resume and reputation seemed to guarantee that any medical emergencies at the Exposition would be dealt with skillfully and professionally.[44]

Not all personnel issues went so smoothly, despite the director general's best efforts. From the outset Buchanan expressed a desire to deal fairly with Exposition laborers. At his insistence the board and executive committee established an eight-hour workday and agreed to pay prevailing wage rates with time-and-a-half for overtime. They also agreed that the Exposition Company and all contractors it engaged would give a preference in hiring to workers who could demonstrate one year's residence in Buffalo.[45]

Union officials generally appreciated Buchanan's policies. Still, an exposition involved tight construction deadlines. Knowing this, some labor leaders and some workers tried to extract further concessions with the threat of strikes. In early May 1900 some 250 day laborers employed by the Exposition Company walked off the job, demanding ten hours' pay for eight hours' work. After leaving their posts the strikers approached a group of men who worked for an outside contractor that was excavating for a lagoon. Between fifty and a hundred of them joined the walkout. Those that did not were pelted with chunks of dirt and stones. A mounted Exposition police officer who tried to disperse the strikers received similar treatment. Yet the effort was all for naught. Union leaders did not support the action, unskilled labor was easy to come by, and the malcontents either returned to work or were replaced.[46]

On August 25 the staff workers, employed by a local contractor, struck. Except for the New York Building, later the Buffalo and Erie County Historical Society Museum and now The Buffalo History Museum, Exposition structures were not meant to be permanent. They were largely constructed of a lath and iron framework covered with a staff substance composed of gypsum, hemp, and plaster, hardy enough to hold up during the few months the Exposition would be open. The staff workers, depending on their specific duties, received anywhere from twenty to forty cents an hour. They demanded raises ranging from ten to fifteen cents. As was the case with the other unskilled workers, management was in a position of strength. When the strike began they had several days' surplus of staff material. Most workers had returned or been replaced before the supply started to dwindle.[47]

As Buchanan dealt with the numerous problems and details of exposition planning, the United States government was making its own plans for the event. Of the $500,000 appropriated by Congress for the Expo, $200,000 was to pay for the construction of the Government Building. It was to be 418 by 130 feet with two pavilions, each 150 feet square, connected by arcades. The interior of the building consisted of one large exposition space, divided into a central rectangle 100 by 140 feet, and ten bays, divided by wooden posts, five on each side of the main space, each thirty feet wide. Every cabinet department would have a display in the building, as would the Smithsonian Institution and the Commission of Fish and Fisheries. At Buchanan's request, the government board of management set aside ten thousand dollars to dis-

Work on the Government Building at the Pan-American Exposition (National Archives and Records Administration).

patch an agent to the Philippines to collect exhibits from this new, mysterious possession.[48]

On June 1, 1900, the Treasury Department awarded the contract for construction of the Government Building to an Omaha, Nebraska contractor, who had submitted a bid of $166,000. By mid–August, despite a shortage of lumber, the work was well under way. So, too, were the Machinery and Transportation Building and the Electricity Building. Contracts for several other structures had been let, and contractors were getting to work. Indeed, with 1,485 men working for various contractors, along with 350 Exposition employees, it appeared that all was well in terms of meeting construction deadlines.[49]

Then came September 11, 1900, bringing to Buffalo perhaps the most unlikely form of natural disaster the city could receive.

10

Exposition: Problems with the Plans

On September 8, 1900, the deadliest storm in United States history struck Galveston, Texas. Likely a Category 4 hurricane on the Saffir-Simpson Scale, it destroyed nearly four thousand homes and left anywhere from eight to twelve thousand dead.

Then the storm turned northeast. On the evening of September 11 it hit Buffalo. At ten o'clock the winds were blowing at thirty miles-per-hour. They had reached fifty to sixty by midnight, and at 3:30 a.m. on the 12th they peaked at 78 miles-per-hour—beyond hurricane force—a velocity sustained for about five minutes. Despite the intensity of the storm, most of the damage in Buffalo was minor. A number of utility lines went down, as did several of the city's chimneys. The *Buffalo Commercial* reported that, "The squatters living on [Grand] Island passed a most terrifying night." They bore the full brunt of the southwest winds, and many homes were badly damaged. The city's only fatality was Rose Markease, a 45-year old housewife, who went outside to gather storm debris to use as firewood. In so doing she touched a downed live wire and was electrocuted. Both her husband and a fireman who attempted to rescue her were shocked but not severely injured.[1]

At the Exposition grounds the Government Building sustained the worst damage. Nearing completion, its walls were blown down and thrown into an adjacent canal. The contractors placed the damage at thirty to forty thousand dollars and the lost time at over a month. The winds also removed one tower of the Electricity Building and damaged another beyond repair. The contractors estimated the loss at $25,000. The Manufactures and Liberal Arts Building, the Horticulture Building, and the Forestry Building also sustained damage. So did the entrance to the Midway. There a tower was blown down, the damage put at ten thousand dollars.

Although the total damage came to about $100,000, John Milburn rushed to assure everybody that, "Work is progressing, and the final completion of the damaged buildings will not be appreciably delayed by anything that has happened." The Exposition president pointed out that none of the landscaping was affected, and concluded, "I am glad to be able to assure the public that notwithstanding the extraordinary violence of the storm, there has been no loss or damage to cause any apprehension or affect the successful prosecution of the work or the plans of the Exposition Company."[2]

Still, time was beginning to catch up with Exposition planners. No major building was finished, many were not even begun, and an unpredictable Buffalo winter was fast approaching. Realizing this, Buchanan requested—and received—the authority he needed to speed things up. On September 20 the board of directors approved his proposal that contractors receive a one-hundred-dollar bonus for every day they completed a building project ahead of schedule. On October 28 the executive committee granted his request for "the widest latitude" in making unilateral decisions concerning construction. In making the request, the director general cited a number of projects yet to be completed. Some 1,200 lamp posts had to go up. Interior work in all buildings remained to be done, and the company was yet to award contracts for

The Electric Tower, the Pan-Am's centerpiece, nears completion (Library of Congress).

livestock buildings and barns. "I am deeply impressed with the responsibility attached to all of us to conclude the Exposition and have it ready for its opening," Buchanan observed, and he promised to "carefully and conscientiously protect the interests of the Exposition in all ways."[3]

The most critical project was the Electric Tower, the focal point of the fair. Work began in early August, and it quickly fell behind schedule. For a time director of works Carlton considered bringing in arc lights to allow the work to go on day and night. He quickly changed his mind. "It would mean death to some of the workmen," he informed one reporter. "No matter how the lights were arranged, shadows would be cast of the most deceptive nature." He concluded, "I am extremely anxious to complete the tower, but I would rather it did not get above the foundations by next May than to think haste had been responsible for a death."[4]

Perhaps God rewards good intentions, because favorable weather settled over Buffalo for much of September and October. On October 18 workers began "framing the tower proper." The next day there were 75 men at work on the structure. By the end of the month the number had reached 117. Snow halted the work on November 12 and again on November 25 and 26. On November 28 the carpenters on the project struck for five days. The day they returned, December 3, the iron work of the tower reached its maximum height, 335 feet, resulting in a brief celebration among the formerly disaffected laborers. Three days later the *Buffalo Express* reported that workmen had completed half the tower's woodwork, and the staff workers were not far behind. Buchanan cut corners, in terms of time, by awarding the contract for painting the tower to the Niagara Construction Company. The same firm was doing the staff and carpentry work and already had scaffolding in place. The action paid off—aided by a relatively mild winter. By the end of March the structure was virtually completed except for statuary work. On the 29th the *Buffalo Express* gushed, "Most of the staging has been stripped from the Howard tower, and its graceful outlines stand out against the blue sky in imposing grandeur."[5]

By then an unanticipated culprit was threatening the grandeur of the entire Rainbow City. Smoke from New York Central locomotives, the American Radiator Company, and the Exposition's own power plant was covering Turner's beautifully colored buildings with a sooty residue. The railroad, when alerted to the problem, quickly agreed to equip its engines with smoke arresters, which mitigated the situation somewhat. However, it was the power plant that was doing the bulk of the damage. There smoke arresters did little good. Neither did switching to cleaner anthracite coal. In early April concessionaires began to complain about the damage the smoke was doing to their wares. This forced Buchanan to switch to natural gas at the power plant. It was an action he took reluctantly because of the expense involved, but circumstances made it necessary. The executive committee voted to allow Turner ten thousand dollars to repaint affected buildings, but he ended up completing the work for $5,300.[6]

In early March Turner faced a different challenge to his color scheme. The director of color had planned for the United States Government Building to be painted yellow with a green dome. This way it would correspond with the Horticulture Building at the opposite end of the esplanade. At first John Taylor Knox, architect for the structure, approved of the plan. Later he decided a "soft gray" would be more appropriate for the entire building. "The scale of the exposition as a whole," he explained, "is such that the Government building in this warm gray will in no wise conflict with the stronger-color structures adjoining."[7]

Turner disagreed, noting, "It was my plan that [the Exposition] should be carried out under one general color scheme." He added, "When you eliminate all color and make [the Government Building] gray, you do not conform to the general color scheme as agreed upon in the beginning." A series of meetings followed, but Knox barely budged, offering only to add a bronze coloring to the building's statuary. Turner appealed to the Exposition's advisory board of color and its board of architects, both of which supported the director of color. Meanwhile, observed the *Buffalo Express*, "forty industrious painters have been vigorously plying their brushes on the west facade of the stately national structure," their brushes dipped in soft gray.[8]

Then, following an April 7 meeting with Knox, Turner announced that the government architect had agreed to adopt the director's plans. "The color scheme of the exposition will be complete," he proclaimed. In reality, all the director of color had gained was a weak compromise. The dome would be blue, not green as Turner desired, and the rest of the building would remain, in the words of the *Express*, "the obnoxious gray," with occasional yellow trim. In an article published near the end of the Exposition, Turner tried to put the best face on things, writing, "The Government Building has mild gray for the structural portions to relieve the yellow, and … where it is possible, the green note is introduced in the sashes and domes." In another article, a more impartial observer wrote, "The Government Building is unfortunately out of chromatic harmony with the others, because the Government architect did not fall in with the general plan." He added, "This is the single instance where there was a failure on the part of anybody to work towards the common end."[9]

Turner also had difficulty finding good help. The requirement that the

Exposition hire only Buffalo labor limited the pool of painters. The city's brutal cold added to the problem, coupled with the fact that the entire city was sprucing up for the expected deluge of visitors. Anyone who could find work painting the interior of a hotel or department store would leap at the chance as opposed to braving the wind and the cold to help create Turner's Rainbow City.[10]

Those painters the Exposition and its contractors were able to employ had a tendency to strike. On November 20, 1900, about sixty of them walked off, demanding that their hourly wage rate of thirty cents be raised a dime. The strikers did not have the sanction of their union, which had a contract valid through April. Both director of works Carlton and the contractors employing the painters held firm against the painters' assertion that stormy weather and outside climbing entitled them to more than the prevailing wage. The strike lasted until January 7, when the two sides reached a compromise. The deal raised the men's wages to thirty-five cents an hour, provided time-and-a-half for overtime, and included a clause stating that "no strikes or further trouble be caused."[11]

The painters were not alone in their proclivity for striking. On January 25 Exposition plasterers put down their tools. Money was not the problem. Rather, they were upset that carpenters were nailing such things as moldings, cornices, and panels into place, tasks the plasterers insisted belonged to them. The carpenters, of course, felt otherwise. Leaders of both unions met on the night of the 26th, and after "considerable wrangling," they agreed that a plasterer and a carpenter would work together on such projects.[12]

On March 14 about a hundred plasterers struck. This time money was the issue, the men demanding a raise from four to five dollars a day. The action put union leaders in a bind. The previous November they had agreed to a contract establishing the rate and forbidding any work stoppage. Officially the union took a neutral position, pointing out that the agreement did not prevent individual workers from striking. Off the record, many criticized the workers. Bolstered by the lack of union support for the action, Exposition officials threatened to go after out-of-town labor. This, along with a compromise offer, brought the men back to work on April 1. The agreement called for a ten-hour work day at a daily wage of six dollars.[13]

On March 25 it was the plumbers' turn. The journeymen had been making three dollars a day, the master plumbers $3.50. All wanted four dollars, and the entire force of some thirty men went on strike to get it. Although their absence reportedly caused "much annoyance to the contractors," both classes of workers settled when the journeymen got a raise to $3.50. Solidarity was the issue when about fifty carpenters launched a partial strike on April

9. The action was taken in sympathy for striking planing mill workers. The carpenters refused to handle any lumber coming from the offending mills.[14]

However reasonable or unreasonable the laborers' various demands may have been, there is no doubt that the work of assembling an exposition at Buffalo, especially during the winter months, was difficult—and dangerous. On November 21, 1900, another storm struck Buffalo, bringing winds just as strong as those experienced in September. The storm brought down the Cyclorama, a Midway attraction which was under construction, and two smaller Exposition buildings. When the gale hit, an unnamed worker was on the top staging of the Horticulture Building. Nearby was a swaying rope attached to a derrick that was hoisting building material to the top. Suddenly a gust of wind struck the man "and lifted him as though he was a feather." He made a frantic grab for the rope and managed to snag it. The wind sent both him and the rope swinging. Its gusts were so strong that the worker could not safely descend hand over hand. Instead he slid the entire 120 feet, "the rope sawing the flesh from his hands until when he touched the ground the palms were burned to the bone and blood was dripping from them."[15]

On a snowy December 31 a roofer working on the Wisconsin Building slipped on a loose piece of tin tiling. He slid down the slope of the roof and then fell twenty-five feet to the ground. "He struck with stunning force on his right shoulder and arms," one newspaper reported. The man suffered a broken wrist and shoulder blade. The accident put an end to all roofing work that day.[16]

Winter injuries were either rare or unreported. However, with the coming of spring the number shot up. Often accidents came in clusters. "Within the week the business of the exposition emergency hospital has increased at a rapid rate," the *Express* noted on March 31. Although most were "of a trivial character," they were occurring at a rate of four or five a day. In one case a painter at the Ethnology Building allowed a heavily loaded bucket to drop. It hit another laborer in the head, resulting in a painful scalp wound. In another a teamster was trying to extricate a mule that had become mired in the mud. The animal fell over on the teamster, leaving him with severe bruises on his side.[17]

April 9 saw three workers injured at the Exposition grounds. Frank Schwartz, a painter working on the pergola, fell fifteen feet after slipping from a scaffold and sprained his ankle. Joseph Calla, age sixteen, was employed by the Midway attraction Streets of Cairo. While performing his duties he fell thirty feet into a hole. Fortunately he landed in the mud and suffered only a minor scalp wound and a "severe shaking up." The most serious case was that of Thomas McDougall, seventeen years old, an electrician's assistant. McDougall was helping string wires on a tower of the Triumphal Causeway, sixty feet above the ground, when he lost his footing and fell. He suffered a broken arm, a fractured skull, and spinal injuries. The victim was treated at the Exposition hospital before being removed to Buffalo General. There he lingered for twenty days before succumbing to his injuries.[18]

Two days later there was another fatality on the Pan-Am grounds. The victim was Magnus Ohnstein, a sub-contractor on the Government Building. He was working some two hundred feet above the ground, placing sculptured figures on the dome. Somehow he stepped off the platform on which he was standing and fell ninety feet to a lower platform. Suffering a fractured skull, he was instantly killed. His fellow workers lowered his body to the ground with ropes.[19]

Two workers were electrocuted after the Exposition's May 1 opening. On the 13th Martin Kiefig and two colleagues were hauling wheelbarrow loads of dirt along a "rude plank runway" in the basement of the Machinery Building. The area was poorly lit, and wires carrying 1,800 volts hung just five feet overhead. Kiefig brushed against one with his head, and in attempting to get away he apparently grasped the wire with his hand. Two coworkers rushed to his aid, suffering severe burns in their rescue attempt. One was later able to walk home. The other ended up in a Buffalo hospital, where doctors amputated a finger that had been "cooked to a crisp."[20]

Nine days later John Krause, a laborer in the plumbing department, was working with a crew of men that was making alterations to the sewer system under the Agriculture Building. It was dark and wet, and the men had to crawl to stay below a maze of electrical wires that ran through the trench where they were working. Krause was in the lead. Suddenly, "an agonizing cry of pain" alerted his colleagues to the fact that Krause had come into contact with one of the wires. The next man in line tried to pull him free and received a serious shock. The foreman of the work party made his way to the nearest manhole, clambered out, and got a policeman to phone the power plant and have the current cut off. Unfortunately nobody there at the time knew which buttons to push, and it was a half hour before anybody stopped the charge. An Exposition ambulance crew attempted to revive Krause, but to no avail. Pan-Am officials did take steps to make sure that such an accident did not occur again. That same day a directive went out to the heads of all departments that electricians must accompany any crew doing subterranean work in the vicinity of live wires.[21]

As the Exposition approached, the board of directors was finally forced to confront an issue that had first been raised two years earlier. On April 25, 1899, the New England Sabbath Protective League wrote to John Milburn, asking that the fair be closed on Sundays. A similar request came one year later from the Tremont Temple in Boston. At the time Buchanan recommended to the executive committee that "no action whatever should be taken upon the subject for the time being."[22]

The matter lay largely dormant for the remainder of the year, but as 1901 dawned the Exposition Company began receiving several petitions asking that the gates be closed on the Sabbath. Many came from individual churches, others from such religious organizations as the Epworth League, the Sabbath Union, and the Women's Christian Temperance Union. Despite being Christian organizations, some were not hesitant about threatening a boycott or legal action. In the latter case they cited a state law that prohibited "shows" on Sundays as well as "all noise disturbing the peace of the day."[23]

Proponents of Sunday opening also proved willing at times to take the low road. If the Exposition was a "show," one pointed out, a similar interpretation might apply to sacred concerts in churches or even church services themselves. In January 1901, as such leaders as Milburn and John Scatchard, chairman of the executive committee, were denying that Exposition officials had even discussed the subject, the *Pan-American Magazine* was taking direct aim at the opponents of Sunday opening. In an editorial entitled, "No Bigots Need Apply," came the sub-head, "Ministers Who Loaf Six Days a Week and Work One Would Close the Glories of the Exposition to the Man Who Works Six and Loafs One." The piece concluded, "There are probably 60,000 [working] men in Buffalo, who if not allowed to see the glories and beauties of the Exposition on Sundays will never see them at all."[24]

As the holy war intensified, David T. Day, the Exposition's superintendent of mines and metallurgy, proposed a compromise. Why not, Day asked, use the Exposition's stadium for "Great religious gatherings, the best preachers in the United States being invited to address the crowds?" Meanwhile the people of Buffalo were providing the proponents of Sunday opening with statistical ammunition. Although the Exposition was incomplete and not formally opened, visitors were allowed, for a slight admission fee, to enter the grounds and view the scene. On March 31, a Sunday, some 15,000 showed up. That same day a meeting held at the Delaware Avenue Baptist Church to protest the possibility of Sabbath fair days attracted only eight hundred. Two weeks later the Sunday Exposition crowd grew to 25,000.[25]

On April 27, with opening day fast approaching, the board of directors met in special session to decide the issue. Mayor Diehl moved that the Exposition open at one o'clock on Sundays. Hoping to assuage opponents, he further moved that the Midway be closed and that the sale of all items except food be prohibited. President Milburn led the opposition to the motion, repeating the protests of religious leaders and expressing his belief that the Exposition constituted a "show" under state law. Although he was considered the pre-eminent barrister in western New York, Milburn lost this case. Following a four-hour meeting the board voted 16–3 to open the gates on Sunday afternoons. Although disappointed, Buffalo's ministers chose to turn the other cheek. They announced that they would take no legal action to close the fair on Sundays.[26]

If the Sunday controversy was a nuisance for Exposition officials, the company's finances were emerging once again as a source of deep concern. On February 25 Buchanan informed the executive committee that income, mostly from the sale of stocks and bonds, came to $3,629,319.26. The company had spent thus far $3,370,641.81. This left just $258,677.45 in the till. At the same time unpaid contracts totaled just over a million dollars, with many more bills on the way.[27]

The company applied to the U.S. government for a loan of $500,000, but the senate rejected the bill in early March. Adding insult to injury was the fact that they approved four million for the upcoming fair in St. Louis. The board responded with a resolution to issue $500,000 in second mortgage bonds. To sell them Milburn called an April 6 meeting of the original Pan-Am incorporators. He laid out the financial plight of the Exposition but assured those gathered that all would end well. If there were eight million admissions to the fair, he asserted, all bonds would pay at par. He added that "careful and thorough investigation made by the exposition officials ... showed conclusively that 15,000,000 admissions could be expected." The crowd cheered—and they invested. By the end of the day the company had sold over $200,000 worth of bonds. By mid April the sales reached $427,000.[28]

As Milburn tried to shore up Exposition finances, workers were rushing to get everything ready for opening day on May 1. As March came to an end, so did most of the company's labor troubles. Meanwhile warmer weather melted the blanket of snow that had covered the grounds for several weeks. This revealed an accumulation of scrap lumber and other junk that no one had bothered to remove during the construction process. Five hundred men were soon at work tidying up, prompting the *Buffalo Commercial* to report in early April that the formerly litter-strewn vistas "now stretch away like a well-kept garden."[29]

With both the snow and the debris gone, landscape architect Rudolf Ulrich was able to get to work. He had a narrow window of time in which to complete his task, but according to the local press, Ulrich possessed "a preparation which makes grass grow rapidly." He started about April 1 to get the grounds in shape, and continued mild weather aided his efforts. By the 15th the *Commercial* was reporting, "The shrubs have braced up, the crocuses have burst from their veils, and tulips and other posies have risen promisingly from their beds so recently covered with snow."[30]

Also well along was the electrical wiring on Exposition buildings. This was the responsibility of consulting engineer Luther Stieringer and Henry Rustin, chief of the mechanical and electrical bureau. Their lighting effects at Omaha's Trans-Mississippi Exposition had been considered "uniquely beautiful." With the harnessing of Niagara power and the miracles it made possible major themes of the Pan-Am, the electricians' contributions would be critical to the event's success.[31]

Buchanan started reasonably early to make sure Stieringer and Rustin would have everything they needed to light up the Rainbow City. In July 1900 he contracted with the Safety Insulated Wire & Cable Company of New York to supply electrical wire. The selling point in the arrangement was that the firm agreed to rent the wire rather than sell it. This made sense for a temporary exposition. It also cut the cost by two-thirds, which was significant since the Pan-Am would require over four hundred miles of wire. Two months later General Electric agreed to furnish 200,000 incandescent bulbs at 14.4 cents apiece. These would supply the nighttime lighting effects on the Exposition buildings. At eight candle-power they were about half as bright as the standard incandescent bulb in use at the time. "The light, therefore, is not concentrated or glaring, and it is not wearisome to the eye," one reporter would observe. As a more wordy Stieringer noted, "From the structural and decorative standpoint, to secure the best results we must have a lamp so small … that it gives but little light individually, but is capable of being so grouped, massed or distributed as to produce the desired effects and diffusion without raising any point of space to a brilliancy disagreeable to the eye to rest upon."[32]

To achieve these "desired effects," the Exposition Company would pay the Niagara Falls Power Company $25,000 a month. The electricity was generated twenty miles away at the company's central plant, where Power House No. 1 produced five thousand horsepower of current. Starting as two-phase alternating current at 2,200 volts, it was increased to 22,000 volts by means of step-up transformers. Upon reaching the terminal station in Buffalo, step-down transformers reduced the voltage to 11,000. The current then traveled 13,000 feet to the "rheostat house" on the west side of the Exposition grounds.

Buchanan authorized the purchase of a "water rheostat" from General Electric in February 1901. At $560 it was a bargain. A new and novel piece of technology, it allowed the Exposition's outside lights to be raised from zero, to a dim glow, and gradually up to full intensity, a metamorphosis achieved every evening of the fair at dusk. The rheostat system consisted of three tanks, each three feet wide, seven feet long, and three feet deep, holding a total of 1,400 gallons of water. Metallic blades, six feet long, in the tanks could be raised or lowered by an electric motor. When lowered into the water they lessened the distance the current had to travel through the water, making it stronger. Full metallic contact would bring the lights up to maximum intensity.

From the rheostat house the current traveled underground through three lead-covered copper cables. It ended up at a transforming sub-station in the Electricity Building, part of General Electric's display. There eighteen transformers reduced the voltage from 11,000 to 1,800. Adjacent to the transformers was the distributing switchboard, from which the power was sent to about forty transformer pits located throughout the grounds. These reduced the voltage to 104 to supply the bulbs that would create the fair's nighttime show of light and color that one observer would refer to as "nocturnal architecture."[33]

On March 22 the *Buffalo Express* reported that Rustin was "getting the big buildings wired and dotted with incandescents," adding that his work "has progressed as far as the other construction work will allow." The latter observation was telling. With opening day some six weeks away, it was becoming obvious that the Exposition buildings would not all be completed on time. In fact, the day after the *Express* reported Rustin's progress, the *Courier* told its readers that 150 buildings were yet to be finished. In most cases the major construction work was done, and the staging was coming off many of the main Exposition structures. But this still left statuary, painting, and other finishing touches. In addition to these details, the Electric Tower remained without elevators or its restaurant.[34]

Farthest behind were the state and national buildings, over which the Exposition Company had little control. In some cases state legislatures initially appropriated only enough money to send displays, then decided at the last minute to vote additional funds to erect a building. Michigan representatives did not select the site for theirs until March 10. Three days later Chile awarded the construction contract for its building. On the 20th Buchanan advanced the Puerto Ricans two thousand Exposition dollars "for the rapid completion" of their building. He added, "The architect will reach here in a few days." By then three thousand men were at work on state and foreign buildings. Despite that none would be complete by opening day.[35]

As the work continued on the exteriors of Exposition structures, other groups of laborers were adding display booths, draperies, and bunting to the interiors. Meanwhile the many displays that would fill those booths were making their way to Buffalo—but at a trickle. Many exhibitors planned to come to Buffalo to oversee personally the installation of their displays. Wanting to spend as little time as necessary, they held off shipping, creating visions of epic last-minute traffic jams in the minds of Exposition officials. The concerns were justified. Through much of March freight cars in the single digits arrived daily in Buffalo. The number increased in April, fifty-five arriving on the 10th. Not all could be switched to the grounds, so transportation companies were called upon to supply extra teams and trucks.

The shipments were diverse, ranging from artillery pieces, to three freight cars of ocean water for the government's fisheries display, to "a Los Angeles orange as big as a man's head." In some cases they were potentially overwhelming. By November 1900 the inquiries for space in the manufactures division would have covered three times the area available. The interior court, designed for fountains and flowers, was utilized for some of the overflow, as was a nearby building. Applications for space in the Machinery and Transportation Building totaled four times what was available. A separate structure for railroad equipment went up at the north end of the grounds. Unfortunately it proved to be too small to house large passenger cars. In the end only locomotives were displayed there.[36]

Despite the delays and difficulties, officials remained hopeful that the Exposition would be ready in time for opening day on May 1. On the last day of March both President Milburn and director of works Carlton assured reporters that, barring inclement weather, all would be in readiness. Buchanan echoed their thoughts. On April 15 he observed, "If this mild weather holds out, so we can get some substantial roads under us, we will have the exposition grounds looking handsome on the first day of May, and will have the interiors of the buildings so nearly complete that no one can tell that a single thing remains to be done."[37]

The mild weather didn't hold out; and on April 20, Milburn, Carlton, Buchanan, and all the other folks connected with the Pan-Am were reminded that they were indeed holding their fair in Buffalo.

11

McKinley: Journey to San Francisco

In January 1901 President McKinley developed a cold, which soon grew into a case of influenza. His recovery was slow, and the illness left him bedridden for over a week. Fortunately the Twentieth Amendment was still more than three decades away, and the patient was fully recovered by March 4, 1901, the day of his second inauguration. The weather that day could have sent the second-term president back to his sickbed. A light rain grew in intensity, and McKinley began his inaugural address in a downpour. Not learning from his predecessor William Henry Harrison, he spoke bareheaded as the rain turned to sleet.[1]

Perhaps the president, who loved to travel and meet the people he served, was buoyed by the prospect of his upcoming six-week trip. The journey would take him through the heart of the Confederacy, across the desert Southwest, and up the Pacific coast. At San Francisco McKinley was to witness the launch of the battleship *Ohio*. He would then turn east and conclude his tour at Buffalo, where on June 13 the president was scheduled to deliver a major address at the Exposition. Along the way he planned to take on ossified senate Republicans on the subject of reciprocity, spending much of the political capital his decisive re-election proved he possessed. McKinley's plan was to start slowly, speaking of foreign markets as he traveled through the South. The serious discussions would take place on the return trip from San Francisco, building to a crescendo and setting the stage for a major address at Buffalo.[2]

At 10:30 a.m. on April 29 a presidential party of 43 left Washington's Union Station on a special train. Ida's health was always precarious, but she shared her husband's love of travel. The first lady also had a strong supporting cast. In addition to a personal maid, Ida's niece Mary Barber, a special favorite, would accompany her on the trip. Also in attendance was Dr. Presley M. Rixey, a Navy surgeon who was serving as the White House physician. The first lady felt very secure under his care, and this had made him a critical member of the executive staff.[3]

Crossing the Potomac immediately put the presidential train into what had been, 36 years earlier, Confederate territory. But the sectional divide was forgotten as the party rode the rails of the Southern Railroad. "Large crowds assembled at every station," wrote a reporter for the *New York Times*. "The

The president and the first lady pose at the White House (Library of Congress).

countryside and crossroads each had its little group of watchers straining their eyes to catch a glimpse of the Chief Magistrate as the train whisked by." At Charlottesville a group of students from the University of Virginia offered a warm greeting. At Roanoke, where thousands had gathered, two bands competed for the honor of serenading their special guest with "Hail to the Chief."[4]

The only reference to earlier hostilities that day was made by the president. At Lynchburg, where the train stopped for ten minutes, McKinley said he was "very glad … to meet the people of the city of Lynchburg." Then he deadpanned, "The first time I ever tried to come to Lynchburg, I did not succeed. I came here with a number of other gentlemen who sought entrance, but the gates were closed. And so we departed to seek another host, if not more hospitable, less formidable than the one that greeted us here."[5]

Heading deeper into the South, McKinley continued to receive warm and enthusiastic greetings. For the president reunification remained an important theme. At Corinth he told listeners, "The valor and the heroism of the men of the South and the men of the North have within the last three years been shown in Cuba, in Puerto Rico, in the Philippines, and in China, and when we are all on one side we are unconquerable." At Huntsville, Alabama, where Confederate veterans composed the guard of honor, the president said, "I am glad to see the boys in gray uniting in giving the reception," adding, "Once foes, now friends forever."[6]

The presidential train reached New Orleans on May 1. The party remained there for two days, sightseeing and attending various events. "Never, except in Mardi Gras times, were the streets so choked and jammed with surging humanity," one observer noted. Among the places the president visited was Southern University, a black college that boasted an enrollment of five thousand. The fact that he visited the institution did credit to the president. His talk to the students who gathered to hear him would be viewed today as condescending, but it reflected the views of such black leaders of the day as Booker T. Washington. "I am glad to know that all over the South, where most of you dwell," the president said, "the states have provided institutions of learning where every boy and girl can prepare themselves for usefulness and honor under the Government in which they live." He added, "What you want is to get education, and with it you want good character, and with these you want unfaltering industry."[7]

From the Crescent City the train continued west into Texas, where the travelers caught their first glimpses of cowboys and long-horned cattle. At Prairie View, a short distance west of Houston, the president addressed students at the "State Normal and Colored Industrial School." He spoke outside, and the audience included nearly a thousand horses used to transport the majority of the people gathered. McKinley offered the same type of paternal advice he had at New Orleans. He also noted that, "In our recent war with Spain your race showed distinguished qualities of gallantry upon more than one field."[8]

Arriving at El Paso on the 6th, the president was greeted by thousands of Mexican citizens who had crossed the bridge from Juarez to see him. McKinley, who desired to take a look at Mexico, was taken to the bridge. There, from the U.S. customs office, he peeped across the bridge, viewing the Sierra Madre Mountains, far to the south. Customs of the times prevented any American president from venturing onto foreign soil. Ten years earlier Benjamin Harrison had walked halfway across the bridge, but McKinley preferred to remain one hundred percent on American *terra firma*.

The itinerary next took the presidential party into a pair of American territories, New Mexico and Arizona. In Deming, New Mexico, McKinley was greeted by the territorial governor and by a banner at the train station reading, "New Mexico Demands Statehood." He told those gathered that he hoped their territory would someday achieve their goal, but he could not promise when. However, the chief executive assured them that, state or not, "You are part of the seventy-five millions that constitute the greatest free government on the face of the earth." (New Mexico would become a state ten years later.)[9]

After traveling through Arizona, including a visit to a gold mine and to Aztec ruins, the train rolled into California on May 8. It was Fiesta Week in Los Angeles, and the prominent visitors were treated to parades, receptions, and outpourings of enthusiastic Angelinos. The president appeared at the head of a floral parade in a coach drawn by six horses. Upon reaching the reviewing stand he was showered by rose petals until they covered the tops of his shoes. Less fortunate was Secretary of Agriculture James Wilson, who lost his wallet to a pickpocket during the festivities.[10]

Wilson was not the only prominent individual who found cause to complain. Arriving in California the same day as the presidential train was the train bearing Ohio governor George K. Nash and about a hundred other Buckeye dignitaries. It had left Cincinnati four days earlier, following a route more northerly than the president's. At several stops along the way, the governor's train had been greeted by a number of former Ohioans who had moved west. At Los Angeles, however, the bulk of the attention went to the president, and Governor Nash became chagrined. "At Los Angeles it was all McKinley," an Associated Press reporter wrote, "and the Ohio gubernatorial party felt slighted." When a third train bearing the Ohio congressional delegation was attached to the Ohio Special, an unnamed passenger traveling with the governor complained that they "now were given third place." Tensions escalated further when the local committee of arrangements would not allow the governor's train to depart on the evening of May 9 because the presidential train had not yet left the city. This delayed the Ohio contingent until the following morning. Meeting with a delegation from San Jose, representatives of the governor insisted that his arrival in that city precede that of the president.[11]

McKinley's reaction—if any—to the political tempest was not recorded. It is unlikely he gave it any thought at all because Ida's health had once again worsened. This crisis apparently began with a "felon" (infection) on her forefinger. Dr. Rixey had lanced it as the train crossed the desert of New Mexico or Arizona. The operation brought no relief, and she soon developed a fever and a case of diarrhea. On Saturday, May 11, the first lady collapsed. The next day the devout president violated his self-imposed rule against traveling on the Sabbath. Abandoning the presidential train, which continued on its scheduled visits, McKinley took his wife directly to San Francisco, arriving two days ahead of schedule. H. T. Scott, president of the Union Iron Works, the firm that had built the *Ohio*, made his home available to the president and his stricken wife. There she was placed in bed, with Dr. Rixey and a phalanx of nurses at her side.[12]

Ida's illness quickly became front page news all across the country. Her husband vastly curtailed his public schedule to remain at her bedside. Planned speaking engagements at Stanford University and the University of California at Berkeley were canceled. So, too, was a parade for the city's school children and a number of banquets and receptions. Meanwhile the first lady appeared to rally. Medical bulletins issued to the press were cryptic yet optimistic. For example on the 14th her doctors announced, "Mrs. McKinley has lost nothing but gained a little since last night's rest."[13]

With that bit of reassurance, the president decided to go ahead with his official entry into San Francisco. At 3:20 that afternoon he left the Scott residence for a carriage ride to the Townsend Street depot. There he met the presidential train as it arrived. However, since this was where the original schedule had called for him to disembark, McKinley did not board the train. Rather he stepped into a waiting carriage for a parade which he was both to lead and review.

Along the way the city police and McKinley's Secret Service detail kept vigilant—and for good reason. At one point the security force spotted a man who was following the presidential carriage. At times he would "glide up closely in a stealthy manner." Finally Agent George Foster "hustled him out of the line." Later along the parade route, a boy with a "devilish toy," which produced a loud explosion when dropped to the pavement, startled a policeman. The boy received a stern lecture but was allowed to keep his noisemaker on the condition that it remain in his pocket. Another officer became concerned when he spotted "a round black object as big as a stovelid and twice as thick" rolling into the center of the street. It turned out to be the bottom of a Japanese lantern that had surrounded an overhead arc light. "It's from 'an-arc-y' light," the policeman quipped, a joke that would not be so funny four months later.[14]

McKinley shared the viewing platform with Governor Nash—apparently no longer pouting—and Governors Henry Gage of California and T. T. Geer of Oregon. (Even when he was the center of attention, Nash could not catch a break. On May 13 the governor was taken to visit California's giant redwood trees. One of them, standing near the famous General Grant tree, was named in his honor. Three days later Nash came down with a case of poison oak. It left his eyes so swollen that the governor was partially, but temporarily, blinded, and it kept him bedridden for two days.) Although McKinley loved a parade, an observer described him as "uneasy" on the viewing platform. He spent only a few minutes there before calling for a carriage to take him back to his wife's bedside.[15]

Following an uneventful day on the 15th, Ida's condition worsened again the next day. At about five in the morning the knot of reporters gathered outside the Scott home noticed "a stir in the house." Lights flickered, and one of the attending physicians arrived on the scene. Secretary Cortelyou issued an understated medical bulletin four hours later: "Mrs. McKinley's condition not so favorable, she having had a sinking spell at 5 o'clock this morning." The Associated Press reported, "Mrs. McKinley's life hangs by a thread, and she is liable to expire at any moment." The wire service added, "She is unconscious most of the time and is just hovering between life and death." A reporter for the *San Francisco Examiner* went further, writing that it was "almost a certainty Mrs. McKinley is going to die." Indeed, as local officials considered postponing the launching of the *Ohio*, White House staff members quietly made tentative plans for a funeral train.[16]

Then, as she had often done in the past, Ida rallied once again. The administration of "heart stimulants" was given much credit for her improvement. Late on the afternoon of the 16th, as the AP reported her near death, the first lady sat up and was able to speak. Citing her doctors, the press reversed itself the next day, reporting that her life was out of danger. They also announced that, barring a change for the worse, the president would attend the launching of the *Ohio*, scheduled for the next day, Saturday, May 18.

Back in Ohio, the *Columbus Dispatch* saw the executive decision as the best possible news about the first lady's condition. "The president's actions seemed to give more assurances of Mrs. McKinley's improvement than any statement from her doctors could have done," the paper's traveling correspondent wrote. In an editorial the paper waxed eloquent about the vessel the president was about to help launch. "It is a big addition to Uncle Sam's growing and now powerful navy," the paper boasted. Even *Dispatch* advertisers were caught up in the excitement. Lazarus Department Store announced "a Saturday launching of bargains at the Big Store."[17]

May 18 dawned bright in San Francisco, the physicians remained optimistic, and at 10:35 the president of the United States boarded the tug *Slocum* at the Spear Street wharf, bound for the yards of Union Iron Works. As he crossed the bay a number of ships fired salutes in honor of the commander-in-chief. Among them was the transport *Sheridan*, named for McKinley's fellow Ohioan and just back from service in the Philippines. As stirring as the brief voyage was for the president, it was also tinged with anxiety. It and the return trip were the only times that the devoted and worried husband was out of telegraphic communication with the Scott house.

As at the other presidential events in the city, thousands of spectators turned out for the festivities. "Every available boat on the bay was pressed into service and carried its sightseers toward the focal point," the *San Francisco Chronicle* noted.[18]

Arriving at the landing, McKinley was greeted by an escort of flag-waving employees of the Union Iron Works. They preceded him to the dry dock, which had been converted into an amphitheater for the event. One of the laborers, a machinist, delivered a brief welcoming speech, and on behalf of his colleagues, presented the guest of honor with a gold plate. In responding, McKinley's thoughts first went out to his ailing wife. "I am inexpressibly thankful to the ruler of us all," he told the crowd, "for His goodness and mercy, which have made it possible for me to be with you here today." He then saluted "the loyal patriotism of the people of San Francisco" and offered thanks to "the people of this coast for their noble work during the Spanish war." In particular McKinley commended the employees of the Union Iron Works. "No one can stand surrounded by the workmen of this great establishment without recalling the splendid work done by the ships you have builded and their priceless services to the country," he enthused. "When Admiral Dewey was directed to go to Manila and destroy the Spanish fleet, he made the *Olympia*, which you builded, his flagship; and his command from that ship accomplished one of the most brilliant achievements in the annals of the American navy."[19]

The president and John Davis Long, his secretary of the navy, then watched as many of those same workmen, armed with sledges, dislodged blocks under the *Ohio*'s keel in preparation for the launching. At 12:26 Mary Barber, McKinley's niece, pushed "the magic button" that released the ship into the harbor. As the vessel glided by, Miss Helen Deshler, a niece of Governor Nash, christened the ship with a bottle of California champagne. "I baptize thee, and name thee Ohio," Miss Deshler cried. "May God speed thee on thy way." All was momentarily silent, then, as the ship slipped into the drink, steam whistles shrieked and cannons boomed, all signaling that America's newest battleship was now afloat. A Marine band played The Star Spangled Banner, and the crowd began singing "until it seemed as if the anthem pealed to the skies."[20]

With that the brief ceremony was over. The president paused briefly, looking over the rail at the place where the ship had been built. The workmen below spotted him and began to cheer. He removed his hat to salute them, then said, "You are the men who launched the *Ohio*. I am proud and glad to meet you for I think you have done a noble work. She is a magnificent ship, as are all those that have been built by the Union Iron Works."[21]

Heading back aboard the *Slocum*, the presidential party passed a number of Navy ships in formal review. Blue clad sailors stood at attention at the rails, marine guards were at present arms, and there were drum and trumpet salutes aplenty. "It was a glorious spectacle," one reporter wrote, "and it was a poor sailor whose pulse did not beat faster at the sight of it." Grand though the scene may have been, it presented itself before a president who was preoccupied. Anxious to return to his wife's bedside, McKinley did not wait for the gangplank to be rolled out when his boat arrived at the wharf. Instead, he leapt over the rail to the pier and virtually ran to his waiting carriage for the return trip to the Scott house.[22]

Ida's condition forced the first couple to remain in San Francisco for another week. The president used some of the time to reschedule events circumstances had forced him to skip. On May 21 he took part in a parade that allowed him to greet the children of San Francisco. Some 45,000 lined the route. Three days later he crossed the bay to participate in a similar parade in Oakland. Between those two events McKinley spoke to a gathering of the Knights Templar and greeted two regiments of soldiers returning home from the Philippines. He also paid a visit to the military hospital at the Presidio. "This is a young boy to be a soldier," he observed at one point. A reporter for the *San Francisco Chronicle* observed, "The President's eyes glistened more than once" as he visited with the youthful wounded men.[23]

The McKinleys departed the city on May 25 along a carefully chosen route, selected so Ida would travel only upon smooth, paved streets, that took them to the ferry dock. By then the people of San Francisco had developed a deep and protective bond with the couple. The *San Francisco Examiner* explained, "For over a week the President of the United States has been a citizen of San Francisco—as we might say, one of ourselves. It was not in his official relation that we considered him mostly," the paper went on. "It was for the husband rather than the President that we were concerned." That concern had not lessened. The people's cheers as the presidential carriage headed to the ferry dock were restrained so as not to disturb the first lady. Accompanying them, according to the *Chronicle*, was "a murmur of affection that came from a feeling of companionship with the president in his lonely vigils of last week."[24]

A ferry carried the president and Ida to Oakland, where they boarded an eastbound train. A planned excursion to the Pacific Northwest was canceled, and the president's visit to the Pan-American Exposition would have to be rescheduled. The first couple would return to Washington as directly and quickly as possible. Although the decision was sound, it left many disappointed. The route of the return journey had been made public, and telegrams poured in requesting that the president stop at various communities along the way. The ever protective Cortelyou was having none of it, and the requests were uniformly turned down. Indeed, as the party continued east, train crews were changed a few miles from the end of each division to avoid crowds that had gathered. Only at the larger communities did the train slow down and the president appear on the rear platform, waving to the people who had turned out to greet him. Many communities received a consolation prize. Governor Nash, still hungry for attention, made numerous stops as he and his party returned home to the Buckeye State.[25]

At 7:30 on the morning of May 30 the presidential train arrived back in the nation's capital. Assisted by several men, the president and Dr. Rixey carried Ida, seated in a chair, from the private car *Olympia* to a waiting carriage. To avoid the rough cobblestone streets, police cleared the more smoothly paved sidewalk of spectators, and the carriage glided off toward the White House. Once there, Dr. Rixey and a number of attendants bore Ida, still in her chair, inside. The doctor remained for an hour. As he departed, Rixey told a group of reporters that the first lady was "resting very comfortably." He added, "She is better today than when she left San Francisco." Although Ida was still very weak, Dr. Rixey assured the reporters that she was "in no immediate danger."[26]

The president returned to a capital awash in rumors that he was considering running for a third term. They gained a certain credence by the fact that such McKinley allies as Rep. Charles Grosvenor and Sen. Chauncey Depew were encouraging the talk. Democratic newspapers were beginning to accuse McKinley of stirring up "a third-term mania." This troubled the president, who had an ambitious second-term agenda in mind. Third term talk would add an unneeded political taint to any program he pushed. After calling an emergency cabinet meeting to discuss the matter, he issued a statement that was uncharacteristically blunt and unequivocal. "I will say now, once and for all, expressing a long settled conviction," McKinley wrote, "that not only I am not and will not be a candidate for a third term, but would not accept a nomination for it if it were tendered to me."[27]

The Shermanesque disclaimer struck a resonant chord with the public, and with the latest political crisis out of the way, McKinley's thoughts turned to the personal. On July 5 he and Ida returned to Canton for what would be his longest time away from the capital as president—a scheduled three months. There the McKinleys would enjoy their home and their friends. At the time nobody knew that William and Ida's respite would prove to be a benediction.

12

Exposition: Deadlines and Delays

At about 11:00 p.m. on April 18, 1901, snow began to fall in Buffalo. The following morning it intensified, and on the 20th the city awoke to find eight inches on the ground. The wet snow and the winds that accompanied it brought down trees, telephone and power lines, and trolley wires. Telegraph service was affected to the point that the Weather Bureau was unable to report how far the storm extended beyond western New York.

At the Exposition grounds the Rainbow City suddenly bore more resemblance to Chicago's White City of 1893. Damage, however, was minimal. Indeed, Exposition officials were pleased the roofs held up under the onslaught. Skylights were a different story. At the Horticulture Building snow falling from the steeply slanted dome crashed through a skylight, and the rain that followed damaged a display of California fruits and grains, along with shelves and draperies. The snow also claimed a forty-foot section of skylight on the Mines and Graphic Arts Building, but it did virtually no damage to the interior. If the actual loss caused by the storm was slight, the potential loss was horrendous because fire apparatus could not travel through the accumulation of snow. As a preventive measure the department set up a "rigid patrol" around the grounds.

The greatest loss to Exposition officials was time, which they were already fighting to get everything complete. For contractors the delay was just two days—bad enough with opening day just over a week away. The landscaping department faced a longer wait since they could do little until the snow melted. Landscape architect Rudolph Ulrich told a reporter, "We were in hopes that we would be pretty well prepared for opening day, but at present the outlook is problematic." The excessive moisture in the ground sidelined all paving work. Also temporarily halted were Henry Rustin's electrical wiring crews. And when they returned to work they had to repair a number of smaller wires the snow had snapped. The storm brought the transportation department to a standstill. As the wagons sat idle, 250 freight cars waited on the tracks north of the grounds.[1]

On April 21 members of the executive committee toured the grounds before meeting with the director general to decide if they should postpone the fair's opening day. The result was a compromise decision. The Exposition would open on May 1, as advertised, but there would be no opening day ceremonies. Those events would take place on May 20, already scheduled as the Pan-Am's Dedication Day. In making the announcement Buchanan assured reporters, "We are going to open on the first of May, you may be sure of that. We immediately will put on double shifts of men, if necessary work 10,000 men day and night, and, in short, do everything within human power to make up for the time that has been lost."[2]

The next day warm and sunny weather returned to Buffalo, justifying the committee's decision to go ahead with the May 1 opening. By that afternoon not only was the snow gone, but the ground was dry in most places. Work on the buildings resumed, as did paving. The transportation department contracted for extra wagons to haul the glut of displays from freight cars to the proper buildings. Among the items moved were two carloads of siege and field guns from the Rock Island, Illinois arsenal, part of the U.S. government display. Symbolically the most important work done on the 22nd was the installation of the statue Goddess of Light to her perch atop the Electric Tower. Actually only the bottom half of the 28-foot statue went up that day. The top followed on the 23rd. In each case, as the crane lifted the figure skyward, men stood on the pinnacle of the structure and guided it into place. They accomplished the dangerous task quickly, without incident or injury. The Niagara Construction Company earned $1,500 for its efforts, and Exposition officials were content with the knowledge that the main structural features of their most prominent building were complete.[3]

At the same time carting companies were working twelve to sixteen hours a day to keep ahead of arriving freight cars. Occasional shortages of teams hindered the effort, but the crews did yeoman work. On Sunday, April 28, with no competition from Buffalo's commercial interests, the wagons delivered thirty-five carloads to the grounds. Included were donkeys for the Midway attraction Beautiful Orient and two engines from the Schenectady Locomotive Works. They nearly duplicated the effort the following day, despite the fact that businesses were again competing for teams and wagons.[4]

Although the crews worked long and hard, the Exposition was still a work in progress when the gates officially opened on May 1. Coming through the main entrance at the southern end of the grounds, visitors stepped onto solid pavement; but before long it gave way to slag. Yet such was the progress—even on opening day—that by day's end only the north Midway remained to be surfaced.

That progress, of course, required workers. And as opening day visitors wended their way through the grounds they encountered, according to one reporter, "gardeners with plants, painters with pots, carpenters with saws, rakers with gravel, diggers with picks, and plasterers with staff." At the entrances to every major Exposition building two or more wagons were parked, workmen scurrying to unload their contents. Inside those buildings carpenters were still putting booths in place as employees from various firms unpacked boxes to be ready to fill them. Some were further along than others. The Machinery Building was virtually filled, a task accomplished in just over a week. In the Manufactures and Liberal Arts Building well over half the booths were in place. None of the displays were yet complete, but many were very close. There were also no finished exhibits in the Agriculture Building, although Michigan's, Oregon's, and Argentina's were well under way. The story was the same in the Electricity Building, where exhibitors were trying to install numerous pieces of heavy machinery. At the Ethnology Building officials blamed Central and South American countries for the unfinished condition of things. After committing for display space in the building, many decided to combine their ethnological exhibits with items they were showing in other buildings, hoping to make their exhibits more impressive.[5]

Outside, many Exposition buildings still wore scaffolding, as did the Propylaea, a curving colonnaded structure garnished with statuary and panels bearing messages reflecting the Pan-American spirit. Unfortunately it and its scaffolding were at the entranceway where visitors traveling by train would arrive. Scaffolding also covered portions of the Stadium. Most disappointing, perhaps, was the scaffolding around the lower portion of the Electric Tower, where workers were putting sculpture in place. The structure itself was closed to the public as crews worked inside to finish the restaurant and the elevators.[6]

Electric lighting proved to be another area of trouble. For the first half hour after the exterior lights came on they would occasionally die down and go out, a problem likely caused by the rheostat. Power failures also plagued several Midway attractions. Both problems repeated themselves from time to time as the month went on. The situation was especially vexing for the Midway concessionaires, most of whom depended on electricity to keep their shows open. Sunday closing was already taking money from their coffers. Now power failures were adding to their financial woes. The problem hit its peak on the 29th, when a short circuit near the Electricity Building during the early evening hours produced a power failure that lasted several hours. It also caused a minor fire, but crews quickly extinguished the blaze. Buchanan

The Pan-American Exposition's Grand Canal flowing past the Horticulture Building (Library of Congress).

had much greater difficulty attempting to mollify disappointed Midway show-men.[7]

With the actual opening day behind them, Exposition officials now set their sights on May 20, the advertised Dedication Day. On Sunday, May 5, and again on the 12th, most buildings were closed to allow carpenters to install booths and exhibitors to fill them. On the 10th the canals that encircled the grounds were filled and ready for the gondolas that would offer rides to Exposition visitors. At the same time workers were rapidly completing the bridges over the waterways. Elsewhere crews were putting the many fountains that dotted the grounds into operation, including those in the grand basin in front of the Electric Tower. The stadium opened on the 15th, and a crowd of eight thousand turned out for a three-hour "carnival of sports." The event included genuine athletic contests, such as races both on foot and on bicycles, plus a number of shows presented by Midway performers.[8]

On May 17 the *Buffalo Express* announced, "The heavy work at the exposition ended yesterday." All that remained, the paper added, were "light finishing tasks." To support its contention, the *Express* noted that five out of every six freight wagons rumbling through the grounds were now hauling debris out, while only one was bringing exhibits in. Director of works Carlton offered a similar sentiment, although more curiously phrased. Speaking of Dedication Day, he told a *Courier* reporter, "Our work will be done, but it will not all be completed."[9]

Landscape architect Ulrich had nine hundred men laying walkways, leveling ground, and setting out flowers and shrubbery. Nevertheless, he had to concede that the grounds would not be fully ready by Dedication Day. "I have tried very hard to get finished," he explained, "but it is impossible. There will be no bad spots, but planting will not all be done." Karl Bell, superintendent of sculpture, offered a similar report. "All the big groups," he explained, "have been placed and pointed and the only work remaining to be done is on some of the single figures."[10]

In most departments all that remained were details; but the list of details was daunting. On May 2 Buchanan and the executive committee arranged to have 902 lamp posts painted at a cost of $4,500. Five days later the board of directors met to consider other last-minute arrangements. They voted to purchase 2,500 additional shrubs and $2,070 worth of plants, along with seventeen ducks and fifty Toulouse geese. The electrical department received more utility poles and an additional 30,000 feet of wire. The board approved contracts for "sculptural figures" to place on bridge pylons and for cast inscriptions for mounting on a variety of buildings. Many of their actions involved painting. Included was the interior of the Women's Building, the exteriors of the Bazaar Building and the Stadium, the metal roofs on the five largest Exposition buildings, and the railings of the Electric Tower stairway. The Scott Paper Company received the contract to supply toilet paper. The firm agreed to provide the first twenty cases as well as "all fixtures" for free. Finally the board tabled a request to grant a contract for a concession called "Palmistry and Mind Reading" to allow Buchanan time to "investigate the character of the proposed entertainment and submit a recommendation."[11]

Some details having to do with the Midway were less easily handled. One problem involved concessionaire Frank Bostock and his boa constrictors. Bostock's show featured exotic animals from around the world. Most stayed put, but on at least two occasions the snakes did not. The first one, said to be seven feet long, was found on May 4 by a city police officer on night patrol. It was lying motionless on a paved street. Authorities returned the reptile to its owner, who assumed it had fallen from a wagon that was delivering his creatures to the Midway.

It soon developed that two boas had gotten loose *en route* to the fair; or such was possibly the case. Midway showmen, hungry for publicity, were not above planting stories in the local press, so the tale of the second snake may be apocryphal. In any event, the boa in question was said to be Bostock's personal pet, "kind-faced [and] mild-mannered." Local livestock may have disagreed, because on the 11th the *Commercial* reported that a Bostock representative had ventured to Tonawanda to pay for two head of cattle and five sheep that had been "hugged to death." Three days later the paper announced that the wayward serpent had been found by a hotel employee in nearby Echota. Here matters grew complicated as the boa's captor demanded a five-hundred-dollar reward for its return. Bostock threatened a lawsuit, and the man with the newfound snake, who was reportedly holding it hostage in a boat in the Niagara River, threatened to turn it loose in a Canadian swamp. That never happened. Although short on details, the *Express* reported on the 17th that the reptile was safely back with its owner.[12]

Far more serious was the outbreak of measles that struck the Canadian First Nations natives who composed the Midway's "Eskimo Village." Exposition officials concluded that they had been exposed to the disease while waiting for transportation at Ellis Island. Eventually eleven cases were reported. Dr. Park ordered that the village be quarantined and treated the most severely affected at the Exposition hospital. Sadly, one victim died from the effects of the disease. Sebelia Nikolemik, of the Labrador region of Newfoundland, at first showed signs of recovery. Then she developed pneumonia, dying on May 11. She was seven months old. Sebelia was buried the next day, her mother too ill to attend the service.[13]

The Exposition's sprawling Machinery Building (Library of Congress).

May 19 was a busy day at the Exposition grounds, and so was the night that followed, as Buffalo got ready to greet the world—or at least that portion of it bearing the fifty-cent admission fee. An army of workmen, armed with brooms, scoured the landscape. Meanwhile painters finished coloring the two bandstands on the Esplanade. "The people of Buffalo will see a beautiful Exposition," Carlton promised, while also admitting, "There will be minor details in construction work and groundwork that will not be complete." However, "There will be no unsightly scaffolding to offend the eye." A break in a steam pipe connecting the boiler house with pumps outside the Machinery Building threatened to shut down the Fountain of Abundance. Then a crew of efficient steamfitters arrived and had everything repaired before dark. After dark Rustin put the exterior lighting to its final, successful test.[14]

At 10:06 a.m. on May 20, 1901, "the finest carriage that could be procured" halted in front of Buffalo's city hall. Exposition president John Milburn stepped out, along with U.S. Vice President Theodore Roosevelt. Four minutes later the Dedication Day parade started north toward the Exposition grounds. Military men were at the head of the column, with soldiers representing both the United States and Mexico. They totaled two thousand, including four martial bands. Politicians, among them Sen. Henry Cabot Lodge of Massachusetts and Mark Hanna, followed. Behind them were representatives from foreign countries and a delegation promoting the 1904 Louisiana Purchase Exposition to be held in St. Louis. Exposition directors and officers came next, along with assorted editors, mayors, judges, and bands.

Right behind the formal parade came the far gaudier—and far more fun—Midway parade. Put together the two processions formed a column stretching nearly four miles. The Native Americans of the Indian Congress were at its head; and a young girl on horseback was at the Indians' head. A group of chieftains, riding single file, followed. Fair Japan sent "Geisha girls, swordsmen and wrestlers attired in their native costumes." The residents of the Eskimo Village, accompanied by panting sled dogs, wore their furs. Bostock brought a group of zebras and two elephants, one of which carried a caged lion on its back. His was not the only animal act. The Streets of Cairo entry included camels, elephants, and donkeys, "accompanied by Asiatic bands and tribes of Turks, Bedouins, Egyptians, Moors and other representatives of the historic lands of the East."[15]

At exactly twelve noon the parade reached the Esplanade of the Exposition. Fifteen minutes later Milburn escorted the vice president to the platform in the Temple of Music reserved for VIP's. Soon after that the 71st Regiment Band opened the ceremonies with Handel's Hallelujah. Then the Rev. C. H. Fowler, a Methodist bishop, offered a prayer so lengthy that it took up nearly two newspaper columns. The invocation had twelve "Thous," fifteen "Thys," and twenty-nine "Thees." The bishop asked God's blessing on Buffalo, the Exposition's board of directors, the presidents of all American republics, and "all who take part or have interest in these ceremonies." The most prescient injunction was, "Bless our vice president, who may become our president."[16]

Poems and more musical numbers followed. President Milburn read letters from a number of Latin American leaders and one from the president of the United States. McKinley was still in San Francisco with his perilously ill wife. He nevertheless took time to send a message to Buffalo. "I earnestly hope that the great exhibition may prove a blessing to every country of this hemisphere," the president wired.

Following a few remarks from Mayor Diehl, the vice president took to the podium. Although Teddy generally spoke purely on behalf of Teddy, he seemed to promote McKinley's ideas of reciprocity when he said, "This twentieth century is big with the fate of the nations of mankind, because the fate of each is now interwoven with the fate of all to a degree never even approached in any previous stage of history." He welcomed the participating neighboring countries to the United States and then bragged a little. "I think that we have reason to be satisfied with the showing made in this exposition," Roosevelt proclaimed, "of the results of the enterprise, the shrewd daring, the business energy and capacity, and the artistic, and above all the wonderful mechanical skill and inventiveness of our people."[17]

Teddy remained for several hours, taking in the evening's fireworks display, a feature that would become a staple of the Exposition. The show capped a hugely successful day. Dedication Day went off without a hitch, and paid admissions totaled 101,867. The crowd was so big that some of the restaurants ran out of food. Unfortunately the six-figure attendance numbers were not the start of a trend. On May 21 the attendance fell to 20,991, and that figure remained close to the norm. On May 26 the *New York Times* reported, "There still remains much to be done both inside and outside. Many important exhibits are not ready." That and similar stories appearing in other newspapers discouraged potential visitors. The Pan-Am was an artistic, creative, and technical triumph. However, press reports of an unfinished exposition would make it very difficult for the Exposition to be a financial success.[18]

13

Czolgosz:
The Path to Anarchy

Anarchy. In the late 1800s and early 1900s the word had the same visceral effect on people that terrorism does today—and for good reason. The concept went back to ancient Greece, the term coming from the Greek words *an* ("not") and *archos* ("government" or "rule"). The idea of utopian societies free of government constraints has bobbed up time and again throughout history. It has never, however, been tried on a large scale. That is in large part because the freedom-craving idealists have never been able to agree on how their society should be formed. And even if they did, such an agreement would constitute a governmental framework, exactly what they purport to oppose.[1]

As the 1800s wore on the radicals could not even agree on who the enemy was. One school of thought was led by Mikhail Bakunin. A member of an aristocratic Russian family, he nevertheless called for "the absolute destruction" of all governmental institutions. Espousing a different view was Karl Marx, who saw capitalists as the true enemy of the working class. Speaking of Marx, Bakunin conceded, "He wants what we want, the total triumph of economic and social equality." But, he quickly added, Marx sought that equality "through state power, through the dictatorship of a very strong and, so to speak, despotic government."[2]

Radicals were also reevaluating their tactics. In 1849 German Karl Heinzen wrote an article bearing the blunt title "Murder." Recent revolutions had failed, he concluded, because radicals had rejected murder as a tactic. "Even if we have to blow up half a continent or spill a sea of blood in order to finish off the barbarian party," Heinzen asserted, "we should have no scruples about doing it."[3]

It took time, but a growing minority of anarchists came to agree with Heinzen. When their planned "Bologna rising of 1874" was betrayed to police, Italian radicals realized the people were unlikely to rise up in mass support of revolution. Instead they turned to a tactic known as "propaganda by deed."

131

In 1878 a 29-year old cook attempted to stab King Umberto I but managed only to scratch him slightly. When a celebratory parade was held in Florence to recognize the king's good fortune, a bomb thrower had more success, killing four and injuring ten.[4]

Beginning in 1879 The People's Will, a Russian terrorist organization, made eight tries in 18 months to assassinate Tsar Alexander II. On one occasion a member of the group did not show up on time to set a fuse on a mined bridge the tsar was about to cross. The man explained that he did not own a watch. Despite this and similar episodes of incompetence, the group finally managed to kill Alexander, and 20 others, in a March 1, 1881, bombing.[5]

Spain witnessed a series of bombings in the 1890s. In one case, after a bomb thrower was executed, another got revenge by tossing a bomb into a theater, claiming 20 lives. Meanwhile France was experiencing similar acts of violence. One involved Emile Henry, who put a bomb in the offices of a mining company. The police discovered it and took it to their station, where it blew up, killing five. In 1893 Auguste Vaillant brought a bomb of his own design to the Chamber of Deputies. He hurled the device, designed to scatter projectiles, from a balcony. Nobody died, but many were hurt. Like Henry before him, Vaillant was executed, exclaiming, "My death will be avenged!"[6]

In a sense it was. On June 24, 1894, an Italian anarchist stabbed to death Sadi Carnot, the French president of the republic, who refused to extend mercy to Vaillant. It marked the beginning of a busy period for Italian assassins. Over the next six years they also killed the prime minister of Spain, the Queen of Hungary, and Italy's King Umberto I.[7]

In the post–Civil War years Europe's industrial revolution crossed the Atlantic. America's corporate profits soared, working conditions stagnated, and soon a nascent labor movement was struggling to correct the inequalities. Often the result was violence as union activists attacked strikebreaking "scabs," and the industrialists employed Pinkerton detectives or persuaded governors to call out state militias to protect their interests.

Into this environment sailed a number of European anarchists. One of the first—and one of the loudest—was Johann Most. A native of Bavaria, Most was twice imprisoned for "antigovernment agitation." He then went to London, founding the journal *Freiheit* ("Freedom"). When he used it to celebrate the murder of Russia's tsar, Most found himself imprisoned for 18 months. In 1882 he set sail for New York. If his locale was new, Most's message was not. Only violence could lift the yoke of oppression from the working class. Not only did he advocate violence, Most published guidebooks and articles delineating how to make it happen. His works included how-to guides on bombmaking, arson, and poisoning.[8]

Among those influenced by Most was another immigrant anarchist, Emma Goldman, a native of the Russian province of Kovno, who arrived in Rochester, New York, on New Year's Day, 1886. Under Most's tutelage, Goldman received lessons in anarchist literature and public speaking. She at first adhered to his endorsement of violence but later distanced herself from that view and from Most himself. When Goldman became involved with Alexander Berkman, a compositor at *Freiheit*, Most ended their relationship.[9]

As Emma Goldman arrived in America, so, too, did a large number of working class immigrants, many German, imbued with revolutionary ideas brought with them from the continent. Several ended up in Chicago, which was soon a hotbed of radical ideology. The Windy City became a tinderbox, and on May 4, 1886, it exploded.

It started with Cyrus McCormick, Jr., inheritor of his father's reaper works and an industrialist so ruthless in his labor policies that he made his fellow capitalists blush. On May 3 McCormick summoned police to deal with strikers who had assaulted strikebreakers with rocks. The responding officers opened fire, killing two to four laborers. Chicago radicals responded by calling for a rally to be held in an alley adjacent to Haymarket Square the following evening. Its main speaker, Albert Parsons, spoke against violence. This led Chicago's mayor, Carter H. Harrison, who had stopped by the rally out of concern, to head for home, relieved that cool heads had apparently prevailed. Parsons finished his talk and headed for a local tavern.

Then a subsequent speaker talked in more radical tones, and undercover police officers rushed to headquarters to summon some 180 cops to the scene. They arrived as the meeting was winding down but demanded that it be broken up immediately. As the demonstrators prepared to depart, someone casually lobbed a bomb. It killed at least one policeman, injured many others, and prompted the officers who were still able to empty their revolvers in a frenzy of fire. In so doing they likely killed far more of their colleagues than the bomb had. In the end some seven officers died and about 60 were wounded. Civilian casualties were about seven dead and 30–40 injured.[10]

Four individuals, including Parsons, were executed following a trial that the governor of Illinois later conceded was a sham. Among those following the case closely was Emma Goldman, who later wrote that the executions "crystallized my views ... and made me an active Anarchist." She was only eighteen at the time.[11]

Five years later a bitter strike at a Homestead, Pennsylvania steel mill owned by Andrew Carnegie turned violent after Henry Clay Frick, on Carnegie's behalf, locked the workers out of the plant and engaged Pinkerton men to protect the scabs he planned to hire. The Pinkerton force—three hundred strong—arrived at dawn on July 6 aboard two Monongahela River barges. The strikers were waiting for them, and shots soon rang out from both sides. A day-long battle ensued, leaving seven Pinkertons and nine strikers dead. Altogether some 60 people were shot.

As the debate over the Homestead battle raged in the press and on the floor of Congress, it prompted a "psychologic social moment" in Alexander Berkman, Emma Goldman's comrade and lover. He determined to assassinate the "tyrant" Frick and at the same time become a martyr for the cause. Berkman planned to use a bomb to do the deed, but even with Goldman's assistance and Most's terrorism handbook, he was unable to produce anything that would explode. In the end he boarded a train for Pittsburgh with a revolver and a nitroglycerin cartridge, which he planned to use to take his own life.

Berkman gained admission to Frick's office by posing as an employment agent for strikebreakers. He fired three shots, two finding their target, and managed to stab Frick with a dagger as the wounded man and a fellow executive who happened to be in the office wrestled with him for control of the gun. Workers from nearby offices rushed to the scene, as did the police. They subdued Berkman and seized the nitroglycerin cartridge before he could put it to use. Following a hasty trial he was sentenced to 22 years in prison. Meanwhile Frick recovered from his wounds.[12]

Although she did not discuss her role in Berkman's attempt for several decades, Emma supported him faithfully during the fourteen years he served in prison. When Johann Most, the forceful advocate of violence, deplored the act, Goldman appeared at one of his lectures with a horsewhip, lashed him with it, then broke the weapon over her knee and threw the pieces at him. Less dramatically, she lobbied to get Berkman's sentence commuted.[13]

With one lover and role model estranged and another cooling his heels in the penitentiary, Goldman stepped out on her own. She traveled widely, lecturing on anarchy and the injustice of Berkman's conviction. Later America's imperialism growing out of the Spanish-American War proved a frequent topic. She was loud and dramatic but undoubtedly sincere and possessed of intelligence and a biting wit. As one biographer noted, her "blunt, earnest, 'sledge-hammer' platform style ... created a sensation." Her theatrics attracted many who disagreed with her just because they wanted to see "Red Emma" perform. Her lectures also generally attracted the local police. Indeed, she was arrested so many times that Goldman took to bringing a book with her so she would have something to read while biding her time in some dank cell.[14]

On May 5, 1901, Goldman delivered the lecture "Modern Phases of Anarchy" at the Franklin Liberal Club in Cleveland. Among those in the audience was Leon Czolgosz.[15]

In the weeks leading up to the Goldman meeting Czolgosz had become "quite restless," according to his brother Waldeck. He would disappear, at first just one day a week, then later for two or three days or even a full week. When family members asked him where he went, Leon would only tell them "to attend meetings." He volunteered nothing more, and the family did not press the issue.[16]

At the same time Czolgosz began demanding his share of the investment in the family farm. Repeatedly in March and April he informed them that if he could not secure the funds immediately he had to have them by summer so he could go west. "He kept up this talk about getting his money," Waldeck recalled, "at times getting quite put out that he could not realize on his share." When Waldeck asked why he wanted to leave, Leon pointed to a dying tree and explained, "Look, it is just the same as a tree that commences dying, you can see it isn't going to live long." Waldeck tried to reason with him on another occasion, explaining that his share would not take him far. To this Czolgosz replied, "I can get a conductor's job or binding wheat or fixing machines or something." If this seemed odd to Waldeck, who had long observed his lethargy on the farm, he did not say. Finally Waldeck bluntly asked, "Why you got to go so far, what is the matter with you?" The response was equally blunt: "I can't stand it any longer."[17]

Finally, in July, Czolgosz got his money and left home on the 11th. His sister-in-law, Jacob's wife, advanced it to him. She immediately noticed that "a change had come over him and he seemed quite happy." Waldeck observed that his brother "brightened up a good deal." He went upstairs, put on his best clothes, and walked out of the house with nothing but what he was wearing. He told his sister-in-law he was going to Kansas and told his sister he was bound for California. His father and step-mother he told nothing, wanting to keep the latter entirely in the dark. A few days later his sister Victoria received a letter from Fort Wayne, Indiana, in which Leon claimed not to know where he was headed. It was the last his family ever heard from him. Later Czolgosz told Buffalo police superintendent William Bull he had spent most of the summer in the Buffalo area and Chicago, although he took a one-day trip to Cleveland just to secure an anarchist newspaper.[18]

What is more clear is that Czolgosz departed holding increasingly radical ideas. His newspaper reading, Vernon Briggs learned, had become more voracious, "suicides and murders especially." The assassination of King Umberto he found particularly fascinating. Czolgosz kept a newspaper account of the deed for several months, taking it to bed with him every night. He allowed his brothers and sisters to read it if they desired, but, characteristically, he never shared his views of the event. Books that he owned, found after the assassination, included numerous accounts of revolutionaries. There was also a pamphlet put out by the Social Labor Party, numerous biographies of social-ists, and works on anarchy.[19]

Perhaps it was during one of his extended absences from the farm that Czolgosz attended Goldman's May 5 lecture. At it she said, "We merely desire complete individual liberty and this can never be obtained as long as there is an existing government." On the question of how to achieve this goal, she was less certain. Goldman first denied that all anarchists supported bomb throwing and other acts of violence. However, she went on to detail recent violent crimes committed by radicals, declaring their motives to be pure and declaring the acts to be "a matter of temperament."[20]

Goldman later recalled encountering Czolgosz during the intermission between her lecture and the discussion session. She noticed him looking over a group of pamphlets and books on sale near the speaker's platform. "Will you suggest something for me to read?" he asked her. "He was very young, a mere youth, of medium height, well built, and carrying himself very erect," Goldman recalled three decades later. "But it was his face that held me, a most sensitive face, with a delicate pink complexion, a handsome face, made doubly so by his curly golden hair. Strength showed in his large blue eyes." Goldman selected some books for him, and although she did not see him during the discussion session, "his striking face remained in my memory."[21]

Emma Goldman remained in Leon's memory as well. Later a purported "full confession" published in the *New York Times* and several other newspa-pers claimed that Czolgosz had stated that Goldman's lecture had "set me on fire." Neither Buffalo newspapers nor the city's police records corroborate that account. However, superintendent Bull, who held numerous conversa-tions with Czolgosz, noted that he "spoke of Emma Goldman in rather a touching way." Bull further asserted that "it was plain to anyone who heard him talk about Emma Goldman that he was in love with her."[22]

Two weeks after attending Goldman's lecture Czolgosz sought out Cleve-land anarchist Emil Schilling. As Schilling later recalled, Czolgosz talked about capitalists and laboring people in a manner he considered "revolution-ary." Schilling invited Czolgosz to have dinner with his family and gave him a book to read about Chicago's Haymarket martyrs. "I thought he was all right when he called on me this time," Schilling remembered. His attitude began to change when Czolgosz returned some three weeks later. This time he asked about anarchists "forming plots" and holding "secret meetings." Schilling noted that when he answered Czolgosz's queries, "He was always laughing at my answers as if he either felt superior or had formed a plan and was putting out a feeler." Schilling also did not like the fact that the young man returned his book, blithely explaining that he did not have time to read it.[23]

Czolgosz returned again about a week later, staying only about an hour. He opened up to Schilling, saying his step-mother abused him and his father did not have the will to put a stop to it. Czolgosz said he was "tired of life." He also spoke of Emma Goldman, telling Schilling he had heard her speak. "He was taken in. Her speech took him," Schilling observed. Czolgosz asked him for a letter of introduction to the fiery female anarchist who had captured his imagination—and likely his heart. Perhaps because of the suspicions he harbored, Schilling replied that he never introduced anyone by letter. Goldman was in Chicago at the time, and when Schilling told Czolgosz he could meet her himself, his unusual guest simply replied, "I go to Chicago."[24]

He did. Goldman had been spending several weeks in the Windy City with Abraham Isaak, who published the newspaper *Free Society*, and his family. On July 12, as she was packing to leave to visit family in Rochester, the doorbell rang. It was Czolgosz, still using the name Nieman. Goldman immediately recognized him as "the handsome chap of the golden hair" who had attended her Cleveland meeting. She invited him to accompany her as she rode the elevated train to the depot. During the ride Czolgosz said he had belonged to a socialist club in Cleveland but had "found its members dull, lacking in vision and enthusiasm." He was eager, the youthful visitor went on, to "get in touch with anarchists" in Chicago.[25]

Goldman asked her friends to look after Czolgosz. They did, but Isaak and others soon became suspicious, feeling, like Schilling, that he was likely a police spy. The eager young radical called Isaak "comrade" and again asked about "secret meetings." Isaak wrote to Schilling, who Czolgosz claimed was a friend, and the Cleveland anarchist wrote back, expressing the same misgivings. The result was the following editorial that appeared in *Free Society* on September 1:

> The attention of the comrades is called to another spy. He is well dressed, of medium height, rather narrow shouldered, blond and about twenty-five years of age. Up to the present he has made his appearance in Chicago & Cleveland. In the former place he remained but a short time, while in Cleveland he disappeared when the comrades had confirmed themselves of his identity, & were on the point of exposing him. His demeanor is of the usual sort, pretending to be greatly interested in the cause, asking for names, or soliciting aid for acts of contemplated violence. If this same individual makes his appearance elsewhere, the comrades are warned in advance, & can act accordingly.[26]

In August Czolgosz made his fourth and final visit to Schilling. His host was reading Isaak's letter when he arrived, and he suspected that Czolgosz might have somehow intercepted it. Schilling invited him in and asked where he had been for the past two months. Czolgosz said he had been working at a cheese factory, then laughed. From Isaak's letter Schilling knew this was not true, further fueling his suspicions. Hoping to catch him in another lie, Schilling invited Czolgosz to take a walk with himself and a neighbor. He revealed little, however, and when the trio returned Czolgosz "seemed tired and went home. I ask[ed] him where he was going," Schilling later recalled. "He said maybe Detroit, maybe Buffalo."[27]

One person far less dubious of the young man calling himself Nieman was the subject of his infatuation, Emma Goldman. Upon reading the notice in *Free Society*, she later wrote, "I was very angry. To make such a flimsy charge on such grounds." She immediately wrote to Isaak, demanding proof of his claims. He lamely responded that he believed Czolgosz was untrustworthy because of his loose talk about acts of violence. Goldman responded with another vitriolic missive, and the next issue of *Free Society* contained a retraction.[28]

In reality both Isaak and Schilling had always had mixed feelings about this mysterious young man who had appeared at both their doors. Despite his doubts—and his warning—Isaak believed Czolgosz'z "eyes and words expressed sincerity." Schilling had listened as Czolgosz told him "things were getting worse and worse," and he had come to believe that "something must be done." Schilling later admitted, "Then I did not think he had a plan; afterward I did."[29]

14

Exposition: Midway, Carnival and Controversy

For William Buchanan and the board of directors the purpose of the Pan-American Exposition was to "educate, uplift, and benefit the millions who were to see it." Beyond that they also wished to "unify, elevate, develop, and Americanize the Americas."[1] For the concessionaires operating attractions along the fair's Midway, the twin goals were far less noble and far more simple. They wanted visitors to have as much fun as possible, allowing themselves to make as much money as possible. These diverse motivations led to numerous conflicts between the two groups.

By the time Buffalo began planning for its exposition the lavish midway was a staple of such events. It had come into its own at Chicago's World's Columbian Exposition in 1893. Ironically the White City's "Midway Plaisance" was at first intended to be an educational feature, headed by a Harvard University professor. His task was to gather ethnological displays from all corners of the globe and showcase them along the Midway. Financial concerns changed things, leading concession fees and the potential of increased attendance to trump cultural goals. The fair hired Sol Bloom, himself a veteran showman, to run the Midway. Under his guidance the ethnology of the world gave way to such attractions as the Hagenback Animal Show, the Congress of Beauty, and numerous ethnic "villages," more stereotypical than educational.[2]

Because of his experiences in Chicago, Buchanan was eager from the outset to include a midway as part of the Pan-Am. That experience also enabled him to recommend certain concessionaires he remembered from the White City. Yet at the same time, the director general realized the hazards of dealing with the denizens of the Midway, whose profit motives often overruled any qualms concerning taste. Under Buchanan's direction the Exposition Company adopted strict rules for the "Lane of Laughter." They required each concessionaire to submit plans for their buildings and to sign a contract

139

stipulating that "all features of the concession were in every sense and at all times … subject to the approval of the Exposition." To drive home the point, the directors employed an "Inspector of the Midway" to "see that the conduct of the entertainment and the language of the spielers be proper and decent."[3]

If Sol Bloom was the driving force behind the Chicago midway, Frederic Thompson was the guiding light in Buffalo. Thompson was born in Ironton, Ohio on Halloween, appropriately enough, in 1873. His father was an English immigrant who worked in a number of Midwestern iron mills, serving in management in later years. In 1887, when the family lived in St. Louis, Fred dropped out of school. He went to work in factories and was an apprentice for a stained glass maker. The Thompsons move to Nashville in the late 1880s. There Fred worked in his uncle's architectural office and was a salesman. He also ran up huge debts, to which gambling and drinking largely contributed.

In 1893 he headed to Chicago and its world's fair. Thompson worked as a janitor and a "demonstrator" at an industrial exhibit. The experience did not spur his interest in shows, at least not at first. He continued to pursue a variety of occupations, and he spent a year studying art in Cincinnati before returning to Nashville in 1894.

Once again he worked in his uncle's office, but the upcoming Tennessee Centennial and International Exposition captured his interest. Thompson formed a partnership with John J. Dunnavant, a local builder, to secure contracts for the 1897 event. He ended up designing a number of fair buildings, but it was the fair's midway, called "Vanity Fair," that caught his eye. Many of the pair's contracts were with its concessionaires. One proved unable to pay, and the two men acquired his show. Thompson reworked the unsuccessful attraction, adding, among other things, a "thinly clad girl." Attendance picked up. He also offered a "Giant Seesaw" at the Nashville fair, placing large cars at each end of an 80-foot steel arm, resting on a 75-foot tall fulcrum. The attraction took riders up 150 feet.

In 1898 Thompson and Dunnavant headed to Omaha for the Trans-Mississippi and International Exposition. This time it was the concession California Gold Mine that the two acquired from a bankrupt proprietor. Thompson stocked the concession's tunnels with coffins and skeletons, added a "celestial auditorium" with dancing girls to the top and renamed it "Heaven and Hell." Local ministers protested the depiction, and Thompson latched on to the free publicity. He changed nothing, instead instituting a well-advertised campaign to come up with a new name for the show. "Darkness and Dawn" won, and in the end, so did Thompson and Dunnavant as people flocked to their attraction.[4]

Thompson arrived in Buffalo during the spring of 1900 to bid for concessions. Soon he became, in the words of his biographer, "the principal architect of the Pan-American midway," designing the majority of its attractions. He was also the owner of two of its most visited amusements. One was the Aerocycle, an updated version of the Ferris wheel and his Nashville "Seesaw." George W. Ferris had introduced his ride at Chicago in 1893. Its diameter was an impressive 264 feet, and its 36 cars could each hold 60 passengers. Thompson combined Ferris's invention with a teeter-totter, placing Ferris wheels at each end of a 240-foot beam held up by a 140-foot tower. Each wheel had four cars capable of carrying eighteen riders apiece. At its apex the Aerocycle carried passengers to a height of 275 feet, eleven feet higher than the Chicago Ferris wheel. Striking ironworkers delayed its construction, and the ride did not open until May 21. Once it did the Aerocycle proved popular, creating "a sensation at the exposition [that was] daily taxed to its utmost capacity."[5]

Thompson's other attraction was A Trip to the Moon. According to Thompson himself, the idea had come to him as a vision. In it he saw an airship traveling through the night sky. Where should it go? he wondered, deciding "to the moon." The result of his fantasy was a 40,000-square-foot structure that cost $84,000 to construct. Passengers, each paying fifty cents, entered the airship *Luna*, "a green and white cigar shaped thing, the size of a small lake steamer with a great cabin in the middle." Large, flapping red wings garnished its exterior. A gong sounded, and the ship, held by guy wires, began to rock and seemingly ascend. Visual effects allowed the riders to view the Exposition, Buffalo, Niagara Falls, and finally an ever-shrinking earth as they soared toward their destination. Hidden fans blew on the passengers' faces, further simulating the sensation of motion. Electrical effects supplied lightning and thunder, adding a touch of imagined danger. "So considerable is the illusion produced," one reporter noted, "that an elderly lady next to me expressed alarm and could not be convinced by her friends or the attendants that the air-ship ... was stationary."[6]

As their journey neared completion, passengers saw the Man in the Moon. Then the ship slowed and struck with a thud, followed by the announcement that the *Luna* had reached her destination. The travelers stepped out and were greeted by "Selenites." Thompson had employed 60 little people to serve as the moon's residents. They uttered "queer twitterings" and offered green cheese to their guests before conducting them to the Palace of the Man in the Moon. There they viewed the "Geisler electric fountain," which displayed all the colors of the rainbow through its waters, and watched the "maids of the Man in the Moon" perform "a rhythmic graceful dance." All in all, it was a spectacular achievement, one that resulted in 400,000 admissions. The *denouement*, however, left at least one passenger slightly disappointed. His complaint was that, after enjoying the wonders of the moon, the visitors were conducted from the palace directly outside to the sunlit, terrestrial Midway.[7]

The variety of amusements was impressive. The House Upside Down was just that—with a hall of mirrors included. The National Glass Company set up a working glass factory on the Midway. Rival concessionaire Elmer "Skip" Dundy outbid Thompson for the Buffalo version of Darkness and Dawn. Like the Omaha concession, it followed a resurrected corpse on its journey through hell and heaven. Missionary Ridge offered a cyclorama of the Civil War battlefield. Other cycloramas depicted Jerusalem on the Day of the Crucifixion and, with dramatic special effects added, the Johnstown Flood.

Animal acts were numerous. Frank Bostock's menagerie featured hundreds of beasts from all over the world, including a boxing kangaroo which scored a number of knockouts over its human competition during its time in Buffalo. The Ostrich Farm featured two dozen of the ungainly birds in a

A view of the Exposition Midway showing the Aerocycle and A Trip to the Moon (Library of Congress).

quarter-acre space. Bonner, billed as "the educated horse," could reportedly add a column of eight figures with three numbers in each row. Wild Water Sports also featured a well-trained horse, this one named Trixy. But its main attraction was a group of diving elks that plunged twenty feet into a shallow pool.[8]

Offering a unique take on what would come to be known as the health care debate was Martin A. Couney, proprietor of the Infant Incubators show. Born in Germany, Couney received his MD in his native land then studied under Dr. Pierre Budin, a highly respected Paris pediatrician. It was Budin's mentor, E. S. Tarnier, who had first developed the idea of infant incubators. Visiting an exhibition, he had spotted a warming chamber for poultry. Tarnier asked its inventor to build a similar contraption, this one large enough to hold two premature babies. In 1896 Budin sent Couney and a group of nurses to Berlin's World Exposition. There he set up six incubators for a show called *Kinderbrutanstalt*, "Child Hatchery." The display caught on with visitors. More important, every baby brought there lived. The following year Couney set up another incubator infant show at London's Victorian Era Exhibition. In 1898 Couney brought his show to the United States, exhibiting at the Trans-Mississippi Exposition in Omaha. He returned to Europe for the 1900 World Exposition in Paris before crossing the Atlantic once again for the Pan-Am.[9]

Couney's exhibit in Buffalo included a dozen incubators, each consisting of a glass case with a metal frame supported by metal legs. In each was a well-padded woven wire cot. A large pipe from outside the building supplied fresh air. The air first passed through "an antiseptic fluid" and then through cotton filters. Meanwhile thermostats guaranteed that the temperature in the incubators would never vary by more than two degrees. A small nursery adjoined the main room. There the patients were fed and weighed every two hours as nurses checked the cleanliness of their tiny quarters.[10]

Most of the infants at the Pan-American came from Buffalo and vicinity. They were cared for free of charge and reportedly admitted without regard to race or class. It is not clear how many Couney housed during his time in Buffalo, nor how many survived. Couney's overall survival rate was 85 percent, better than three times the rate without incubators. Indeed the only sour note came from the *Buffalo Medical Journal*, which editorialized, "The question naturally presents itself as to whether this is worthwhile; whether the race as a whole does not suffer from the preservation of these weaklings to perpetuate their kind." There is no doubt that several Buffalo parents could have provided the *Journal* with a definite answer.[11]

As at Chicago, ethnic "villages" made up a large portion of the Buffalo Midway. Among them were the Hawaiian Village, the "Filipino" Village, and the Eskimo Village. All featured natives and colorful reproductions of their homelands. Alt Nuremberg recreated a German village. Its Royal Bavarian Band offered daily performances of Wagner, Brahams, and Mozart. Its pricey restaurant was the scene of numerous banquets for VIP visitors. Fair Japan included geisha girls and a tea house. As one observer noted, the attraction contained "none of the rougher elements of a midway show. Its pleasure is refined, its life smooth and flowing." At Venice in America, "The Venetian gondoliers chant[ed] their gay songs, and many a carol of midnight joy [rang] through the streets." The reproduction of the Italian city was a main landing dock for the boats that operated on the canal surrounding the Exposition.[12]

The largest Midway attraction was Gaston Akoun's Beautiful Orient. Akoun had taken his show to Chicago in 1893 as The Streets of Cairo. Now Cairo was joined by Tunis, Algiers, Damascus, Morocco, and Constantinople. Camel and elephant rides were available for fairgoers. A parade went by every half hour, featuring dancing girls, sword fighters, and several of the attraction's eight hundred residents. Souvenir hunters had 120 bazaars from which to acquire exotic trinkets. One portion of the Beautiful Orient was closed to the public—and even to Akoun. The concessionaire was required to build a Muslim temple for the faithful among his troupe. According to one report an electrician who accidentally ventured inside nearly lost his life at their hands.[13]

One concession that Buchanan and the board of directors were eager to welcome to Buffalo was The Streets of Mexico, which fit with the theme of Pan-Americanism. The director general consulted the Mexican government before recommending the attraction. They asked that "it should not bring ridicule on Mexico, its streets, or buildings," which the diplomat assured them he would not countenance. Ironically, in light of today's immigration issues, they also wanted concessionaire H. F. McGarvie to guarantee "to return to Mexico all Mexicans there employed."[14]

Like many of its ethnic counterparts, The Streets of Mexico featured a band, dancing girls, a restaurant, and numerous shops. Unlike other Midway attractions, it also boasted a bull ring, where bull fights were a daily feature. It appears that the bulls were not harmed. In fact, they became so tame over time that McGarvie placed ads in Buffalo newspapers seeking to purchase "fierce, vicious bulls" from local farmers.[15]

Visitors to the Midway's Indian Congress bore witness to an era that was sadly in eclipse. Forty-two nations participated in the attraction that strove to be both educational and respectful of the Native Americans. Seven hundred Indians and a thousand horses participated. The natives built the village themselves, and most of them lived in its 163 teepees. The Congress had a theater for native dances and a stadium for parades and sham battles. Among the show's inhabitants were fifteen prisoners of the U.S. government. Perhaps the most famous was the Apache chief Geronimo, who arrived in Buffalo on June 27. He had spent the previous fourteen years under guard on his farm near Fort Sill, Oklahoma; and although his family placed his age at about 88, he was escorted to the Exposition grounds by a baker's dozen troopers.

Geronimo asserted that he had put the past behind him and bore the white man no malice. In fact he gave strong evidence that he had adopted some of their ways. In early September a Buffalo pastor held a special evening service for members of the Midway's Philippine, African, Indian, and "Eskimo" residents. When it was over a photographer wanted to take a group photo. He had just lit the fuse to his flash pan when the chief suddenly stepped out of the shot. The photographer tried to explain that he hadn't made his picture yet. At that point a member of the congregation explained that Geronimo wanted money before he would participate. "How much?" the minister asked. The chief held up five fingers. Geronimo got his five dollars, and the photographer got his picture.[16]

The Exposition Company charged $25 per front foot for Midway space and also received 20 percent of the concessions' gross receipts. This made the "Lane of Laughter" a cash cow for the board of directors. At the same time it was the source of numerous headaches. Some were medical, such as the measles suffered among the First Nations inhabitants. Members of the Indian Congress fell into the habit of eating discarded fruit from the Horticulture Building. In early August a child became seriously ill as a result. The parents refused treatment by the Exposition medical department, and a native medicine man took charge of the case. Within 24 hours the child was dead. In July eight Native Americans were returned to their reservations during an outbreak of tuberculosis. Yet, according to Dr. Park, the Indian Congress was not the primary area of concern. "Our principal trouble," he wrote after the Exposition closed, "was to maintain reasonable cleanliness among the inhabitants of the Beautiful Orient." On several occasions the medical staff seized rotten fruit sold at their stands. Park termed them "absolutely incorrigible and incapable of appreciating the ordinary laws of health."[17]

Despite all the precautions he took, Buchanan later conceded that "a few concessions were let which were unsatisfactory both in their operation and in the tone they gave the Exposition." In extreme cases the director general attempted to shut them down, but the concessionaires had competent lawyers, and they "found no difficulty in using the courts as a shield to cover their defiance of the orders of the Exposition." One such case involved the Ideal

Palace, an attraction that billed itself as "a Parisian Art Studio," and insisted it was not meant "for theological students or superintendents of Sunday schools." Buchanan agreed, and on June 19 he shut it down. At that point the concessionaire changed the description of his attraction to "artistic living pictures" and sought legal counsel. On September 3 it was the dance hall of the Streets of Mexico that incurred the wrath of Exposition officials. La Petite Americaine, a dancer who had previously been removed from the Beautiful Orient, was at the center of the controversy. Not only was her dancing "objectionable to the director general," but he further asserted that it was "not in keeping with Mexican culture."[18]

The Streets of Mexico was also the scene of one of the most serious incidents to occur at the fair. It happened at about 8:00 p.m. on July 18. Ernesto Zozaya, a Mexican resident, had enjoyed a casual relationship with Isabelle Gallardo, a singer and dancer at McGarvie's attraction. Zozaya had become infatuated with her, and in late June he arrived in Buffalo to look for her. The couple was reunited, but Gallardo was not thrilled about the reunion. Soon after Zozaya showed signs of deep depression. Soon after that he purchased a .38-caliber revolver.

Zozaya's advances became so troubling to Gallardo that he was eventually banned from The Streets of Mexico. Despite that he managed to get in on July 18, brandishing his pistol and announcing that he was going to kill Isabelle. Someone alerted McGarvie, who went looking for the unstable young man. He found him, and Zozaya fired, missing the concessionaire by a few inches. Zozaya then put the muzzle of the revolver to his chest and fired again. He staggered backward, then fell on his back and died a few minutes later. When his body was searched at the morgue investigators found a note explaining nothing but asking that his baggage be sent "by express Wells-Fargo" to his family.[19]

Most Midway controversies came down to the clash between the concessionaires' profit motives and the Exposition Company's sense of propriety and decorum. One involved spielers, also known as ballyhooers. These were the individuals who stood outside the shows, beckoning the crowd to enter their attraction. The spielers' tactics were not always entirely honest. Between concerts one day John Philip Sousa decided to check out the Hawaiian Village. Soon an immense throng began to form inside. Upon departing, the March King found out why. Spieler W. Maurice Tobin was shouting, "Sousa is inside! Sousa! The superb Sousa, king of the band masters." Tobin further promised that the bandleader would offer a souvenir to every lady entering the attraction. When Senator Chauncey Depew visited the Hawaiian Village Tobin eagerly announced his presence, this time promising the ladies a kiss from the politician.[20]

Of course the spielers were competitive, and their competitions for the visitors' attention occasionally got out of hand. On the evening of June 28 Frederic Thompson complained to Buchanan that residents of the Streets of Mexico began firing guns in the middle of his barker's ballyhoo. The Mexicans countered with the charge that the denizens of the moon turned a foghorn in their spieler's direction as he extolled the merits of their attraction. Meanwhile an enterprising reporter from the *Buffalo Courier* did some counting and discovered that there were eighty sources of sound on the Midway at any time. Spielers accounted for 38 of them, along with various bands, gongs, drums, and phonographs. Buchanan responded with an order disallowing bands, pans, guns, and foghorns outside the concessions. Women could also no longer be a part of the ballyhoos. The Midway quieted down, but not for long. Three days after the director general issued the new regulations the *Courier* reported, "The Midway has reverted to the old noisy ways." Not only that, but the ballyhooing had spread beyond the Midway. For example, Louisiana had an extensive display in the Agriculture Building, one which the state's commissioners felt was not attracting enough visitors. They solved the problem by installing a phonograph "with a large and varied repertoire of popular rag-time tunes."[21]

The main area of contention between the concessionaires and Exposition officials was the latter group's decision to close the Midway on Sundays. Sabbath or not, a day without paying customers seemed sinful to the showmen, and they were determined to fight. The battle began on May 5, the first Sunday after the Exposition formally opened. E. W. McConnell sent spielers out to announce that Jerusalem on the Day of the Crucifixion and Missionary Ridge would be open to the public. An Exposition policeman attempted to shut down both attractions, but McConnell ignored the officer. He did pay attention when director of works Carlton showed up, and there the incident ended.[22]

The Midway apparently remained quiet for the next few Sundays. Then on June 16 the controversy flared up in dramatic fashion. The incident appears to have been a misunderstanding. J. J. Dunnavant had some of his employees doing repair work on Darkness and Dawn, and to allow them to pass in and out, he had one of the entrances open. An Exposition policeman noticed the open gate and ordered Dunnavant to close it under threat of arrest. When he refused, the cop grabbed the showman and drew his nightstick. Dunnavant broke away, and the officer called in a reserve of six men. Meanwhile some of the concessionaire's workers, including two armed with wrenches, rushed to their boss's aid.

The fracas attracted a crowd of visitors and Midway workers. When an officer threatened to club one of the employees, the man reportedly shouted back, "If you hit me with your club I'll kill you. I am doing nothing." Fortunately a precinct captain with a cool head arrived just as the situation was threatening to get out of hand. He first persuaded Dunnavant's workers to back off, then instructed the individuals from neighboring shows to go back to them and ordered the police to lower their clubs.[23]

On July 7 the Aerocycle, Bostock's animal show, and Venice in America attempted to open. Exposition officials quickly shut down all three. At that point "Skip" Dundy, who was running Frederic Thompson's Aerocycle, went to the Electric Tower and purchased a ticket to ride the elevator. He then strolled over to the canal landing, bought another ticket, and enjoyed a gondola ride. Following his excursion Dundy explained to reporters, "I believe that I have demonstrated that a discrimination has been made and that I have grounds for a suit." A few days later Dundy announced that he planned to open on July 14 and donate all of his ride's profits to charity, a ploy that many other show operators soon adopted.[24]

At three o'clock on the afternoon of July 14 Dundy opened the Aerocycle. Five of his fellow concessionaires bought the first tickets, claiming that they wanted to "help the children." An Exposition police captain was waiting and ordered Dundy to cease operations. Dundy refused. The captain placed him under arrest and escorted him to the Service Building, where the director of concessions virtually begged him to shut down the ride. Dundy again refused, demanding instead that he be transferred to Buffalo police headquarters, where he could be formally charged and allowed to post bail. This the director refused to do, probably because he himself was dubious as to whether or not a crime had been committed. Dundy was instead released. He returned to the Aerocycle and ran the concession until a cordon of police physically capable of blocking every entrance arrived to keep the crowds out.[25]

Two days later the concessionaires met to discuss strategy, all but one agreeing that they would open the following Sunday. A representative of the Indian Congress sounded a defiant note by asserting, "They have a certain number of police and we have 700 Indians. They are looking for trouble, I think, and they can get it quick." Despite the apparent threat of a second Little Bighorn, the Congress also had a pair of lawyers in attendance. The following day many of the leading showmen, including Dundy, McGarvie, McConnell, and Gaston Akoun, along with one of the Indians' lawyers, met with Milburn, Buchanan, and other Exposition officials. The latter group asked the concessionaires to close on the 21st to give the board of directors time to consider the Midway men's grievances. The showmen agreed.[26]

A week went by, a week that included a meeting of the board of directors that produced no decision. The Midway operators met again on July 25. The directors of the Indian Congress announced that they would open on July 28, and a number of other concessionaires said they would open their shows in support. The stage was set for another Midway battle.

It began on the afternoon of July 28. The Indian Congress opened at one o'clock as the spieler announced that the natives were conducting a "religious ceremony" that could be witnessed for a quarter. Jerusalem on the Day of the Crucifixion and the Ostrich Farm soon followed suit, both offering to let visitors in for free. Jerusalem's spieler, after a brief sojourn to police headquarters, informed the crowd that had gathered to witness the controversy, "The exposition company permits you to ride on gondolas, to go up in the tower and to buy [beer], but it says you cannot come in here to see a magnificent painting which has a purely religious character."[27]

Although the 28th passed without serious incident, both sides braced themselves for an expected battle on August 4. Meeting on July 30 the Exposition board of directors voted to close everything on the Midway, even restaurants, on Sundays. That same day the concessionaires met, and all resolved to open the following Sunday.

Then, just three days later, the showmen abruptly backed down, agreeing to close on Sundays. Their stated reason was that an attempt to open "would lead to personal conflict and consequent injury to the exposition." A more likely explanation was that the Exposition's "Midway Day" had attracted 106,315 visitors. The operators wanted to promote similar special—and profitable—days, and to do so they needed the cooperation of Pan-Am officials. Whatever the true motive, Sunday, August 4, passed quietly along the Midway, as did all the Sabbaths that followed.[28]

15

Exposition: Racism vs. Respect

In addition to the Midway attractions mentioned in Chapter 14, there were two which featured black performers—often in blatantly stereotypical roles. One was concessionaire Xavier Pene's Darkest Africa. The attraction was similar to an African-themed exhibit Pene had operated at the World's Columbian Exposition. The difference was that his Buffalo concession strove for scientific legitimacy. Pene operated Darkest Africa in affiliation with the Buffalo Society of Natural History, promising to donate to the society the "collection of African implements" that was part of the attraction. In his pamphlet promoting the concession, Pene asserted, "The scientific features of Darkest Africa differentiate it altogether from the common Midway show.… Of course, the dances and songs have only a show feature to those who do not understand their social or religious meaning.… Those who want to show their children the people among whom the missionaries live and work, as well as the students of Ethnology and Anthropology, will find a wide field for thought and speculation in Darkest Africa."[1]

Pene's brochure went on to claim that the village included 98 natives, representing "11 of the most primitive and least known African tribes." They arrived on June 10, delayed by bureaucratic red tape as Pene labored to get them into the country. Combining racism with redundancy, the *Buffalo Express* described them as "black as the ace of spades, black as ebony, black as dulled tar, black as charcoal, black as cinders, black as crows, black as anything that will convey to the mind absolute undiluted sunless, moonless, starless bleakness." The *Buffalo Commercial* noted that their leader, one Chief Ogndaza, brought three of his 55 wives to Buffalo with him, although the paper later reported that he had sent for three more.[2]

Even the *Buffalo Courier*, a paper that had editorially criticized the State of Virginia for denying blacks the right to vote, described a Darkest Africa religious service this way: "Heathen negroes, black as murkiest night and

150

ugly as sin, idolized and offered sacrifice to weird, uncouth graven images." Later, when a missionary reportedly converted one of the Africans to Christianity, the *Courier* asserted, "The sun went down on one less heathen on the Exposition grounds last night." Concessionaire Pene was less enthusiastic. He believed the conversion was nothing more than an attempt on the part of the converted to get out of participating in the attraction's dances.[3]

As September drew to a close the natives began to suffer from the Buffalo cold. Pene did not supply them with proper clothing, perhaps because he wanted to perpetuate the stereotype of half-naked savages. Instead, according to the *Courier*, they wore "all the clothes they have been able to rake and scrape from any source and present a most ludicrous appearance." The concessionaire did provide the Africans with a gas stove. Because it contained a chamber in which gas would accumulate if not quickly lit, Pene would not allow them to operate it. If they desired warmth, the natives were informed, they must call a white show attendant to light the stove. On a cold September 26, with no attendants in sight, one of the Africans decided to light the stove himself. After starting the gas, he struck a match, then lit his pipe before tossing the match into the stove. The resulting explosion blew off the door, and the flame that shot out badly singed the man's hair and whiskers.[4]

Directly opposite the African Village was the Old Plantation. The Exposition's official guide book described it as "a veritable Old Southern Plantation, representing the 'South be'fo de Wah,' introducing 150 Southern darkies in their plantation songs and dances." Of course the attraction was more minstrel than educational. Families were not separated there. Nobody found himself or herself at the end of a cowhide whip. Instead, as the *Buffalo Express* noted, "If you like coon songs and dances and banjo music go to the Old Plantation and spend a very pleasant hour or so." The stereotyping was so blatant that Richard Barry, who wrote a generally positive guide to the Midway, reported that the concession harkened back to those before the war who "gave slavery the deceptive hue of contented and oft-times happy dependence."[5]

The black residents of the Old Plantation took part in a parade that was part of the Midway Day celebration on August 3. As the *Buffalo Express* described it, "On foot ... came 100 darkies, cantankerous coons, singing, laughing, dancing, whooping, all gorgeous and gay." Other members of the attraction rode on a float. Some played the banjo. Others were live props. The bulk of the float was a reproduction of a slice of watermelon. The *Express* portrayed it thusly: "It was 50 feet long and fifteen feet wide. Its rind was as green as the sea and its core as red as a bullock's heart. The seeds—prepare to laugh—the seeds were the heads of live darkies, sticking out with a grin as broad as the sunset over Tierra del Fuego."[6]

With the Midway portraying blacks as either savages or buffoons, it is not surprising that leaders of Buffalo's black community wished a more positive and accurate depiction. That community was a small one. According to the 1900 census, only 1,698 of Buffalo's 352,287 residents were African American.

Many, however, were politically active. Among them was Mary Talbert, a graduate of Oberlin College in Ohio and a former high school principal. She was corresponding secretary of the Phyllis Wheatley Club, a black women's organization that combined charitable work with political activism. On November 11, 1900, the club hosted an interracial meeting at Buffalo's Michigan Street Baptist Church. There Talbert read an essay entitled, "Why the American Negro should be represented at the Pan-American Exposition." She pointed out that other fairs had "made early provisions for a negro exhibit." One of them, she added, the Negro Exhibit at the Paris Exposition, had "attracted the notice of the world."[7]

It had indeed. America's Negro Exhibit had received a grand prize in Paris, and individual sections of it had earned more awards. One of the driving forces behind the Paris display was Thomas Julius Calloway, a clerk in the War Department. He had formerly worked as an agent of Tuskegee Institute, and in a letter to Booker T. Washington, Tuskegee's principal, Calloway explained his motives. "Europeans think us a mass of rapists, ready to attack every white woman exposed, and a drag in civilized society," he wrote. A well designed exhibit, Calloway believed, would help dispel such notions by painting a more accurate picture of black America. With Washington's blessing, Calloway sold the idea to the United States Commission and—far more impressive—sold the Congress on the need for funding. A bill to appropriate $15,000 for the exhibit easily cleared both houses. Meanwhile the Commission named Calloway "Special Agent for the Negro Exhibit." Not only had he achieved his goal for such a display, Calloway would be in charge of it.[8]

The special agent sought displays in thirteen categories: education, homes, farms, skilled trades and organized labor, domestic service, business, arts, professions, military life, politics, churches, literature, and women. Calloway's call for materials produced an overwhelming result. According to one historian of the display, "The exhibit included displays of various black schools and colleges, displays of agricultural and industrial products, statistical charts examining almost every aspect of African American life, a multitude of pamphlets, a transcribed copy of the black code of Georgia, hundreds of volumes of black literature, lists of African American patents, and dioramas of black history built by schoolchildren."[9]

It also reflected an emerging split in black leadership in America. One

The "War Dance" performed at the Midway attraction Darkest Africa. Midway shows tended to portray blacks as either savages or buffoons (Library of Congress).

school of thought, which Washington propounded, urged African Americans to learn a trade and move slowly, if at all, on any attempt to correct racial injustice. The other, being put forward by W. E. B. Du Bois, sought to challenge discrimination and fight for equality. Calloway was a friend of both men, and his display reflected both points of view. However, as his letter to Washington had hinted, he was more sympathetic to the Du Bois philosophy.[10]

For his part, Du Bois sent to Paris a group of charts created by his students at Atlanta University. They offered empirical evidence to battle racial stereotypes. One pointed out that the rate of literacy among American blacks was higher than that of Russia. Another showed that the marriage rate of African Americans was higher than the rate for Germany. In addition to charts, Du Bois drove home his point with a bibliography of African American works totaling 1,400 titles and with a list of over 300 black patent holders.[11]

In light of the Negro Exhibit's content and success, it is not surprising that Buffalo's black leaders wanted it brought to their city. They apparently appealed to President McKinley. On January 22, 1901, J. H. Brigham, chairman of the Board of Management for the U.S. Government display, wrote to George Cortelyou concerning the matter. "The communication in regard to the negro exhibit at the Pan-American Exposition referred by you at the suggestion of the President has been received," he wrote. "As soon as possible I will lay the matter before the Government Board ... and advise you of their opinion in regard to the same."[12]

In March 1901, at the 19th meeting of the Government Board, Brigham referred to a petition "by certain colored citizens" on behalf of the exhibit. They asked the government for $5,000 to overhaul the display. The exhibit, they explained, had already been sent to Buffalo. The board forwarded the petition to the Interior Department to consider the Negro Exhibit as part of the Bureau of Education display. Interior replied that funds could not be allocated because all monies had been appropriated before the petition arrived.[13]

By then Dr. Selin H. Peabody, head of the Exposition's Liberal Arts Division, had agreed to bring the exhibit to Buffalo. In early January he announced that it would be housed in the Manufactures and Liberal Arts Building "under the supervision of some person, not yet designated by the Exposition company, of the Negro race." That person appears to have been James A. Ross, a local businessman, politician, and publisher. Ross had been active in the campaign to bring the exhibit to Buffalo. He was also a member of the Committee of Public Comfort, a group set up to secure lodgings and provide hospitality for blacks visiting the fair. Calloway's involvement at this point is unclear. The *Buffalo Express* reported that Calloway was in charge of the exhibit when it was installed in late April. An article describing the exhibit appeared under his byline in the same paper on May 5. After that his name disappears from the local record. Later press accounts named Ross as the man in charge, and he presented himself as "Assistant in charge of the Negro Exhibit, Pan-American Exposition."[14]

Ross made some changes in the arrangement of things and added a portrait of Abraham Lincoln. He also took a more commercial approach, a move perhaps made necessary by the failure to secure government funding. Ross tried to get Booker T. Washington to lend his name and image to a brand of cigars he hoped to sell at the Exposition. The Tuskegee educator declined. Ross had more commercial success with a souvenir pamphlet he produced to promote the exhibit. Unlike most other Exposition pamphlets, this one included advertising. Some 40 local businesses ponied up to help make the public aware of the exhibit.[15]

It is not clear how many Pan-Am visitors made their way to the Negro Exhibit. Reviews in the press, at least those discovered for this work, were universally positive. Most national magazines ignored the exhibit, focusing instead on the Midway, the electrical effects, or other more eye-catching features. One local Buffalo publication, *Our Record,* ran an article in August 1901 entitled, "Some Educational Exhibits at the Pan-American." The piece termed the display "an exhibit of very great social value." Somewhat less enthusiastically, the article continued, "It is extensive, well installed, and arranged on those principles of development and the preservation of distinctive characteristics, which make even a dull subject interesting."[16]

The day the exhibit was installed the *Express* also mixed high praise with a measure of condescension—or at least a prediction that its appeal would be limited. "An exhibit more complete, valuable or far reaching in its effects could scarcely be imagined," the paper observed, "and it, undoubtedly, will be a center of interest and attraction for the thousands of negroes who visit the exposition."[17]

The most thorough and positive account of the exhibit filled one column of the *Courier* on May 28. Under the headline "NEGRO RACE SHOWS GREAT PROGRESS," was a vivid description of the "instructive and entertaining study." The reporter was particularly impressed by the "nine plaster of paris groups" used to chart "the rise of the race from ignorance to enlightenment." It started with "Emancipation," showing a "poverty-stricken family of ex-slaves encamped in a field, without so much as a roof over their heads." The last three groups were devoted to education. "Progress of Education" featured a white frame Southern schoolhouse. "Educational Results" showed "a crowd of well dressed, intelligent boys and girls who are attendants at the negro high school in Washington, D. C." A model of the high school itself was the display for "Investment in High School Education." Between emancipation and education were sections covering such topics as whites who assisted blacks and the life of a pioneering black farm family.[18]

"To show the present prosperity of the industrious, educated negro, there is a series of photographic frames giving views of the homes ... of well-to-do negroes in many of the large southern cities," the article explained. "None of these is palatial," it continued, "but all of them show the comfort and good taste of the occupants."[19]

The *Courier* was also impressed with a series of pictures depicting "business institutions owned and operated by colored men." They included iron foundries, laundries, hotels, and "stores of all kinds." The largest was a black-owned cotton mill in North Carolina. "People who think the negro is without capacity for business will have something to ponder upon after they have seen [this] series of pictures," the reporter concluded.[20]

That conclusion alone made the Negro Exhibit well worth the trouble it took to get it to Buffalo.

16

McKinley: Respite in Canton

"NO FORMAL Demonstration for the President and Wife," read the headline of the *Canton Repository* on the evening of July 5, 1901. With that the paper warned its readers that Ida McKinley's health was still precarious. Therefore, when the president and the first lady arrived in their hometown the next morning, the family desired a low key reception. Flags in abundance would be on display, but only a few personal friends would gather at the depot for the arrival.[1]

Soon after the evening *Repository* hit the streets, the McKinleys were on their way home. At 7:45 that evening two private cars were attached to the Pennsylvania Railroad's regular western express train for the overnight journey to Canton. Secretary Cortelyou, Dr. Rixey, and a contingent of clerical workers and personal servants accompanied the president and the first lady.

"Mrs. McKinley as she boarded the train showed unmistakable evidences of her recent severe illness," a reporter at the Washington depot observed, "but she moved with alacrity from the carriage, boarded the train without any material assistance, and appeared to be in a contented and cheerful state of mind." During the fifteen-minute wait before the train pulled out, Ida "cordially acknowledged the greetings of friends who had assembled at the station."[2]

As requested, the first couple received a welcome home that was "informal and undemonstrative" yet "most warm and cordial." The party arrived Saturday morning, July 6, their Pennsy train, scheduled for 9:58, pulling in just a few minutes late. Canton's mayor, the city's postmaster, and a few other local officials composed the welcoming delegation, purposely kept small in number. The couple walked through the station to their waiting carriage. "Mrs. McKinley seemed to be none the worse for the trip from Washington," the *Repository* reported, adding, "It was said by members of the party that she passed a good night and that her condition continues favorable."[3]

156

Indeed, Ida felt so well that she received a number of visitors that evening, her first guests outside the immediate household since her illness on the western trip. All were relatives or close friends of the McKinleys. They greeted their callers on the front porch made famous during the 1896 campaign. The first couple remained there for several hours, standing frequently to bow and smile at acquaintances who walked or drove past the house. According to the *Repository*, the evening was a tonic for Ida. "The informal little visits seemed to give her much pleasure, and she seemed to be in most excellent spirits," the paper observed.[4]

The first couple returned to a house that had been prepared to receive them. Their carriage and their piano had been shipped to Canton from the White House, and at least three horses would soon follow. Work on the Market Street home came to over $1,600, including $458 for stonework, $360 for cutting down and repaving the driveway, and $253 for sodding and grading. The project required $423 worth of lumber, the cost of painting was $206, and the bill for plumbing work came to $113.[5]

Meanwhile the McKinleys' absence from the White House provided an opportunity for a number of repairs and improvements to the Executive Mansion. The exterior received fresh paint, and new ranges went into one of the kitchens and the butler's pantry. Painters also kept busy in the main first floor corridor. Several second floor rooms got new carpeting, and some also were given a good cleaning.[6]

William and Ida quickly fell into a relaxed pattern of life. Daytime often included a drive through the city, and nighttime brought more front porch visitors. Abner McKinley arrived on the 10th to spend a few days with his brother and his sister-in-law. On the evening of the 16th the Thayer Military Band marched to the McKinley home following their weekly rehearsal and offered an impromptu concert. The president "thanked them most heartily for the serenade, and told them Mrs. McKinley had thoroughly enjoyed it." The Grand Army of the Republic Band scheduled another concert for ten days later, but the event had to be canceled. Leopold Biechele, a neighbor who lived diagonally across the street from the McKinleys, died shortly before the concert was scheduled to begin. Indeed, a crowd had already begun to gather on the lawn when the announcement of the postponement was made. The president then walked over to the Biechele home to express personally his and Ida's sympathies to the family.[7]

On July 13 the president was out for a walk when Zebulon Davis, an old friend, drove by. Davis was part owner of a Cleveland automobile manufacturer, and he offered the chief executive a ride. McKinley had never ridden in a car before, and he didn't seem anxious to do so. The president smiled and tried to demur, but Davis was persistent, and he finally acquired a reluctant passenger. "During the trip," the *Washington Post* reported, "the President was noticed to keep a firm grip on the seat of the vehicle, seemingly being careful lest he might be toppled out by any sudden lunge of the machine while turning corners." His caution proved wise. At one point a bicycle rider got in the way of the vehicle, forcing Davis "to do some quick steering in order to avert an accident." Otherwise the brief ride went without incident.[8]

After about a week a sprinkling of congressmen and other government officials mixed in with the family and social visitors. Attorney General Philander Knox arrived on the morning of July 18 and remained most of the day. He and the president reportedly discussed pending justice department appointments. Secretary of State John Hay came to Canton on August 21. Like his cabinet colleague, he caught an afternoon train back to the nation's capital. Although the secretary and the president discussed several matters "of importance," the *Repository* reassured its readers that none were of "special significance calling for a declaration of policy."[9]

When Mark Hanna and his wife came down from Cleveland on August 2, the senator took pains to inform reporters, "This visit is purely social, and there was nothing either political or official to cause me to come at this time." Still, the old friends were joined in the president's library by Sen. Shelby Moore Cullom of Illinois, a powerful and prominent member of the upper chamber. And although Hanna insisted that the arrival of both senators in Canton was coincidental, he did concede that the three men had discussed upcoming legislation.[10]

Those who spent time with the president in Canton that summer agreed that the respite from Washington was good both for him and for the first lady. On August 12, Charles G. Dawes, who was serving as McKinley's comptroller of the currency, paid a visit. He remained for two days, finding the president in "his best mood" and Ida "very much improved in health." He felt the couple was "passing a quiet and pleasant summer." On the 13th Dawes wrote in his diary, "We had a jolly evening with euchre and Cortelyou playing the 'Caecilian,' a kind of piano."[11]

On August 26, writing to a Boston reporter, Cortelyou observed, "The President has had a very quiet and restful summer here, and both he and Mrs. McKinley have been much benefited." Although presidential duties occasionally intruded, Cortelyou concluded, "There are many pleasant features to a change of this sort."[12]

The main presidential duty McKinley performed during his time in Canton was crafting his speech to be delivered at the Pan-American Exposition. Reciprocity, a theme the president had developed during his west coast trip, was to be the main focus of the address. The former frontman for Republican protectionism had become an enthusiastic convert. The war had made the United States a world military power. Reciprocity, McKinley came to believe, would make it a world economic power. At Buffalo the president hoped to convince his fellow citizens of the wisdom of his position.[13]

On August 9 a delegation from Buffalo arrived in Canton to work out the final details of McKinley's visit. It was a blue ribbon committee, including Chairman Milburn, Director General Buchanan, Mayor Diehl, and John Scatcherd, chairman of the executive committee. The president was scheduled to leave Canton on the morning of September 4, arriving in Buffalo that evening. After two full days of activities, including a visit to Niagara Falls, the presidential train would depart on September 7. McKinley would not return immediately to Canton. Instead he would go to Cleveland to participate in the national encampment of the Grand Army of the Republic.

Milburn told the *Repository* that he expected a quarter of a million people to show up September 5 for President's Day at the fair. "Buffalo will be given over to holiday attire," he promised, "and every courtesy possible will be shown the distinguished guests. President McKinley will be escorted to and from the exposition grounds in a manner befitting the dignity of the chief executive of a country as large and as prosperous as the United States."[14]

Nine days after the Canton meeting Buchanan informed Cortelyou that the Exposition's committee on ceremonies was at work on the program for the president's visit. Meanwhile the secretary had aides busy scrounging copies of speeches that had been delivered at the fair. On August 24 the director general sent Cortelyou a tentative schedule of activities along with a copy of the schedule arranged by the government board for the presidential reception in the Government Building. These Cortelyou willingly approved, but he did have two concerns. One was presidential security, which had troubled him since McKinley first announced plans to attend the fair. "I assume the city authorities as well as Exposition Management will give every attention to discreet and thorough precautionary measures during the President's stay in Buffalo," he wrote on September 2. The other was the constant worry over Ida's fragile health. Cortelyou requested that if there were any demonstrations planned on the ride from the depot to the Milburn house that were "likely to make the horses uneasy," that the first lady be taken directly from the depot to her host's home. Also, because of her condition, Ida would likely not be attending any receptions that might be planned for her. "Please see that this is fully understood," Cortelyou beseeched Buchanan, "so that there may be no misapprehension or embarrassment." Finally, the presidential secretary instructed, "Suggest that any salutes fired should be at such a distance as not to frighten horses or disturb Mrs. McKinley." Buchanan assured him that, "I am arranging personally [to] devote myself to Mrs. McKinley's comfort and wishes."[15]

The Pan-American was not the only exposition to occupy the president's time that summer. Five days after the Buffalo contingent paid its visit, a delegation representing the Louisiana Purchase Exposition, to be held in St. Louis in 1904, arrived in Canton. Former Missouri governor David R. Francis and Sen. Thomas H. Carter of Montana represented the exposition company. Their mission was to give the president formal notification that the group had perfected its plans for the fair. This would qualify the exposition for federal funds, provided the president issued a formal proclamation. McKinley assured his visitors that the proclamation would be forthcoming.[16]

The president also heard from the South Carolina Inter-State and West Indian Exposition, scheduled to open at Charleston on December 1. The board of directors wanted him to take part in "the ceremonies of our 'Opening Day.'" McKinley also received a number of invitations from Buffalo and Exposition interests, all eager to receive a presidential visit. During a previous trip to the city, the president had stayed at the Niagara Hotel, and the hostelry's manager was desirous that he return. "We have a choice of desirable suites we can offer," the manager assured Cortelyou, "and are prepared to place a good private waiter at his disposal and insure the highest grade of service." An official of the Lenox Hotel also extended an invitation. He assured Cortelyou that the Lenox was "in every way the finest and best located hotel in Buffalo" and "the best adapted to the requirements of the President and his party." Of course, the denizens of the Midway appreciated the kind of publicity a presidential visit would provide. Frank Bostock offered to give a special performance of his wild animals. Frank Cummins of the Indian Congress was more creative. "I am at a loss to know what to do with 700 Indians," he wrote. "Almost every day they hold a meeting and pass a resolution about the Great Chief of the Nation. They know you are coming here September 5th and are very anxious to have you and your party at the Congress at a Special Exhibition."[17]

McKinley also heard from a Prof. Gustave Meyer, who described himself as a "Scientific American Astrologer." On July 16 he warned of "much trouble to our soldiers, also strikes, riots, and bloodshed, with mob violence and lawlessness." He also predicted "much trouble in Turkey, also in the City of Paris, in France, and the West Indies." Most presciently, he wrote, "We shall further hear of much trouble to our dear President, and it will be well for our Chief Executive to guard himself from all harm during the whole summer, and to be ever watchful and prepared for trouble from any source."[18]

On Tuesday, September 3, the presidential staff began packing the office equipment in use at the McKinley home for the trip to Buffalo and Cleveland. Although the exact itinerary was not announced, it was expected that the president would be away from Canton for between ten days and two weeks.

Before the first couple departed for the big fair, they took time to attend a much smaller one. The Stark County Fair was under way, and on the afternoon of the 3rd the McKinleys, accompanied by Dr. Rixey, took their carriage to the local event. They arrived at three o'clock and rode around the grounds. The party drove past several outdoor displays, halting at one point to watch a harness race. "Children's day was at its height," the *Repository* reported, "and several times the carriage was halted that the occupants might witness the pleasures of the little people. The children ran after the President's carriage, and he waved and smiled greetings to them."[19]

The following morning at ten the special presidential train left Canton, bound for Cleveland along the Pennsylvania Railroad. Cortelyou and Dr. Rixey accompanied the president and the first lady, as did a maid and a nurse for Ida and three clerical aides. Also aboard were three family members, Miss Sarah Duncan, the president's niece, and Mary and Ida Barber, nieces of Mrs. McKinley. There was no formal send-off. Indeed, the time of departure had not been announced to the public.

The train reached Cleveland at just after noon and was shifted onto a siding. Meanwhile a crowd swarmed the depot, vainly seeking a glimpse of the president. Those who were patient enough were finally rewarded when the presidential cars were switched into the depot. The president and Cortelyou stepped out onto the rear platform and doffed their hats to the crowd. Ida remained inside the Pullman, bowing to the crowd from the window. Soon their cars were attached to "one of the swiftest engines on the Lake Shore Road," the line that would take them to Buffalo.[20]

17

Exposition: The Good

On July 13, some ten weeks after the Pan-Am's opening day, the board of directors announced, "The Exposition exhibit buildings, the installation of exhibits therein, the landscape work, and the electrical illumination … are complete." Eleven days later came word that all state and national buildings, beyond the direct control of the board, were open to visitors. The news was good, but it came too late. Word of an unfinished exposition had radiated from Buffalo, severely curtailing attendance during the early weeks.[1]

The various state buildings proved popular, especially to visitors from the states they represented. The structures seldom contained extensive displays. Rather, as the *Buffalo Courier* observed, they were "rest houses pure and simple." Weary Exposition patrons found easy chairs, ice water, and writing tables for individuals wishing to drop a line to the folks back home. Those eager to find out what was happening in their home states could peruse the principal daily and weekly newspapers. New York, in its stately building meant to be permanent, entertained visitors with a $2,500 piano made of mahogany and trimmed in gold.[2]

New York appropriated $350,000 for the Exposition. Twenty-four of the other 44 states in the Union at the time also voted funds to participate. They ranged from the one thousand dollars that Delaware spent to the $75,000 invested by Illinois. With only nine states erecting buildings, and the six from New England sharing another, many states were limited to displays in other Exposition buildings, Agriculture and Mining housing most of the exhibits.[3]

Florida, not surprisingly, offered an extensive collection of fruits and vegetables. But the state also had a display of artifacts from the Seminole tribe. California's honey-making entry was so large that the bee keepers decided to build a separate building to house it. New York sought to inform with its exhibit in the Agriculture Building. In addition to a large number of crops, the displays also included seeds, samples of threshed grain, and a group of models loaned by the Cornell Agricultural College tracing the history of the plow. Corn figured prominently in a number of states' offerings. Nebraska used ears to spell out the message, "Corn is King in Nebraska." Illinois artists enlisted cobs, husks, and kernels to create a nine-by-six-foot work of art. Visitors marveled at the realism of the farm scene it depicted. North Dakota displayed a cow made of corn, and Alabama used the crop to create a five-foot high replica of the state's capitol building.[4]

Although many of the national buildings at the Exposition, most notably Canada's, had parlors for visiting citizens, most also found space for displaying their national wares. However, like the states, other countries also placed exhibits in major Exposition buildings.

Much was predictable. Argentina showed two hundred samples of wool and a variety of cereals and minerals. Bolivia also had mineral products on display, along with raw rubber, alpaca wool, and coffee plants. In addition, the *Buffalo Courier* noted, "Coco leaves bespeak the source of the world's pain-killing cocaine." Often the expected was mixed with items visitors were less likely to anticipate. For example, at Peru's display in the Agriculture Building, along with corn, coffee, tobacco, and wool, was an Incan mummy said to be four hundred years old. Chile's exhibit included a miniature salt petre factory and the first locomotive ever run in South America. The latter was removed from the Chilean Building and placed in the Transportation Annex alongside the *DeWitt Clinton*, which held the same honor in the United States. Chile's most impressive display was its art work, which drew "immense crowds" to the building. According to one reporter, "The [Chilean] art gallery ... is said by some to rival the Exposition art gallery." Ecuador also offered an "especially fine" collection of oil paintings and water colors, along with cocoa beans, deer skins, and leather goods.[5]

The decision of the Honduran commissioners to distribute cigars at their nation's building led to a minor controversy. Customs officials held up the initial shipments, believing the stogies were intended for resale. They were not, and once officials were convinced that the smokes were to be given away "as samples of one of the great industries of their republic," they waived the duty.[6]

Canada, after recovering from their pique at not being formally invited in a timely manner, threw themselves wholeheartedly into the effort, appropriating $112,000. The main floor of the country's building was "devoted to a comprehensive agricultural exhibit," featuring all the grains grown by America's northern neighbor. As a tribute to the host city, the ground floor also included "a monster stuffed buffalo," owned by the government and never before displayed at an exposition. Minerals from the Canadian Shield region, gold from the Klondike, and numerous artworks rounded out Canada's contribution to the Pan-Am.[7]

Within the drab walls of the United States Government Building was an impressive display. It included exhibits from every cabinet department, as well as other agencies. The result, according to one observer, was an exhibit of "extraordinary completeness."[8]

Many of the displays were of both historical and monetary value. The State Department booth had proclamations signed by every president from Washington through McKinley. It also contained a collection of autograph letters from foreign leaders. At the Treasury Department display visitors could see samples of every coin ever produced by the United States government, plus many foreign coins. Similarly, the Post Office Department had a collection of all American-issued postage stamps, valued at over fifty thousand dollars.[9]

Within the Interior Department display, the Bureau of Education had the usual paper-and-pencil type of materials shown at previous expositions. In addition the bureau offered "biograph" and "graphophone" exhibits. The former showed "moving pictures" of the Washington, D.C., schools, exercises at the Carlisle, Pennsylvania Indian School, and drills at the Naval Academy. The Geological Survey printed a thousand maps a day of the Niagara from Buffalo to its mouth and distributed them to eager visitors. But it was the Patent Office that stole the show. At previous expositions its exhibit had consisted only of "motionless models, a display of little interest to the average visitor," the government conceded. At Buffalo the office showcased "various machines in actual operation," representing the cutting edge of American ingenuity and technology at the dawn of the twentieth century. Among them was an "Electrograph," which transmitted photographs by wire, and the "Telautograph," which could "send a message in one's own handwriting over any distance which a Morse code line can be worked." Electric typewriters were also on display, as were working models of up-to-date harvesting machines. In June inventor Frederick E. Ives placed his "kromskop," a device for printing color photographs, on display, along with some finished prints. Ives had been working on the process since the mid–1880s, and his entry attracted several visitors. Perhaps the most popular inventions on hand were the gramaphone and the graphaphone, both early day phonographs. "The space in front of the trumpets leading from those two busy machines is crowded all the time," the *Buffalo Express* observed.[10]

The military was well represented. The Navy Department's display included the original plans of the *Monitor* and the *Merrimac* (later the *Virginia*), the ships which fought the first battle between ironclads on March 9, 1862. There were also models of 26 Navy vessels, ranging from first-class battleships to unarmored gunboats. An eight-by-twenty-foot map of the world featured 307 lead models showing the positions of every U.S. Naval ship, including those under repairs or under construction. The display was updated daily. The "central figure" of the exhibit, at least in the opinion of the Navy, was a cyclorama showing the quarter-deck of an armored cruiser, the flagship of a squadron. A canvas background was painted to show the other vessels of the squadron against a seascape. Life-sized wax figures manned the ship, working eight-inch guns.[11]

The War Department had on hand an extensive collection of uniforms dating back to the Revolution. There was also a "very complete and instructive" display of small arms and projectiles. Especially popular with visitors was a set of ceremonial swords presented to Civil War generals Ulysses S. Grant, William T. Sherman, Philip Sheridan, Henry W. Halleck, George Thomas, and George G. Meade, plus Admiral Dewey and other Spanish-American War heroes. Just north of the building the department assembled an impressive group of artillery. The largest was a twelve-inch seacoast rifle weighing 115,000 pounds. Also included were a ten-inch gun, a twelve-inch mortar, a five-inch "rapid fire" gun, as well as several older seacoast defense

Ohio was among a number of states erecting their own buildings at the Pan-American Exposition. The state's pennant-shaped flag made its debut at the fair (Library of Congress).

guns. Beginning May 28 gun crews conducted daily drills for Exposition visitors. A detail of enlisted men also performed daily drills at a model brigade field hospital. Included were first aid for the wounded, litter drill, and demonstrations of tent pitching and hospital establishment.[12]

Early on the morning of August 15 the cadets of West Point arrived at the Exposition grounds, pitched 215 two-man tents, arranged their camp, and marched off for breakfast. Two days later was Army Day at the fair, and tens of thousands, the *Buffalo Express* reported, viewed the martial parade that wound through the city. At its head were Gen. Nelson A. Miles, commander of the Army, Director General Buchanan, and Mayor Diehl. The West Point band was a short distance behind, followed by the cadets, "their feet rising and falling with a precision equal to the ticking of time in a perfect clock." They marched to the Exposition Stadium, where they were joined by other outfits, including the local Buffalo militia, in a day of inspections and drills. The West Point drills became a daily feature at the Exposition, so popular that the Stadium was sometimes filled to capacity—and beyond. Infantry, artillery, and cavalry were all included, along with demonstrations on setting up camp. As the cadets prepared to depart on August 28, the *Express* observed, "The memory of their visit will endure as one of the brightest chapters in the history of ... the exposition. By the great horn spoon and the great cream-colored mule, it is the truth."[13]

The Commission of Fish and Fisheries had a very popular display, one that occupied the entire south annex of the Government Building. Railroad tank cars brought fresh water from Lake Erie and salt water from Woods Hole, Massachusetts, to fill its 32 tanks. "The many curious specimens of fishes make this exhibit one of very unusual interest," noted one observer. However, the commission contended, "The primary purpose of the exhibit is to show the functions of the commission." As a result the display included models of vessels used in scientific research and methods of hatching fish. In fact, during the run of the Exposition, several million eggs were hatched at the exhibit.[14]

Also popular with visitors was the lifesaving station, then a part of the Treasury Department. Every afternoon at two an "announcement gun" was fired at the station, located on Mirror Lake. At that point, according to the Department's final report, "the other parts of the exposition grounds were, to a great measure, deserted." A half hour later the crew of eleven picked men from Great Lakes and Atlantic coast stations began its demonstration. It took them six minutes to fire a life line from a gun and bring ashore in the breeches buoy a man from a mast in mid lake. They also put on a capsize drill and demonstrated methods of resuscitation. The station included a gasoline powered lifeboat, which the *Courier* termed "the latest innovation in life-saving appliances."[15]

Most people visiting the Exposition, especially those from out of town, arrived at the north entrance, where the railroads disgorged their passengers. The Pan-Am's architects preferred that fairgoers enter at the Lincoln Avenue gate on the south side of the grounds. There lush landscaping, well garnished with flowers, provided a subtle introduction to the scenes that lay ahead. As one observer noted, "By entering from the north ... you are plunged at once, without preparation into the midst of the Exposition. From the south it unfolds like a flower."[16]

The process became complete at the Triumphal Bridge, which, despite its lofty moniker, spanned only a shallow section of the artificial waterways traversing the grounds. The original idea had been for the bridge to commemorate Dewey's victory at Manila, a concept later considered impolitic in light of the Latin American participation at the fair. If the theme was toned down, the gaudiness was not. Four pylons, one hundred feet high, punctuated the corners. A statue of a rider on a rearing horse topped each. Below were bronze-colored trophies and more statuary in the niches. Cables linking the pylons bore polished copper shields and flags and coats of arms of participating countries, "the whole expressing the triumphal struggle of the people of the United States to free themselves from institutions of despotic ages and governments."[17]

At the bridge, according to Pan-Am historian Joann Marie Thompson, the Exposition grounds "would be fully and dramatically revealed." In the foreground the Horticulture Building stood to the left of the Esplanade, the Government Building to the right. A short distance north came the Temple of Music and the Ethnology Building, both sporting domes and using vivid colors to reflect Turner's vision of the "savage" taste. These two structures marked the southern end of the Court of Fountains. As one continued north, the Machinery and Transportation Building sat to the west, the Manufactures and Liberal Arts Building opposite. Both were rectangular with a 500-foot facade and a central court. Beyond these structures the Mall intersected the Court of Fountains, the Electricity Building appearing on the left, the Agriculture Building on the right. By that point Turner's harsh colors had given way to subtler, more pastel hues as one approached the Electric Tower.[18]

Beyond the Tower was an open area known as the Plaza, which offered seats for weary visitors. It also provided the entrances to the Midway and the Stadium. As was the case at the south entrance, flower beds dotted the Plaza. Indeed, flowers and other plant life could be found throughout the grounds. Some twenty acres were devoted to this purpose, not including areas adjacent to and inside the Horticulture Building. In all the Exposition boasted nearly two hundred flower beds, ranging from one hundred to six thousand square feet. Tulips lined the canals, offering a colorful show to the Exposition's spring visitors. A bed of Crimson Rambler Roses, planted in the fall of 1900, yielded some 300,000 blooms at its peak, according to Frederic Taylor, the Exposition's superintendent of horticulture. About ten thousand cannas occupied 35 different beds. Among them was the McKinley, a bright scarlet dwarf, named for the man who always wore a carnation in his lapel and often gave it to children he met. There were also pansies and geraniums, including a half dozen new varieties of the latter. Water lilies decorated the Exposition's lakes and basins. In addition to the flowering plants, visitors found shrubs and nearly a hundred species of evergreen trees. Nor were the displays limited to indigenous species. A sole exhibitor from Mexico supplied nearly fifty varieties of cactus. The greenhouses grouped around the Horticulture Building offered displays of tea plants, coffee trees, pineapple plants, coconut trees, and cotton plants.[19]

Sculpture also graced the grounds. Like Turner's color scheme, the goal of the statuary was to "tell the story of Man and his Rise to Civilization." Sadly, as with the "savage colors" giving way to more gentle hues, elements of racism entered into the equation. For example, Story of Man, the group in front of the Government Building, began with the Savage Age, which featured Far Eastern warriors and American Indians, the former attacking dead enemies. The Despotic Age portrayed slave owners—but of the Roman Age. The Age of Enlightenment highlighted the "civilizing" influence of Western Europe. Similarly the Electric Tower was flanked by figures portraying starkly different visions of Niagara Falls. One was called Primeval Niagara, or The Great Waters in the Days of the Indian, which purported to represent the falls in "its mythical sense." The other was Niagara To-day, or The Great Waters in the Days of the White Man. It featured a youth rising from the water holding in one hand a hammer and in the other a woman with a globe in her hand. All of this was meant to represent "Niagara conquered by the white man and harnessed to his work."[20]

Elsewhere the works were designed to punctuate the buildings near which they were located. Groups outside the Mining and Horticulture buildings represented "man's conquering of the elements." Among the pieces at the entrance to the livestock barns was one called Horse-Trainer. Adjacent to the Temple of Music were four groups representing Heroic Music, Sacred Music, Gay Music, and Lyric Music. Another quartet, these flanking the Ethnology Building, featured "the four races of men." As a tribute to the host city, statues of American bison graced the south entrance to the grounds and the exteriors of many buildings.[21]

One of the unique structures at the Pan-Am was the Stadium, which seated 13,000 and made possible an impressive schedule of sporting events spanning the run of the Exposition. It was the brainchild of Director-general Buchanan, who "conceived the idea of having an Athletic Congress ... which would eclipse any athletic carnival heretofore attempted." A "base-ball" game between the Carlisle Indian School and Cornell University on May 17 was the initial contest. The American Athletic Union sponsored a number of events, including basketball games and track meets. Intercollegiate football games filled the October portion of the calendar, while much of August was devoted to bicycle races. The second week of September was set aside for automobile shows, including the conclusion of a race from New York City to Buffalo. Among those participating were millionaires John Jacob Astor and William K. Vanderbilt, Jr. Unfortunately, the McKinley assassination overshadowed the event.[22]

A short distance south of the Stadium stood the Agriculture Building and the Dairy Building. The original plan called for just one structure, but it soon became apparent that the dairy exhibits required their own facility. It was constructed in the style of a Swiss chalet and included a restaurant and, for reasons that are unclear, dormitories of Exposition police. Two large refrigerated glass cases, running the length of the 150-foot building, displayed butter and cheese. Among the highlights was a butter sculpture of the Minnesota State Capitol. In addition to the various state displays, the Agriculture Building had a large entry from the American Sugar Beet Association and numerous exhibits of seeds and leaf tobacco. The Vermont Maple Syrup Association displayed its wares, and many bee-keeping societies had live bees busy at their occupation.

Nearby were seventeen livestock barns, covering ten acres of ground. Frank A. Converse, the superintendent of livestock, had originally intended to have animals present from all participating Pan-American countries, but strict quarantine laws made this impossible. Instead Converse focused his attention on collecting as large an exhibit as he could from the United States and Canada. The Dominion cooperated, setting aside $50,000 for the effort, and Converse visited numerous meetings of state and national livestock associations. As a result so many exhibitors came forward that the superintendent was forced to show one class at a time. The swine show came first, running from August 26 to September 7. It was followed by cattle, sheep, poultry and pigeons, and "pet stock." Because of limited space, horses and cattle were shown in the Stadium. The four thousand entries in the poultry and pigeon show strained the capacity of the barns.[23]

Because the various livestock associations could not agree on the ground rules, Converse had to abandon his plans for breed tests for dairy cattle.

The War Department's extensive display included this collection of small arms (National Archives and Records Administration).

Instead he established a "model dairy," the purpose of which was "to illustrate every phase of dairy work, from the feeding of the animals to placing the finished product on the market." In the end a committee of judges determined that the Guernseys made the best showing in the production of both butterfat and churned butter. The cost of the model dairy, including staff and feeds, came to four thousand dollars. However, sales of milk and other products reduced the deficit to just one thousand.[24]

Adjacent to the Lincoln Parkway gate the Exposition established a military camp, inviting hundreds of units to come and participate. Pan-Am officials agreed to supply tents, cots, flooring, and sanitary items. In return the visiting units agreed to remain in uniform during their time there and to give a military exhibition daily. Usually performed on the Esplanade, these exhibitions included parades, reviews, guard mounting, rifle drills, bayonet exercises, and close order drills. Every participant paid a one-time admission fee, but the outfits could stay for up to six days. At first the visiting units named the camp whatever they saw fit, but on June 9 Buchanan designated it Camp Fillmore in honor of the thirteenth president.

Forty-eight organizations, including the West Point cadets, representing a dozen states and Ontario, participated, their visits often overlapping. The community of Dwight, Illinois sent its camp of Spanish-American War veterans. Toronto dispatched the 48th Highlanders to Buffalo, and Troy, New York sent the Poke Hook and Ladder Company. Private schools and colleges were also represented at Camp Fillmore. Among those making an especially positive impression were the cadets from Virginia Polytechnic. On their last day at the Exposition, the *Buffalo Express* observed, "Visitors will be sorry to lose the natty looking fellows in the white trousers and blue jackets." The paper went on to explain, "Their exhibition of the manual [of arms] has called forth expressions of astonishment from old military men. 'Order arms' is like the motion of a single piece of machinery."[25]

A variety of bands also contributed to the martial atmosphere of the Exposition. Music was an important part of Buchanan's background, and the director general made it a major component of the Buffalo fair. The bands were diverse, including the Carlisle Indian Band, the Boston Ladies' Band, the Newsboys' Band of Grand Rapids, and the Puerto Rican String Band. Summoning his diplomatic skills, Buchanan also secured the Mexican Artillery Band and the Municipal Band of Havana. Both groups had sixty members, and both remained in Buffalo for several weeks. Most groups received between five hundred and a thousand dollars per week for their services—with one notable exception. John Philip Sousa's Band was paid $30,000 for a four-week engagement.[26]

The March King made his first appearance at three o'clock on June 10, performing outdoors at the bandstand on the Esplanade. The concert lasted two hours and concluded with "The Invincible Eagle," a march in the 6/8 tempo that Sousa composed in honor of the Exposition. Both the afternoon performance and another given that evening attracted thousands of wildly appreciative audience members. Two days later the *Buffalo Courier* made arrangements with the bandmaster to take requests from its readers, who were invited to submit titles of songs they would like played. The *Courier* published the requests, which Sousa agreed to clip from the paper, playing as many as he could.

Perhaps the highlight of Sousa's time at Buffalo was his band's Fourth of July concert in the Stadium. Some 12,000 people show up for the 8:15 p.m. show, which opened with "America." Midway through the program the spectators and a somewhat startled Sousa heard another band approaching the Stadium. It was the Bavarian Band from the Alt Nuremburg Midway attraction, which came to pay its compliments to the bandmaster. Sousa responded by having his band play the German national anthem, and the Bavarians returned the favor with "America" before marching out playing "Stars and Stripes Forever."[27]

During their first three evenings at the Exposition, Sousa's band played "Nearer My God to Thee" as the lights outlining the major buildings were brought up. Buchanan decided that it would be "peculiarly appropriate and desirable" that "The Star Spangled Banner" be offered instead, and he sent instructions to that effect to Sousa. The March King complied, as did other bandleaders booked by the Exposition. Eventually even the bands connected with the Midway attractions joined in, creating what the director general would term "an emotional, uplifting, exquisite feature of the Exposition."[28]

Early on the morning of August 25 the 52-car train bearing Col. William F. Cody and his Buffalo Bill's Wild West and Rough Riders Show arrived near the Exposition grounds. There were cowboys and Indians, soldiers from all over the world, a herd of bison, and over six hundred horses. Within a few hours a crew transformed a large vacant lot adjacent to the East Amherst gate into an impressive tent city.

Cody had planned to promote his appearance with a downtown parade, but the Midway men, sensing a mutually beneficial opportunity, offered their resplendent venue. Buffalo Bill accepted, and his exotic riders, blaring bands, and prancing horses fit right in with the scene. That evening some eight thousand attended the troupe's initial performance of a two-week booking. Sharpshooter Annie Oakley was on hand to display her prowess with a rifle. There were horse races, sham battles between cowboys and Indians, lasso throwing, bronco busting, and Native war dances. A lifesaving crew reenacted a rescue from a shipwreck, and "a company of Arabs illustrated the riding and games of their native land." The only negative note came just before the performance, when a cannon used to announce the show discharged prematurely. An employee was tamping powder with a ramrod when the blast occurred. The ramrod shot out, badly lacerating the man's arm, and the fire that belched from the muzzle burned his head and face. Though painful, the injuries were not life threatening.[29]

Another frontier celebrity present at the Pan-Am was Martha Jane Canary, better known as Calamity Jane. A skilled horsewoman and excellent shot, she had spent time at various western forts, reportedly serving as a scout for Gen. George A. Custer. She had also spent time in Deadwood, South Dakota during the 1870s gold rush. The Indian Congress booked her as an attraction, and on July 31 she arrived in grand style, driving a one-hundred-mule team through the Exposition grounds.[30]

"The Pan-American Exposition," observed one visitor, "is a comprehensive glance of American life." Most of that comprehensive glance, of course, celebrated the wonders of the contemporary era, but at the Ethnology Building visitors could examine the artifacts of earlier eras and peoples. Arthur Lincoln Benedict, a Buffalo physician, was the curator of the display. Although Benedict was not a professional ethnologist, he was a serious amateur, whose excavations at Native American sites in western New York led to several published articles. He threw himself into the project, contacting scholars and institutions to secure displays. The results were mixed, many collections being committed to museums and therefore unavailable.[31]

Still, Dr. Benedict amassed an impressive collection to fill his gaudy building. Native American arrow points, spear points, and drills, along with other tools, were on display. So were clothing, baskets, and pottery of more recent vintage from Zuni, Navajo, and Apache tribes. Closer to home, Benedict acquired masks from the Iroquois nations. As for foreign countries, Mexico was the only one to offer collections on a large scale. America's southern neighbor sent pottery, woven fabrics, and gold and silver ornaments crafted by native peoples. For visitors wishing to expand their horizons even further, Benedict included a library section with books, reports from the Bureau of Ethnology, and reprints of Benedict's own articles on his digs.[32]

The ethnology exhibits were not all confined to the indoors. In May 1900 Benedict asked Newcomb Carlton to construct a Native American mound on the Exposition grounds. The director of works agreed, and the earthwork went up near the Alaska Building. The project was so successful that plans were made for two famous effigy mounds, Ohio's Serpent Mound and the Eagle Mound of Wisconsin. The former ended up being razed because of inaccuracies. The latter was never entirely completed and became covered with grass as the summer wore on.[33]

Natural resources were on full display at the Forestry Building and the Mines Building. The former had exhibits from throughout the Western Hemisphere. Not only were wood samples and forest products available for viewing, but there were also reports on efforts to preserve and manage woodlands. The Mines Building was replete with samples, including two of the largest gold nuggets ever found in the American West and a silver nugget weighing three hundred pounds. One of the more interesting cases on display was empty when the Exposition opened. Over the summer it filled with new minerals discovered during the run of the fair. Also on hand were examples of mining machinery and tools, a model of the first petroleum well, and an electrical map of the mineral resources of the Americas.[34]

One-fourth of the Manufactures and Liberal Arts Building was devoted to items in the latter category. Education was the main display subject, with exhibits covering primary grades through college. There were also models

A view of the Exposition from the bandstand, showcasing the Electric Tower (Library of Congress).

and plans for up-to-date school buildings as well as library displays. Musical instruments were the second most important category. Ten exhibitors brought pianos to the fair, including an improved player piano "upon which the effect of four-hand playing can be obtained." Also on display were organs, strings, and band instruments. Advances in medicine were also chronicled, particularly hospitals established to treat consumption (tuberculosis). Other displays recognized progress in the area of sanitation, including a group of photographs showing how towns in Massachusetts were turning raw sewage into "the most practical and perfect agricultural fertilizer that has yet been discovered."[35]

The goal of the Division of Graphic Arts, according to Thomas M. Moore, who had charge of it, was to demonstrate "the means, methods, materials, machinery apparatus and appliances for printing and the results obtained." The displays were located in two buildings. The "Gallery" housed papers, ink, and "the products of the printing, engraving and book binding arts," but no machinery. The "Workshop" was at first located close by, but just before the Exposition opened it was moved to a site on the Midway. This relocation prompted a number of exhibitors to withdraw, but there were, nevertheless, several printing presses in operation. Among them was a press that could turn out 50,000 sixteen-page, four-color forms of paper in an hour. The Dow composing machine reportedly could set and justify in a column at a rate greater than any other. Also on display was a machine that was capable of producing eight thousand envelopes an hour.[36]

Early in 1900 Algar M. Wheeler, superintendent of the Division of Manufactures, sent letters to over thirty thousand American producers. By early November requests for space totaled three times the amount available. Fountains and flowers came out of the building plans, freeing up more room, and participants were limited to just enough space for "the best products, as well as the latest improvements and achievements." At the same time, several large firms declined to participate. Because of good economic times, many companies were too busy, while others saw little need for the advertising benefits of the Exposition. As Wheeler later explained, "A time of great industrial prosperity is clearly not the best for Expositions. Men and means cannot well be spared in such prosperous times for exhibition purposes."[37]

The perils of prosperity notwithstanding, the scope of manufacturing displays was impressive. It ranged from extensive exhibits of silverware, to sewing machines, to pottery. There were looms producing hammocks and mosquito netting, large displays of pottery, and a complete shoe factory in operation. The J. B. Williams Company of Glastonbury, Connecticut had a booth looking like a Grecian temple made entirely of soap. The cash register was about two decades old when the Exposition opened, and exhibits of the devices offered "stereopticon" views of their construction. There were heavy duty steel mail boxes on display, made for the new rural delivery service being instituted. Modern locks were designed so "the key enters the door knob, thereby preventing the marring of the door-fittings"; and modern type writers were designed so "the writing surface unrolls in sight of the operator" and "paragraph beginnings are located automatically."[38]

New foods were also on display, including instant coffee, onion salt, coffee and tea tablets, "both useful in traveling," and "health breads." "Cereal breads" were claimed to be "a perfect substitute for real coffee." Aunt Jemima offered "pancakes [made] out of some new process flour." Many of the food manufacturers offered free samples, including "biscuits made from the 'finest baking powder on earth,'" and pancakes made from "the only pancake flour that wouldn't result in sinkers." As a result of all the handouts, the building became a magnet for visitors desiring a free lunch, producing this scene described by a reporter: "'Well,' said a fat lady from Seneca County, 'that meal's the first thing I've got for nothing since I landed in Buffalo.'"[39]

In the Machinery and Transportation Building machinery occupied about two-thirds of the space. Most of it was industrial, including "engines and motors driven by air, gas, gasoline, oil, steam, and water." Both metal and woodworking devices were on display, as were machines for turning out horseshoes, clocks, jewelry, and pins and needles. Machines for making brick, tile, and pottery were also on hand. So were bottling and corking machinery and spinning and weaving appliances.[40]

With railroad cars dispatched to a separate building, the transportation section included automobiles, ambulances, bicycles, and watercraft. Since the horse remained a prominent source of transportation in 1901, harness and saddlery were also included. Forty automobile manufacturers participated, showing off the latest in electric, steam, and gasoline powered horseless carriages.

Bicycles were well represented by local firms, Buffalo having gained a reputation as "the Greatest Wheel City in the World" as the fad developed in the 1890s. Flat terrain and a wealth of paved streets provided an eager market for the city's manufacturers. Perhaps best known among the plethora of firms was the George N. Pierce Company. A longtime maker of housewares, in 1896 Pierce added bicycles to his company's line. The Pierce display at the Exposition showed "automatic figures of the two wheelmen" with background scenery that moved "in a constantly changing procession, giving just the motion effect that is needed." One rider, perched on a competitor's product, was suffering from the "severe vibrations" of the road. The other, mounted on a Pierce "Pan-American Special," glided along "serenely and smoothly." A "handsome display" of Pierce bicycles sat nearby. Also present was the recently introduced two-speed "Motorette" automobile, Pierce's first entry into that field. Three years later he would introduce the luxury "Great Arrow," and in 1908 the firm would be renamed the Pierce Arrow Motor Car Company.[41]

Another novel form of transportation could be found in the Agriculture Building. The Stair Lift Company of Philadelphia installed "moving stairs," charging three cents for a ride or a nickel for two tickets. The *Buffalo Courier* boasted that the escalator could lift a thousand people an hour, adding, "It will please bulky folk who do not love to climb stairs."[42]

Electricity, of course, was a centerpiece of the Pan-Am, and the Electricity Building did not disappoint those who were curious about the relatively new technology. Among the many displays were entries from the two bitter rivals, Westinghouse and General Electric. Many of the Pittsburgh company's latest improvements in railway technology, including electric brakes, steam couplers, and semaphore signals from Union Switch and Signal were found in the Railway Annex. In the Electricity Building the company occupied six thousand feet of space, containing engines, generators, transformers, and alternators. Most visitors were attracted to a "high-voltage sign," consisting of two large glass plates covered on the back with metal foil and bearing the name "Westinghouse." As AC current was sent through it a tinge of violet light at first glowed around the letters, shooting out showers of sparks as the voltage was brought up.

General Electric's display stressed its most recent improvements, particularly in the field of incandescent and arc lighting. GE did not concede the rail industry to Westinghouse, showing its own line of brakes, switches, and a "modern electric mining locomotive." However, the company did make an implicit concession in another area, displaying a large variety of alternating current lamps and motors.[43]

One of the booths in the Electricity Building belonged to the Edison Manufacturing Company, and it contained one of the Wizard's latest inventions. The 1890s had seen the prolific inventor launch an ambitious but largely unsuccessful iron ore milling business and work to make improvements in cement. In 1899 Edison turned his attention to developing an improved stor-

The Electricity Building displaying its nighttime illumination (Library of Congress).

The Exposition's Pergola and one of many utility poles on the grounds (Library of Congress).

age battery, a type of battery which is recharged by running a current through it. His goal was to produce one about half as heavy as the lead-acid models then in use but fully as powerful. The future of the automobile, Edison believed, was in electric cars, and he wanted his batteries to power them. Characteristically, the still energetic inventor plunged wholeheartedly into the effort. He purchased an abandoned brass mill, converting it into the Edison Storage Battery Company, prepared other buildings for manufacturing, and launched experiments with a variety of metals.

In July 1901 Edison placed an iron-nickel model on display in his Exposition booth. It was under a glass case, and it reportedly attracted hundreds of visitors daily, although likely not as many as did his phonograph. Early on the battery was withdrawn from competition with other batteries on display at the Exposition. The stated reason was that, "Mr. Edison is not yet quite prepared to give the world and the jury of awards all of what are now secrets of the laboratory in connection with the battery." It was equally likely that the battery itself was not ready for public scrutiny. Edison would spend another decade on the project, rejecting one prototype after another. In 1904 he would voluntarily recall 14,000 of one model following reports of acid leaks and other problems. Then, once the battery was perfected, Henry Ford's assembly line and the internal combustion engine rendered it obsolete—at least for large-scale automobile production. Still it found life in electric trucks designed for intra-city deliveries, as well as railroad signaling, miners' lamps, and various military uses.[44]

Edison made at least two visits to the fair while passing part of his summer at the nearby Chautauqua. During his first sojourn, on July 20, he stayed for the evening illumination, admitting that it surpassed any idea he had formed. "It is a wonder," he told a *Courier* reporter in speaking of the fair. "As for the illumination, it's a record breaker." During an August 6 visit, Edison met Henry Rustin, superintendent of the Exposition's mechanical and electrical bureau. Perhaps channeling his inner hippie, Edison told Rustin, "This is out of sight."[45]

The telephone was about a quarter of a century old in 1901, and the Pan-Am boasted an exhibit that one observer termed "probably [the] greatest ever made at any Exposition." Among its highlights was a booth where the roar of Niagara Falls could be heard from a transmitter installed at the Cave of the Winds. The Kellogg Switchboard and Supply Company of Chicago had an elaborate display, one good enough to earn a gold medal from Exposition judges. It featured one section of the largest multiple switchboard ever built, with a capacity of 12,000 lines. There was also a complete switchboard, designed for smaller communities, capable of handling 160 lines. The company had several other switchboards on view, along with 36 models of "wall sets" and storage batteries. Branch booths in different sections of the building demonstrated the quality of the company's service.[46]

The Bell Telephone Company was also present, offering an exchange, "in restricted proportions," with a capacity for six hundred subscribers. Otherwise, it was "complete in every detail." The company was eager to point out that the batteries of all the exchanges in Buffalo and Niagara Falls were charged by motor generators powered by the falls.[47]

Exposition visitors also had the opportunity to observe firsthand the latest breakthrough in communication, wireless telegraphy. Versions of Marconi's landmark invention could be found in the Electricity Building and as a part of the War Department exhibit in the Government Building. Messages were exchanged from both locations with Fort Porter, located about three miles away.[48]

Sunset at the Pan-Am brought not just the amazing illumination of the buildings, but other light shows as well. One was offered by the thirty-inch searchlight perched at the 360 foot level of the Electric Tower. Its beam was clearly visible at Niagara Falls, and on the night of August 9 the light was directed toward Toronto, a distance of 58 miles. It was a cloudy evening, which clearly separated the Exposition beam from the reflections of the city's arc lights.[49]

During the course of the fair fireworks lit up the night skies on 31 occasions, usually capping a special day. They opened with "Niagara Falls in Liquid Fire" and "Pan-America Welcomes All," featuring maps of North and South America, and closed with "Farewell to the Beautiful City of Light." Between were such displays as "Naval Bombardment of Manila," "Fountain of Fire," held in the middle of Exposition Lake, and "Destruction of the Pirate Fleet at Tripoli." Most were supplied by Henry Pain of Manhattan Beach, whose pyrotechnics had long delighted visitors to Coney Island and other vacation spots. The typical cost of his Exposition shows was $1,200, but officials allocated $2,500 for President's Day.[50]

Even with the additional allotment, the show honoring McKinley fell far short of the display put on for Grover Cleveland at the World's Columbian Exposition. The White City had laid out ten thousand dollars for its President's Day spectacular. Unfortunately for Buchanan and the board of directors, red ink was trumping spectacle, and by mid-summer Exposition officials were force to pinch pennies.

18

Exposition: The Bad and the Costly

"Special" days, dates set aside to honor various places or groups, were common at the Exposition. Many participating states and countries were so recognized, although all of Central America shared September 30. Among the communities saluted were Toronto, Hamilton, Erie, Batavia, Rochester, and of course Buffalo. Scandinavians, Welsh, juveniles, and "old folks" each had their own day. So did insurance agents, Spanish-American War veterans, New England grocers, nurses, hotel men, electrical contractors, and mining engineers. Often multiple groups were honored on the same day. October 10, for example, was Dunkirk Day, Delaware Day, and National Paint, Oil and Varnish Association Day.[1]

Next to President's Day, the most significant special date was Midway Day, held on August 3. A very profitable day for the Pan-Am, it also highlighted the differing philosophies between the Midway men and Exposition officials concerning the purposes of the fair and how to promote it. The board had a publicity bureau that eventually boasted a hundred employees. They worked with the railroads to produce travel folders advertising the fair, placed brochures in hotels, and visited every large town in the United States within 150 miles of Buffalo. Their printed matter ended up in 19,854 publications. They even engaged Charles Stow, who had prepared advertising for P. T. Barnum's circus, to design banners which were displayed in major cities.[2]

The showmen did not think the Exposition's efforts were particularly effective, and as their day approached they determined to give Exposition officials a lesson in publicity. Frederic Thompson took the lead, explaining, "An exposition is not, nor should it be, a serious thing. Amusement should predominate. It should be billed like a circus." Thompson and his fellow denizens of the Midway met on July 21 and designed a poster informing the public of "the many millions of marvelous, merry, mystifying, thrilling, scenic, spectacular features" of their planned special day. The concessionaires promised a day of pure mirth, assuring potential visitors that "even the organ in the Temple of Music will forget the symphonies and rhapsodies of the masters and tear loose with the popular jingle." Fast presses in five cities immediately went to work churning out the alluring posters. On July 26 some twenty wagons departed Buffalo, and the *Commercial* predicted that "the fence or barn within [50 miles] without a poster will be a rarity." Three days later "the most beautiful girls from the different shows and bally-hoos" left to visit surrounding cities and to pin ribbons promoting Midway Day "into the buttonholes of everyone whom they meet."[3]

The effort paid off. Midway Day resulted in an attendance of 106,315, the largest since Dedication Day, when just 102,000 went through the turnstiles. The festivities began with a parade, which got under way at 10:30 and lasted over an hour. The *Buffalo Commercial* described it thusly:

> Nothing like it was ever seen in Buffalo before, and in all probability nothing like it will ever be seen again. White men and black men, yellow men and red men, men from all corners of the globe, attired in native costume and carrying native implements of war or peace, marching to their own tongue—gaily dressed women from the East and West, the North and the South—wild animals from the jungles of India and Africa, the white plains of the far North and the wildernesses of the Americas.[4]

The Carlisle Indian band provided music, as did groups from several Midway attractions. The Indian Congress had representatives of 42 nations, "in an extra coat of paint and all the feathers and ornaments they could lay hands on." Both Geronimo and Calamity Jane were on hand. Frank Bostock paraded his lions, bears, and baby elephants. Fair Japan offered Geisha girls, "attired in fanciful but neat and dainty Japanese costumes," along with acrobats, tumblers, and other performers. The Hawaiian Village float featured guitar players and troubadours "singing soft Hawaiian airs." The Old Plantation entered the aforementioned watermelon themed float that so amused the *Buffalo Commercial* reporter.[5]

For the rest of the day the Exposition grounds went from the cultural to the colossal. The canal, normally the scene of tranquil gondola rides, became the venue for swim meets and a canoe race featuring "an Eskimo, a Filipino, an Indian, one of the gondoliers from Venice, and one of the Hawaiians." The First Nations native from the far North won. At the Stadium athletic events gave way to a "grand circus," a spectacle that opened with the release of several thousand homing pigeons. There were horse and camel races and exhibitions of trick riding and lasso throwing. A balloon went up, and a parachutist jumped out. Even the Electric Tower, the serious centerpiece of the Exposition, was not immune to the fun. Matt Gay, a high diving performer leapt from a platform installed at the 118-foot level into the canal, but only after a work crew had deepened that section of the waterway. A Senor Cameroni slid down a rope—by his teeth—from near the top of the structure, alighting in the Stadium. Human cannonballs, a wedding ceremony in a hot-air balloon, and a greased pole contest, with the pole suspended over the lake and a ham as the prize, rounded out an unforgettable, and very profitable, day.[6]

At least one Exposition official was convinced. John Scatchard told the *Buffalo Courier*, "There has been enough periodical advertising. Intelligent thinking people have had their fill of descriptions, if they took the time to read all the papers and periodicals. What is necessary now is to reach the class that attends an exposition for the fun and amusement there is in it. And this subject will be taken up immediately." Nothing came of it. The Midway men offered a number of suggestions—host a children's day, have a different special day with unique features every day, hold a week-long Pan-American carnival fashioned after the Mardi Gras. All the talk was for naught. Despite Scatchard's conversion and bold promise of action, the staid board of directors appears never to have given the showmen's suggestions serious considera-tion.[7]

They should have. Disappointing attendance figures were already forcing Buchanan and the board into difficult decisions. It was not entirely their fault. May and June of 1901 were the wettest Buffalo had experienced for seven years, and June was the coldest in the thirty years that records had been kept. Those statistics, along with unfinished displays much of that time, contributed to a daily attendance that averaged under 11,000 during the first two months of the Exposition. July and August saw the figures improve, but the damage had been done. In early August a committee appointed by the board to cut expenses recommended "discharging" 38 employees in various departments and "reducing staffs in various offices in unknown numbers." They also called for the closing of several offices in Ellicott Square, moving some to the Service Building, and the "reduction of some salaries." Although the board did not make public the total number of jobs cut, the *Buffalo Commercial* reported that "about 300 employees" were let go. In his final report Buchanan wrote that the number of Exposition employees went from a high of 2,742 persons in May 1901 to 1,521 in September, although the completion of construction projects had much to do with the decline.[8]

On September 23 the board learned that construction indebtedness exceeded half a million dollars. They voted to pay thirty percent to each com-pany. Meanwhile the board played rough with two Midway shows that owed them money. The Johnstown Flood owed the Exposition Company eight hun-dred dollars, and the War Cyclorama was short $160. Their power was cut off until they paid. Buchanan asked the executive committee to reconsider its decision to lease no more space in Exposition buildings for selling concessions. He wrote, "I beg to respectfully present my belief to your committee that in view of the financial condition of the Exposition ... that it might be the wish of your committee to ... authorize this office to dispose of such space as in my judgment might be compatible with the interests of the Exposition." The committee agreed, as did the board, and contracts were soon let to sell Oriental rugs, turquoise jewelry, ladies' hat fasteners, and numerous other products.[9]

One of the unsung heroes of the financial crisis was Henry M. Nicholls, an assistant to Exposition treasurer George Williams. Nicholls salvaged some $100,000 in Pan-Am funds and in the process prevented a precedent that could have closed the fair. Recalling the events half a century later, Nicholls was unsure of the exact date; but the board had just learned of its construction debts, so it was likely late September. In any event, one of the Exposition's special days was expected to result in a large gate.

Most contractors were willing to give the company a little extra time, but two of them were somewhat less patient. They sued the Exposition Company and secured a judgment. The Erie County sheriff planned to send deputies to seize the 3:00 p.m. gate receipts on the big day, a fact that Nicholls was somehow made aware of. The company, he knew, could sustain the loss, but it could not have survived the wave of suits that would have been sure to follow. In all likelihood the fair would be forced to close. Realizing this, Nicholls contacted Col. John Byrne, commandant of the Exposition police, who agreed to send a lieutenant and a squad of police to each gate to escort the ticket sellers to the Service Building. Aware that a levy could not legally be made on something contained on one's person, Nicholls instructed the ticket sellers to place the receipts in a parcel and put it in their pockets. The deputies also knew the law, and they made no attempt to interfere with the three o'clock deposit.

Nicholls had taken the first trick, but the sheriff took the next one. The American Express and Wells Fargo Express companies were engaged to collect and become the custodians of the daily receipts. An armored car was scheduled to arrive at six. It didn't, and when Nicholls called to find out why, he was informed that the sheriff had warned the companies not to accept Exposition funds. As the assistant treasurer pondered his dilemma, the 9:00 p.m. receipts also came in. Meanwhile he learned that the bank with which the Exposition was dealing would not take the money until morning. Desperate, Nicholls called Williams to seek guidance. "If you can get the receipts down here," the treasurer offered, "you can put them in the vault in my basement."

This led to a brainstorming session in the Service Building and eventually to a plan. The hospital was next door, and Nicholls and associates decided to borrow its ambulance. Two staff members sneaked over to secure the driver's cooperation, which he willingly offered. The funds were gathered and taken to a back office opposite the ambulance garage. Nicholls and the other staffers formed a line, passing the money bags one by one, like a bucket brigade, and loading them in the vehicle. Then the men jumped in atop the bags, the garage door flew open, and the ambulance sped through the Exposition grounds and out onto Delaware Avenue. They made it safely to the Williams home and deposited the money. A few days later, smarting from adverse publicity over their actions, the two contractors withdrew their suits.[10]

The Exposition was a relatively safe place to visit. Major crimes were rare, but minor thievery was not. Of the 351 arrests made by Pan-Am police, 79 were for petty larceny, followed by disorderly conduct (72), fence jumping (65), intoxication (27), and "suspicious persons" (25). Among those arrested, 134 were discharged and 89 were ejected from the grounds. Only six were imprisoned; and of course one was sentenced to death for murder.[11]

Pickpockets were responsible for many of the thefts. A number of visitors reported stolen purses, cash, and stick pins. Items displayed in various buildings also went missing, often overnight. A favorite target was foodstuffs. During the early weeks of the fair, fruit frequently disappeared from the Horticulture Building. In the Agriculture Building thieves made off with a variety of items. The New York display lost potatoes, cucumbers, corn, and other vegetables. Sixty cans of salmon were taken from a Canadian booth, and representatives of the Overholt Whiskey Company reported two or three empty bottles several mornings. The Farrar Cigar Company lost between thirty and forty rare and expensive stogies one night. In the Manufactures and Liberal Arts the losses included fifty cakes of toilet soap, fifty packages of Kato Coffee, and several bottles of Mohican Mineral Water. The stealing was not limited to the indoors. Thieves broke into several nut vending machines on the Esplanade and the Midway.[12]

Some of the most serious thefts occurred in the Government Building. On the evening of August 17 detectives arrested a man after witnesses saw him remove the micrometer from a $700 theodolite, a surveying instrument. The suspect, M. W. Monahan, claimed to be a surgeon from Atlanta. Detectives searched him and found five valuable lady's rings, a steel saw, several duplicate keys, $280 in cash, and a bottle of chloroform. Subsequent investigation revealed that Monahan was indeed a doctor, "one of the leading physicians in the city" and head of Atlanta's Homeopathic School of Medicine. He told detectives that he was in the habit of taking chloroform and likely stole the micrometer while under its influence. The good doctor agreed to pay the cost of repairing the theodolite. That satisfied the United States district attorney and Buffalo's police court judge. As for the rings and other items, no questions appear to have been asked. As for Dr. Monahan, he announced plans for "an extended trip through the West."[13]

Sometime during the night of July 3–4 thieves made off with four sheets of stamps, valued at between three and four thousand dollars, from the Government Building. The same stamps had been stolen at the Paris Exposition, but they were later recovered and the thief arrested. The government was not so lucky this time. An investigation revealed numerous problems with the guard force in the Government Building, who were frequently asleep on duty. Two were fired and one suspended for a week following the incident. The charge of sleeping guards was confirmed by Theodore Sheldon, a gossipy Government Building guard and diarist, who recorded such an incident on September 25. He also noted that on at least two occasions one Colonel Peabody sneaked in a lady and spent the night with her in the State Department section.[14]

Perhaps the youngest Exposition thieves were the three teenagers and 22-year old arrested on August 23. They were popcorn vendors, two working at the headquarters of the concessionaire, two working in the small wagons that distributed the product in numbered bags. The latter two persuaded the former pair to steal a quantity of the bags and sell them to them for a penny apiece. The boys on the wagons then sold them for a nickel, pocketing a four-cent profit. Exposition police believed the youthful crooks cleared about five hundred dollars before they were caught. They might have made much more, but they attempted to enlist a fifth cohort, who promptly reported them.[15]

Occasionally Exposition officers found themselves under arrest. The Pan-Am cops were a diverse lot. Only three of the men hired were police officers, although 57 were listed as soldiers. Another 57 were clerks, 41 were students, and 26 were farmers. Also included were 21 salesmen, eight painters, five electricians, two butchers, a baker, a barber, a "base-ball" player, a druggist, a decorator, an upholsterer, and an undertaker. They were charged 59 times with neglect of duty, 32 times with conduct unbecoming an officer, ten time with sleeping on duty, and six times with intoxication. Fifty ended up being dismissed from the force, and fifteen resigned while facing charges.[16]

On July 13 a former Exposition officer, previously suspended for absence without leave, found himself under arrest, charged with stealing a diamond ring from a concessionaire. The ticket from a Rochester pawn shop was found in his possession. Another Pan-Am cop was arrested on August 4 and charged with stealing a can of preserved meat from a booth in the Manufactures and

Liberal Arts Building. The theft occurred on a Sunday, when only guards and exhibitors were permitted in the building. Detectives caught him in the act.[17]

Buffalo's city police were not entirely above suspicion either. On July 15 the *Courier* reported that members of the municipal force were on the payroll of various boarding houses. According to the newspaper, they were receiving kickbacks from "inferior rooming hotels" to steer visitors in their direction. Fair visitors would naturally ask the men in blue to direct them to reputable hostelries near the Exposition grounds. Instead the cops were sending them to inferior establishments, many a great distance away from the grounds.[18]

Of course none of this mattered to a pair of visitors destined for Buffalo. One was Leon Czolgosz, who would first find quarters outside the city. The other was William McKinley, who would have no trouble securing lodging.

19

Czolgosz:
Two Trips to Buffalo

Leon Czolgosz made two trips to Buffalo during the summer of 1901. It is not clear what attracted him to the city, although cheap rail fares offered in conjunction with the Exposition may have been a motivating factor. He arrived the first time in July. On either July 16 or 17 he uncharacteristically struck up a conversation with a young man waiting for a street car. Czolgosz asked the man where he lived, and he replied that he boarded in the country near the community of West Seneca with Antoine Kazmarek. The two stopped at a saloon for a glass of beer before heading for West Seneca.

Czolgosz, still using the name Fred C. Nieman, made arrangements with Mrs. Kazmarek to provide him with a room and do his washing for three dollars a month. The only catch was that the new boarder would have to share his bed with either his newly found friend or with one of the Kazmarek children. Czolgosz's personal habits had not changed. He subsisted on milk, crackers, and cake and refused to eat with the other occupants of the house. The front room had once served as a store, and he took his meals there, eating by himself at the counter. Kazmarek later said his solitary roomer usually arose before seven, washed very carefully, dressed neatly, and stood before a mirror for a minute or two before going out. On days he spent at West Seneca, Czolgosz sometimes took a walk in the morning but spent most of his time on the piazza, tipped back on a chair, reading pamphlets and newspapers. He paid one of the children to fetch him a newspaper, which he "read very carefully." Three or four days a week he left early for Buffalo, returning between 9:30 and 10:30 at night. Asked why he went to the city so often, Czolgosz simply replied, "To attend some meetings."[1]

Czolgosz largely kept to himself, avoiding conversation to the extent possible in the crowded house. When drawn into talk, he would steer the discussion away from himself. For example, he would ask Antoine about his work as a section hand on the Lake Shore Railroad, a topic that was likely of little interest to him. Once Kazmarek asked his tenant how he got along without a job. He responded dishonestly, claiming he worked during the winter months and lived off his earnings during the summer.

One morning in late August Kazmarek came downstairs at seven o'clock to find Czolgosz arranging his clothes in front of the mirror. His bag was packed, and he announced that he was leaving. When Antoine asked where he was going, Czolgosz's reply was typically cryptic. "Maybe Detroit, Toledo, Cleveland, or Baltimore, maybe Pittsburgh," he answered. Kazmarek did notice that Czolgosz was in "fairly good spirits for him." When Mrs. Kazmarek asked their departing boarder to settle up his remaining debt, which totaled $1.75, he said he could not pay. Instead, Czolgosz left behind a revolver, which the couple later discovered did not work.[2]

He ended up taking a steamer to Cleveland for what proved to be a very brief visit. Czolgosz later said that he returned to the Ohio city to "look around and buy a paper." He also apparently secured funds from an unknown source, because when he returned to Buffalo witnesses saw him flash an impressive bankroll. Some have since speculated that he may have received the final installment on his share of the family farm, but his siblings and his parents would later insist that they never again saw Leon after he left home.[3]

Czolgosz was back in Buffalo on August 31. He entered John Nowak's saloon on Broadway, which contained six rooms for boarders, and said he would like a room and wished to have his washing done. Nowak informed him that the rate was two dollars a week and asked what name he should write on the receipt. "John Doe," the stranger replied. This, of course, raised a red flag with the proprietor. Still, his prospective tenant was well dressed and came across as "a fair sort of man." To be safe, Nowak asked him for a reference. "Oh, Dalkowski of Toledo told me to come here," he responded. "You know, he left last night." Mr. Dalkowski had indeed left the previous night. A postal employee from Toledo, he was a frequent boarder, staying with the Nowaks when he was in Buffalo to attend "singing conventions." Later, at the request of the police, Nowak wrote Dalkowski, who denied knowing anybody by the name of Nieman or Czolgosz.[4]

Frank Walkowiak, a law student who worked for Nowak, was immediately suspicious of Czolgosz—or so he would later insist. As he led the new tenant to his room, Walkowiak asked, "What made you say John Doe?" Czolgosz answered, "Well, I'll tell you, I'm a Polish Jew and I didn't like to tell him or he wouldn't keep me in the house." When Walkowiak asked his real name, Czolgosz once again resorted to Fred Nieman. Continuing his impromptu examination, Walkowiak asked him what he was going to do in Buffalo. "I'm going to sell souvenirs," Czolgosz replied. Walkowiak continued to harbor suspicions, but Nowak wasn't interested. When his young clerk/bartender/bellhop raised concerns, the owner simply replied, "He pays his bills, doesn't he?"[5]

Indeed, despite a bogus reference and a vague background, Czolgosz proved to be a model boarder. Nowak recalled that he never drank to excess, or even came close, and that when he had whiskey at the bar, it was never the cheap five-cent-a-glass rotgut. In fact, at the time, the landlord was "quite proud" to rent to "so young a man who was so temperate." Czolgosz left most mornings at seven and returned at about 10:30 p.m. In coming and going he seldom spoke to anyone, and never without being spoken to first. If he did not go out, Czolgosz remained sequestered in his room. He never ate in the saloon. The Nowaks concluded that he was "too proud" to be associated with them. By his neat manner of dressing, they felt he must be a waiter or a barber, perhaps even a writer. The couple had first assumed that he was a visitor to the fair, but his regular hours suggested otherwise.[6]

Only once did Czolgosz deviate from his usual schedule. It was on a Sunday evening, and he returned early to the saloon. A picnic was going on, and the business was crowded. Czolgosz sat at a table, listening to one of the conversations. When the talk turned to religion, one of the picknickers observed that he did not believe much in priests. "If you have got any money," he said, "it is all right with them. If you haven't, they have no use for you." After taking in a bit more of the conversation, Czolgosz said he had attended services at St. Casimir Church recently and all the priest talked about was money.[7]

A few people in the neighborhood later recalled encounters with Czolgosz. One was John Romantowski, who said he had engaged the visitor in conversation one day while out for a walk. As Romantowski remembered it, Czolgosz suggested that they go to a nearby saloon for a beer. While there the visitor flashed a roll of bills that included a fifty and proposed a future excursion to Niagara Falls, a trip that never materialized. Another was Joseph Rutkowski, a barber who gave Czolgosz a shave. He described his customer as "very quiet," adding that he "was always sober and spoke intelligently." On one occasion Czolgosz asked Rutkowski about socialists in Buffalo, quickly adding that he did not believe in socialism himself.[8]

As Czolgosz roamed the streets of Buffalo, Emma Goldman was enjoying a sojourn to Rochester. Oppressive summer heat had led to the cancellation of her latest speaking tour, prompting her to visit her sister and other relatives. Rather than stirring up audiences, "Red Emma" went on picnics with her nephews and engaged in friendly debates with one of the boys, a devout McKinley Republican. Through the generosity of a Buffalo friend, Goldman was able to spend a week in the city, taking in Niagara Falls and the Pan-American. Police and reporters would later attempt to connect her with Czolgosz in Buffalo, but no evidence was ever uncovered. Indeed, there was nothing to contradict Goldman's later claim that her time in western New York was no more than "a new and exhilarating experience, to which I completely abandoned myself." The only thing which "somewhat marred" Goldman's holiday was the "warning against Nieman" in *Free Society*, which she was able to get retracted.[9]

On September 3 Czolgosz visited the Walbridge Company's Main Street hardware store. He purchased a nickel-plated, six-shot, .32-caliber Iver Johnson revolver, the same weapon Bresci had used to assassinate Italy's King Umberto I. It was small enough to be easily concealed, and Iver Johnson had a reputation for quality. The weapon cost $4.50. Czolgosz also bought a box of cartridges.[10]

William McKinley was due to arrive in town the next day.

McKinley:
Sojourn to Buffalo

At 5:55 p.m. on September 4, 1901, the Lake Shore train bearing President McKinley and his party pulled into Buffalo's Central Station. Exposition President Milburn was already on the train, having boarded with Mayor Diehl and other officials at Dunkirk, some fifty miles down the tracks. As crowds cheered and whistles from lake steamers and factories shrieked, William Buchanan clambered aboard the presidential train. The director general was likely relieved that, after spring's setback, President's Day was about to become a reality. He was also hopeful that McKinley's appearance at the fair would swell attendance numbers and Exposition coffers. In an attempt to do so, Buchanan had approved promotional flyers well into six figures and advertisements in over 800 newspapers.[1]

Ida had borne the trip well. According to the *Buffalo Express*, "Mrs. McKinley was bright and cheery and was interested in a first glimpse of the Rainbow City." Although its language was more restrained, the *Buffalo Courier* reported, "Mrs. McKinley was not more fatigued than was expected." Following a good night's rest, the newspaper predicted, "she would be able to take part in the [next day's] programme."[2]

Then came an incident that not only shattered the first lady's nerves, but a good bit of glass as well. The train pulled out of the station, headed for the Exposition grounds. A short distance down the tracks were three large cannons from the seacoast artillery. The intent was to fire a 21-shot salute in honor of the president. Unfortunately the guns had been placed far too close to the tracks, and as the train reached the spot, a booming report shattered all seven windows on the right side of the first car. Only two people occupied that coach, a reporter for the *Buffalo Courier* and an official of the Lake Shore Line. The blast knocked both down, but there were no injuries.

The engineer quickly brought the train to a stop. Meanwhile Thomas J. Lightfoot, a member of the White House staff, rushed through the train shouting, "Where is Dr. Rixey?" The Navy physician was quickly located. "The terrific concussion of the firing had distressed Mrs. McKinley greatly," the *Courier* man reported. "She was temporarily prostrated by the noise." Cortelyou rushed to the rear platform and motioned to the commanding officer to cease fire. The officer apparently took it as a signal to continue, and all 21 rounds were fired. Nevertheless there was no further damage, and thanks to her husband's soothing presence and Dr. Rixey's "restoratives," Ida quickly regained her composure. There was some talk of an investigation, but the realization that McKinley would likely balk at the idea of punishing anyone for the mistake ended the discussion. The president dismissed the incident with a smile and the observation, "They had more powder than they thought."[3]

The train continued on to the Exposition grounds, where a growing crowd filled the area from the Propylaea to the Esplanade. People seeking a better vantage point climbed posts, benches, and statues. It took two platoons of Exposition police, but a path was cleared through the middle of the throng so the carriages that would deliver the prominent party into the grounds would be unobstructed.

At about 6:30 the special train came to a stop at the north end Exposition station. After Milburn, chairman Scatchard of the executive committee, and a nurse alighted, the president stepped off the train. He waved to the crowd with both hands then turned to lift Ida down to the platform. An Exposition roller chair was waiting for her, but Mrs. McKinley refused it, preferring to walk to her carriage.

The tour of the grounds was a quick one. The procession never stopped. Upon leaving the Exposition, the carriages continued straight to Milburn's Delaware Avenue home, where the McKinleys would stay for the duration of their visit. Following dinner, which wrapped up at about 9:30, the president met with the Exposition's committee on ceremonies, going over the schedule of events for the next two days.[4]

That schedule was printed in detail the next day in the city's newspapers. It was also included in the Exposition's daily program. That published itinerary called for the president to "leave the house of Hon. John G. Milburn, No. 1168 Delaware Avenue," at ten the next morning. Before departing McKinley took a short walk around the grounds. He carried with him the speech he was to deliver that day, stopping from time to time to jot down a new word or phrase. "I never have overcome the nervousness that comes over me before making a speech," he remarked.[5]

At 10:00 a.m., as published, the doors of the Milburn home opened for the president, the first lady, and the Exposition president. McKinley supported his wife as the trio walked to the waiting carriage. Thousands, some climbing trees and roofs, lined Delaware Avenue as the presidential carriage and those that followed, bearing government and Exposition officials, headed toward the grounds at a trot. Upon reaching the Lincoln Parkway gate, the president was greeted by yet another battery of artillery ready to salute him. This one did no harm.[6]

The party proceeded to a specially constructed platform at the Esplanade. It was at once gaudy and impressive, purple in color and capable of seating over 500 VIPs, the handiwork of Newcomb Carlton. As the party approached two thousand infantrymen snapped to attention, and martial music pierced the air. As the presidential carriage halted, so did the patriotic serenade. Once again William McKinley helped his wife out of the carriage. The two spoke briefly before parting. Then, at 10:39, John Milburn offered perhaps the briefest introduction in the history of executive speechmaking: "Ladies and gentlemen, the president."[7]

McKinley began innocuously, telling the crowd how nice it was to be back in Buffalo. He then turned to the event that had brought him there.

President McKinley extols the virtues of reciprocity during his Exposition speech as reporters listen and take notes (Library of Congress).

"Expositions," he intoned, in a line often cited, "are the timekeepers of progress. They record the world's advancement." Buchanan and Milburn must have been pleased when he added, "The Pan-American Exposition has done its work thoroughly, presenting in its exhibits evidences of the highest skill and illustrating the progress of the human family in the western hemisphere."[8]

Soon the president got down to business. The original plan had been to use his California trip as a springboard for discussing reciprocity, letting his rhetoric on the issue rise to a crescendo at Buffalo. Events had denied him his prelude, but McKinley would still bring the subject to *forte*, if not *fortissimo*. "My fellow citizens," he said, "trade statistics indicate that this country is in a state of unexampled prosperity." In a statement that likely shocked many of his fellow Gilded Age Republicans and the businessmen that supported them, he added, "The figures are almost appalling." But the president was not calling for policies that would short-circuit prosperity. Rather, the challenge was to maintain it in an ever-shrinking, increasingly interdependent world. "Our capacity to produce," he explained, "has developed so enormously and our products have so multiplied that the problem of more markets requires our urgent and immediate attention. Only a broad and enlightened policy will keep what we have." Put simply, McKinley asserted, "Isolation is no longer possible or desirable." After again praising the work of the Exposition, he concluded, "Our earnest prayer is that God will graciously vouchsafe prosperity, happiness and peace to all our neighbors, and like blessings to all the peoples and powers of the earth."[9]

Upon concluding his address, McKinley turned immediately to Ida, who, "with the applause still resounding," smiled and nodded. Her husband and Dr. Rixey helped the first lady up and escorted her to her carriage. Mrs. McKinley returned to the Milburn home to rest. "She was not seized with sudden weaknesses," the *Express* reassured its readers, "but simply was following the dictates of prudence in not overtaxing her strength by endeavoring to accompany the President through the trying ceremonies at the Stadium."[10]

Those ceremonies included a review of over two thousand members of the armed forces, under the command of Gen. Samuel M. Welch. Infantry, artillery, signal corps, and Marines were all represented. The Marine Band provided music. Welch put his men through "a brief manual of arms" before the commander-in-chief inspected the troops.[11]

The president then shifted to his role as chief diplomat, visiting the buildings of Canada, Honduras, Chile, Mexico, the Dominican Republic, and two new American possessions, Cuba and Puerto Rico. He also stopped at the Agriculture Building, where many foreign countries had displays. He did not remain long in any building, five minutes being typical. He was in the Dominican Republic Building long enough to be served coffee. In the Cuban Building McKinley and his entourage received cigars. While visiting the Agriculture Building the president took just a cursory look at most displays. However, when he spotted the Puerto Rican display he bolted ahead of his party and stepped in for a careful examination. "I am glad to see this," he said.[12]

A luncheon at the stately New York Building followed, an affair which included 210 invited guests. Among them were five cabinet members, six Supreme Court justices, three U.S. senators, and numerous foreign diplomats. Breast of spring turkey, farcie, brown sweet potatoes, and asparagus francaise composed the main course, and Old English Sherry, 1878, was likely a popular feature. Following a reception at the Government Building and a tour of its displays, McKinley returned to the Milburn home, arriving at 4:35. Dinner was served before six because the president's day at the fair was not over.

Shortly after 7:00 p.m. the presidential carriage again entered the Exposition grounds. This time the president and the first lady were to be treated to the nightly illumination of the buildings. At 7:30, late dusk that September 5, the rheostat began to do its work, and a faint orange glow became visible. Gradually the lights came up. "Richer and brighter," the *Express* waxed, "it rose into a steady shine of beauty, beyond the glories of the gems of earth." Then a fuse blew, and the Ethnology Building went dark. "That will break Rustin's heart," Milburn told McKinley. "It always is on such occasions that accidents happen," the understanding president replied. The problem was quickly corrected, and soon Ethnology was again resplendent.[13]

After the first couple had a few minutes to take in the scene, they headed to the Park Lake and boarded a surfboat, one of a fleet that took the various dignitaries to the life-saving station. From there they would be treated to Pain's fireworks show, featuring a set-piece portrait of the guest of honor. *En route* the 74th Regiment band serenaded them from a floating platform. After the show was over and the McKinleys were leaving the grounds, Ida turned to take a final look at the Rainbow City. "Oh, it is beautiful," a reporter heard her say. The first couple's visit was also beautiful for Exposition officials. President's Day saw a paid attendance of 116,660, an Exposition record.[14]

September 6, William McKinley believed, was to be "the restful day" of his sojourn to Buffalo. The schedule included no speeches, no official duties, just a visit to Niagara Falls, a longtime desire of the first couple, and the public reception at the Temple of Music. The latter, which involved meeting the people, was the sort of thing the president genuinely enjoyed. "Everyone in that line has a smile and a cheery word," he had explained to Henry Stoddard. "They bring no problems with them; only good will. I feel better after that contact. It is the visitor to the Cabinet room pressing some policy or seeking some office who tires."[15]

At about 8:30 a carriage bearing the McKinleys, John Milburn, and presidential niece Mary Barber departed from the Milburn home. Other members of the presidential party followed. At the Exposition depot some one hundred diplomats, Exposition officials, and assorted big shots joined them. Also waiting were four large Pullmans, courtesy the New York Central, which would deliver their passengers to Lewiston, some five miles north of Niagara Falls. From there they would transfer to the cars of the Great Gorge Route, an electric trolley line, which would take them along the banks of the Niagara to the falls.[16]

The train arrived at Lewiston shortly after ten. There the party encountered a delay. A misunderstanding had arisen over where the New York Central train was to arrive. As a result the Great Gorge Route cars had to be pushed down the tracks to meet the train. Nobody was aware of this when the presidential party arrived; and the McKinleys had already stepped down from the car before the mistake was discovered. Chairman Scatcherd rushed to locate a chair for Ida, and the president opened his wife's black silk parasol to shield her from the intense sun. Meanwhile a phalanx of detectives surrounded the McKinleys. Scatcherd did double duty. Joined by George Urban, Jr., an Exposition director, he pushed the cars down the tracks and into position. Railroad employees and one of the detectives got the other three into place.

Gliding south to the falls, the four trolley cars passed the Whirlpool, numerous rapids, and stretches of tranquil waters. The president and the first lady were, of course, in the lead car, "an observation car with open sides and big easy chairs." The other three followed at 300-foot intervals. As their trolley descended into the Niagara gorge, the grade became frighteningly steep, so much that McKinley feared his wife might panic. She assured him that she was "greatly enjoying" the spectacular view. At that point, according to one witness, "His eyes lighted with satisfaction."[17]

The president and his party were greeted at the city of Niagara Falls by the mayor and a mounted military escort. Carriages were waiting to take them through town to the falls. The short journey led to an executive decision. During his California trip, McKinley had declined to take a single step onto the international bridge at El Paso. But here the suspension bridge to Canada offered the best views of both the American and the Canadian Horseshoe Falls. This time the presidential carriage ventured onto the span, turning around about ten feet shy of the midpoint.

The morning's activities both delighted and fatigued Ida. Before continuing on with the day's itinerary the president first took his wife to the International Hotel—aptly named considering the coterie of diplomats that would soon be visiting—where a quiet room awaited. The tourist-in-chief then rejoined the party for an excursion to Goat Island. There, despite his formal attire, McKinley clambered over the rocks. Following a luncheon at the hotel, the president delivered the first lady and Mrs. Buchanan to the train. He and the rest of the assembly then toured the Niagara Falls power house. After viewing the switchboard, they inspected the dynamos, then rode the elevator 145 feet down to the bottom of the wheelpit, "where the waters rush and roar." Upon departing, McKinley told William Rankine, "This is a great and marvelous work."[18]

It was 2:55 when the president boarded the train that was to return him to the Exposition. Ida, still feeling the strain of an eventful morning, decided not to accompany her husband to the afternoon public reception. It was a fortuitous decision.

That reception, the one Cortelyou had so dreaded, was to take place in the gaudy, cavernous Temple of Music. Louis Babcock, marshal of the Pan-

The Exposition's Temple of Music (Library of Congress).

Am, had spent the day supervising the gang of laborers that was getting the facility ready for the presidential reception. They first removed the chairs from the main floor, creating an aisle twelve to fifteen feet wide starting at the east doors. Midway in the building the aisle turned toward the south doors. The president was to be stationed at that point. There Babcock's workers erected a stand and draped a large American flag, so McKinley could not be seen from behind. Palms and two bay trees were also part of the background.

When the work was finished Babcock and James L. Quackenbush, a Buffalo lawyer, had a late lunch at a restaurant near the esplanade. Over sandwiches and "a glass of imported Pilsner beer," the two men discussed the impending reception. As they did, Quackenbush quipped that it "would be Roosevelt's luck" to have someone shoot the president that afternoon. At that point the reception was less than one hour away.[19]

21

Convergence:
Assassination

A minute or two before 4:00 p.m. on September 6 the presidential carriage arrived at the Temple of Music. After returning from Niagara Falls McKinley had paid a brief visit to the Exposition's Mission Building. There he viewed various displays, was serenaded by a quartet from the Streets of Mexico, and enjoyed some light refreshment and a cigar. When a Pan-Am official said, "I'm glad to see you back in Buffalo," McKinley joked, "Yes, I don't know whether I will ever get away."[1]

Louis Babcock was waiting at the Temple of Music to greet the president, now accompanied only by John Milburn and the ever-present George Cortelyou. The reception about to occur had been a source of consternation for the presidential secretary. Twice he had removed it from the official schedule, and twice McKinley had reinserted it. The second time, as Cortelyou later explained to Babcock, "the direction was well nigh imperative."[2]

Presidential security was a relatively new concept at the time, giving Cortelyou ample cause for concern. During his first term Grover Cleveland had requested two or three guards for his summer home in Massachusetts. The rash of death threats during the Spanish-American War prompted Cortelyou to ask for a quartet of Secret Service agents at the White House. This protection, however, was discontinued after the war. After that the Washington police force was responsible for presidential security, although the Secret Service assigned details for presidential trips.

At Buffalo George Foster, McKinley's usual bodyguard during his travels, was joined by a pair of agents, Samuel Ireland and Albert Gallaher. Additional security at the Temple seemed more than ample. The crowd, entering the building at the east door, would immediately be flanked by eighteen Exposition guards, nine on each side of the aisle. They would then encounter seven soldiers from the 73rd Seacoast Artillery and a number of Buffalo detectives. More detectives milled about close to the president. Agents Foster and Ireland stood opposite McKinley, with Gallaher closer to the south exit, through which the crowd would depart.[3]

Cortelyou stood to the president's right, Milburn to his left. This would enable the Exposition president to identify prominent local residents for McKinley. Agent Ireland later told some political and military officials that the positioning went against usual procedure. A reporter for the *Buffalo Courier* overheard the remarks, converting the comments into "an interview" with the agent. "It has been my practice to stand immediately at the President's left where I could see the right hand of those who approached him," he was quoted as saying. "Today, however, Mr. Cortelyou insisted that Mr. Milburn should have that place, and I was placed where I could not see the right hands of those who approached the President." The article earned Ireland a letter of reprimand from John E. Wilkie, head of the Secret Service, who termed the remark "a pitiful attempt to shift responsibility," one which would not have occurred had the agent "wisely heeded the general Rules and Regulations as to reticence."[4]

As he entered the Temple of Music, none of these details mattered to the president. The veteran politician immediately sized up the situation, walking straight to his position. Temple organist William Gomph began a Bach sonata, William McKinley said, "Let them come," and the east doors opened for the ten-minute reception. The time would be brief, but the president was sure to make the most of it. He had perfected "the McKinley grip," with which, it was said, he could shake fifty hands a minute. Grasping a person's hand, he quickly pulled it down, then sideways, almost pushing away the recipient. No one complained; the thrill of shaking hands with the president and the warmth of his smile dominated the moment.[5]

It was a warm day, and as the people in line entered the relatively cool building, it was natural that they would take out handkerchiefs to wipe the perspiration from their foreheads. As a result, Babcock would recall, "handkerchiefs were much in evidence." Leon Czolgosz had one, and he used it to conceal his recently purchased Iver Johnson revolver.[6]

At Cortelyou's insistence, the guards hurried along the crowd, which made it more difficult for those same guards to scrutinize the individuals. At the same time McKinley's hand shaking skills sped people on their way, creating occasional gaps in the vicinity of the chief executive. All of this played into Czolgosz's hands. The guards would have little time to size him up, and the likely open space in front of the intended victim would allow him freedom of movement. Even the individual standing in line immediately in front of Czolgosz inadvertently acted in the assassin's favor. Foster later described him as "a dark complexioned man with a black moustache." He looked enough like an Italian to send up an anarchist alarm in the agent's mind, and Foster later recalled that he had "taken [the] fellow past the President" because his "general appearance did not suit me." Police would later look for the man, without success, believing him to be a possible accomplice.[7]

Czolgosz, by contrast, aroused no suspicion, and Agent Ireland was bluntly honest about the reason why. The assassin, Ireland noted in his official report, "had a good, clear complexion," adding, "There was nothing suspicious in his countenance." A reporter overheard Ireland describe Czolgosz as possessing "a boyish, innocent looking face." He conceded that after first noticing Czolgosz his attention was "called to the man … who looked like an Italian."[8]

As Czolgosz approached the president, he had his right hand wrapped with a white handkerchief. He extended his left hand, and McKinley, with an "expression of sympathy" on his face, turned slightly to reach his right hand toward the young man's left. Suddenly Czolgosz pushed aside the president's outstretched arm with his left hand, raised his right hand, and fired two shots in rapid succession.[9]

At that point there was what one witness termed "a regular football scrimmage." The scene was confusing at the time, and it has confounded historians of the assassination ever since. Soldiers, Secret Service agents, and Exposition guards all rushed toward the assailant. So did one James Parker, a black waiter in one of the Pan-Am's restaurants. The Secret Service would later launch a monumental effort to discredit Parker and diminish his role, but overwhelming eyewitness testimony suggests otherwise.[10] (See Appendix.)

In the melee Foster shouted to Gallaher, "Get the gun, Al! Get the gun!" Gallaher tried to comply, but he was only able to secure Czolgosz's handkerchief, which he kept until the trial. Still smoldering from the gunfire, it burned his hand. Private Francis O'Brien of the Seacoast Artillery finally got the gun. Apparently he and others in the pile mistook the agent for the assassin or an accomplice. They choked and shoved him until Foster interceded. By then Czolgosz had been totally subdued. Foster realized this and gave instructions to stand him up. However, as they lifted him, Czolgosz "took a quick look back at the President … to see if he had done his work well." This enraged Foster, and he "smashed him right in the jaw."[11]

It was McKinley's words which eventually spared his assailant any further rough treatment. As soon as the shots were fired, Ireland related that evening, "I saw the President give Czolgosz a startled look which changed to one of contempt and draw his hand up against his breast." A reporter wrote, "At the first report the President shivered from heels to head, his shoulders leaped upward, his head flung backward, [and] his left hand clutched at his breast." De Witt Colegrove, who had been second in the receiving line, turned to see McKinley "with his hand slowly moving over and around his abdominal wound." Colegrove added, "I think he was looking to see if blood might be issuing."[12]

Buffalo detective John Geary caught the stricken president, and with the aid of Milburn and Cortelyou, assisted him to a chair. Watching Czolgosz take a pummeling, McKinley said either—eyewitnesses disagreed—"Don't let them hurt him," or, addressing the officers directly, "Go easy on him boys."[13]

His thoughts then turned to Ida. Here, too, witnesses did not agree as to the exact wording, but a preponderance remembered him telling Cortelyou something like, "I trust Mrs. McKinley will not be informed of this; at least I hope it will not be exaggerated."[14]

Exposition guards Homer James and James McCauley took the still unconscious Czolgosz to the office of Harry Henshaw, the Exposition's super-intendent of music, and placed him on a table. McCauley searched him, turning over to Agent Ireland $1.46 in coin, a letter from the Cleveland Knights of the Golden Eagle that certified his membership, and cards advertising a local hotel and a Turkish bath. The prisoner was still bleeding from Foster's blow. From time to time, after regaining consciousness, he put his sleeve to his lip, presumably removing blood. To any inquiries he remained totally silent.[15]

Meanwhile word of the shooting spread quickly around the Exposition grounds, and a lynch mob mentality grew just as quickly. Midway concessionaires were closing their shows, and the people turned away swelled the crowd forming around the Temple of Music. Soon it reached an estimated fifteen to twenty thousand. A resident of nearby Jamestown later related, "The crowd, men and women, cried 'Hang him!' 'Kill him,' and they were just wild with rage." Guard James recalled, "The crowd on the outside were crazy with anger. Oaths upon top of oaths rang through the air." More ominous were the faces pressed up against windows, awaiting any sign that the prisoner was about to be removed.[16]

"Only a leader was lacking to set the crowd in hostile motion," Louis Babcock later wrote, "and while there was sufficient force to hold the prisoner, many might have been killed or injured had the Temple been stormed." A call went out to the Service Building for all reserve Exposition police to report. A company of the Seacoast Artillery was also summoned. Meanwhile officials found some rope normally used to shut off sections of the Esplanade during military drills. As the reinforcing artillerymen, bayonets fixed, pushed back the crowd, police used the rope to clear a space in front of the south entrance.

At the same time the police parked a patrol wagon at the east entrance, diverting the crowd's attention.[17]

Everybody present realized the mood of the crowd was getting uglier and that their opportunity to get the prisoner safely away might soon vanish. They also felt the sight of a battered and bloody Czolgosz might incite the mob further, so they decided to clean him up first. Then a carriage pulled up, piloted by "a stockily-built little Irish driver," and James and McCauley escorted the prisoner outside. A reporter claimed Czolgosz was "almost as white as the President had been" following the shooting. Bartlett Sumner, a roller chair guide at the Exposition, had reached the scene a few minutes earlier, watching as the crowd pushed up against the line of soldiers stationed at the south entrance. Czolgosz struck him as "a young looking fellow." Despite the guards' efforts to make their prisoner presentable, Sumner added, "One could tell that there had been some sort of trouble for his face was red, almost purplish. Streaks of blood showed on the side of his face." James and McCauley virtually threw him into the wagon. At that point, Sumner observed, "The mob swayed forward and the men made a dive for the cab." An order for the artillerymen to "load rifles" and the subsequent click of breeches sent most of them back. Nevertheless, Agent Gallaher reported, "I was compelled to draw my gun to check the mob from the side of the carriage which I was protecting."[18]

Its human cargo secure, the carriage departed at full speed across the Esplanade toward the Triumphal Bridge. The mob followed, redoubling its cries of "Lynch him!" Soldiers ran alongside the vehicle as long as they could, using their weapons to trip anybody who got close. When the wagon reached the bridge its pursuers were only twenty feet behind. Thanks to Newcomb Carlton, that was as close as they would get. The director of works ran to a telephone and ordered that the Lincoln Park gate be thrown open then immediately closed as soon as the carriage passed through. This was done, leaving the mob to mill about the Exposition grounds.[19]

Carlton's quick thinking may have hemmed in one mob, but another soon formed around police headquarters. William S. Bull, Buffalo's superintendent of police, was ready for them. As soon as he received word of the shooting, at about 4:20, Bull ordered out reserves of officers, both mounted and on foot. He had the building roped off and dispatched officers to patrol a two-block perimeter surrounding the building. The precautions paid off. Twice the crowd attempted to storm the jail, their leaders holding a section of rope for a lynching on one occasion, but the officers on horseback had little difficulty in dispersing them.[20]

When the wagon delivered Czolgosz to police headquarters, it was a

The Exposition's Triumphal Bridge on President's Day (Library of Congress).

New York City cop who took charge of the prisoner. James Vallely was a sergeant of detectives in the Big Apple but had been put in charge of the detective bureau at the Exposition. He conducted Czolgosz to a cell, sat down with him on a cot, and asked if he smoked. When his prisoner replied, "Yes, sir," Vallely produced two cigars, lit them both, and joined him in a smoke. The two chatted briefly. Czolgosz once again identified himself as Fred Nieman and claimed to be a blacksmith. Asked why he shot the president, he replied, "I only done my duty." When the detective asked if he was an anarchist, Czolgosz said, "Yes, sir."[21]

After his short conversation with Vallely, the prisoner, Bull recalled, was "not disposed to talk until he was given something to eat." The officers obliged him, and Czolgosz ate everything they brought. After that he "seemed more pleasant and willing to talk." As always he was concerned with his personal appearance, asking to be allowed to wash up and get some clean clothes. At first the police denied this request, but when Czolgosz produced some money, they dispatched a guard to get the change of clothing. When it arrived the prisoner disputed the amount of change he got back. The police gave him the price of each item, to which he replied, "Oh, that's right. Let it go."[22]

The interrogation took place in Bull's office. Assistant District Attorney Frederick Haller began the questioning. Sometime between ten and eleven Haller's boss, D. A. Thomas Penney, who had been taking measurements and questioning witnesses at the crime scene, showed up and took charge. James L. Quackenbush, a local attorney who had been at the Temple when the shooting occurred, accompanied him.

"The prisoner was at all times cool and collected," Bull would write, "showing no indication of feelings of remorse for the crime he had committed." Asked if he comprehended the enormity of his crime, Czolgosz said he did but added that people sometimes escaped being hanged. For the first time since his arrest he dropped the Nieman moniker and correctly identified himself. Although he often hesitated, he answered every question put to him. Czolgosz recounted his life's story, including his problems with his stepmother. He told of listening to Emma Goldman and being influenced by her teachings. He also spoke of other anarchists he knew, Abraham Isaak among them. The prisoner professed to believe in neither government nor marriage, claiming he was an advocate of free love. He also told of his disenchantment with the Catholic Church. Czolgosz said he had come to Buffalo from Chicago, adding that he visited the Exposition several times before the president arrived in town.[23]

His interrogators, of course, were particularly interested in the crime. Czolgosz said he shot McKinley because he thought it was right, repeating his belief that it was his "duty." The president, he asserted, "was a tyrant and should be removed." He said he had been present at McKinley's speech the previous day and had followed him to Niagara Falls that morning; but his intent from the start had been to do the deed at the reception in the Temple. Czolgosz detailed how, as he waited outside for the event to begin, he placed his revolver in his right hand, covered it with his handkerchief, and stuck his hand in his right pocket. When he reached the point inside where the line was reduced to single file he took his right hand from his pocket and held it against his stomach, his finger on the trigger of the concealed weapon. Czolgosz remained in this stance until he reached the president and opened fire. He intended to fire more shots, but the men who subdued him acted quickly, preventing him from doing so.[24]

At one point Quackenbush asked the prisoner if he would make a statement for the press. "He thought, evidently, that I was a newspaper man," the attorney later recalled, with apparent pride over his deception. Czolgosz, who was not represented by counsel, agreed to implicate himself not just to those gathered in Bull's office but for the entire world. He started to write, but his hand shook, so he dictated two sentences to a stenographer. It stated, "I killed

President McKinley because I done my duty. I didn't believe one man should have so much service and another man should have none."[25]

By the time Czolgosz reached police headquarters the president had been at the Exposition hospital for over an hour and was undergoing surgery. Soon after he had been assisted to a chair at the Temple of Music, Cortelyou asked, "Do you feel much pain?" McKinley slipped his hand through the front of his shirt. One witness claimed to have heard him say, "This wound pains greatly." Another said his words were, as he pointed to his chest, "I feel a sharp pain here." At the same time a short, white-haired man broke through the crowd. It was Don Manuel Aspiroz, Mexico's ambassador to the United States. "Oh, my God, Mr. President," he exclaimed, "Are you shot?" McKinley stoically replied, "Yes, I think I am." Then he sank back in the chair, gripping its arms tightly in a battle to remain conscious.[26]

An electric ambulance from the Exposition hospital quickly arrived. Its attendants put the stricken president on a stretcher, which Cortelyou and Milburn helped bear to the vehicle. Those still in the Temple receded as the victim was carried out. A hush fell over the crowd, and men removed their hats. As he was placed in the ambulance, Foster later recalled, McKinley looked plaintively at the agent, "as much as to say, 'Why don't you come with me?'" Foster jumped in and held his arms under the president's head, putting him in a position which McKinley said "felt a great deal better."[27]

T. F. Ellis, a medical student, drove the ambulance. According to Dr. Nelson Wilson, the Exposition's sanitary officer, he "handled the steering bar with the utmost skill. No chauffeur, however expert, ever drove an automobile with more speed and more wisdom through dangerous places than did Ellis." As the young driver guided the vehicle safely past the throng of onlookers, the patient was thinking ahead. "Be careful of the doctors," McKinley told Cortelyou. "I'll leave all that to you." It is likely the president was recalling the shooting of his friend James Garfield twenty years earlier. Conventional wisdom at the time—largely supported by subsequent historians—was that Garfield's doctors performed indecisively and poorly. In any event the twentieth president, shot on July 2, 1881, had lingered until September 20.[28]

The ambulance reached the hospital at 4:18 p.m., some ten to fifteen minutes after the shooting. Roswell Park, the respected surgeon who was serving as the Exposition's medical director, was performing an operation in nearby Niagara Falls. Dr Wilson "assumed responsible charge of the hospital pending his [Park's] arrival." Also on duty were Dr. George M. Hall; E. C. Mann, a medical student; Ellis; and seven nurses. Adelle Walters, an 1890 graduate of the Buffalo General Hospital Training School for Nurses, supervised the nursing staff.[29]

An Exposition ambulance sits outside the hospital. The facility was really little more than a clinic (Library of Congress).

The president was placed upon the operating table and undressed. In the process a bullet fell to the floor. It had not penetrated the skin, perhaps being partially deflected by a button, but left a bruise above the breastbone. Agent Foster, who took charge of the slug, later recalled McKinley dryly observing, "That only leaves one." The medical students cleansed the bruise and what was obviously a more serious wound below, to which they also applied gauze dressing. Although just a senior student, Mann instructed one of the nurses to administer .01 gram of morphine and .001 gram of strychnine. The former was for pain, and the latter was commonly used as a heart stimulant.[30]

Calls had gone out to a number of physicians, but it was 22 minutes before the first two arrived. At 4:45 Dr. Herman Mynter, a native of Denmark who had lived in Buffalo over twenty years, walked into the Exposition hospital. Accompanying him was Dr. Eugene Wasdin of the Marine Hospital. Mynter examined the patient and concluded that the wound was deep and serious. He recommended immediate surgery.

A number of doctors soon reached the hospital. Among them were Peter

W. Van Peyma, a Buffalo obstetrician who had been enjoying the fair when the ambulance sped by. Drs. Joseph Fowler and John Parmenter, also Buffalo physicians, arrived soon after. So did one Edward Wallace Lee of St. Louis, who said, Dr. Park later recalled, he had been "medical director of one of the western Expositions." Park would write of Lee, "He manifested a tremendous amount of nerve in almost forcing his way into the operating room, talking with the president, and virtually offering to do the operation himself." He further annoyed Park by traveling on to New York and doing "a lot of talking," despite the physicians' self-imposed gag order. Lee was, Park concluded, "more hindrance than help."[31]

This flood of medical talent posed a problem for Cortelyou. He remembered the president's admonition to be careful of the doctors, but he realized he had no way to assess their abilities—or lack of the same. Taking Milburn aside, he said, "You know all these men. When the right one arrives, tell me." Soon after that Dr. Matthew D. Mann walked into the hospital and Milburn told Cortelyou, "That is the man for the operation."[32]

Fifty-six years old, Dr. Mann specialized in gynecology and obstetrics but also practiced in other fields. Colleagues considered him to be a "beautiful operator." At the same time many also labeled him as petulant, a characteristic he would demonstrate before the day was over. Although choosing a physician of his specialties to perform surgery on a gunshot wound to the abdomen would not be common practice today, it made sense to a certain degree in 1901. At the time gynecologists carried out abdominal surgery more frequently than other specialists. Mann had a reputation for performing hysterectomies in under twenty minutes, the speed of the procedure limiting the amount of blood loss at a time when intravenous fluid had not been perfected. Still, it appears likely that William McKinley was to be Mann's first gunshot patient.[33]

Mann agreed with Mynter that surgery was called for. That left just two Questions: When? and Where? Although it had an operating room of sorts, the Exposition hospital was little more than a clinic. Poorly lit and underequipped, it was designed more for skinned knees, heat prostration, and other ailments associated with a fair than it was for a serious gunshot wound. A transfer to the Buffalo General Hospital would have resulted in superior facilities, but Mann felt time was of the essence. Mynter and Parmenter agreed. Medical journals of the day cautioned that delay in such cases was not advised. The danger of a hidden hemorrhage was a real one, especially with the relatively soft, slow traveling bullets fired from a handgun, which made ragged tears as they flattened following contact.[34]

Cortelyou informed McKinley of the doctors' opinion that the operation should be performed immediately. To this the president replied, "Gentlemen, I am in your hands."[35]

Mann selected Mynter and Parmenter to assist him and asked Wasdin to administer ether as an anesthetic. Mann requested that Dr. Wilson keep a record of the procedure. Wilson later sent a minute-by-minute account to Park. Miss Walters supervised her team of nurses as they sterilized instruments, prepared dressings, and made other preparations. Wilson would later report that Walters "displayed excellent judgment in the disposition of the nurses and in the preparations which were immediately begun under her directions for the operation."[36]

At 5:20 Dr. Wasdin began administering the ether, which took nine minutes to do its work. As they waited the doctors scrubbed thoroughly with soap and water before immersing their hands in a solution of bichloride of mercury. At 5:30 the field of operation was shaved and scrubbed with green soap, and Mann began the operation. He stood on the right side of his patient, and Parmenter stood to Mann's right. Opposite were Mynter and the persistent Dr. Lee. They were made responsible for sponging and caring for instruments. As Mann began to operate Dr. Rixey arrived. The president's physician had gone to the Exposition grounds after accompanying Mrs. McKinley to the Milburn home, and it took some time to locate him. As the afternoon light dimmed, he aided Mann by using a mirror to direct what sunlight remained to the area of the incision. Later he helped string up one of the Exposition's weak electric lights.[37]

According to the doctors' "Official Report on the Case of President McKinley," the wound "was on a line drawn from the nipple to the umbilicus. It was about half-way between these points, and about 5 cm. to the left of the median line. A probe showed that this wound extended deeply into the abdominal walls, and that the direction was somewhat downward and outward."[38]

At 5:33, after probing the wound, Dr. Mann made a three-inch vertical incision from the edge of the ribs downward, passing through the wound. Parmenter and Lee sponged, and Mynter "caught up bleeding points." A "deep layer of fat" was opened, and a piece of cloth, obviously from the president's clothing and carried in by the bullet, was removed. Mann extended the incision by an inch.[39]

Mann reached the patient's stomach at 5:41. Reaching his finger into the wound, he immediately discovered a hole made by the bullet in the front wall. He was somewhat relieved to discover that "its edges were clean-cut and did not appear to be much injured." Mann closed the wound with a double row of silk sutures. In order to locate a potential bullet hole in the rear of the stomach, he increased his incision by three inches and pulled the organ up "into the operation wound." He then pulled the omentum and the transverse colon "well out of the abdomen." Mann discovered the wound in the posterior wall, this one "somewhat larger than that in the anterior wall" and with "frayed and blood-infiltrated edges." Dr. Mann sutured this wound in a manner similar to the first, but the challenge was greater. The posterior hole was "down at the bottom of a deep pocket." The lack of medical instruments, particularly retractors, also hindered the effort. The team of physicians had no way of knowing that Dr. Park's housekeeper, being told he was wanted at the Exposition hospital, had sent his bag there.[40]

Mann then inserted his hand deeply into the wound in an attempt to discern the track of the bullet. He could find no trace of it. Further, "The introduction of the hand in this way seemed to have a bad influence on the President's pulse," so Mann backed off. He asked each of the surgeons present "whether he was entirely satisfied that everything had been done which should be done and whether he had any further suggestions to make. Each replied that he was satisfied," and Mann began to close.[41]

At that point, 6:23 according to Wilson, Roswell Park arrived on the scene. At the time of the shooting he had been at Memorial Hospital in Niagara Falls. Along with Dr. W. R. Campbell and Dr. A. L. Chapin, Park was removing a cancerous tumor from William Powley of nearby Ransomville. One of the two assisting surgeons later told Park's son, Julian, "Dr. Park was half-way through the operation when someone burst in and said, 'Doctor, you are wanted at once in Buffalo.' Before he could continue Dr. Park said, 'Don't you see that I can't leave this case if it was for the President of the United States?' 'Doctor, it is for the President of the United States.'" Although an interesting story, it is one Dr. Park never recorded himself.[42]

Dr. Park asked Dr. Campbell to make arrangements for a special train to Buffalo. He completed the operation, leaving the dressings to Dr. Chapin, and hastened to the railroad station. There he found everything in confusion, but eventually a train showed up, although the delay greatly annoyed Buffalo's leading physician. The situation Park encountered at the Exposition hospital did not improve his mood. "Just as I entered the operation room," the doctor later recalled, "the first incident that attracted my attention was Dr. Mann rapping Dr. Mynter's fingers with one of the instruments because said fingers were apparently in his way." More troubling, both Parmenter and Wilson later told him that they saw perspiration from Mynter's forehead fall into the wound. Park also believed the doctors had acted with "undue haste" to operate. He never expressed any criticism publicly. However, in an account he later edited for publication, Park wrote that his colleagues had moved ahead with the surgery to preclude his participation. Specifically, "Not a few have not hesitated to express their unreserved opinions to the effect that it was simply a matter of jealously rather than of urgent haste because of the President's symptoms."[43]

Park retained his composure and his professionalism in the operating room, perhaps to his patient's detriment. Mynter strongly recommended inserting an abdominal drain to remove any body fluids that could produce infection. Mann was just as adamantly opposed. Asked to break the impasse, Park demurred with the weak explanation that the doctors performing the operation were in the best position to decide. Mann declined to drain, later asserting, "There had been no bleeding nor oozing; there was nothing to make any discharge or secretion."[44]

Although he kept his counsel at the time, Park later termed the decision not to drain "unfortunate." Had it been done, he added, "the patient's chances would have been improved rather than the reverse." Park noted that six weeks later he had a case involving a woman who attempted suicide, shooting herself in the abdomen in the same location where the president had been wounded. Park made posterior and anterior drainage, and the patient recovered. Still, he conceded, "[McKinley's] body was so stout that to have made it in this case would have been difficult." He concluded, "Whether this would have saved the patient or not I cannot say, but I have always regretted that it was not put into practice."[45]

At 7:01, according to Wilson's careful record keeping, bandaging was completed. Fourteen minutes later nurses and sickroom supplies were dispatched to the Milburn home, where McKinley would be sent to recover. At 7:32 McKinley, still under the effects of the ether, was placed in an ambulance for the trip to his host's home. As the hospital doors opened, soldiers and police moved back the crowd that had pushed forward, hoping to catch a glimpse of the wounded chief executive. At Rixey's request, Park and Wasdin rode with the president. The other doctors followed. A mounted military escort moved out, and the ambulance followed. A hushed crowd was waiting at the Milburn home as ambulance attendants, aided by Milburn himself, gently bore the stretcher from the vehicle into the house. As the president was carried in, witnesses clearly heard him groaning.[46]

Now it was a matter of waiting.

22

McKinley: Week of Hope and Agony

As the sun rose over Buffalo, New York on September 7, 1901, William McKinley was still alive. This was good news for all concerned, and it gave the president's doctors reason to believe that, rather than simply comforting a dying man, they may become part of a lengthy recovery. Rixey and Cortelyou had issued two bulletins during the night. Tersely worded, they gave the assurance that the patient was "resting well" and listed his vital signs. Dr. Park added his name to the 6:00 a.m. bulletin. It said, "The President has passed a good night; temperature, 101.6; pulse, 110; respiration, 24."[1]

McKinley was in a large rear room on the second floor, one which connected with an equally large front room. Dr. Park had dispatched Catherine Simmons and Adele Barnes to the Milburn residence with a hospital bed, bedding, and other sickroom supplies. According to Park, "When we reached the house with the ambulance conveying the President everything was ready down to the smallest detail for his reception." A representative of General Electric had installed electric fans, which were in operation before the ambulance arrived. Not on hand was an x-ray machine. Thomas Edison had offered one, but it was not accepted. The reasons behind this rejection are unclear. X-rays had been used in surgery since 1896 and were utilized frequently during the Spanish-American War. Not only would the device have located the bullet, but it might have also suggested damage done along its track.[2]

The Milburn family abandoned their home for a Buffalo hotel, and the house became both a hospital and an informal nerve center for the government. Ropes blocked off the neighborhood, preventing any traffic that might disturb the convalescing president. The 14th U.S. Army Regiment, stationed at nearby Fort Porter, paced up and down the sidewalks along Delaware Avenue and West Ferry Street. The Milburn barn became a telegraph station, keeping Cortelyou in touch with Washington. Two tents went up on a vacant lot across the street to shelter the newspapermen swarming in from across the country.

213

Most of the cabinet arrived during the day on September 7, as did Mark Hanna and Myron Herrick, two of the president's closest friends and political allies. McKinley's two sisters accompanied Herrick, but neither they nor any of the other visitors were allowed into the sickroom. The only exception was Ida. Early in the morning McKinley asked to see his wife. The doctors consulted, agreeing to a brief visit. The couple reportedly held hands but spoke little, the president telling the first lady, "You know you must bear up well." Ida returned for another short visit in the afternoon but otherwise spent most of the day sleeping.[3]

Shortly after noon a special train bearing Theodore Roosevelt pulled into the New York Central station. The vice president had been on an island in Lake Champlain, speaking to the Vermont Fish and Game Club, when he was notified of the assassination attempt. He immediately cut short his visit and made his way to Buffalo. Once there he was uncharacteristically quiet. To a reporter who caught up with him as he rushed through the depot, he announced, "I have nothing to say. Nothing to say. Nothing to say at present." A waiting carriage delivered him to the Milburn home, where he received encouraging news about the president's condition. He stayed just thirty minutes, again refusing to talk to the press as he departed. Rooms were waiting at the Iroquois Hotel, but the vice president instead accepted an offer from Ansley Wilcox, an attorney and personal friend, to stay at his Delaware Avenue home.[4]

Many of the cabinet officers stayed at residences near the Milburn home. Alice Sprague later recalled that Secretary of War Root, a family friend, spent the week at their home at 810 West Ferry Street. The home became a gathering point for government officials, and she remembered John Hay's stories of Abraham Lincoln, Teddy's tales of San Juan Hill, and Root's tales of Teddy. When they had business to conduct, the cabinet ministers went to the Buffalo Club, which had made rooms available to them.[5]

The Pan-Am opened Saturday morning, but both attendance and enthusiasm had waned, at least for the time being. "My interest in the Ex was gone," one fair visitor wrote to his daughter. Another wrote that the shooting had "cast a gloom over every one." Admissions were off Saturday, and the Sunday total of 25,146 was the smallest Sabbath crowd in several weeks. "All spoke in low tones," the *Commercial* reported, "and gazed silently at the closed Temple of Music." Souvenir sellers who had anything bearing the likeness of the president or the Temple of Music did a brisk business. Portraits of McKinley that originally had sold for a nickel increased to a quarter and then to fifty cents. Small trays with pictures of the Temple of Music, once selling at three for a quarter, were now fetching twenty-five cents apiece. Also attracting attention were the five bulletin boards put up to display the latest medical reports. One man, visiting from the country, read the largely positive one o'clock bulletin. Then he spotted an American flag flying from atop a pole on the Esplanade. "Thank God, it's there yet," he said through tears. "I hope it will never fly at half mast."[6]

By then Czolgosz's reported leanings toward anarchy in general and Emma Goldman in particular had thrown the country into a red scare. Police in major cities arrested purported anarchists, and mobs pelted others with stones or threatened to lynch them. Johann Most made the mistake of publishing in *Freiheit*, one day before the shooting, an old essay defending the assassination of kings. That unfortunate coincidence ended up costing him a year in prison.[7]

Although the term had not yet been coined, Goldman was clearly public enemy number one. She was in St. Louis at the time and was shocked when she spotted a newspaper headline that blared "ASSASSIN OF PRESIDENT McKINLEY AN ANARCHIST. CONFESSES TO HAVING BEEN INCITED BY EMMA GOLDMAN. WOMAN ANARCHIST WANTED." On an inside page she saw a picture of the assailant. "Why, that's Nieman," she gasped, remembering the compelling young man who had attended her Cleveland lecture. Learning that friends were being held without bail in Chicago, she decided to head there and turn herself in. On the way she heard a fellow passenger describe her as, "A beast, a bloodthirsty monster." Another said, "She should have been locked up long ago," to which a third replied, "Locked up nothing! She should be strung up to the first lamppost."[8]

Arriving in Chicago, Goldman did not immediately turn herself in to the authorities. She spent a great deal of time destroying papers that might in any way implicate friends or acquaintances. Through an intermediary, she also tried to arrange an interview, for which the *Chicago Tribune* was willing to pay five thousand dollars, money Goldman feared she would need for her defense. It never happened. On September 10, as she waited for the reporter at a friend's apartment, police charged in and took her away.

The officers took Goldman to police headquarters, where she "was kept in a stifling room and grilled to exhaustion from 10:30 a.m. till 7 p.m." Detectives walked by, shaking their fists and making threats. A few tried to trick her into confessing by insisting they had arrested a third conspirator who "confessed everything." Goldman endured five days of similar treatment before Chicago's chief of police showed up at her cell and calmly asked for an account of her movements since the May 5 lecture in Cleveland. The prisoner complied, leaving out only the names of "comrades who had been my hosts." When she was finished, the chief replied, "Unless you're a very clever actress, you are certainly innocent. I think you are innocent and I am going to do my part to help you out." After that her treatment changed drastically. Goldman was allowed to order food, receive visitors, and "lead the life of a society lady." Meanwhile, the country was recovering somewhat from its panic, and the Buffalo district attorney was starting to realize that, other than Czolgosz's name dropping, he did not have any real evidence against her. He still went through the motions, dispatching a subordinate to Chicago for a hearing. The judge and the lawyer sparred verbally for some two hours before the judge set Goldman free.[9]

On September 8 Dr. Charles McBurney, described by one reporter as "the celebrated New York surgeon," arrived at the Milburn home. The title was fitting. McBurney was credited with pioneering the diagnosis and treatment of appendicitis. Indeed, the arrival of such a prominent physician led some to speculate that the president's condition had worsened. Milburn tried to reassure nervous reporters, explaining, "He came because, well, you know, it's the President of the United States who lies over there." McBurney proved to be a big mouth. After examining the patient, he proclaimed, "The operation performed by Dr. Mann at the exposition hospital marked the epoch of the century in surgery. In my opinion the President surely will recover." He went on to predict that McKinley would be back at his desk in six weeks.[10]

The vital signs suggested a different prognosis. The president's temperature had remained high since surgery, ranging from 101 to 102.8 degrees that Sunday. The doctors attributed this to "surgeon's fever," a natural increase in temperature following abdominal surgery because of dehydration. A pulse rate that went from 122 to 132 during the day was, according to McBurney, normal considering McKinley's constitution. At one point, as Mann and Mynter tried to explain to reporters that the president was not entirely out of danger, McBurney interrupted them with more rosy pronouncements.[11]

Ida got out of the house that Sunday, buoyed by the positive medical reports. She and Mrs. Lafayette McWilliams, a family friend, took a carriage ride through a nearby park. Milburn and Dr. Rixey assisted the first lady to the carriage, but the two women rode accompanied only by their driver. They were gone just under an hour. "Mrs. McKinley looked pale and weary, but cheerful," one reporter observed. "She walked very feebly, leaning heavily upon the arms of her escort and raising her feet into the carriage with great difficulty." The rides would become daily occurrences.[12]

The positive reports continued over the next three days. On Monday, the 9th, the patient was given a "nutrient enema," consisting of egg, whiskey, and molasses, the first nutrition he had received since the shooting. The 3:00 p.m. medical bulletin reported, "The President's condition steadily improves and he is comfortable, without pain or unfavorable symptoms. Bowel and kidney functions normally performed." Asked about his friend's condition by a reporter, Mark Hanna replied, "Just glorious," and announced plans to return to Cleveland. Cabinet members and the president's sisters also left Buffalo that day, as did the vice president, who was off to climb the 5,344-foot Mt. Marcy in the Adirondacks.[13]

As the other cabinet members departed, John Hay, who had remained in Washington to keep U.S. diplomats and foreign leaders apprised of any developments, arrived in Buffalo. He told a newsman, "The reports of the doctors are so encouraging that I see no reason for alarm or fear that the President will not recover." Speaking to Louis Babcock, the secretary of state was far less optimistic. "The President will not live," he bluntly asserted. "I was one of the secretaries to President Lincoln. He was shot and died. I was a close friend of Garfield, who tendered me a post under him. He was shot and died. Now I am Secretary of State under President McKinley. He will surely die for it has been the fate of the Presidents with whom I have been associated to be assassinated."[14]

There was a slight setback on September 10, but the doctors rushed to assure a nervous public that it posed no threat to ultimate recovery. When the operation had been performed at the Exposition hospital, they explained, the surgeons had removed a fragment of fabric torn from the president's coat. It produced "a slight irritation of the tissues ... the evidence of which appeared only tonight." They removed a few stitches and "partially" opened the wound to address the situation. "This incident cannot give rise to other complications," the physicians asserted, "but it is communicated to the public as the surgeons in attendance wish to make their bulletins entirely frank."[15]

The president also received his first nourishment by mouth on the 10th. It came in the form of "pure beef juice," given every hour. Ida continued to see her husband twice a day, but the doctors were the only other visitors. The medical bulletins continued positive on the 11th. A sample of blood taken from the president's ear demonstrated "the absence of any blood poisoning." The doctors added, "His stomach tolerates the beef juice well and it is taken with great satisfaction." The next day McKinley informed them that he would enjoy "a nice mild cigar." He didn't get one.[16]

No sooner had the president's request for a stogie hit the wires than a Chicago tobacconist shipped off a box of "Perla de Montanas," which he somehow knew was a favorite of McKinley's. It was one of a number of gifts and offers the chief executive received, ranging from the thoughtful to the bizarre. A Washington, D.C., store owner sent a bottle of port to Cortelyou to pass on to his boss. "I feel sure if a little be given in between meals it will give strength and make new blood." He added, "Get the doctor's opinion on this." Noticing that the president was being nourished in part with whiskey, the Green River Distillery in Owensboro, Kentucky sent a case of their oldest. A German-American resident of the nation's capital forwarded "several packages of genuine German 'Zwieback,' a twice baked bread famed for its nutritious, health-giving properties." The *Buffalo Express* reported that two bottles "of brown stuff" arrived on the 11th from Indiana. Enclosed was note saying, "I am quite sure if you will take a little of this after each meal, you will improve rapidly." Another parcel, this one from New Jersey, contained "a bottle of liquid which smelled strongly of carbolic acid." Its purported contents was a fast-healing liniment. A Buffalo dry cleaner offered to clean the president's clothes free of charge, and a Detroit organ manufacturer made available "a Cecilian ... for his as well as Mrs. McKinley's entertainment."[17]

With the president apparently on the road to recovery, Buffalo began planning for a long convalescence. Secretary Root was quoted as saying the city would be "the summer capital," although fall was rapidly approaching. The calendar notwithstanding, residents looked forward to their community's role in the president's healing process and to its new status in the government. Meanwhile Exposition officials were making plans for Jubilee Day, a celebration of the president's recovery, scheduled for September 21. As Buchanan described it, "It is proposed that the day shall be devoted to thanksgiving, and the expression, through such forms as may be decided upon, in dignified manner of the joyousness of the occasion." Religious services in the Stadium and the Temple of Music, a children's chorus of 3,000 or more, and a special fireworks display were all part of the tentative plans.[18]

Jubilee Day never happened. On Thursday, September 12, McKinley received his first solid food, toast, reportedly taken with chicken broth and coffee. A few hours later the ebullient Dr. McBurney boarded a train for New York, proclaiming as he left the Milburn home, "The President is out of danger."[19]

McBurney had been gone but a short time when his former patient began to complain, "I am tired, so tired." His pulse was back up to 130, but it was considerably weaker. McKinley had also not digested the food given him that day, nor had he passed any intestinal gas since the early morning hours. The doctors diagnosed the president's condition as intestinal toxemia and ordered another enema, but it did not achieve the desired results. They then called in an expert, Dr. Charles Stockton, a respected stomach specialist and professor at the University of Buffalo School of Medicine. Despite his area of expertise, Stockton was more concerned about the president's apparently failing heart. McKinley's physicians had already administered digitalis and strychnine. He ordered more, along with calomel and other strong laxatives.[20]

Thursday afternoon's three o'clock medical bulletin cryptically announced, "The President's condition is very much the same as this morning," subtly adding, "His only complaint is fatigue." By 8:30 that night circumstances forced a more honest assessment. "The President's condition this evening is not quite so good," it began. "His food has not agreed with him and has been stopped. Excretion has not yet been properly established." Even if that bulletin had not been issued, the coterie of reporters camped across the street knew something was up. "The apprehension which was felt ... for the President was apparent in everything about the Milburn house," a *Commercial* representative wrote. The number of visitors picked up, and "expressions of cheerfulness" gave way to countenances "of alarm and anxiety." Every room in the house was lit, and the physicians who emerged waved off all questions.[21]

Calls went out to family members who had returned to Ohio, to cabinet members who had departed for Washington, and the vice president, who was somewhere on Mt. Marcy. On Friday, September 13, the public, which had gone to bed full of optimism, awoke to the words of the 2:30 a.m. medical bulletin, which stated, "The President's condition is very serious and gives rise to the gravest apprehension." It went on to explain, "His heart does not respond properly to stimulation." The doctors were working tirelessly to stimulate McKinley's heart. In addition to the digitalis and strychnine, they administered nitroglycerine, adrenalin, and even brandy. Believing, as did most physicians at the time, that the contents of the bowels were toxic and could lead to intestinal poisoning, they continued to administer stronger enemas. All of this missed the mark. According to Dr. Jack C. Fisher, a retired professor of surgery who became a scholar of the assassination, "Most physicians today will recognize that McKinley was in shock, but because of the development of a pathologic third space with several liters of fluid having accumulated deeply within an inflamed retroperitoneum. What McKinley had needed desperately, and did not receive, was intravenous fluid in a significant quantity." That knowledge remained decades away.[22]

The board of directors of the Pan-American Exposition held an emergency meeting, voting to close the fair "in the event of the death of President McKinley." The doctors continued to struggle, but their patient knew it was hopeless. At one point, as they administered oxygen, he asked, "What's the use?" The 2:30 bulletin stated, "The President has more than held his own since morning and his condition justifies the expectation of further improvement." But three hours later: "The President's physicians report that his condition is grave at this hour." Most of the time he was unconscious. At around six that evening a rumor that McKinley had died began making the rounds. It was slightly premature.[23]

At about seven the president asked for Ida. Cortelyou brought her in, and everybody else stepped out. From the next room, some thought they heard whispers from the couple; others were not so sure. Ida may have been the last person McKinley recognized. Family members and cabinet officers went in to say their farewells. So did Mark Hanna, described as "ashen-faced." He went to his dear friend and political partner. "Mr. President! Mr. President!" he called out. Then, emotion overcoming protocol, "William! William!"[24]

The 9:30 bulletin was blunt. "The President is dying." He had been unconscious for an hour and a half and would never regain consciousness. His heartbeat grew fainter, and his extremities chilled. During those final hours the doctors heard him faintly murmur a few lines from "Nearer My God to Thee," his favorite hymn. Later some on the scene, abetted by the press, would craft from this the more eloquent final words, "Good-bye, all. Good-bye. It is God's will. His will be done, not ours." Not that he would not have said that had he been able. Recalling his most prominent patient several years later, Dr. Park would write, "He bore his illness and such pain as he suffered with beautiful, unflinching Christian fortitude, and no more tractable or agreable patient was ever in charge of his physicians. No harsh word of complaint against his assassin was ever heard to pass his lips.... Up to this time I had never really believed that a man could be a good Christian and a good politician."[25]

The final medical bulletin was released at 2:15 a.m. on September 14: "The President is dead."

At that moment the 26th president was dashing down Mt. Marcy, some 400 miles to the northeast. Right then Theodore Roosevelt did not know that he was president, but he was certain that he soon would be. He had left in a blinding rain shortly before midnight after receiving a telegram from the cabinet members present in Buffalo summoning him to the scene. A relay of drivers piloted him down hazardous mountain roads, Teddy urging them to, "Hurry up! Go faster!" despite boulders and other obstructions brought out by the storm. He reached North Creek at dawn, where both a special train and a telegram announcing McKinley's death awaited him.[26]

Arriving at Buffalo, Roosevelt made his first two executive decisions. First, he would take the oath of office at the home of his friend, Ansley Wilcox. The cabinet wanted him to be sworn in at the Milburn home, but Teddy strongly objected to having the ceremony take place in the same residence where McKinley's body lay. Second, he would go to the Milburn home before being formally sworn in so he could pay his respects to Ida McKinley as an individual, rather than as her husband's successor. But he had to get cleaned up first. Wilcox had formal clothes that fit the new chief executive, but all of his hats were too small. John S. Scatchard, a neighbor and chairman of the Exposition's executive committee, came to the rescue.[27]

Cortleyou greeted Roosevelt at the Milburn house, explaining that the new president could not view McKinley's body because the doctors were performing an autopsy. Further, Ida was in no condition to receive visitors. He did meet with a few cabinet members, once again rejecting their suggestion that he take the oath of office there. Then, cabinet officers in tow, he departed for the Wilcox residence.

The swearing in, according to Louis Babcock, posed a logistical problem. The Pan-Am marshal later wrote that the cabinet was uncertain as to the proper way to administer the oath, so Milburn dispatched Babcock to the library for an 1881 *New York Herald*, chronicling Chester Arthur's swearing in following the Garfield assassination. They figured it out, and at 3:30 Roosevelt took his position in Wilcox's library. Secretary Root broke down in tears, then composed himself and formally requested that the vice president take the oath of office. In words the two men had previously discussed, Roosevelt responded, "And in this hour of deep and terrible national bereavement, I wish to state that it shall be my aim to continue absolutely unbroken the policy of President McKinley for the peace and prosperity of our beloved country." The words, which Roosevelt likely did not mean, went a long way toward calming shaky financial markets and nervous Republican politicians. Following this abbreviated inaugural address, Judge John R. Hazel, at 41 the youngest federal judge, administered the oath of office to America's youngest president.[28]

Despite her deep grief, Ida McKinley knew what she wanted, a simple funeral service for her husband. It was not to be. On Sunday, September 15, there was the type of service the first lady desired at the Milburn home. Only cabinet officers, family members, and such close friends as Mark Hanna attended. After that, William McKinley became public property. The body was taken to city hall, where the slain president lay in state before being returned to the Milburn home at six that evening. The funeral train, bound for Washington, D.C., departed the next morning. The casket remained overnight in the East Room of the White House. The following morning, September 17, a military escort led the hearse to the Capitol, where the casket was placed in the Rotunda, where thousands filed past to pay their respects.[29]

That evening William McKinley started for home. The funeral train went via Baltimore, Harrisburg, and Pittsburgh and arrived at Canton at noon on the 18th. It was a city deep in mourning. Church bells had begun tolling upon word of the president's death. Factories shut down, and stores either closed or saw business fall to virtually nothing. There was one exception. Dry goods stores did a booming business, besieged by those seeking black crepe and other symbols of mourning. A swarm of visitors descended on the small city, prompting the Committee on Hotels and Restaurants to appeal to local citizens to open up their homes.[30]

Ida went straight to the North Market Street home with the famous front porch. Abner McKinley and Dr. Rixey assisted her inside. According to the *Canton Repository*, "The late residence of the dead president was the only house as far as the eye could see which bore no signs of mourning." Rixey told reporters Mrs. McKinley had borne the trip well, "although she frequently gave way to grief and sobs."[31]

Some seven thousand individuals filed past the home the next morning, most to pay their respects, some to gather pebbles or grass from the property. Police were on hand to prevent them from taking anything else. Meanwhile the former first lady was steeling herself for a private prayer service, which she had requested. Only a few close friends and family members were present. Then, at about a quarter after one, William and Ida McKinley parted one last time, the widow too grief stricken to attend the public services.

The Thayer Military Band, police and military units, and the carriages bearing President Roosevelt and his cabinet rode in advance of the hearse. The funeral took place in the Methodist Church, where the president had been a member. The procession then went to Westlawn Cemetery, where a Grand Army band played "Nearer My God to Thee" before William McKinley was laid to rest.[32]

The next day Ida was stronger. Shortly before noon she went for a drive with her sister, Mrs. M. C. Barber, and Dr. Rixey. They stopped at her husband's grave, which she and her sister briefly visited. Ida would live, largely as a recluse, until May 26, 1907. Family legend holds that she never suffered another seizure.[33]

23

Czolgosz:
Trial and Execution

Leon Czolgosz had confessed to murder the night of the McKinley shooting, and with a plethora of witnesses it seemed that district attorney Penney had an open-and-shut case. Still, there was one question—the issue of sanity. Dr. Joseph Fowler, the jail physician, wanted it addressed, and he persuaded Penney to grant him and two "alienists," as doctors who dealt with mental diseases were then termed, access to the prisoner. Fowler summoned Drs. Floyd Crego and James Putnam to take part in the examinations. Both were associated with the University of Buffalo, and both arrived with sterling reputations in the field.[1]

Although Czolgosz had talked openly about his crime ever since his arrest, his always capricious attitude again shifted when the three doctors showed up on Monday, September 9. Fowler opened the interview by asking why he had shot the president. "Did I shoot the President?" Czolgosz replied. For the next half hour he denied any knowledge of the crime. Fowler, believing the examination "was all up," resorted to desperate measures. The doctor "went for him quite severely, telling him that he had signed his confession and reminded him that he had made the statements before many witnesses." The tongue lashing changed Czolgosz's attitude. He admitted that he had shot McKinley and answered questions as he had before. When it was all over the trio concluded that anarchy, not insanity, had led him to commit the crime.[2]

The alienists were not Czolgosz's only visitors. The morning after the shooting Walter Nowak, described by the press as a Cleveland cigar maker, arrived at Police headquarters and asked to see the prisoner. Chief Bull allowed it. As he later recalled, Nowak castigated his former acquaintance, saying, "I have always been a friend of yours. Why did you do this? ... Why have you committed an act that is going to bring disgrace upon the Polish race?" Nowak continued along this line as Czolgosz sat silently and smiled.

The visitor, perhaps speaking as much for the benefit of the police present as for his one-time friend, added, "You and I belonged to the same society, attended the meetings together, but it became so radical…. I gave it up." Driving home the point, he added, "I am a Republican, not a Socialist or Anarchist." To this Czolgosz responded, Oh, yes, you are a Republican for this (indicating with his fingers)," explaining Nowak was a Republican "for the money in it."[3]

Nowak later told reporters he had known Czolgosz for two years, repeating his assertion that he had belonged to the same club as the prisoner but left when it became "a little too rabid to suit his taste." He insisted that Czolgosz belonged to "anarchistic organizations" in Cleveland, Chicago, New York, and Patterson, New Jersey. He also claimed, ridiculously, that Czolgosz's father had "been a crank on the subject of anarchy all his life. It's bred in the bone."[4]

Nowak was not the only Polish-American upset by Czolgosz's action. On September 8 a group of prominent Buffalo Poles met and announced that Polish Day at the Pan-Am would be postponed "for an indefinite time." In making the announcement, they added, "We hereby pledge our sincerest sympathy for His Excellency, the President, and furthermore … emphasize our grief and sympathy."[5]

Even in jail, Czolgosz remained fastidious about his appearance. Bull later noted that he was "most immaculate about his dress and person, washing himself and 'fixing himself up' a good deal of the time." Dr. Fowler concurred, saying he exhibited "extreme pride about how he looked," requesting a brush and a comb because his hair had become "disheveled" in jail.[6]

On September 13 officials decided to move their prisoner. The medical bulletins were far less encouraging, and "signs of unrest began to appear," along with "muttered threats against the assassin." At 11:00 a.m. Czolgosz was removed to the Erie County Penitentiary. He was not handcuffed for the trip but was informed that the officers accompanying him were armed and would not hesitate to pull the trigger. Few people at either facility were aware of the move, but the *Buffalo Express* spilled the beans. The next day the newspaper ran a story headlined, "Where is Czolgosz?" The article went on to answer the question accurately, citing as its source a man doing repair work at the penitentiary. He told the *Express* "he had had to work overtime to fix up a special cell for Czolgosz."[7]

Although their prisoner was gone, the Buffalo police wanted to avoid violence. Toward that end Bull again employed the tactics he had the night of the shooting. He doubled the reserves at the station and dispatched heavy patrols, both mounted and on foot, to the surrounding streets. Heavy ropes went up around the building, all doors were locked, and a knot of officers stood just inside every entrance. The headquarters, one observer noted, "was garrisoned like a fort in war time. It simply overflowed with men." The precautions were wise. Just after midnight a mob of some two thousand made a charge down Franklin Street toward the station. Only half a dozen officers were present at the section toward which they were heading, but they quickly sounded the "reserve alarm." Almost instantly a hundred men on foot, plus a dozen on horseback, appeared. The police went on the offensive, rushing straight toward the crowd, shouting and waving their nightsticks above their heads. At this display of force, the *Commercial* reported, "The mob melted away like snow." Those who remained gathered around the bulletin boards reporting the president's deteriorating condition. When word of his death arrived, Bull later recalled, "the crowds quietly dispersed. Vengeance was turned to sorrow; it was as if death had entered every household."[8]

Buffalo's legal community had definite goals in mind for Czolgosz's trial. When word of the shooting reached District Attorney Penney, he wrote later, "I recalled to mind the disgraceful scenes that surrounded the detention and trial of the assassin of President Garfield." Charles J. Guiteau served as his own attorney during a sensational 54-day trial that both captivated and offended the American public. His jail cell interviews with reporters produced the same results. Penney was determined to keep the prisoner sequestered and to make his trial "an orderly, dignified procedure that could in no way bring criticism upon our own community or upon our form of government generally." He consulted with Root, Cortelyou, and Roosevelt, "and I was very glad to find that my own ideas of how the procedure for the prosecution of this man should be conducted were approved by all of them."[9]

Attorney Adelbert Moot, president of the Bar Association of Erie County, shared Penney's views. He also realized how important it was that the defendant be represented by competent defense counsel—if only for the sake of appearances. To that end he approached Judge Loran L. Lewis and Judge Robert C. Titus. Both men had served New York in the state senate and the supreme court. Both were also reluctant to take on the assignment. Lewis was 76 years old and, as he later recalled, his sons feared that the trial "would make serious drafts on my nervous system." Moot later recalled that Titus, then 62, was being seriously considered by the Democratic Party as its next candidate for governor. Defending the anarchist murderer of a beloved president, therefore, could have made "serious drafts" on his political future. Titus was out of town, attending a Masonic convention, when he received word of his selection. Returning to Buffalo, he met with Lewis and Moot. "After quite a long conversation with Judge Titus," Moot later remembered, "Judge Lewis turned to [him] and said, in substance, 'Judge, we are not cowards, and if it is our duty to defend Czolgosz, we will defend him.'" This simple reasoning persuaded Titus, and he agreed to take on the case. Each man would receive $350 for his services.[10]

By the time he convinced Titus of his responsibilities, Lewis already knew how difficult those responsibilities would be. Soon after the appointment, before Titus returned to town, he had gone to the jail to meet with Czolgosz. Lewis explained who he was, adding that he had come so they could plan a defense. The prisoner "looked me in the eyes but made no reply." The counselor made "several attempts" to get him to talk before finally giving up.[11]

On September 16, following just under five hours of testimony, the grand jury of Erie County returned an indictment against Leon Czolgosz in the murder of William McKinley. In keeping with Penney's view to keep the defendant secluded to the extent possible, he was taken from the jail to city hall via what the police termed "The Tunnel of Sobs," a dank passageway under Delaware Avenue. Czolgosz arrived about an hour after the indictment had been handed down. Penney asked him if he had a lawyer, to which Czolgosz only shook his head. The district attorney repeated the question but received no response. At this point Judge Edward K. Emery formally assigned Lewis and Titus as defense counsel.[12]

Czolgosz returned the next day for his arraignment. After the indictment was read to him, Penney asked, "How do you plead?" The prisoner maintained his silence. "Do you understand what I have read to you?" the frustrated prosecutor asked. "Do you understand that you are charged with the crime of murder in the first degree? You can say yes or no." Czolgosz remained unresponsive, but Lewis stepped in. He explained that he had met with his client but had been unable to ascertain his wishes. Lacking any guidance, he entered a plea of not guilty on Czolgosz's behalf.[13]

Having secured two respected, albeit reluctant, jurists as defense counsel, the Bar Association of Erie County went a step further. Apparently not satisfied with Fowler, Crego, and Putnam's earlier interview, Moot summoned Dr. Carlos F. MacDonald, professor at Bellevue Hospital Medical College in New York. The doctor who had been present at William Kemmler's botched execution in 1889 had, despite that debacle, remained an advocate for electrocution. He had also gained a reputation for supporting the insanity defense and interpreting it liberally. The bar association wanted him to examine their court's prominent prisoner. This he agreed to do, but realizing the resentment the Buffalo medical community felt toward Gotham doctors, he asked that Arthur W. Hurd, superintendent of the Buffalo State Hospital, assist him in the examination.[14]

Unable to make contact with Dr. Hurd, MacDonald examined Czolgosz alone on Saturday, September 21. Hurd joined him the next day. The prisoner repeated his life history and "admitted to having had sexual intercourse with women, but denied masturbation or other unnatural practices." The doctors found no "evidence of delusion, hallucination, or illusion." In addition, "He evinced no appearance of morbid mental depression, morbid mental exaltation, or of mental weakness or loss of mind; nor did he display any dictation of morbid suspicion, vanity or conceit, or claim he was 'inspired' or had 'a mission to perform,' or that he was subject to any uncontrollable impulse." Czolgosz's insistence on personal cleanliness and his fastidiousness about his clothing could have been viewed as "vanity," and his claim that, "I done my duty," could have been construed as "a mission," but Hurd and MacDonald overlooked both. Instead they settled upon "the existence in him of the social disease, Anarchy, of which he was a victim."[15]

Following the examination, which was conducted in private in the district attorney's office, reporters asked Titus if the defense would be calling Dr. MacDonald. "We are not calling adverse witnesses," he replied. MacDonald had refused to comment upon the results of the examination. However, the *Buffalo Express* believed defense counsel's statement justified "the supposition ... that he found the prisoner to be sane."[16]

Czolgosz's trial began on Monday morning, September 23. The courtroom events were just a formality in the opinion of the local press, which had already delivered its own verdict and, for good measure, pronounced sentence. Six days earlier the *Buffalo Commercial* had informed its readers that the grand jury had "indicted the murderer," noting that "the electric chair is not far distant." As the trial opened the *Express* reported, "His conviction is foreordained.... After the verdict will come his sentence and after the law's decree will come his death." Not to be outdone in undermining the judicial process, the *Evening News* ran this headline: "Czolgosz, the Anarchist Who Shot Down the President, Faces the Court That Will Sentence Him to Death for His Crime."[17]

If a bit short on journalistic impartiality, the Buffalo papers were not lacking in accuracy. The trial would last just two days, a total of only about eight hours in session, and when it was over everything would happen just as the press said it would.

At 10:00 a.m. Judge Truman C. White asked District Attorney Penney, "Mr. District Attorney, have you any business for the Court?" Penney replied, "I desire to arraign the prisoner Leon F. Czolgosz, your Honor." Penney informed the defendant that he had been indicted on the charge of murder and asked, "How do you plead?" At that point Lewis tried to intercede, but the judge cut him off, saying, "I think the prisoner was about to speak. Czolgosz, did you understand what the District Attorney said to you?" To this Czolgosz replied, "I didn't hear it." Penney repeated himself, and this time the prisoner responded, "Guilty." A guilty plea could not be accepted in a capital case, so White brusquely intoned, "The clerk will enter a plea of not guilty and we will proceed with the trial."[18]

Then Titus announced that he wished to make a statement on behalf of Lewis and himself, "not in the way of apology, but as a reason why we are here in defense of this defendant." He went on to make a statement that, if not an apology, certainly came close:

> I at first declined absolutely to take part in the defense of this case, but subsequently it was made to appear to Judge Lewis and myself that it was a duty which we owed alike to our profession, to the public and to the Court, that we accept this assignment, unpleasant though the task is for us, and we therefore appear in accordance with that assignment to see that this defendant, if he is guilty, is convicted only by such evidence as the law of the land requires in a case of this character, and that in the trial of this case the forms of law shall be observed in every particular and that no act or bit of evidence shall be introduced here upon the trial of this case and accepted against this defendant unless it is such as would be introduced and accepted upon the trial of the meanest criminal in the smallest case.[19]

Jury selection came next, a process which produced one moment of humor. The district attorney was questioning prospective juror Richard J. Garwood, which led to this exchange:

Q. Sir, are you hard of hearing?
A. Sir?
Q. Are you hard of hearing?
A. Yes, sir; a little.[20]

Garwood was one of many called for jury duty who admitted he had formed an opinion in the case, likely one against the defendant. Nevertheless, defense counsel made no objection, and he was seated. The defense did excuse seven potential jurors. Three said their opinions were so fixed they could not likely be changed, even by evidence, two were less than convincing in contending that their views could be changed, and one insisted that he had not formed an opinion but admitted he had expressed an opinion to others "in an off-hand way." The seventh was a cop. The prosecution excused eight jurors.[21]

In the middle of jury selection Lewis chimed in with a request that the court limit the hours of the trial to ten to twelve in the morning and two to four in the afternoon. "Neither Judge Titus or myself are young men," he explained, "and we are neither of us in perfect health." Perhaps more honestly, he added, "I mention four because my home—my summer home—is in

Lewiston, and my train leaves at 4:40, and I am not inclined, unless I am absolutely compelled to do so, to find an abiding place here in the city." Even with this interruption, it took just two hours and a half to seat the jury, a remarkably quick time in a capital case. The *Evening News* considered this a positive thing. "Not a needless question is asked; not a word, scarcely, is spoken that is unnecessary," the paper reported. "Technicalities were not raised by counsel for the accused as is customary in many murder cases." Indeed, the *News* implied that everybody was working as a team, stating, "All credit should be accorded to District Attorney Penney and Judges Titus and Lewis."[22]

Although likely intended as a compliment, the implication that Titus and Lewis were rolling over and playing dead for the prosecution was not entirely accurate. Titus's assertion that the task assigned them was "unpleasant," and Lewis's preoccupation with not missing his train may have helped send that signal. Still, considering the legal hand they were dealt, the attorneys made an honest, if futile, attempt to poke a few holes in the prosecution's case.

For example, Dr. Harvey R. Gaylord, who had performed the autopsy, told Penney plainly that, "The cause of death was a gunshot wound leading to changes in the important viscera." Under cross examination Lewis got him to concede that wounds in the stomach "had adhered and were in a process of healing." He also elicited testimony that the kidneys showed "no loss of continuity which would enable me to say [they] had been perforated." Finally Lewis got the doctor to profess, "I don't think that I could state specifically that the death of the President was due to injury in any organ made directly by the bullet," though he added, "The changes caused by the bullet, which resulted from the passage of the bullet through that space back of the stomach was what caused his death."[23]

On re-direct Penney was able to undo much of the damage. "What is your conclusion as to the cause of death?" the district attorney queried. "He died as a result of absorption of this breaking down material in this area back of the stomach." Penney then asked what caused "the breaking down of the material." Injury to the tissue was the reply. "What was the cause of the injury to the tissues?" Penney continued. Finally he secured the answer he was seeking: "That I should attribute to the bullet."[24]

Lewis tried a similar tactic with Dr. Mann, asking him if the breaking down of tissues found during the autopsy was "to be expected from the nature of the wound the President received?" Mann conceded, "They were not to be expected, and that was an unusual, unexpected condition." He also brought up Mann's earlier testimony that McKinley's body was in a "debilitated condition." Lewis asked, "Do you mean that there were indications that his body was in that condition before he was assaulted?" Mann admitted, "The President probably was not in a very good physical condition, he was somewhat weakened by hard work, want of exercise and conditions of that kind." When Lewis continued, "[Do] you think that had something to do with the result?" Mann answered, "I think undoubtedly that had something to do with the result." Again, Penney effectively countered: "From your knowledge of the autopsy and the history of the case, was there anything that would have saved the life of the President known to medical or surgical sciences?" Mann responded, "There was not."[25]

When the prosecution rested, Lewis immediately responded, "If your honor please, the defendant has no witnesses that he will call." Instead, he asked permission "to make some remarks to the jury in summing up this case," promising they would be "very brief."[26]

At first Lewis's remarks seemed like the tired *apologia* he had already offered: "This being the first time in over twenty years that I have had occasion to address a jury as counsel in a case, you may imagine that I feel somewhat in a strange position, especially in a case of the importance of this. A great calamity has befallen our nation. The President of our country has been stricken down and died in our city."[27]

He conceded that "beyond any peradventure of doubt," that the murder occurred "at the defendant's hand." Therefore, "The only question that can be discussed or considered in this case is the question whether that act was that of a sane person." At that point Penney likely perked up. The alienists had concluded that Czolgosz was sane, precluding the defense from calling them as witnesses. The prosecution had failed to call them, considering their testimony moot. This opened the door for Lewis to attempt a "Hail Mary" closing argument. Again, he asserted that the duty assigned to Titus and him was "an exceedingly unpleasant one." He referred to the fact that his client's guilty plea had been rejected "because the law is so merciful." He suggested that mobs who asserted "that a man, charged with the crime that this defendant is, should not be permitted to have a trial before a court of justice ... are a more dangerous class of community than the anarchists about whom we read so much."[28]

He then invoked nostalgia. "I remember," Lewis said, "when I was a young man living in the city of Auburn ... that the news came that a colored man had gone up the shore of the Owasco Lake and there had murdered practically an entire family." A lynch mob quickly formed but was dissuaded by William Henry Seward, the New York political icon who became Lincoln's secretary of state. Seward went on to volunteer his services on behalf of the accused, recognizing, Lewis insisted, "an opportunity to give an object lesson to the world as to the proper disposition of such a case." The trial dragged on for two months. Seward was there for the duration, "not that he cared anything for the negro but he wanted to teach the people of the country the sacredness of the law."[29]

Lewis did not give the verdict, but he termed the case "a great object lesson to the world." Counsel went on, "Here is a case where a man has stricken down the beloved President of this country, in broad daylight, in the presence of hundreds and thousands of spectators," he explained. "If there ever was a case that would excite the anger, the wrath, of those who saw it, this was one, and yet, under the advice of the President, 'Let no man hurt him,' he was taken, confined in our prison, indicted, put upon trial here and the case is soon to be submitted to you whether he is guilty of the crime charged against him." Ignoring the mob scene in the minutes following the shooting, Lewis observed, "That, gentlemen, speaks volumes in favor of the orderly conduct of the people of the City of Buffalo."[30]

"The law," Lewis reminded the jurors, "presumes that this man is innocent of the crime and we start, in investigating this case, with the assumption that for some reason or other he is not responsible for the act which he performed on that day." He went on to suggest that Czolgosz was not responsible. Every human being, defense counsel asserted, possesses "a strong desire to live." Yet the defendant had committed a capital crime in the presence of hundreds of witnesses. "Now, could a man, with a sane mind, perform such an act?" He even suggested that a verdict of not guilty by reason of insanity would provide solace to a grieving public:

> If it can be that you find that this defendant was not responsible for the crime, for this act, you would aid in uplifting a great cloud off from the hearts and minds of the people of this country and of the world. If our beloved President had met with a railroad accident coming here to our city and had been killed, we should all regret very much, we should mourn over the loss of such a just man, but our grief would not begin to compare with the grief that we have now, that he should be stricken down by an assassin, if such were the case. That adds poignancy to our grief—it does in my case, to a very large extent. But if you could find that he met his fate by the act of an insane man, it would amount to the same as though he met it accidentally, by some accident, and passed away under such circumstances.[31]

Titus was either impressed or lazy, stating that Lewis's remarks "so fully and completely covered the ground.... I intended to present to the jury myself," that he had nothing to add.[32]

The district attorney, on the other hand, had plenty to say. He realized he would have to counter an unexpected defense of insanity by implication. Lewis had rhetorically introduced that which he could not through sworn testimony.[33]

"Gentlemen of the jury," Penney intoned, "this is not a case for oratorical flights or vivid imagination." Then he went on to assert that "the noblest man, I believe, that God ever created upon the soil of the United States was taken from our midst." He spoke of crowds that collected to view the casket or the funeral train. "I have seen people mourn and shed tears for hour after hour who never saw that great man," he emoted, "and I am convinced, if I never was before, that there is such a thing as a national heart and that that great national heart has been weeping as it never wept before." And what had brought about "such a great calamity?" Here Penney appealed not just to emotion but to prejudice. From the Know Nothings of the 1850s to the contemporary Tea Party and Fox News, there has been an anti-immigrant strain in this country, and the prosecutor rushed to exploit it.

> Brought by what? By this instrument (pointing to defendant) of an awful class of people that have come to our shores, a class of people that must be taught, that should be taught and shall be taught that it is entirely foreign to our laws, to our institutions and to the laws and institutions that evolved such a man as William McKinley, that they have no place upon our shores, that if they cannot conform to our laws and our institutions, then they must go hence and keep forever from us; that they will not be permitted to come here, to stay here to educate themselves into the notion that they can take the life of any individual irrespective of consequences, and come into a court—think again, gentlemen.[34]

When Penney had finished, Judge White made his instructions to the jury. This led to some verbal sparring over the issue of sanity. Penney asked the judge to charge the jury that "the law presumes every individual sane" and that "the burden of overthrowing the presumption of sanity and of showing insanity is upon the person who alleges it." Titus objected to the latter, and Penney, after planting the notion in the jury's mind, agreed. Titus then asked White to charge "that if the Jury are satisfied from all the evidence in the case that at the time of the committing of this assault he was laboring under such a defect of reason as not to know the quality of the act he was doing or not to know the act was wrong, that then he is not responsible and they must acquit him." White replied, "I so charge," adding with apparent annoyance, "I intended to make it very plain to the jury in the first place."[35]

With the jury charged to everybody's satisfaction, the twelve men retired to deliberate upon Leon Czolgosz's fate. They weren't gone long. Thirty-five minutes later the jury foreman announced that they had found Czolgosz guilty of murder in the first degree. According to press accounts, it did not take even that long for the jurors to reach a verdict. They delayed in returning only "for the sake of appearances." All that was left was to set the date of sentencing. It would be two days later, Thursday, September 26, at 2:00 p.m. When that was done, according to the *Buffalo Commercial*, "As always before, the prisoner arose and mechanically extended his wrists for the steel handcuffs."[36]

Czolgosz broke his silence at the sentencing, but his behavior remained peculiar. He gave curt, often one-word, answers when Penney questioned him. Then, when the clerk asked if he had any legal cause to show why sentence should not be pronounced, he pointed to the district attorney and said, "I would rather this gentleman speak." Titus persuaded the judge to allow Czolgosz to make "a statement in exculpation of his family." It was brief: "I would like to say this much: That the crime was committed by no one else but me; no one told me to do it and I never told anybody to do it." After a bit more discussion, Titus going out of his way to make sure Czolgosz's family was in no way implicated, White sentenced the convicted man to death "in the week beginning October 28, 1901."[37]

That night, shortly after ten, Czolgosz was taken from the rear entrance of the Erie County Jail to a railway car parked close by. The car was backed to the New York Central station and attached to Train 12, bound for Auburn State Prison. The town's chief of police, along with eighteen other officials, had arrived to escort the prisoner to his final destination. According to the chief, Czolgosz "ate and smoked almost every minute of the trip," receiving all the sandwiches and cigars that he desired. He answered questions, all trivial in nature, but did not speak otherwise. The chief denied press accounts that a large mob accosted the assassin, some delivering blows. Between 150 and 200 people were waiting at the station when the train arrived, but he termed them "mostly respectable people." A policeman from Buffalo drew his gun upon spotting the crowd, but the chief immediately persuaded him to put it back.[38]

Respectable or not, the crowd apparently unnerved Czolgosz. J. Warren Mead, the warden at Auburn, later recalled that when the prisoner was brought in, "he shook or shivered, and trembled and went all to pieces." He was, the warden observed, "completely undone."[39]

Soon Czolgosz settled into a routine not unlike that at Buffalo. He got up about seven every morning, washed, dressed, and ate breakfast "with apparent relish." He then smoked, exercised, and enjoyed a "hearty" lunch. After that he smoked two pipe bowls of tobacco, lay down on his cot, ate dinner, and smoked some more before retiring. The prisoner maintained a "stoic silence." He would answer questions, but often paused up to a half hour before responding. Despite this Mead concluded that Czolgosz was "way above" the ordinary criminal in intelligence. Dr. John Gerin, the prison physician, agreed. After meeting Waldeck and learning anecdotally of his parents and other siblings, Gerin concluded that he "was far above his family in intelligence."[40]

One day Mead told Czolgosz he was going to send a priest to visit him.

"If you send a priest down here I'll smack his head," he replied. Czolgosz later apologized "for saying he would smack anyone's head," but when a local priest showed up, Czolgosz would not talk with him. The cleric sent for "the Polish priest of Buffalo," and Czolgosz did speak with him. However, Warden Mead related, the interview was "not … at all satisfactory to the Polish priest." On another occasion, Dr. Gerin recalled, the prisoner asked to see a priest "at once." The warden was not present, and by the time he returned and sent for the priest, Czolgosz refused to see him. Something about his refusal, Gerin noted, led the doctor to believe he would have seen the priest had the clergyman arrived at once. The delay, he believed, led Czolgosz to suspect his visitor might be a detective in disguise, "ready to hear his confession."[41]

As he languished in the Auburn prison, awaiting his fate, "poor Leon" had at least one defender. Had he known, Czolgosz would likely have been very pleased to realize that Emma Goldman was on his side. As her biographer suggests, Goldman's sympathy may have grown out of guilt, the realization that her words may have led him to shoot America's ultimate figure of authority. Whatever the motive, she threw herself into the effort. Her first salvo was an article entitled "The Tragedy of Buffalo," which appeared in *Free Society*. "Leon Czolgosz and other men of his type," she wrote, "far from being depraved creatures of low instincts are in reality supersensitive beings unable to bear up under great social stress. They are driven to some violent expression, even at the sacrifice of their own lives, because they cannot supinely witness the misery and suffering of their fellows." She concluded, "My heart goes out to him in deep sympathy, as it goes out to all victims of oppression and misery."[42]

Before the piece appeared, Goldman learned her friend Abe Isaak had attempted "to tone down the article" with some creative editing. She got everything restored, but the incident was an omen. Her attempts to raise funds for the assassin or to organize public meetings on his behalf went nowhere. Many radicals repudiated Czolgosz's act. Those who did not were caught in what Goldman termed "an epidemic of abject fear that could not be overcome."[43]

At about midnight, as October 28 was ending, Warden Mead went to Czolgosz's cell. The condemned man told him he "wanted to make an anarchistic speech on the scaffold in public." When Mead told him he could not, the prisoner "resumed his sullen almost ugly mood and refused to talk anymore."[44]

Five hours later the warden and a guard woke Czolgosz. The guard gave him a pair of dark trousers with a slit in the left leg, "so as to allow the free application of the electrode," and a light gray shirt. He asked to see the prison superintendent, who also turned down his request to make a speech. Soon the invited witnesses, including state officials, physicians, press representatives, the Erie County sheriff, and other assorted dignitaries, gathered in Mead's office. They were conducted to the death chamber, which Czolgosz entered a few minutes after seven, a guard to each side. The witnesses could not have been more divided as to the prisoner's demeanor. Dr. MacDonald later wrote, "As Czolgosz entered the room, he appeared calm and self-possessed, his head was erect and his face bore an expression of defiant determination." Sheriff Caldwell told a *Commercial* reporter, "I was impressed with the idea that the assassin was a man of great nerve. Although guards had hold of his arms, the prisoner could have walked unaided to the chair." Another witness from Buffalo, Charles Huntley, agreed. Czolgosz did not show any signs of fear and he did not "tremble or turn pale." Prison officials offered a different perspective. Dr. Gerin said he "went all to pieces," insisting his face "was the picture of abject terror," a view shared by John Nelson Ross, who "took all measurements and descriptions of the prisoners at Auburn." Mead said Czolgosz was so close to physical collapse that the guards virtually had to carry him to the chair.[45]

He did have enough presence of mind to begin his "anarchistic speech." Accounts vary, but the most accurate is likely the one Ross took down in shorthand at the time. "I shot the President," Czolgosz said, "because I thought it would help the working people and for the sake of the common people. I am not sorry for my crime." He was then seated in the chair, adding, "That is all I have to say." Then, as the guards adjusted the straps to his head and chin, he said, "I am awfully sorry because I did not see my father."[46]

At that moment Mead gave the signal to pull the switch. This, according to MacDonald, a longtime observer of executions, threw the prisoner's body "into a state of toxic spasm, involving apparently every fiber of the entire muscular system." As the *Commercial* reported, "The rush of immense current threw the body so hard against the straps that they creaked perceptibly. The hands clenched up suddenly and the whole attitude was one of extreme tenseness." Grisly descriptions notwithstanding, this Auburn electrocution was not botched, as William Kemmler's had been a dozen years earlier. As MacDonald noted, "That conscious life was absolutely destroyed the instant the first contact was made, was conceded by all of the medical witnesses present; also that organic life was abolished within a few seconds thereafter."[47]

An autopsy followed, alienists believing they could learn a lot by studying the brain. Czolgosz's was found to be "above normal" and slightly heavier than averages noted for "Polish brains." All this seemed to confirm that the defendant was indeed responsible for his crime. Only one more duty remained to be performed. State officials, likely fearing macabre souvenir hunters, had ordered Mead to see to it that Czolgosz's body was not merely buried but destroyed. This the warden accomplished, with the aid of sulfuric acid.[48]

24

Exposition: The Final Weeks

When the Exposition reopened on September 16 the crowds were ready to return. In fact, despite the three-day shutdown, September admissions nearly equaled those of August. Part of it was morbid curiosity. Visitors crowded into the Temple of Music, seeking the exact spot where McKinley fell. Exposition officials had covered the location with seats and instructed employees not to point it out to visitors. On September 20 Buchanan proposed to the executive committee that they may wish to consider marking the spot and railing it off. At the same time he feared potential criticism "that we were trading, in a commercial sense, upon the disgraceful act committed upon that spot." After considering the matter, both the executive committee and the board of directors decided to enclose the location and have it "marked with some simple marker."[1]

Meanwhile, Exposition offices were "besieged with ambulance chasers from New York." They sought to purchase the cot on which the president had rested after the shooting, his pillow, and any other souvenir that might be available. The requests were ignored.[2]

It did not take long for the Pan-American to return to its usual routine of the uplifting, the gaudy, and those events that straddled the line between the two. On September 29 Frank Bostock hauled a cage of lions to the Esplanade, where it became the scene of a wedding ceremony. In a strange bit of symbolism, a Presbyterian minister performed the nuptials as the tamer cracked his whip to keep the beasts at bay. The Exposition staged a baby show on October 1. It is not clear how many infants participated, but twelve came up missing during the festivities. All were recovered. Prizes went out in a variety of areas, including "fattest baby," which went to a four-month-old weighing 24 pounds. Visitors wanting more refined forms of entertainment were likely pleased when Victor Herbert and his orchestra arrived on October 14 for two weeks of concerts in the Temple of Music.[3]

Special days continued to dot the Exposition's calendar, and they often produced large crowds. Railroad Day, held on September 28, saw an attendance of 117,678. On October 9 New York Day attracted 129,576. Ten days later Buffalo Day shattered all records as 162,652 souls entered the six Exposition gates. The lessons of Midway Day were well learned, and spectacular entertainment marked the big days. On Railroad Day "Marvelous Marsh" rode a bicycle down a 130-foot incline before jumping off and diving into a pool. There was a water sports show on Mirror Lake, a balloon ascension and parachute jump, and a performer who belted a punching bag while perched near the top of the Electric Tower. New York Day included a balloon race, and Buffalo Day featured a children's parade, canoe races, and a Victor Herbert concert.[4]

Occasionally the only people not enjoying the various state days were those states' governors. On October 6, the day before Illinois Day, Gov. Richard Yates decided to make a side trip to Niagara Falls. The governor, along with several staff members and their wives, were well on their way when the train came to a sudden halt, the victim of "a disarranged dynamo." A six-mile walk followed. As New York Day was drawing to a close, Gov. Benjamin Odell and his wife headed to the life saving station to view the evening fireworks. Unfortunately neither had secured a ticket, and the federal guard in charge of the station refused to let the couple through the gate. Exposition officials vouched for the Odells, but to no avail. The guard had his orders, he asserted, and he was going to follow them to the letter. Finally the governor's party broke the impasse, surrounding the first couple and pushing them past the obstinate gatekeeper.[5]

As October wore on, and the Exposition's days became numbered, some members of the executive committee and the board of directors suggested extending the fair until November 15. They argued that the extension could add a badly needed $150,000 to the company's coffers. Those opposed not only doubted the math but pointed out that the Exposition would have to renegotiate dozens of contracts with concessionaires.

Meanwhile, proposals ranging from fire to ice began to emerge. A stock company formed with the goal of burning the Exposition to the ground as a pyrotechnic closing ceremony. Their plan called for the placement of "huge mines" in the buildings. "All about," they added, "would be scattered tanks of oil and other inflammable materials." As the mines were simultaneously detonated and the buildings went up in flames, a fireworks show would add to the festivities. Spectators would pay a dollar or more depending on how close they were to the conflagration. At the other extreme, an unnamed Midway showman suggested holding a winter ice carnival on the grounds. Under his plan the fire department would douse the Exposition buildings "until they become coated with so many thicknesses of ice as to resemble ice palaces." Fountains and lakes would become skating rinks, and a "toboggan slide" would be attached to the Electric Tower.[6]

In the end the obstacles to extending the Exposition proved insurmountable. The government exhibits were committed to the Charleston fair. New leases would have been required for everything from electric power to turnstile rental. On October 22 the board of directors voted unanimously to extend the fair just two extra days. The Pan-Am would close at the stroke of midnight, November 3.[7]

As the newly announced closing day approached, both Exposition offices and concessionaires began winding down their operations. On October 22 the board of directors voted to end fireworks shows except on Saturdays and to cut back on the number of band performances. Meanwhile souvenir dealers, not wishing to be stuck with merchandise stamped "Pan-American Exposition," made drastic price cuts. Bargain hunters also headed for the various state and national buildings, where furniture and other items could be had

The Indian Congress puts on a sham battle in the stadium (Library of Congress).

for half price. A few concessionaires began packing up and leaving, which led to a new problem. Some of them did not just haul away their own stock but other people's as well; and some of the teamsters, who mainly worked at night, helped themselves to merchandise, as well as planking, building materials, and wire.[8]

When closing day arrived it was a day of socializing as Exposition employees, Midway workers, and other individuals connected with the Pan-Am bid farewell to each other after half a year together in Buffalo. The day's highlight, from the standpoint of entertainment, was a sham battle in the Stadium. United States regulars took on members of the Indian Congress, some of whom had once been part of the real thing.

The official closing ceremonies got under way at 11:00 p.m. in the Temple of Music. Victor Herbert's orchestra opened the program. Then came a surprise announcement. J. N. Adam, a local businessman, had purchased the Temple's organ and was donating it to the city of Buffalo. Speeches by Mayor Diehl and President Milburn followed. Milburn then walked to the Triumphal Bridge and, as ten buglers sounded "Taps" from the Electric Tower, threw the switch that dimmed the Exposition lights for the final time.[9]

The Pan-American Exposition was officially over, but much of the crowd lingered and gradually turned into a mob. They stole tiny electric lights that decorated lamp posts, dug up plants, and carried off benches. At about two in the morning the marauders invaded the Midway. They tore down cloth signs and used them to entangle and throw down unsuspecting victims, took men's hats, and prowled in packs, roughing up anybody who got in their way.

One of the mob's primary targets was Pabst-on-the-Midway, a beer and restaurant concession that was crowded with customers. The problems began when waiters tossed out one of the rowdies, depositing him on his face. This offended his friends, and they demonstrated their chagrin by throwing chairs from outside porches through the windows. Passersby soon joined in, attacking anyone resembling a Pabst employee. An Exposition guard, displaying more courage than prudence, charged into the melee and was promptly laid low with a chair. He recovered and "used his club freely on the group before him." A police reinforcement soon arrived on the scene. A resourceful waiter aided them by turning a large hose on the crowd. As he aimed it at one portion of the mob, the others assailed him with bottles and chairs, but his fellow waiters rallied to his aid, returning the volleys. By the time things were under control about fifty people had been hurt, cuts and bruises accounting for most of the injuries. Pabst-on-the-Midway was wrecked.[10]

Beautiful Orient received the brunt of the next attack. "A sort of guerrilla yell" was the signal for the charge. When it was over, displays were missing, ticket boxes were scattered, and one ticket taker was trampled although not seriously injured. The rioters then directed their attention to the House Upside Down, but employees, taking a page from the Pabst waiter's playbook, used a hose to keep them at bay. The mob did manage to wrench a large clock from the outside of the show and carry it away in triumph.

The next morning revealed the damage. Even concessions that had not been entered, including A Trip to the Moon and Darkest Africa, sustained damage to exterior decorations thanks to bricks and rocks. Some fifteen thousand light bulbs were gone from the grounds, along with electrical wire. Hay, straw, and rare plants, purloined from the Agriculture and Horticulture buildings, dotted the landscape, as did glass and broken furniture. Here and there could also be found upended mineral water booths. An *Express* writer summed up the scene, writing, "The Midway ... resembled a beach upon which the tide had tossed the odds and ends of many wrecks."[11]

The Exposition allowed visitors into the grounds for twenty-five cents beginning November 3, but there was soon little to see, and workers easily outnumbered tourists. Many of the Midway attractions were bound for Charleston, and a number of ethnic shows were obligated to return performers to their native countries. By the end of the day, the *Commercial* reported, "The Mexicans, Eskimos, the Hawaiians, the Filipinos, the Japs, most of the Indians, and many of the Orientals have departed." A group of concessionaires booked a special train, with freight cars for structural material, a passenger coach for speilers, and stock cars for the animals. The Indian Congress avoided the problem of transporting stock by holding a horse auction on November 7.[12]

Many exhibitors also planned to move on to Charleston, and the work of removing displays from the major buildings got under way at 8:00 a.m. on the 3rd. To prevent theft, Exposition officials instructed those taking down exhibits to supply the building superintendent with a list of items to be removed. This was checked as the display items were loaded and again when the wagons left the grounds. Two special guards were stationed adjacent to Tiffany & Company's extensive jewelry and gemstone exhibit as it was packed for shipment. After just two days of work Buffalo newspapers reported that virtually all of the displays were at least partially gone, and many had been totally removed. This was bad news for a couple from Carthage, Missouri. A train wreck *en route* and a death in the family had forced them to return home twice. They finally reached Buffalo on November 7 but remained positive. "Of course the fair's over, but there's a whole lot to be seen here," the gentleman told a reporter. "There's nothing in my part of Missouri that can come up to these buildings of yours."[13]

On November 4 crews began removing the lights, fixtures, and wiring used to illuminate the major buildings. The Exposition Company had leased all the wire, so it had to be carefully rolled up for its safe return. The board closed the hospital on November 3 and disbanded the police force on November 15. With post-fair admissions averaging under a thousand a day, the company announced that the gates would close for good on November 17. The board agreed to sell flags, turnstiles, office furniture, and 265 "comfort cots" to the Charleston exposition. They rejected a proposal to sell the lamps in the Temple of Music to be resold as souvenirs. On November 26 the board entered into a contract with the Chicago House Wrecking Company, which purchased "buildings and other material" for $93,000.[14]

As he prepared to ship his animal show to Charleston, Frank Bostock had a serious problem. Jumbo II, a large African elephant, had attacked at least three individuals in recent weeks. Two were animal keepers who worked for Bostock. One suffered head injuries and several broken ribs; the other had his arm broken in two places. The last straw came when Jumbo seized the eleven-year-old daughter of one of his employees. He grabbed the girl with his trunk and would likely have killed her had she not slipped out of her dress and rolled to safety. Bostock announced plans to hang the beast in the Stadium, but after consulting with representatives of the Humane Society, he changed the sentence to electrocution. He placed an ad in the *Buffalo Commercial*, announcing that the public could witness the spectacle for fifty cents and informing them that the New York Central would run special excursion trains for the event.

It was all for naught. First, shortly before the scheduled 2:30 execution, Mayor Diehl and other prominent Buffalo residents persuaded Bostock not to make the electrocution a public spectacle. Between seven hundred and a thousand had already paid their admission fee and entered the Stadium. They were conducted back out, their money refunded. Despite the commercial setback, Bostock still intended to do away with his troublesome pachyderm. He rescheduled the execution for sundown and announced that the public would not be admitted. Despite the admonition to stay away, some five hundred souls found their way into the Stadium by dusk. They didn't see much. A 2,200-volt charge from the Exposition's powerhouse surged through the four electrodes attached to Jumbo's hide but didn't faze the intended victim a bit. He threw a trunkful of dirt over his back, glanced at the curious-looking electrical apparatus around him, but otherwise did not so much as blink. Some suspected a flaw in the power delivery, others speculated that the beast's thick rubberlike skin had spared him. In any event, Bostock announced that he would not try to play executioner again. As a result, Jumbo headed to

Charleston more famous than ever; and considering the Midway men's flair for publicity, that might have been the idea all along.[15]

As late as October 20 John Milburn was living in denial, at least publicly, concerning the Exposition Company's financial health. "If we get 10,000 paid admissions a day," he told a reporter, "we will more than pay operating expenses." Then he hedged. "As to the financial outcome, I do not think it proper to make any predictions." With just two weeks to go the Exposition president claimed he was "cudgeling my brain to get up some more big days like Buffalo Day." By the time the fair ended, Milburn had shifted his position somewhat. On the one hand, he proclaimed, "The Exposition was a credit from every point, artistic as well as utilitarian," adding, "In the history of expositions it ranks as one of the greatest that has ever been given, and will take high place as a thing of beauty." As to the bottom line, however, "What might be termed a financial unsuccess will, I am sure, be met by the citizens of Buffalo with the same courage, dignity, fortitude and graciousness with which they built the Exposition."[16]

The Pan-Am had indeed been "a financial unsuccess." Stock subscriptions had resulted in $1,724,770, and first and second mortgage bonds had realized another $3 million. However, as the Exposition was set to open, the projected budget came to nearly seven million. This meant the fair would need eight million paid admissions to break even. It got 5,306,859, plus 2,813,189 unpaid visitors. A total of 296 concessions brought in another $1,345,717. At $89,543, the Bailey Catering Company yielded the most. This was followed by The Beautiful Orient ($54,445), Alt Nuremberg ($50,946), Pabst's-on-the-Midway ($46,480), and Bostock's Animal Show ($41,551). All of this was not enough, and Milburn was forced to concede that the Exposition had lost some six million dollars and would have to default on over $3,500,000 in bonds.[17]

Among the victims were the Rumsey Brothers, on whose property the Exposition had been held. On November 25 the executive committee voted not to restore the Rumseys' property to its original condition, as the company had originally promised to do. The cost which fell upon the brothers was believed to approach six figures. One week later they learned that the Exposition would also default on nearly one-third of the rent, approximately $21,000.[18]

On December 6 the Erie County sheriff took possession of all Exposition buildings and their contents. Deputies occupied every structure, and items in booths which had not been emptied remained in place. So did shrubs and other plants, many of which Buffalo residents and area nurseries had already purchased. A sale of office furniture, held to satisfy one of the Exposition's claimants, resulted in bargain prices and realized only $236. Despite the objections of director of works Carlton, who explained that several cabinets had simply been loaned to the company, a deputy sold them with everything else.[19]

The same day the deputies arrived at the Rainbow City, Milburn departed Buffalo for a trip to the nation's capital. Officially he went to Washington to attend a meeting of the McKinley Memorial Association; but he also planned to do a little lobbying. During his stay Milburn met with members of both houses of Congress, pushing for an aid bill to help with the Exposition's shortfall. Not everybody appreciated the effort. Milburn had been back home only a short time when he received a letter threatening his life "unless you personally see to it that some return is made to those poor workingmen and poor workingwomen who invested in Pan-American stock and to whom silvery promises were made and have been unfulfilled." Still the Exposition president overcame long odds and secured some relief. Both Speaker of the House David Henderson and Rep. Joseph "Uncle Joe" Cannon, chairman of the appropriations committee, opposed sending additional taxpayer money to Buffalo. Nevertheless, on June 30, 1902, the House voted 118–110 for a $500,000 appropriation. The measure won Senate approval, and President Roosevelt added his signature.[20]

Eventually the Exposition Company claimed that its creditors received 97% of what was due them. However, the bill left out a number of claimants. None of the appropriation could be used for either rent or the restoration of property, once again shutting out the Rumseys. In addition the Company defaulted on some $3,500,000 worth of bonds. It appears the only relief the bondholders received was approximately $70,000 divided between them after a tract of Exposition property on the north side of Delaware Park was sold in 1904.[21]

Even with the onset of a Buffalo winter, visitors into the hundreds continued to stroll around the former Rainbow City. The snow was deep, and the once brilliant hues had largely turned pastel, but that seemed not to matter to people longing for one last look at the fair. This opportunity came to an abrupt end on March 2, when the Chicago House Wrecking Company erected signs threatening to arrest trespassers. In addition to all buildings owned by the Exposition Company, the firm also purchased the Government Building for $5,100. On March 5 they began dismantling the fair, starting with the Fine Arts Building. It was one of the few brick structures on the grounds, and the company believed there would be a demand for bricks "in the local spring building boom."[22]

Within a few weeks the Fine Arts Building was a memory, as were numerous state and foreign buildings. The Stadium began coming down at the end of March. By early May Transportation, Horticulture, Ethnology, Manufactures, and the Government Building were all targets of the wrecking ball. Most of the Midway had also fallen. It was against this backdrop that Mr. and Mrs. Adolph von Holbein of Leipzig, Germany arrived in Buffalo on May 10, hoping to visit the newly opened Exposition. Mr. von Holbein, described by the *Courier* as "an intelligent German," told the paper, "I made a mistake in the dates."[23]

Work on wrecking the Temple of Music got under way on April 27. Souvenir hunters had already begun the process. Light bulbs went first, followed by other items that could be carried off easily. Eventually the scavengers pried up floor boards around the spot where McKinley had been standing when he was shot. Meanwhile looters of a different sort were offering to purchase the building, hoping to put it up somewhere else and charge admission. It was rumored to be destined for the St. Louis fair as a midway attraction, but John Milburn squelched the report. A clause in the Exposition Company's contract with the wrecking firm, he explained, stipulated that the Temple could not "be sold or used for exhibition purposes."[24]

At the same time a movement was afoot to save the Electric Tower and make it a permanent part of the Buffalo skyline. One plan called for the city to purchase it and move it to "the Front," where many had originally wanted the fair to take place. Another suggested leaving it where it was and purchasing the surrounding land. The Rumsey family, which had had its fill of everything connected with the Pan-Am, shot down this idea when they flatly refused to sell the property. All plans eventually fell through, and in the spring of 1902 the fair's crowning architectural achievement began coming down. Before the process was complete, two workmen fell from the structure and were killed.[25]

Another victim was the Goddess of Light, the gilded statue perched atop the tower. David Humphrey, a popcorn vendor at a beach near Cleveland, purchased it to put atop the dome of his sales pavilion. There it would join the Forestry Building, which Humphrey planned to convert into a dance hall, as well as several Midway structures. As July dawned and Humphrey had failed to come for the Goddess, the wrecking company secured some rope and attempted to bring her down themselves. It didn't work out well. Soon the once-proud figure lay at the base of the tower, "a mass of galvanized iron." The *Courier*, writing tongue-in-cheek, termed it a suicide from a lady who vowed "never [to] be so humiliated." Driving home the point, the paper explained, "Cleveland—of all places—a popcorn joint—of all thrones."[26]

A thing of beauty that met an unfortunate demise, the Goddess of Light was a fitting, final symbol of the fair she adorned. The Pan-American Exposition had educated, enlightened, and entertained millions. It showed the world the wonders of the chaining of Niagara and of the Industrial Revolution. Its light show inspired nightly, and its Midway produced mirth. Unfortunately, in Buffalo these memories of the fair's triumphs would mix with the reality of "a financial unsuccess"; and with the passage of time America, if it remembered at all, would know it only as the place where McKinley had fallen.

"The Pan" deserved better.

Appendix

The Secret Service, "Big Jim" Parker, the 73rd Seacoast Artillery and Homer James: Who Did What?

In the "interview" overheard by the *Buffalo Courier* reporter, Samuel Ireland drew the wrath of his superior, Secret Service director John Wilkie, for placing implicit blame on George Cortelyou for the positioning of guards in the Temple of Music.

That was not the only statement which upset Ireland's boss. The agent was also quoted as saying, "I reached for the young man [Czolgosz] and caught his left arm. The big negro standing just back of him; and who would have been next to take the President's hand, struck the young man in the neck with one hand and with the other reached for the revolver."[1]

The "big negro" was James Benjamin "Big Jim" Parker, a waiter at one of the Exposition's restaurants, who like his fellow citizens, was anxious to shake hands with the president. In the days immediately following the shooting, Ireland's initial assessment, that Parker acted as a hero, was the general one. The *Express* reported, "James B. Parker, the negro who seized and knocked down Leon Czolgosz ... is greatly admired by visitors at the Pan-American Exposition, to whom he is pointed out." Fairgoers asked him to relate his story, and bolder ones even asked for pieces of the waistcoat he was wearing at the time of the shooting. One offered a quarter for a button off the garment, another upped the ante to a dollar. Even early on, however, there was a cloud on the horizon. "Parker is somewhat indignant," the *Express* observed, "at what he terms the unwarranted action of the Government detectives in attempting to take the credit for the capture of the would-be assassin."[2]

The campaign to discredit Parker was thorough and largely effective. It started with Wilkie. In reprimanding Ireland, the chief wrote that the agent's unguarded words were "largely responsible for the wide distribution of the

247

absurd story of the Negro Parker, which, at least, gave an opening for much undeserved criticism of this Service." Ireland took the not-so-subtle hint. In his official report he wrote of an epiphany. Conceding that he first believed Parker's story that the waiter had struck the assassin, he continued, "Later when over the excitement and my memory being refreshed by the reporters and others, I am sure I recall Parker's having passed in the line some time ahead of Czolgosz and noting his unusual height and peculiar looking face,"[3]

Before the end of the month the *Buffalo Courier* was "reporting," "This negro has been given national prominence by making claims of bravery which on the spur of the moment seemed genuine but have since been shown to be entirely false." The paper added, "Parker is said to be making capital out of the notoriety, which the press unwittingly but generously gave him." Big Jim was not entirely without friends. The *Evening News* published an account of two white southerners, who echoed Parker's story. On September 27 his "colored friends" met at the Vine Street Methodist Church. Parker appeared but declined to speak before the gathering. The group passed a cautiously worded set of resolutions, pointing out that the Associated Press, "a herald of accepted facts," had reported Parker's "heroic acts." They concluded, "That when the American historian shall have written the narrative he may find himself able so to reconcile the conflicting statements as to award honor to whom honor is due."[4]

Unfortunately the details of exactly what Parker—or anybody else—did that afternoon are lost to history. As the resolution asserted, the accounts are conflicting. Still, the earliest stories of witnesses, likely the most accurate, strongly suggest that Parker was very much involved in the effort to apprehend Czolgosz. The *Buffalo Express* reported that Ireland first grabbed the shooter and threw him to the floor. As he fell, "A huge negro named John[*sic*] Parker leaped upon him … and they rolled over on the floor." The *Evening News* said Exposition guard Homer James delivered the first blow. "Before [Czolgosz] could bestir himself," the paper continued, "the groveling coward was pinned to the floor under six feet of the brawn and muscle of James B. Parker." The *Commercial* offered two accounts in the same story. The first one mirrored the version printed in the *Express*. Eleven paragraphs later, it claimed, "Parker, the negro, put his hands on Czolgosz first; he threw his arms about the assailant with a pressure that would have strangled him." Only Foster's intervention, the story went on, saved the assassin. The *Courier* was the only Buffalo paper not to mention Parker, although it did publish Ireland's interview crediting the waiter. Its account identified Foster and Ireland as the first men to reach the assailant.[5]

The *Rochester Union and Advertiser* produced three witnesses who corroborated Parker's account of events. William H. Coon, a resident of Batavia, said he was "looking directly at the President as the shots rang out.... Next he saw the negro hurl himself at the would-be assassin and grasp him by the throat and throw him to the floor." Charles Cooney and Beckworth Trimper, farmers living near Clyde, a village some sixty miles east of Rochester, also witnessed the shooting. "They are both credible persons," the paper asserted, "and they state that the negro John[*sic*] Parker, was the first one to reach the would-be assassin. With two blows he knocked the fellow down and then pounced upon his prostrate form."[6]

Except for one brief reference, Parker was never mentioned at the Czolgosz trial. As Foster was being cross examined by Titus, defense counsel asked if he had noticed a "dark complexioned man with a black moustache." The agent replied that he had seen him and, not liking his looks, passed him along. Foster apparently thought Titus was referring to the man the guards believed to be Italian and, therefore, a potential anarchist. The attorney seems to have been thinking of Parker. As a result, this exchange ensued:

Q. Did you see this colored man?
A. What colored man?
Q. Parker?
A. I noticed a colored man in the line, but it seems to me he was in front of this man.
Q. Instead of behind him?
A. Instead of behind him. I never saw no colored man in the whole fracas.[7]

Bad grammar aside, Foster's voluntary addendum to his final answer was unnecessary. Titus had not asked him about the "fracas." It would appear that the agent was anxious for any opportunity to drive home the Secret Service's version of events.

A number of witnesses contradicted that account, giving credit neither to the Secret Service nor to James Parker. Instead they cited members of the of the 73rd Company, Seacoast Artillery, as the first men to reach Czolgosz. According to Louis Babcock, the military men "centered upon the prisoner from all sides, and almost quicker than I can describe it, bore him to the ground." Secret Service, Buffalo police, and Exposition guards soon joined the fray. James Quackenbush told a similar story, testifying that the artillerymen "lunged forward towards the defendant," followed quickly by Foster and Ireland. Harry Henshaw, the superintendent of music, told the court the first men he saw grab Czolgosz were two soldiers. "At the same instant," he continued, "there was a dozen or more who crowded around and struggled to get at the man also." John Branch, in charge of the Temple toilet rooms, offered a slightly different account: "I saw one of the Exposition guards grab after this man, and at this time this artilleryman got near the man first," bearing him down.[8]

Perhaps because his previously published remarks would have proven troublesome, Ireland did not testify at the trial. Agent Gallaher said he fell as he sprang forward toward the assassin, then heard Foster shouting for him to get the gun. Foster testified that he grabbed Czolgosz first, was soon joined by two unidentified men, and the three of them took the shooter to the floor. This surprised Titus, who had just heard Babcock, Quackenbush, Henshaw, and Branch say the military men had been the first to get to Czolgosz. Under cross examination he asked Foster, "Then you were the man instead of those artillerymen that crushed the defendant to the floor?" That made Foster back off a bit. He replied, "No, sir. When we settled down, I noticed a man by the name of O'Brien ... was lying right alongside of me." He added, "That was the only artilleryman that was seen though."[9]

The man to whom Foster was referring was Pvt. Francis P. O'Brien. According to his own testimony, he was the first man to get to the assassin. "I jumped at him and knocked him over against somebody," O'Brien recalled. He repeated the assertion when cross examined by Titus. Corp. Louis Bertschey, who commanded the small squad sent to the Temple of Music, supported O'Brien's story when he appeared on the stand.[10]

Historians of the McKinley assassination often focus on the contentious claims of Parker and the Secret Service. Occasionally Private O'Brien and the 73rd receive some notice. There is a fourth player, however, whose name has been lost to history. On September 25, 1901, the *Noble County Leader*, a Caldwell, Ohio newspaper, reported that Exposition guard Homer James, a hometown boy, "was who struck down President McKinley's assassin." The story asserted that, almost as soon as the shots were fired, "there was the smack of Guard James' club as he smashed the brute in the face." The story continued, "He staggered back stunned into the arms of the powerful colored man Parker and both went down together." It also predicted, "The Buffalo city police department and the secret service agents will try and rob him of the honor."[11]

James Parker could have appreciated that last statement. However, it may also have been true in the case of Homer James. The guard testified before the grand jury but not at the trial, the account of which was public. His story is also not without corroboration. As mentioned above, the *Buffalo Evening News* reported that James felled Czolgosz with a "blow across the face" from his baton. The magazine *Timely Topics* wrote, "Homer James, an Exposition guard, was probably the first to reach Czolgosz. He sprang across the backs of those who blocked his way and dashed his club upon the anarchist's skull."[12]

It seems likely that James Parker would have lived a happier life—and likely a longer one—had he not been at the Temple of Music that day. At first he did well, lecturing to largely African-American audiences and recounting his story. Mark Hanna reportedly gave him a gift of one thousand dollars. Soon, however, Parker fell on hard times. In 1907 he wrote to Ida McKinley, asking if she could use her influence to secure him a job in the government. The former first lady passed the letter along to Cortelyou, asking if he could help her husband's protector. Through the secretary's influence, Parker got work as a congressional messenger.

Sadly, it didn't last long. Parker had a hard time holding a job, a fact to which heavy drinking likely contributed. Indeed, just a few weeks before writing to Ida, Parker had been arrested in Atlantic City, New Jersey. Police charged him with vagrancy, but a judge refused to sentence him, saying, "A man who tried to do the service for his country that Parker attempted deserves leniency." Following a subsequent arrest, Parker was committed to the "insane department" of a West Philadelphia hospital. It was there that he died in early 1908.[13]

There will likely never be a conclusive answer to the question of exactly who did what that fateful afternoon at the Temple of Music. There seems little doubt, however, that the Secret Service did James Parker a grave disservice. There are simply too many early eyewitnesses, including guard James and the indiscreet Ireland, to suggest otherwise. And in 1901 America it was very unlikely that many people would have lied to make a hero of a black man. Yet in a sense, McKinley's death made the question moot. Big Jim Parker may have prevented Czolgosz from firing a third round. As it turned out, two were plenty.

Chapter Notes

Chapter 1

1. H. Wayne Morgan, *William McKinley and His America* (Kent, OH: Kent State University Press, 2003, repr. of 1963 edition), 2–5; Margaret Leech, *In the Days of McKinley* (New York: Harper & Brothers, 1959), 4.

2. Morgan, *McKinley*, 6–9; Leech, *In the Days*, 5.

3. Murat Halstad, *The Illustrious Life of William McKinley, Our Martyred President* (N.p.: Author, 1901), 113.

4. Morgan, *McKinley*, 13–14.

5. Roger Pickenpaugh, *Camp Chase and the Evolution of Union Prison Policy* (Tuscaloosa: University of Alabama Press, 2007), 13–14; William H. Armstrong, *Major McKinley: William McKinley and the Civil War* (Kent, OH: Kent State University Press), 4, 9–10; H. Wayne Morgan (ed.), "A Civil War Diary of William McKinley," *Ohio Historical Quarterly* 69, no. 3 (1960), 276–277.

6. Armstrong, *Major McKinley*, 15–21.

7. *Ibid.*, 22, 28–29, 36, 38–41.

8. *Ibid.*, 43–44, 50–52; Morgan, *McKinley*, 22.

9. Armstrong, *Major McKinley*, 63–66, 71–75, 82–83.

10. *Ibid.*, 103.

11. *Ibid.*, 104–106.

12. Morgan, *McKinley*, 30–34.

13. Leech, *In the Days*, 11; Morgan, *McKinley*, 35–37.

14. Morgan, *McKinley*, 38–39; Julia B. Foraker, *I Would Live it Again: Memories of a Vivid Life* (New York: Harper & Brothers, 1932), 258.

15. Morgan, *McKinley*, 40–42; Henry L. Stoddard, *As I Knew Them: Presidents and Politics from Grant to Coolidge* (New York: Harper & Brothers, 1927), 229; H. H. Kohlsaat, *From McKinley to Harding: Personal Recollections of Our Presidents* (New York: Charles Scribner's Sons, 1923), 96.

16. Morgan, *McKinley*, 42–43.

17. *Ibid.*, 48–49.

18. *Ibid.*, 54–55.

19. *Ibid.*, 63; Leech, *In the Days*, 19–23.

20. Morgan, *McKinley*, 85–98.

21. *Ibid.*, 104–116; R. Hal Williams, *Years of Decision: American Politics in the 1890s* (New York: John Wiley & Sons, 1978), 44.

22. Morgan, *McKinley*, 117–120.

23. *Ibid.*, 121; Leech, *In the Days*, 58.

24. Charles S. Olcott, *William McKinley*, 2 vols. (Boston and New York: Houghton Mifflin, 1916), I, 281–282; Ivan M. Tribe, *Sprinkled with Coal Dust: Life and Work in the Hocking Coal Region, 1870–1900* (Athens, OH: Athens County Historical Society, 1989), 123–125.

25. Morgan, *McKinley*, 4, 124–125; Leech, *In the Days*, 28.

26. H. Wayne Morgan, "Governor McKinley's Misfortune: The Walker-McKinley Fund of 1893," *The Ohio Historical Quarterly* 69, no. 2 (April 1960), 103–120.

27. Morgan, *McKinley*, 134, 137–139; Williams, *Years of Decision*, 94.

Chapter 2

1. Eric Rauchway, *Murdering McKinley: The Making of Theodore Roosevelt's America* (New York: Hill & Wang, 2003), 120; Scott Miller, *The President and the Assassin: McKinley, Terror, and Empire at the Dawn of the American Century* (New York: Random House, 2011), 38.

2. Miller, *The President and the Assassin*, 39–41; L. Vernon Briggs, *The Manner of Man That Kills* (New York: Da Capo, 1983, repr. of 1921 edition), 289–290.

3. Briggs, *The Manner of Man That Kills*, 290–291.

4. Lloyd Vernon Briggs interviews, Channing Family Papers, Massachusetts, Historical Society (hereafter referred to as CFP, MHS).

5. Briggs interviews, CFP, MHS.

6. Briggs, *Manner of Man*, 314–315.

7. Briggs interviews, CFP, MHS.

8. Rauchway, *Murdering McKinley*, 166.

9. Briggs, *Manner of Man*, 303–305; Briggs interviews, CFP, MHS.

10. Briggs, *Manner of Man*, 305; Briggs interviews, CFP, MHS.

11. Briggs interviews, CFP, MHS.

12. Rauchway, *Murdering McKinley*, 175–176; Miller, *The President and the Assassin*, 231–232; Briggs interviews, CFP, MHS.

13. Briggs interviews, CFP, MHS.

14. Briggs interviews, CFP, MHS.

15. Briggs interviews, CFP, MHS.

16. Briggs interviews, CFP, MHS.

17. Briggs interviews, CFP, MHS.

18. Briggs, *Manner of Man*, 294, 307; Briggs interviews, CFP, MHS.

19. Rauchway, *Murdering McKinley*, 100–101; James W. Clarke, *American Assassins, the Darker Side of Politics* (Princeton, NJ: Princeton University Press, 1982), 42–51.

Chapter 3

1. John W. Percy, *Buffalo-Niagara Connections: A New Regional History of the Niagara Link* (Buffalo: Western New York Regional, 2007), 21–25.

2. J. N. Larned, *A History of Buffalo Delineating the Evolution of the City* (New York: Progress of the Empire State, 1911), 7; Sophie C. Becker, *Sketches of Early Buffalo and the Niagara Region* (Buffalo: McLaughlin, 1904), 106–107.

3. Percy, *Buffalo-Niagara Connections*, 31–35, 44.

4. *Ibid.*, 46; Becker, *Sketches of Early Buffalo*, 108–109; H. Perry Smith, *History of the City of Buffalo and Erie County, with Illustrations and Biographical Sketches of Some of Its Prominent Men and Pioneers*, 2 vols. (Syracuse: D. Mason & Co., 1884), 19–21.

5. Percy, *Buffalo-Niagara Connections*, 48–49; Larned, *History of Buffalo*, 12–13; Smith, *History of Buffalo*, 25.

6. Smith, *History of Buffalo*, 21; Larned, *History of Buffalo*, 12–13; William Ketchum, "The Origin of the Name of Buffalo," *Publications of the Buffalo Historical Society* 1 (1879), 17–19, 26.

7. Larned, *History of Buffalo*, 15–16; Smith, *History of Buffalo*, 36–38; Becker, *Sketches of Early Buffalo*, 114.

8. Becker, *Sketches of Early Buffalo*, 115–116; Larned, *History of Buffalo*, 22; Smith, *History of Buffalo*, 46–50.

9. Louis L. Babcock, *The War of 1812 on the Niagara Frontier* (Buffalo, NY: Buffalo Historical Society, 1927), 116–137; Larned, *History of Buffalo*, 27–30; Becker, *Sketches of Early Buffalo*, 119–131.

10. Becker, *Sketches of Early Buffalo*, 132; Smith, *History of Buffalo*, 76–77.

11. Percy, *Buffalo-Niagara Connections*, 135–136, 146–148; Smith, *History of Buffalo*, 80–95; Larned, *History of Buffalo*, 32–33.

12. Larned, *History of Buffalo*, 37–38; Percy, *Buffalo-Niagara Connections*, 152.

13. Percy, *Buffalo-Niagara Connections*, 153, 155–156; Larned, *History of Buffalo*, 40–43; Henry Wayland Hill, *Municipality of Buffalo, New York, A History 1720–1923*, 2 vols. (New York: Lewis Historical Publishing, 1923), 269–270.

14. Percy, *Buffalo-Niagara Connections*, 167–168.

15. Hill, *Municipality of Buffalo*, 267, 296; Larned, *History of Buffalo*, 43, 59.

16. Larned, *History of Buffalo*, 56–57; Hill, *Municipality of Buffalo*, 295; Smith, *History of Buffalo*, 119–120.

17. Smith, *History of Buffalo*, 120–121.

18. Larned, *History of Buffalo*, 43–44, 60–61; Smith, *History of Buffalo*, 114–115, 121; Hill, *Municipality of Buffalo*, 268, 296; Lewis F. Allen, "The Cholera in Buffalo," *Publications of the Buffalo Historical Society* 4 (1896), 245–255.

19. Smith, *History of Buffalo*, 96–98; Hill, *Municipality of Buffalo*, 297–298.

20. "Francis Joseph Walter," A Social and Cultural History of Buffalo, New York, 1865–1901, Ph.D. diss., Western Reserve University, 1958, 153–154.

21. Percy, *Buffalo-Niagara Connections*, 171; *Buffalo Express*, May 21, 1872, quoted in Walter, Social and Cultural History, 150.

22. Walter, Social and Cultural History, 44, 69–74.

23. *Ibid.*, 173–175, 190–193.

24. *Ibid.*, 151–152.

Chapter 4

1. Morgan, *McKinley*, 140–143; Williams, *Years of Decision*, 101; Paul W. Glad, *McKinley, Bryan, and the People* (New York: J. B. Lippincott, 1964), 98–99.

2. Morgan, *McKinley*, 149–152; Roger Pickenpaugh, "Front Porch Campaign," *Timeline*, October-December 2007, 46.

3. R. Hal Williams, *Realigning America: McKinley, Bryan, and the Remarkable Election of 1896* (Lawrence: University Press of Kansas, 2010), 65; Leech, *In the Days*, 132.

4. Paul W. Glad, *The Trumpet Soundeth: William Jennings Bryan and His Democracy, 1896–1912* (Lincoln: University of Nebraska Press), 54–56; Williams, *Realigning America*, 84–86.

5. Williams, *Years of Decision*, 112; Glad, *McKinley, Bryan, and the People*, 176; Williams, *Realigning America*, 130–131.

6. Lewis L. Gould, *The Presidency of William McKinley* (Lawrence: Regents Press of Kansas, 1980), 11–12.

7. Williams, *Realigning America*, 131.

8. Pickenpaugh, "Front Porch Campaign," 51.

9. Williams, *Years of Decision*, 119; Williams, *Realigning America*, 134; Pickenpaugh, "Front Porch Campaign," 51–55.

10. Williams, *Realigning America*, 136–139; Williams, *Years of Decision*, 121.

11. Stoddard, *As I Knew Them*, 241.

12. Pickenpaugh, "Front Porch Campaign," 57–58.

13. *Ibid.*, 58.

14. *Ibid.*; Williams, *Realigning America*, 147–149.

15. Williams, *Realigning America*, 149–150.

16. Pickenpaugh, "Front Porch Campaign," 59.

17. Leech, *In the Days*, 113.

18. Kohlsaat, *From McKinley to Harding*, 68.

19. James D. Richardson (ed.), *A Compilation of the Messages and Papers of the Presidents*, 10 vols. (Washington, DC: Bureau of National Literature, 1913) VIII, 6236–6238.

20. *Ibid.*, 6239; David Saville Muzzey, *James G. Blaine: A Political Idol of Other Days* (New York: Dodd, Mead, 1935), 431–457; Alice Felt Tyler, *The Foreign Policy of James G. Blaine* (Hamden, CT: Archon, 1965, repr. of 1927 edition), 184–188; Leech, *In the Days*, 141–142; Morgan, *McKinley*, 129–146.

21. Richardson, *Messages and Papers*, VIII, 6240–6244.

Chapter 5

1. Leech, *In the Days*, 134; the quote comes from Gould, *The Presidency*, 52.

2. Morgan, *McKinley*, 191–195; William T. Horner, *Ohio's Kingmaker: Mark Hanna, Man and Myth* (Athens: Ohio University Press, 2010), 213–220.

3. Foraker, *I Would Live It Again*, 256; Leach, *In the Days*, 131–132; Dunn, *From Harrison to Harding*, 224–225.

4. Leech, *In the Days*, 132, 435; Mrs. Garrett A. Hobart, *Memoirs* (NP: Privately Printed, 1930), 14, 29–30, 46–49.

5. Leech, *In the Days*, 127; Gould, *The Presidency*, 39.

6. Leech, *In the Days*, 131; Morgan, *McKinley*, 236–237; *Pittsburgh Times*, March 22, 1897, quoted in Gould, *The Presidency*, 37.

7. Stephen Ponder, *Managing the Press: Origins of the Media Presidency, 1897–1933* (New York: St. Martin's Press, 1999), 3, 5, 6.

8. *Ibid.*, 2, 5, 13–14; Leech, *In the Days*, 230–231; Gould, *The Presidency*, 38.

9. Williams, *Years of Decision*, 132.

10. Gould, *The Presidency*, 13, 27, 40, 42–43; Morgan, *McKinley*, 211–215; Leech, *In the Days*, 141–142; Williams, *Years of Decision*, 132–135.

11. Lyman J. Gage, *Memoirs of Lyman G. Gage* (New York: House of Field, Inc., 1937), 112–114.

12. Morgan, *McKinley*, 238–239.

13. *Ibid.*, 234–237; Foraker, *I Would Live It Again*, 192; Kohlsaat, *From McKinley to Harding*, 156.

14. John Dobson, *Reticent Expansionism: The Foreign Policy of William McKinley* (Pittsburgh: Duquesne University Press, 1998), 30, 153–159; Gould, *The Presidency*, 48.

15. Gould, *The Presidency*, 48–49; Dobson, *Reticent Expansionism*, 15; William Adam Russ, Jr., *The Hawaiian Republic (1894–1898) and Its Struggle to Win Annexation* (Selisgrove, PA: Susquehana University Press, 1961), vii–viii.

16. Dobson, *Reticent Expansionism*, 15, 35, 95–97; Gould, *The Presidency*, 48–50; Russ, *The Hawaiian Republic*, 130–131, 137–138, 143–145, 156, 194, 218–219; Evan Thomas, *The War Lovers: Roosevelt, Lodge, Hearst, and the Rush to Empire, 1898* (New York: Little, Brown, and Company, 2010), 169–171.

17. Dobson, *Reticent Expansionism*, 96–98; Russ, *The Hawaiian Republic*, 343–355.

18. Leech, *In the Days*, 152; Gould, *The Presidency*, 50; Dobson, *Reticent Expansionism*, 28, 33, 37–39.

19. Dobson, *Reticent Expansionism*, 39–42; David F. Trask, *The War with Spain in 1898* (New York: Macmillan Publishing Company, Inc., 1981), 2–6; John L. Offner, *An Unwanted War: The Diplomacy of the United States and Spain over Cuba, 1895–1898* (Chapel Hill: University of North Carolina Press, 1992), 3, 12.

20. Trask, *The War with Spain*, 8–11; G. J. A. O'Toole, *The Spanish War: An American Epic—*

1898 (New York: W. W. Norton & Company, 1984), 56–57; Ivan Musicant, *Empire by Default: The Spanish-American War and the Dawn of the American Century* (New York: Henry Holt and Company, 1998), 67–70; Offner, *An Unwanted War*, 12; Dobson, *Reticent Expansionism*, 44.

21. Trask, *The War with Spain*, 2. For Hearst and Pulitzer see David R. Spencer, *The Yellow Journalism: The Press and America's Emergence as a World Power* (Evanston, IL: Northwestern University Press, 2007).

22. Trask, *The War with Spain*, 13; Stoddard, *As I Knew Them*, 232; Gould, *The Presidency*, 63; Miller, *The President and the Assassin*, 95–96.

23. Offner, *An Unwanted War*, 42–47; Gould, *The Presidency*, 67; Musicant, *Empire by Default*, 103–104; John L. Offner, "McKinley and the Spanish-American War," *Presidential Studies Quarterly*, 34, no.1 (March 2004), 54.

24. Offner, *An Unwanted War*, 48; Offner, "McKinley and the Spanish-American War," 54; Trask, *The War with Spain*, 17; Gould, *The Presidency*, 67.

25. Trask, *The War with Spain*, 17; Offner, *An Unwanted War*, 50–51.

26. Musicant, *Empire by Default*, 108–109; Trask, *The War with Spain*, 19–21; Dobson, *Reticent Expansionism*, 51; Offner, *An Unwanted War*, 80–81.

27. Musicant, *Empire by Default*, 110, 115; Richardson, *Messages and Papers*, VIII, 6,255–6,263.

28. Offner, *An Unwanted War*, 92–93.

29. Musicant, *Empire by Default*, 118–119, 125; Dobson, *Reticent Expansionism*, 55; Trask, *The War with Spain*, 24.

30. Trask, *The War with Spain*, 25; Musicant, *Empire by Default*, 126–130.

31. Musicant, *Empire by Default*, 137–141; Offner, *An Unwanted War*, 122.

32. Thomas, *The War Lovers*, 209; Offner, *An Unwanted War*, 123; O'Toole, *The Spanish War*, 127.

33. Dobson, *Reticent Expansionism*, 29; Offner, *An Unwanted War*, 124.

34. Offner, *An Unwanted War*, 129; Thomas, *The War Lovers*, 233; Trask, *The War with Spain*, 33–34.

35. Thomas, *The War Lovers*, 147.

36. O'Toole, *The Spanish War*, 100, 136; Trask, *The War with Spain*, 80–81, 86; Musicant, *Empire by Default*, 159–160.

37. O'Toole, *The Spanish War*, 146.

38. Offner, *An Unwanted War*, 131–134; O'-Toole, *The Spanish War*, 146.

39. Musicant, *Empire by Default*, 165–166; O'-Toole, *The Spanish War*, 147.

40. Leech, *In the Days*, 173–175; O'Toole, *The Spanish War*, 150.

41. Musicant, *Empire by Default*, 174–176; Leech, *In the Days*, 178–179; Hobart, *Memories*, 60.

42. Musicant, *Empire by Default*, 168.

43. *Ibid.*, 178; Trask, *The War with Spain*, 49, 56.

44. Trask, *The War with Spain*, 40–44; Gould, *The Presidency*, 79; Musicant, *Empire by Default*, 172–173, 176–177.

45. Gould, *The Presidency*, 79, 81; Trask, *The War with Spain*, 40–41, 43–44; Musicant, *Empire by Default*, 176; Offner, *An Unwanted War*, 156–157.

46. Offner, *An Unwanted War*, 157–159, 168; Musicant, *Empire by Default*, 181–182; Gould, *The Presidency*, 81; Hobart, *Memories*, 62–63.

47. Thomas, *The War Lovers*, 235–236, 241; Offner, "McKinley and the Spanish-American War," 60.

48. Trask, *The War with Spain*, 56–58; Musicant, *Empire by Default*, 188–190.

Chapter 6

1. Lewis L. Gould, *The Spanish-American War and President McKinley* (Lawrence: University Press of Kansas, 1982), 6–7; Trask, *The War with Spain*, 145–147; Musicant, *Empire by Default*, 98, 236–237.

2. Musicant, *Empire by Default*, 189; Trask, *The War with Spain*, 158–159; Musicant, *Empire by Default*, 248–251; Dobson, *Reticent Expansionism*, 85.

3. Gould, *The Presidency*, 91–93; Henry S. Pritchett, "Some Recollections of President McKinley and the Cuban Intervention," *The North American Review of Reviews*, March 1909, 397.

4. Leech, *In the Days*, 231–232. The threatening letters can be found in the George B. Cortlyou Papers, Library of Congress (hereafter called LC).

5. Musicant, *Empire by Default*, 198–199; Trask, *The War with Spain*, 100–101; O'Toole, *The Spanish War*, 183.

6. O'Toole, *The Spanish War*, 184–188; Trask, *The War with Spain*, 182–283; Musicant, *Empire by Default*, 222–228.

7. Leech, *In the Days*, 204–205; Trask, *The War with Spain*, 105–106; David J. Silbey, *A War of Frontier and Empire: The Philippine-American War, 1899–1902* (New York: Hill and Wang, 2007), 41; Kohlsaat, *From McKinley to Harding*, 68.

8. Trask, *The War with Spain*, 111, 116, 122–127; Musicant, *Empire by Default*, 324–326.

9. Trask, *The War with Spain*, 172–175.

10. *Ibid.*, 178, 183.

11. Thomas, *The War Lovers*, 277, 281–283.

12. Musicant, *Empire by Default*, 358, 385; Trask, *The War with Spain*, 219–220; Frank Freidel, *The Splendid Little War* (New York: Bramhill House, 1958), 99.

13. Friedel, *The Splendid Little War*, 119, 138; Musicant, *Empire by Default*, 418; Thomas, *The War Lovers*, 324–325; Trask, *The War with Spain*, 243–247.

14. Trask, *The War with Spain*, 250–251; Freidel, *The Splendid Little War*, 189–190.

15. Musicant, *Empire by Default*, 439–465; O'Toole, *The Spanish War*, 337–338; Freidel, *The Splendid Little War*, 229; Trask, *The War with Spain*, 262–268.

16. Musicant, *Empire by Default*, 477–484, 501; O'Toole, *The Spanish War*, 345–346; Freidel, *The Splendid Little War*, 233–253.

17. Thomas, *The War Lovers*, 347, 356–357; Musicant, *Empire by Default*, 511–513, 515; Trask, *The War with Spain*, 324–325, 332.

18. Trask, *The War with Spain*, 333; Freidel, *The Splendid Little War*, 300.

19. Friedel, *The Splendid Little War*, 267; Musicant, *Empire by Default*, 528–539; Trask, *The War with Spain*, 357–364.

20. Trask, *The War with Spain*, 385–386; Musicant, *Empire by Default*, 544–545.

21. Musicant, *Empire by Default*, 567–569, 574–575; Trask, *The War with Spain*, 414–415; Silbey, *A War of Frontier and Empire*, 46–52; O'Toole, *The Spanish War*, 369–371.

22. Musicant, *Empire by Default*, 582–584; Silbey, *A War of Frontier and Empire*, 64–78, 207–208.

23. Musicant, *Empire by Default*, 587–595.

24. Trask, *The War with Spain*, 428–435, 441; Musicant, *Empire by Default*, 596–597, 604.

25. Dobson, *Reticent Expansionism*, 103–107, 112–115; Trask, *The War with Spain*, 453–453, 456; Musicant, *Empire by Default*, 614–616, 619, 622–626.

26. Dobson, *Reticent Expansionism*, 117–120; Trask, *The War with Spain*, 470; Musicant, *Empire by Default*, 628–629.

27. Dobson, *Reticent Expansionism*, 125, 136; Thomas, *The War Lovers*, 393.

28. Leech, *In the Days*, 292; Musicant, *Empire by Default*, 632, 651–654; Gould, *The Presidency*, 123–124.

29. Morgan, *McKinley*, 352; Gould, *The Presidency*, 208–210.

30. Gould, *The Presidency*, 163–164; Morgan, *McKinley*, 365–366.

31. Gould, *The Presidency*, 28, 154–158.

32. *Ibid.*, 215–217; Thomas, *The War Lovers*, 382, 385–386; Leech, *In the Days*, 535–537, 540–541.

33. Leech, *In the Days*, 523, 542–543, 557; Gould, *The Presidency*, 219–220; Morgan, *McKinley*, 358, 387.

34. Gould, *The Presidency*, 229; Morgan, *McKinley*, 388; Leech, *In the Days*, 557.

Chapter 7

1. Jill Jonnes, *Empires of Light: Edison, Tesla, Westinghouse, and the Race to Electrify the World* (New York: Random House, 2003), 328–329; Abram John Foster, *The Coming of the Electrical Age to the United States* (New York: Arno, 1979), 255–256; *Buffalo Commercial*, November 16, 1896.

2. Larned, *Municipality of Buffalo*, 332; *Buffalo Courier*, November 18, 20, 1896; *Buffalo Commercial*, November 19, 1896.

3. Foster, *Coming of the Electrical Age*, 117–120; Jonnes, *Empires of Light*, 56–59, 80–84; Ernest Freeberg, *The Age of Edison: Electric Light and the Invention of Modern America* (New York: Penguin, 2013), 71–72.

4. Jonnes, *Empires of Light*, 84; Foster, *Coming of the Electrical Age*, 117; Freeberg, *Age of Edison*, 72–74.

5. Tom McNichol, *AC/DC: The Savage Tale of the First Standards War* (San Francisco: Jossey-Bass, 2006), 66–67; Harold I. Sharlin, "The First Niagara Falls Power Project," *The Business History Review* 35, no. 1 (Spring 1961), 65.

6. W. Bernard Carlson, *Tesla: Inventor of the Electrical Age* (Princeton, NJ: Princeton University Press, 2013), 13–14, 18, 34–35, 48–50, 63–65; Margaret Cheney, *Tesla: Man Out of Time* (New York: Dell, 1981), 19–20.

7. Carlson, *Tesla*, 69, 72–73; Cheney, *Tesla*, 30–34; Jonnes, *Empires of Light*, 102, 109.

8. Carlson, *Tesla*, 73–75; Cheney, *Tesla*, 35–36; Jonnes, *Empires of Light*, 110–113.

9. Jonnes, *Empires of Light*, 114; Cheney, *Tesla*, 36–37; Carlson, *Tesla*, 77–81.

10. Richard Moran, *Executioner's Current: Thomas Edison, George Westinghouse, and the Invention of the Electric Chair* (New York: Vintage, 2002), 47–48; Jonnes, *Empires of Light*, 118–119.

11. Moran, *Executioner's Current*, 49; Jonnes, *Empires of Light*, 123–124; Foster, *Coming of the Electrical Age*, 196–197; Malcom MacLaren, *The*

Rise of the Electrical Industry During the Nineteenth Century (Princeton, NJ: Princeton University Press, 1943), 172–173.

12. Jonnes, *Empires of Light*, 136–137; Moran, *Executioner's Current*, 49–50; Foster, *Coming of the Electrical Age*, 197–198; MacLaren, *Rise of the Electrical Industry*, 176–177.

13. Jonnes, *Empires of Light*, 136–137; Moran, *Executioner's Current*, 50.

14. Moran, *Executioner's Current*, 50–59; Jonnes, *Empires of Light*, 145, 150–152; MacLaren, *Rise of the Electrical Industry*, 177–179; McNichol, *AC/DC*, 84–85.

15. McNichol, *AC/DC*, 87–90; Jonnes, *Empires of Light*, 165–166; Moran, *Executioner's Current*, 92–93.

16. Jonnes, *Empires of Light*, 169–171; McNichol, *AC/DC*, 91–92.

17. McNichol, *AC/DC*, 103–106; Jonnes, *Empires of Light*, 171–172.

18. Moran, *Executioner's Current*, 70–76; Jonnes, *Empires of Light*, 148–149.

19. McNichol, *AC/DC*, 96, 108–111; Jonnes, *Empires of Light*, 176–177; Moran, *Executioner's Current*, 84–86, 102–103.

20. McNichol, *AC/DC*, 115–116; Jonnes, *Empires of Light*, 178, 189–190; Moran, *Executioner's Current*, 112–113.

21. Moran, *Executioner's Current*, 111–114; Jonnes, *Empires of Light*, 197–198.

22. Moran, *Executioner's Current*, 115–117; McNichol, *AC/DC*, 117–119.

23. Moran, *Executioner's Current*, 119–121; Frederick Drimmer, *Until You Are Dead: The Book of Execution in America* (New York: Citadel, 1990), 3.

24. Moran, *Executioner's Current*, 121; McNichol, *AC/DC*, 121; Jonnes, *Empires of Light*, 186.

25. Jonnes, *Empires of Light*, 187–189; Moran, *Executioner's Current*, 156–160; Arnold Beichman, "The First Electrocution," *Commentary*, May 1963, 413; McNichol, *AC/DC*, 121–124.

26. Moran, *Executioner's Current*, 7, 9–10.

27. *Ibid.*, 12–13; Carlos F. MacDonald, "The Infliction of the Death Penalty by Means of Electricity," *The New York Medical Journal*, May 5, 1892, 506; Robert G. Elliott, *Agent of Death: The Memoirs of an Executioner* (New York: E. P. Dutton, 1940), 26.

28. Beichman, "The First Electrocution," 416–417; Moran, *Executioner's Current*, 13–14; McNichol, *AC/DC*, 124–125.

29. Beichman, "The First Electrocution," 417; Moran, *Executioner's Current*, 15–16; Jonnes, *Empires of Light*, 212.

30. MacDonald, "Infliction of the Death Penalty," 506; Drimmer, *Until You Are Dead*, 15.

31. Jonnes, *Empires of Light*, 159, 218; McNichol, *AC/DC*, 82–84; Carlson, *Tesla*, 105–107, 113–117.

32. Jonnes, *Empires of Light*, 253–256; McNichol, *AC/DC*, 133–135.

33. Jonnes, *Empires of Light*, 257–268; McNichol, *AC/DC*, 135–136; Foster, *Coming of the Electrical Age*, 238–239.

34. Foster, *Coming of the Electrical Age*, 239–240; MacLaren, *Rise of the Electrical Industry*, 186–187; Jonnes, *Empires of Light*, 268; Alexis S. Yaeger, "Showcasing Electricity at the Pan-Am: The Development and Display of Electricity at the Pan-American Exposition of 1901," MA thesis, Buffalo State College, 2010, 38–39.

Chapter 8

1. Yaeger, Showcasing Electricity, 45; Percy, *Buffalo-Niagara Connections*, 218–219; Sharlin, "The First Niagara Falls Power Project," 60–61; Robert Blake Belfield, "The Niagara Frontier: The Evolution of Electric Power Systems in New York and Ontario, 1880–1935," Ph.D. diss, University of Pennsylvania, 1981, 2–3.

2. Belfield, "The Niagara Frontier," 3–4.

3. Sharlin, "The First Niagara Falls Power Project," 62; Belfield, "The Niagara Frontier," 4–6; Edward Dean Adams, *Niagara Power: A History of the Niagara Falls Power Company, 1886–1918*, 2 vols. (Niagara Falls, NY: privately printed, 1927), I, 115–118.

4. Jonnes, *Empires of Light*, 280–284; Belfield, "The Niagara Frontier," 7, 9; Sharlin, "The First Niagara Falls Power Project," 62–63.

5. Jonnes, *Empires of Light*, 283–284; Sharlin, "The First Niagara Falls Power Project," 68–69.

6. Adams, *Niagara Power*, II, 6–7; Jonnes, *Empires of Light*, 284–285; Sharlin, "The First Niagara Falls Power Project," 69–70; Belfield, The Niagara Frontier, 14–17.

7. Sharlin, "The First Niagara Falls Power Project," 70.

8. Jonnes, *Empires of Light*, 284–286; Adams, *Niagara Power*, II, 23–24.

9. Sharlin, "The First Niagara Falls Power Project," 70; Jonnes, *Empires of Light*, 287–288; Belfield, "The Niagara Frontier," 18.

10. Jonnes, *Empires of Light*, 288–289; Carlson, *Tesla*, 159–160; Belfield, "The Niagara Frontier," 21–22; Adams, *Niagara Power*, 174–175, 182.

11. Jonnes, *Empires of Light*, 297, 303–306; Belfield, "The Niagara Frontier," 25–30.

12. Foster, *Coming of the Electrical Age*, 252–254; Jonnes, *Empires of Light*, 286–287, 306;

Sharlin, "The First Niagara Falls Power Project," 73.

13. Foster, *Coming of the Electrical Age*, 254–255; Belfield, "The Niagara Frontier," 30–32; Jonnes, *Empires of Light*, 318–320; "A Souvenir of the Lighting of Niagara Furnace," Buffalo History Museum (hereafter called BHM).

14. Jonnes, *Empires of Light*, 321; Belfield, "The Niagara Frontier," 32–36; Foster, *Coming of the Electrical Age*, 256; Rollin Lynde Hartt, "The New Niagara," *McClure's Magazine* 17, no. 1 (May 1901), 80.

15. Foster, *Coming of the Electrical Age*, 256, 259; Belfield, "The Niagara Frontier," 37; *Buffalo Courier*, December 25, 1896, January 4, 1897; Brett Gowronski, Jana Kasikova, Lynda H. Schneekloth, and Thomas Yots, *The Power Trail: History of Hydroelectricity at Niagara* (Buffalo: Western New York Wares, 2005), 33.

16. Isabel Vaughan James, *The Pan-American Exposition* (Buffalo: Buffalo and Erie County Historical Society, 1961), 1; *Buffalo Courier*, May 1, 1901; *Buffalo Express*, July 5, 1897.

17. *Buffalo Express*, June 26, July 28, September 19, December 12, 1897.

18. *Buffalo Courier*, May 1, 1901; *Buffalo Commercial*, January 5, 1898.

Chapter 9

1. *Buffalo Courier*, May 1, 1901.

2. *Buffalo Express*, January 6, 1899; *Buffalo Commercial*, January 5, 1899.

3. *Buffalo Express*, January 27, February 1, 1899; *Buffalo Commercial*, March 2, 1899; *Buffalo Courier*, May 1, 1901.

4. *Buffalo Express*, March 8, 1899; *The Pan-American*, March 16, 1899; *Buffalo Courier*, May 1, 1901.

5. Proceedings of the Board of Directors, March 9, 18, 1899, Box 1, Vol. 1, PAEC Records, BHM.

6. *The Pan-American*, April 20, 1899, 45–48.

7. *Buffalo Express*, May 2, 7, 18, 1899; *Buffalo Courier*, May 7, 18, 1899.

8. *Buffalo Express*, April 4, 1899; Report on Sites Submitted to the Executive Committee by Messrs. Burnham, Olmsted, and Manning, Box 1, Folder 3, PAEC Records, BHM.

9. Report on Sites Submitted to the Executive Committee by Messrs. Burnham, Olmsted, and Manning, Box 1, Folder 3, PAEC Records, BHM.

10. Proceedings of the Board of Directors, May 13, June 9, 1899, Box 1, Vol. 1, PAEC Records, BHM.

11. WIB to Edwin Fleming, June 13, 1899, WIB to John N. Scatcherd, October 12, 1899, Box 8, Folder 1, WIB Papers, BHM; Proceedings of the Board of Directors, November 8, 1899, Box 1, Vol. 1, PAEC Records, BHM.

12. Harold F. Peterson, *Diplomat of the Americas: A Biography of William I. Buchanan (1852–1909)* (Albany: State University of New York Press, 1977), 7–43.

13. *Ibid.*, 44, 50–56.

14. *Ibid.*, 70–71, 77–80, 102, 106.

15. W. I. Buchanan, "The Organization of an Exposition," *The Cosmopolitan* 31, no. 5 (September 1901), 518.

16. Proceedings of the Board of Directors, May 13, 1899, Box 1, Vol. 1, PAEC Records, BHM; Pan-American Exposition, Report of William I. Buchanan, Director General, Box 8, Folder 13, WIB Papers, BHM (hereafter WIB, Report); Form of Circular Note Sent by the Department of State to the American Governments and to the European Governments Having Colonies in the Western Hemisphere, Box 8, Folder 2, WIB Papers, BHM.

17. WIB to William H. Michael, February 15, 1900, Records of International Conferences, Commissions, and Expositions, RG 43, NA; John Weber, Report of Trip to Ottawa, February 17, 1900, Box 4, Folder 2, WIB Papers, BHM; WIB to Executive Committee, March 27, 1900, Box 4, Folder 4, WIB Papers, BHM.

18. Letters of acceptance and rejection are all in the WIB Papers, BHM.

19. *Collier's Weekly*, 26 (December 1, 1900), 5, quoted in Peterson, *Diplomat of the Americas*, 152.

20. *Ibid.*, 152–153.

21. Joann Marie Thompson, "The Art and Architecture of the Pan-American Exposition, Buffalo, New York," Ph.D. diss., Rutgers, The State University of New Jersey, 1980, 23–24.

22. *Ibid.*, 24–26.

23. *Ibid.*, 26; Proceedings of the Board of Directors, November 8, 1899, Box 1, Vol. 1, PAEC Records, BHM.

24. Proceedings of the Board of Directors, November 8, 1899, Box 1, Vol. 1, PAEC Records, BHM.

25. Proceedings of the Board of Directors, December 5, 1899, Box 1, Vol. 1, PAEC Records, BHM.

26. J. William Fosdick to J. M. Carrere, March 2, 1900, WIB to executive committee, March 7, 1900, Box 4, Folder 2, WIB to C. Y. Turner, April 14, 1900, Box 4, Folder 4, WIB Papers, BHM.

27. Evdokia Savidou, "The Career of the

Painter Charles Yardley Turner (1850–1918)," MA thesis, Queens College, 1986, 15–30.

28. *Ibid.*, 36–43.

29. *Ibid.*, 45–55.

30. Thompson, "Art and Architecture," 91; *Buffalo Express*, July 29, 1900; Walter H. Page, "The Pan-American Exposition," *The World's Work* 2, no. 4 (August 1901), 1030.

31. Thompson, "Art and Architecture," 93–95; C. Y. Turner, The Story of the Color Scheme for the Exposition, WIB Papers, BHM.

32. C. Y. Turner, "Organization as Applied to Art," *The Cosmopolitan*, September 1901, 494–496.

33. Proceedings of the Board of Directors, November 8, 1899, Box 1, Vol. 1, Proceedings of the Board of Directors, March 6, 1900, Box 1, Vol. 2, PAEC Records, BHM; *Buffalo Express*, November 12, December 14, 1899, February 25, 1900.

34. *Buffalo Commercial*, December 15, 1899.

35. WIB to executive committee, March 24, 1900, Box 4, Folder 3, WIB to executive committee, April 16, 28, 1900, Box 4, Folder 4, WIB to executive committee, June 18, 1900, Box 4, Folder 6, WIB Papers, BHM.

36. WIB to executive committee, April 7, 1900, Box 4, Folder 4, WIB Papers, BHM.

37. WIB to executive committee, July 14, 19, 1900, Box 4, Folder 7, WIB Papers, BHM; Proceedings of the Board of Directors, September 20, 1900, Box 1, Vol. 2, PAEC Records, BHM.

38. Proceedings of the Board of Directors, May 1, 1900, Box 1, Vol. 2, PAEC Records, BHM.

39. Proceedings of the Board of Directors, June 27, 1900, Box 1, Vol. 2. PAEC Records, BHM; WIB to executive committee, July 19, 1900, WIB Papers, BHM.

40. Organ Music at the Pan-American Exposition, Box 9, Folder 18, WIB Papers, BHM; *Official Catalogue and Guide Book to The Pan-American Exposition* (Buffalo: Charles Ahrhart, 1901), 57–58; WIB to executive committee, March 30, 1900, Box 4, Vol. 3, WIB Papers, BHM; proceedings of the Board of Directors, April 8, 1901, Box 1, Vol. 3, PAEC Records, BHM.

41. *Buffalo Express*, May 12, August 26, October 9, 1900.

42. Proceedings of the Board of Directors, February 6, September 20, 1900, Box 1, Vol. 2, Report of the Commandant of Police Made to the Director-general, Pan-American Exposition, Box 3, Vol. 29, PAEC Records, BHM.

43. WIB to executive committee, May 15, 27, 1900, Box 4, Folder 5, WIB Papers, BHM; *Buffalo Commercial*, May 29, 1900.

44. Douglas W. DeCroix, "A Legacy of Life and Hope: Dr. Roswell Park," *Western New York Heritage* 13, no. 3 (Fall 2010), 53–59; Edward J. Fine, Debbie Reynolds, Emilio D. Soria, Luke R. Scalcione, Debra L. Fine, "The Contribution of Dr. Roswell Park to Epilepsy and Spinal Surgery," *Neurosurgery* 42, no. 2 (February 1998), 372–375; Donald L. Trump and Edwin A. Mirano, "Dr. Roswell Park, Physician with a Vision," *New York Archives*, Summer 2009, 13–15.

45. Peterson, *Diplomat of the Americas*, 155; WIB to executive committee, May 7, 1900, Box 4, Folder 5, WIB Papers, BHM.

46. *Buffalo Express*, May 3, 1900; *Buffalo Courier*, May 4, 1900.

47. Thompson, "Art and Architecture," 36; *Buffalo Courier*, August 25, 1900; *Buffalo Express*, August 25, 26, 1900.

48. Report of the Board of Management, United States Government Exhibit, Pan-American Exposition, Buffalo, New York, 1901, RG 56, General Records of the Department of the Treasury, NA; WIB to J. H. Brigham, December 5, 1899, Letters Received Concerning Government Participation in the Exposition, in General, 1899–1902, RG 33, NA.

49. Board of Management Report, RG 56, NA; *Buffalo Courier*, August 13, 1900; WIB to executive committee, August 8, 1900, Box 4, Folder 6, WIB Papers, BHM.

Chapter 10

1. *Buffalo Commercial*, September 12, 1900; *Buffalo Courier*, September 13, 1900.

2. *Buffalo Commercial*, September 12, 1900; *Buffalo Express*, September 13, 1900; *Buffalo Courier*, September 13, 1900.

3. Proceedings of the Board of Directors, September 20, 1900, Box 4, Folder 6, PAEC Records, BHM; WIB to executive committee, October 28, 1900, Box 5, Folder 4, WIB Papers, BHM.

4. *Buffalo Courier*, August 29, 1900.

5. Electric Tower Construction Field Book, PAEC Records, BHM; *Buffalo Express*, December 4, 6, 1900, March 29, 1901; WIB to executive committee, January 12, 1901, Box 5, Folder 5, WIB Papers, BHM.

6. *Buffalo Express*, March 12, 20, 24, 25, 27, 1901; WIB to executive committee, April 15, 1901, Box 6, Folder 3, WIB Papers, BHM.

7. *Buffalo Express*, March 21, 26, 1901; *Buffalo Commercial*, March 26, 1901.

8. *Buffalo Express*, March 26, 28, April 3, 6, 1901.

9. *Ibid.*, April 7, 8, 1901; *New York Times*,

April 28, 1901; Turner, "Organization as Applied to Art," 496 (emphasis added); Page, "The Pan-American Exposition," 1032–1033.

10. Turner, Report of the Director of Color, Box 8, Folder 16, WIB Papers, BHM.

11. *Buffalo Courier*, November 21, December 12, 1900, January 7, 1901; *Buffalo Express*, November 21, 1900; WIB to executive committee, January 10, 29, 31, 1901, Box 5, Folder 5, WIB Papers, BHM.

12. *Buffalo Courier*, January 26, 27, 1901.

13. *Ibid.*, March 16, 19, 20, 30, 31, 1901; *Buffalo Express*, March 15, 16, 20, 29, 31, 1901; *Buffalo Commercial*, March 29, 1901.

14. *Buffalo Express*, March 24, 26, 27, 29, April 9, 10, 1901; *Buffalo Commercial*, March 28, April 10, 1901.

15. *Buffalo Courier*, November 22, 1900.

16. *Ibid.*, January 1, 1901.

17. *Buffalo Express*, March 31, 1901.

18. *Ibid.*, April 10, 1901; *Buffalo Courier*, April 10, 1901; *Buffalo Commercial*, April 10, 1901; *Buffalo Evening News*, April 29, 1901.

19. *Buffalo Evening News*, April 11, 1901.

20. *Buffalo Commercial*, May 14, 1901; *Buffalo Courier*, May 14, 1901; *Buffalo Evening News*, May 14, 1901.

21. *Buffalo Courier*, May 23, 1901; *Buffalo Express*, May 23, 1901; *Buffalo Commercial*, May 23, 1901.

22. William S. Hubbell to John G. Milburn, April 25, 1899, Martin D. Kneeland to Directors of the Pan-American Exposition, May 31, 1900, WIB to executive committee, May 31, 1900, Box 4, Folder 6, WIB Papers, BHM.

23. *Buffalo Courier*, January 11, February 20, 22, 1901; *Buffalo Express*, March 11, 29, 1901.

24. *Buffalo Courier*, January 11, February 22, 1901; *The Pan-American Magazine* 3, no. 1 (January 1901), 19.

25. *Buffalo Express*, March 22, 1901; *Buffalo Courier*, April 1, 15, 1901.

26. Proceedings of the Board of Directors, April 27, 1901, Box 1, Vol. 3, PAEC Records, BHM; *Buffalo Courier*, April 28, May 3, 1901; *Buffalo Commercial*, April 29, 1901.

27. WIB to executive committee, February 25, 1901, Box 5, Folder 7, WIB Papers, BHM.

28. *Buffalo Commercial*, March 4, 6, April 2, 6, 1901; *Buffalo Courier*, April 9, 1901; *Buffalo Express*, April 7, 8, 9, 17, 1901; proceedings of the Board of Directors, April 2, 1901, Box 1, Vol. 3, PAEC Records, BHM.

29. *Buffalo Express*, March 24, 1901; *Buffalo Commercial*, March 28, April 3, 10, 1901.

30. *Buffalo Commercial*, April 3, 15, 1901; *Buffalo Courier*, April 1, 15, 19, 1901.

31. Page, "The Pan-American Exposition," 1045; Yaeger, "Showcasing Electricity," 52–53; Thompson, "Art and Architecture," 80–81; Luther Stieringer, "The Evolution of Exposition Lighting," *Western Electrician* 29, no. 12 (September 21, 1901), 189–192.

32. WIB to executive committee, June 25, 1900, Box 4, Folder 6, Newcomb Carlton to Safety Insulated Wire & Cable Company, July 5, 1900, Box 4, Folder 7, WIB Papers, BHM; *New York Times*, January 8, 1901; Proceedings of the Board of Directors, May 1, September 20, 1900, Box 1, Vol. 2, PAEC Records, BHM; Page, "The Pan-American Exposition," 1045; Stieringer, "Evolution of Exposition Lighting," 191.

33. William S. Aldrich, "Mechanical and Electrical Features of the Pan-American Exposition," *The Engineering Magazine* 5, no. 21 (September 1901), 840–844; Yaeger, "Showcasing Electricity," 57–58, 68–69; Donald Murray, "The Automatic Age: Electrical Marvels and Mechanical Triumphs at the Pan-American Exposition," *Everybody's Magazine* 5, no. 26 (October 1901), 388; Orrin E. Dunlap, "The Wonderful Story of the Chaining of Niagara," *The World's Work* 2, no. 4 (August 1901), 1052–1053; WIB to executive committee, February 19, 1901, Box 5, Folder 7, WIB Papers, BHM; Ernest Knaufft, "Artistic Effects of the Pan-American Exposition," *The American Monthly Review of Reviews* 23, no. 6 (June 1901), 686.

34. *Buffalo Express*, March 22, 31, May 2, 1901; *Buffalo Courier*, March 23, 1901; WIB to executive committee, April 17, 1901, Box 6, Folder 3, WIB Papers, BHM.

35. *Buffalo Express*, March 11, 26, May 2, 1901; *Buffalo Courier*, March 18, 1901; WIB to executive committee, March 14, 1901, Box 5, Folder 8, March 20, 1901, Box 6, Folder 1, WIB Papers, BHM.

36. *Buffalo Express*, March 10, 12, 16, 27, 28, 31, April 5, 10, 1901; *Buffalo Courier*, April 13, 15, 1901; *Buffalo Commercial*, April 10, 1901; Report of the Superintendent of the Manufactures Division, April 16, 1902, Box 9, Folder 12, Report of the Superintendent of the Machinery Division, March 8, 1902, Box 9, Folder 11, Report of the Superintendent of the Transportation Division, March 8, 1902, Box 9, Folder 19, WIB Papers, BHM.

37. *Buffalo Courier*, April 1, 1901; *Buffalo Commercial*, April 15, 1901.

Chapter 11

1. Leech, *In the Days*, 567, 574–575.

2. *Ibid.*, 575–576; Gould, *Presidency of McKinley*, 243–245.

3. Leech, *In the Days*, 576–577.

4. *New York Times*, April 30, 1901.

5. *Ibid.*

6. *Ibid.*, May 1, 1901.

7. *Ibid.*, May 2, 3, 1901.

8. *Ibid.*, May 4, 1901.

9. *Ibid.*, May 7, 1901.

10. *Ibid.*, May 8–9, 1901.

11. *Ibid.*, May 12, 1901; *Columbus Dispatch*, May 10, 1901.

12. *Columbus Dispatch*, May 10, 1901; Morgan, *McKinley*, 392; Leech, *In the Days*, 577; *New York Times*, May 13, 1901.

13. *New York Times*, May 13–16, 1901; *San Francisco Chronicle*, May 14, 1901.

14. *San Francisco Examiner*, May 15, 1901; *San Francisco Chronicle*, May 15, 1901.

15. *San Francisco Chronicle*, May 14, 18, 1901; *Columbus Dispatch*, May 14, 1901; *New York Times*, May 17, 18, 1901.

16. *Columbus Dispatch*, May 16, 1901; *New York Times*, May 17, 1901; *San Francisco Examiner*, May 17, 1901.

17. *New York Times*, May 18, 1901; *San Francisco Examiner*, May 18, 1901; *Columbus Dispatch*, May 18, 1901.

18. *New York Times*, May 19, 1901; *San Francisco Chronicle*, May 19, 1901.

19. *New York Times*, May 19, 1901; *San Francisco Chronicle*, May 19, 1901; *San Francisco Examiner*, May 19, 1901.

20. *New York Times*, May 19, 1901; *San Francisco Chronicle*, May 19, 1901; *San Francisco Examiner*, May 19, 1901; *Columbus Dispatch*, May 19, 1901.

21. *New York Times*, May 19, 1901.

22. *Ibid.*, *San Francisco Chronicle*, May 19, 1901; *San Francisco Examiner*, May 19, 1901.

23. *San Francisco Chronicle*, May 21–25, 1901; *New York Times*, May 22–23, 1901.

24. *San Francisco Examiner*, May 26, 1901; *San Francisco Chronicle*, May 26, 1901; *New York Times*, May 26, 1901.

25. *New York Times*, May 26, 29, 1901.

26. *Ibid.*, May 31, 1901; *Washington Star*, May 31, 1901.

27. Leech, *In the Days*, 580–581; Morgan, *McKinley*, 383–384.

Chapter 12

1. *Buffalo Commercial*, April 20, 22, 1901; *Buffalo Courier*, April 20, 21, 22, 1901; *Buffalo Express*, April 21, 22, 1901.

2. *Buffalo Courier*, April 22, 1901; *Buffalo Commercial*, April 22, 1901; *Buffalo Express*, April 22, 1901.

3. *Buffalo Courier*, April 23, 1901; *Buffalo Commercial*, April 23, 1901; *Buffalo Express*, April 23, 24, 1901; WIB to executive committee, April 15, 1901, Box 6, Folder 3, WIB Papers, BHM.

4. *Buffalo Express*, April 27, 29, 30, 1901; *Buffalo Courier*, April 28, 1901; *Buffalo Commercial*, May 6, 1901.

5. *Buffalo Express*, May 1, 2, 1901; *Buffalo Commercial*, May 2, 4, 6, 1901.

6. *Buffalo Express*, May 2, 1901; *Buffalo Commercial*, May 2, 1901. The description of the Propylaea comes from Thompson, "Art and Architecture," 34.

7. *Buffalo Courier*, May 2, 4, 5, 9, 25, 30, 1901; *Buffalo Commercial*, May 21, 1901.

8. *Buffalo Express*, May 6, 9, 11, 12, 14, 16, 17, 1901; *Buffalo Evening News*, May 14, 1901; *Buffalo Commercial*, May 10, 15, 18, 1901; *Buffalo Courier*, May 18, 19, 1901; WIB to executive committee, May 2, 1901, Box 6, Folder 4, WIB Papers, BHM.

9. *Buffalo Express*, May 17, 1901; *Buffalo Courier*, May 18, 1901.

10. *Buffalo Commercial*, May 18, 1901; *Buffalo Express*, May 20, 1901.

11. WIB to executive committee, May 2, 1901, Box 6, Folder 4, WIB Papers, BHM; proceedings of the Board of Directors, May 7, 1901, Box 1, Vol. 3, PAEC Records, BHM.

12. *Buffalo Commercial*, May 4, 6, 9, 11, 14, 15, 1901; *Buffalo Express*, May 5, 15, 17, 1901.

13. *Buffalo Courier*, May 12, 13, 1901; *Buffalo Express*, May 12, 1901; Roswell Park, Report of the Medical Department of the Pan-American Exposition, Buffalo, 1901, Box 9, Folder 13 WIB Papers, BHM.

14. *Buffalo Express*, May 20, 1901; *Buffalo Courier*, May 20, 1901.

15. *Buffalo Commercial*, May 20, 1901; *Buffalo Express*, May 21, 1901; *Buffalo Courier*, May 21, 22, 1901; *New York Times*, May 21, 1901.

16. *Buffalo Commercial*, May 20, 1901.

17. *Ibid.*

18. *Buffalo Express*, May 21, 22, 1901; *Buffalo Commercial*, May 20, 21, 1901; *New York Times*, May 26, 1901.

Chapter 13

1. Milton Meltzer, *The Terrorists* (New York: Harper & Row, 1982), 18.

2. *Ibid.*, 18–22, 27–28.

3. *Ibid.*, 15–16.

4. James Joll, *The Anarchists* (Cambridge, MA: Harvard University Press, 1980, repr. of 1964 edition), 100–105.

5. Meltzer, *The Terrorists*, 37–47.

6. *Ibid.*, 52–57; Joll, *The Anarchists*, 113.

7. Joll, *The Anarchists*, 113–114; Meltzer, *The Terrorists*, 48–49.

8. Meltzer, *The Terrorists*, 66–69.

9. Alice Wexner, *Emma Goldman: An Intimate Life* (New York: Pantheon, 1984), 6, 27, 51–54.

10. *Ibid.*, 33–35; Joll, *The Anarchists*, 123–125; Meltzer, *The Terrorists*, 69–71; Miller, *The President and the Assassin*, 137–143.

11. Meltzer, *The Terrorists*, 72–73; Wexler, *Emma Goldman*, 35–36.

12. Meltzer, *The Terrorists*, 73–76; Wexler, *Emma Goldman*, 64–67.

13. Wexler, *Emma Goldman*, 65–66, 69.

14. *Ibid.*, 85–86.

15. *Ibid.*, 103.

16. Briggs interviews, CFP, MHS.

17. Briggs interviews, CFP, MHS.

18. Briggs interviews, CFP, MHS; Briggs, *Manner of Man That Kills*, 293–294.

19. Briggs interviews, CFP, MHS.

20. Channing Walter, "The Mental Status of Czolgosz the Assassin of President McKinley," *American Journal of Insanity*, October 1902, 251–252.

21. Emma Goldman, *Living My Life*, 2 vols. (New York: Dover, 1970, repr. of 1931 edition), I, 289–290.

22. *New York Times*, September 8, 1901; Briggs interviews, CFP, MHS.

23. Briggs interviews, CFP, MHS.

24. Briggs interviews, CFP, MHS.

25. Goldman, *Living My Life*, 290–291.

26. *Ibid.*, 291; Rauchway, *Murdering McKinley*, 101–102; Miller, *The President and the Assassin*, 285–286; Briggs interviews, CFP, MHS; Channing, "Mental Status of Czolgosz," 251.

27. Briggs interviews, CFP, MHS.

28. Goldman, *Living My Life*, 291.

29. Miller, *The President and the Assassin*, 286; Briggs interviews, CFP, MHS.

Chapter 14

1. WIB, Report, 5–6, Box 8, Folder 13, WIB Papers, BHM.

2. Robert Muccigrosso, *Celebrating the New World: Chicago's Columbian Exposition of 1893* (Chicago: Ivan R. Dee, 1993), 154–158; David F. Burg, *Chicago's White City of 1893* (Lexington: University Press of Kentucky, 1976), 216–225.

3. WIB, Report, 65–66, Box 8, Folder 13, WIB Papers, BHM; proceedings of the Board of Directors, July 16, 1901, PAEC Records, BHM.

4. Woody Register, *The Kid of Coney Island: Fred Thompson and the Rise of American Amusements* (New York: Oxford University Press, 2001), 25–28, 38–43, 52–57.

5. *Ibid.*, 67–68; Richard H. Barry, *Snap Shots on the Midway of the Pan-Am Expo* (Buffalo: Robert Allan Reid, 1901), 142, 145; Muccigrosso, *Celebrating the New World*, 176; Norman D. Anderson, *Ferris Wheels: An Illustrated History* (Bowling Green, OH: Bowling Green University Popular Press, 1992), 116–120; *Buffalo Commercial*, May 21, 1901; *Buffalo Express*, July 10, 1901.

6. Register, *Kid of Coney Island*, 68–71; Barry, *Snap Shots on the Midway*, 39–40; Frank H. Winter and Randy Liebermann, "A Trip to the Moon," *Air and Space*, October/November 1994, 62–65; Robert Grant, "Notes on the Pan-American Exposition," *The Cosmopolitan* 31, no. 5 (September 1901), 460–461.

7. Winter and Lieberman, "A Trip to the Moon," 64–66; Barry, *Snap Shots on the Midway*, 40–42; Register, *Kid of Coney Island*, 71.

8. The descriptions of Midway attractions come from Barry, *Snap Shots on the Midway*.

9. William A. Silverman, "Incubator Baby Side Shows," *Pediatrics* 64, no. 2 (August 1979), 127–132; Richard F. Snow, "Martin Couney," *American Heritage*, June/July 1981, 90.

10. Silverman, "Incubator Baby Side Shows," 132; "Baby Incubators at the Pan-American Exposition," *Scientific American* 85, no. 5 (August 3, 1901), 68; "Exhibit of Infant Incubators at the Pan-American Exposition," *Pediatrics* 12 (1901), 414–419; "Some Medical Aspects of the Pan-American Exposition: Infant Incubators," *Buffalo Medical Journal* 57, no. 1 (August 1901), 55.

11. "Some Medical Aspects, 55.

12. Barry, *Snap Shots on the Midway*, 80–99.

13. *Ibid.*, 75–78; *Buffalo Commercial*, May 17, 1901; Mary Bronson Hartt, "The Play-Side of the Fair," *The World's Work* 2, no. 4 (August 1901), 100.

14. WIB to executive committee, March 26, 1900, Box 4, Folder 3, WIB Papers, BHM.

15. Barry, *Snap Shots on the Midway*, 57–59; Jean Dickson, "When Mexico Came to Buffalo," *Western New York Heritage* 10, no. 1 (Spring 2007), 42–48.

16. Karolina Roman, "The Impact of the Pan American Exposition of 1901 on the City of Buffalo, New York," MA thesis, Buffalo State College, 2003, 24–25; Barry, *Snap Shots on the Midway*, 63–67; *Buffalo Courier*, June 28, September 2, 1901; *Buffalo Express*, June 30, 1901; *Buffalo Commercial*, June 28, 29, July 1, 1901.

17. WIB to executive committee, April 16,

1900, Box 4, Folder 4, WIB Papers, BHM; Park, Report of the Medical Department, Box 9, Folder 13, WIB Papers, BHM.

18. WIB, Report, Box 8, Folder 13, WIB Papers, BHM; Barry, *Snap Shots on the Midway*, 135–136; *Buffalo Courier*, June 20, 1901; *Buffalo Express*, September 4, 1901.

19. *Buffalo Commercial*, July 19, 1901; *Buffalo Courier*, July 19, 1901; *Buffalo Express*, July 19, 1901; Dickson, "When Mexico Came to Buffalo," 47–48.

20. Barry, *Snap Shots on the Midway*, 81–82.

21. *Buffalo Courier*, June 27, 29, July 1, 4, 1901; *Buffalo Express*, June 29, 1901.

22. *Buffalo Commercial*, May 6, 1901; *Buffalo Courier*, May 6, 1901.

23. *Buffalo Express*, June 17, 1901.

24. *Buffalo Courier*, July 8, 16, 1901; *Buffalo Express*, July 8, 1901; *Buffalo Commercial*, July 13, 16, 1901.

25. *Buffalo Express*, July 15, 1901; *Buffalo Courier*, July 15, 1901; *Buffalo Commercial*, July 15, 1901.

26. *Buffalo Express*, July 17, 18, 1901; *Buffalo Courier*, July 17, 18, 1901; *Buffalo Commercial*, July 17, 18, 1901.

27. *Buffalo Commercial*, July 25, 29, 1901; *Buffalo Courier*, July 26, 29, 1901; *Buffalo Express*, July 29, 1901.

28. Proceedings of the Board of Directors, July 30, 1901, Box 1, Vol. 4, PAEC Records, BHM; *Buffalo Commercial*, July 31, August 2, 5, 1901; *Buffalo Express*, July 31, 1901.

Chapter 15

1. Keturah Beth Cappadonia, "Timekeeper of Progress: The Fight for Inclusion of the 'Negro Exhibit' at Buffalo's Pan American Exposition, 1901," MA thesis, University of Rochester, 2006, 54–55; Matthew R. Bigham, "'Savagery' in the Shadows of 'Civility': Africans on the Midway," MA thesis, University of North Carolina at Wilmington, 2000, 60–61. The Pene quote comes from the latter source.

2. Bigham, "'Savagery' in the Shadows of 'Civility,'" 61; *Buffalo Express*, July 12, 1901; *Buffalo Commercial*, June 11, 14, 1901.

3. *Buffalo Courier*, June 17, July 6, 1901.

4. Cappadonia, "Timekeeper of Progress," 46, 58–59; *Buffalo Courier*, September 27, 1901.

5. *Official Catalogue and Guide Book*, 45; *Buffalo Express*, June 30, 1901; Barry, *Snap Shots on the Midway*, 125–127.

6. *Buffalo Express*, August 4, 1901.

7. Barbara A. Seals Nevergold, "'Doing the Pan': The African-American Experience at the Pan-American Exposition, 1901," *Afro-Americans in New York Life and History* 28, no. 1 (January 2004), 24–25; Lillian Serece Williams, *Strangers in the Land of Paradise: The Creation of an African American Community, Buffalo, New York, 1900–1940* (Bloomington and Indianapolis: Indiana University Press, 1999), 183–184; William H. Loos, Ami M. Savigny, and Robert M. Gurn, *The Forgotten "Negro Exhibit": African American Involvement in Buffalo's Pan-American Exposition, 1901* (Buffalo: Buffalo and Erie County Public Library, 2001), 10–12; Cappadonia, "Timekeeper of Progress," 79–80.

8. Miles Everett Travis, "Mixed Messages: Thomas Calloway and the 'American Negro Exhibit' of 1900," MA thesis, Montana State University, 2004, 14–15.

9. *Ibid.*, 19–20.

10. *Ibid.*, 3–4, 41.

11. *Ibid.*, 46–48, 63–65.

12. J. H. Brigham to George B. Cortelyou, January 22, 1901, Letters Sent by the Board of Management, 1899–1902, RG 33, NA.

13. Heidi A. Bamford, Behind the Scenes: Federal Planners of the Pan-American Exposition of 1901, Heidi A. Bamford Papers, BHM; 6.

14. Cappadonia, "Timekeeper of Progress," 86–87; *Buffalo Express*, April 24, 1901; Travis, "Mixed Messages," 71–72; Nevergold, "'Doing the Pan,'" 28–29.

15. Travis, "Mixed Messages," 72, 74–75.

16. Elizabeth M. Howe, "Some Educational Exhibits at the Pan-American," *Our Record* 33, no. 5 (August 1901), 84.

17. *Buffalo Express*, April 24, 1901.

18. *Buffalo Courier*, May 28, 1901.

19. *Ibid.*

20. *Ibid.*

Chapter 16

1. *Canton Repository*, July 5, 1901.

2. *New York Times*, July 6, 1901.

3. *Canton Repository*, July 6, 1901.

4. *Ibid.*, July 7, 1901.

5. E. F. Droop & Sons to William McKinley, June 24, 1901, McKinley to H. R. Jones, July 7, 1901, Wheeling & Lake Erie Railroad Co. to McKinley, July 26, August 17, 1901, William McKinley Papers, LC.

6. Memorandum for Secretary Cortelyou, Executive Mansion, Washington, D.C., August 21, 1901, McKinley Papers, LC.

7. *Canton Repository*, July 10, 11, 17, 27, 1901.

8. *Washington Post*, July 14, 1901.

9. *Canton Repository*, July 18, August 21, 1901.

10. *Ibid.*, August 3, 1901.

11. Charles G. Dawes, *A Journal of the McKinley Years* (Chicago: Lakeside, 1950), 274–275.

12. Cortelyou to Morton E. Crane, August 26, 1901, Cortelyou Papers, LC.

13. Morgan, *McKinley*, 352.

14. *Canton Repository*, August 10, 1901.

15. WIB to Cortelyou, August 18, 24, 1901, Cortelyou to WIB, September 2, 1901 (three messages), McKinley Papers, LC.

16. *Canton Repository*, August 15, 1901.

17. J. C. Hemphill to McKinley, August 15, 1901, manager, Niagara Hotel, to Cortelyou, August 10, 1901, George Duchscherer to Cortelyou, August 22, 1901, Frank C. Bostock to McKinley, August 14, 1901, Frank J. Cummins to McKinley, August 21, 1901, McKinley Papers, LC.

18. Gustave Meyer to Cortelyou, July 16, 1901, McKinley Papers, LC.

19. *Canton Repository*, September 3, 4, 1901.

20. *Ibid.*, September 4, 1901.

Chapter 17

1. *Buffalo Courier*, July 13, 1901; *Buffalo Express*, July 25, 1901.

2. *Buffalo Courier*, September 2, 1901; *Buffalo Commercial*, July 18, 1901.

3. WIB, Report, 29–30, Box 8, Folder 13, WIB Papers, BHM; *Buffalo Commercial*, June 17, 1901. Oklahoma, New Mexico, Arizona, Alaska, and Hawaii were yet to be admitted as states. Alaska had a building at the Pan-American Exposition.

4. *Buffalo Express*, May 27, 31, June 28, 1901; *Buffalo Courier*, May 30, June 8, 1901; Richard Gibson, "The Pan-American Exposition," *Overland Monthly* 37, no.1 (January 1901), 650.

5. *Buffalo Commercial*, July 6, August 10, 1901; *Buffalo Courier*, May 24, June 11, August 10, 25, 1901.

6. *Buffalo Commercial*, July 25, 1901.

7. *Buffalo Courier*, August 25, 1901; *Buffalo Commercial*, June 21, 1901; *Catalogue and Guide Book*, 31.

8. F. W. Clarke, "The Government Exhibit at Buffalo," *The Forum* 31, no. 6 (August 1901), 655.

9. Report of Special Jury of Awards on United States Government Exhibits, RG 56, NA; Mark Bennitt, *The Pan-American Exposition and How to See It...* (Buffalo: Goff, 1901), 42–43.

10. Report of Special Jury of Awards on United States Government Exhibits, RG 56, NA;

Buffalo Courier, May 28, 1901; *Buffalo Express*, May 30, June 22, 1901; *Buffalo Commercial*, June 21, 1901.

11. Report of Special Jury of Awards on United States Government Exhibits, RG 56, NA; Bennitt, *The Pan-American*, 42; *Catalogue of the Exhibit of the U.S. Navy Department, Pan-American Exposition, Buffalo, N. Y. 1901* (Washington, DC: Government Printing Office, 1901), 3–8, 25.

12. Report of Special Jury of Awards on United States Government Exhibits, RG 56, NA; Bennitt, *The Pan-American*, 45; *Buffalo Courier*, May 10, 1901; *Buffalo Express*, May 28, 31, August 15, 1901.

13. WIB, Report, 77, Box 8, Folder 13, WIB Papers, BHM; *Buffalo Express*, August 16, 18, 28, 1901.

14. Report of Special Jury of Awards on United States Government Exhibits, RG 56, NA; Bennitt, *The Pan-American*, 44.

15. Wallace H. Hill to Secretary of the Treasury, February 12, 1904, Miscellaneous Records Relating to the Exposition, 1900–1901, RG 56, NA; *Buffalo Courier*, May 13, July 25, 1901.

16. Joe Mitchell Chapple, "Personal Impressions of the Pan-American Exposition," *The National* 14, no. 4 (July 1901), 329; Bennitt, *The Pan-American*, 5.

17. Thompson, "Art and Architecture," 30–31, 46–47; Bennitt, *The Pan-American*, 6.

18. Thompson, "Art and Architecture," 31–33.

19. *Ibid.*, 33–34; Eugene Richard White, "Aspects of the Pan-American Exposition," *Atlantic Monthly* 88 (July 1901), 89–90; Frederic W. Taylor, "The Horticultural Exhibits at Buffalo," *Everybody's Magazine* 26 (October 1901), 405–415.

20. Page, "The Pan-American Exposition," 1038–1040; Knaufft, "Artistic Effects," 687–688; John M. Carrere, "The Exhibition at Buffalo: Some of the Ideas Which Have Determined Its Artistic Character," *Scribner's Magazine* 29, no. 6 (June 1901), 767–768; Talcott Williams, "The Pan-American Exposition: Architecture and Sculpture," *The Churchman* 83, no. 18 (May 4, 1901), 558–560.

21. Page, "The Pan-American Exposition," 1041–1044; Knaufft, "Artistic Effects," 687–688.

22. James E. Sullivan, "Athletics and the Stadium," *The Cosmopolitan*, September 1901, 501–508; Bennitt, *The Pan-American*, 23; Thompson, "Art and Architecture," 50; *Buffalo Express*, June 4–5, 1901; *Buffalo Commercial*, September 3, 1901; WIB to executive committee, September 11, 1901, Box 6, Folder 7, WIB Papers, BHM.

23. Report of the Superintendent of Live Stock, Pan-American Exposition, Box 9, Folder 10, WIB Papers, BHM; Bennitt, *The Pan-American*, 36–37.

24. Report of the Superintendent of Live Stock, Pan-American Exposition, Box 9, Folder 10, WIB Papers, BHM; Arthur Goodrich, "Short Stories of Interesting Exhibits," *The World's Work* 2, no. 4 (August 1901), 1057–1058.

25. Charles J. Wolf to WIB, May 3, 1902, Report of the Military Bureau, Box 9, Folder 15, WIB, Report, 77–78, Box 8, Folder 13, WIB Papers, BHM; Proceedings of the Board of Directors, June 9, 1901, PAEC Records, BHM; *Buffalo Courier*, June 12, July 12, 1901; *Buffalo Commercial*, June 12, 1901; *Buffalo Express*, June 13, 1901.

26. Buchanan, Report, 69–71, Box 8, Folder 13, WIB to executive committee, February 12, 1901, Box 5, Folder 7, WIB Papers, BHM; *Buffalo Commercial*, June 20, 1901.

27. *Buffalo Commercial*, June 11, 1901; *Buffalo Courier*, June 12, 14, July 5, 1901; *Buffalo Express*, July 5, 1901.

28. Buchanan, Report, 72–73, Box 8, Folder 13, BHM; *Buffalo Express*, July 14, 1901.

29. *Buffalo Courier*, August 26, 1901; *Buffalo Commercial*, August 27, 1901; *Buffalo Express*, August 26, 27, 1901.

30. *Buffalo Commercial*, July 30, August 1, 1901; *Buffalo Express*, July 30, 1901.

31. Chapple, "Personal Impressions," 338; Virginia L. Bartos, "'A Fine Exhibit by the Bureau of Ethnology': Dr. A. L. Benedict and the Presentation of Culture at the Pan American Exposition," Ph.D. diss., State University of New York at Buffalo, 2004, 61–63, 118–123.

32. Bartos, "'A Fine Exhibit,'" 131–133, 135–136, 137–138.

33. *Ibid.*, 142–147; Report Regarding Mounds, Box 5, Folder 3, PAEC Records, BHM.

34. Bennitt, *The Pan-American*, 34–35, 40; Goodrich, "Short Stories," 1063.

35. Report of the Division of Liberal Arts, Pan-American Exposition Company, Box 9, Folder 9, WIB Papers, BHM; Bennitt, *The Pan-American*, 30–31; Goodrich, "Short Stories," 1056.

36. Report of the Divisions of Manufactures, Pan American Exposition Company, Box 9, Folder 12, WIB Papers, BHM.

37. Bennitt, *The Pan-American*, 29–30; *Buffalo Express*, May 21, 1901; Goodrich, "Short Stories," 1055; *Buffalo Courier*, August 3, 1901.

38. Mrs. L. O. Harris, "New Foods at the Pan-American Exposition," *Boston Cooking School Magazine* 6, no. 3 (October 1901), 106–108; Lavina Hart, "The Exhibit of Human Nature," *The Cosmopolitan* 31, no. 5 (September 1901), 531–532.

39. Report of the Division of Graphic Arts, Pan-American Exposition Company, Box 9, Folder 5, WIB Papers, BHM; Bennitt, *The Pan-American*, 22; Goodrich, "Short Stories," 8; Murray, "The Automatic Age," 400–401.

40. Report of the Machinery Division, Pan-American Exposition Company, Box 9, Folder 11, WIB Papers, BHM; Bennitt, *The Pan-American*, 32–33.

41. Bennitt, *The Pan-American*, 33, 58; Percy, *Buffalo-Niagara Connections*, 213–214; *Buffalo Express*, June 6, 1901.

42. Proceedings of the Board of Directors, May 7, 1901, Box 1, Vol. 3, PAEC Records, BHM; *Buffalo Courier*, May 28, 1901.

43. "Pan-American Exhibit of General Electric Company," *Western Electrician*, 28, no.4 (June 15, 1901), 406–407; "Westinghouse Pan-American Exhibits," *Western Electrician*, 29, no.5 (August 10, 1901), 65–67.

44. Andre Millard, *Edison and the Business of Innovation* (Baltimore and London: The Johns Hopkins University Press, 1990), 129–131, 186–187, 191–193; Wyn Wachhorst, *Thomas Alva Edison: An American Myth* (Cambridge, MA: MIT Press, 1981), 91–93, 99–101; Martin V. Melosi, *Thomas A. Edison and the Modernization of America* (New York: Pearson-Longman, 2008), 148–153; Murray, "The Automatic Age," 396–397; "The Edison Storage Battery at Buffalo," *Western Electrician*, August 10, 1901; "Edison Storage Battery Not in Competition at Buffalo," *Western Electrician*, August 3, 1901.

45. "Edison at the Pan-American Exposition," *Western Electrician*, August 17, 1901; *Buffalo Courier*, July 21, 1901.

46. Bennitt, *The Pan-American*, 26; "Telephoning the Roar of Niagara," *Western Electrician* 28, no. 24, 405; "Kellogg Telephone and Switchboard Exhibit at the Pan-American Exposition," *Western Electrician* 29, no. 16, 261–262.

47. *Buffalo Commercial*, August 24, 1901.

48. Bennitt, *The Pan-American*, 57.

49. *Ibid.*, 49; "Pan-American Exposition Searchlight Signals to Toronto," *Western Electrician* 29, no. 8, 114.

50. Fire Work Exhibitions, Box 8, Folder 16, WIB to executive committee, August 27, 1901, Box 6, Folder 7, WIB Papers, BHM; *Buffalo Express*, June 3, 1901.

Chapter 18

1. WIB, Report, 74–76, Box 8, Folder 13, WIB Papers BHM.

2. Report of the Advertising Bureau of Publicity, Frank R. Rosseel Papers, BHM; "The Newspapers and the Exposition," *Profitable Advertising*, June 1901; Publicity Through the Press, Box 5, Folder 2, PAEC Records, BHM.

3. Register, *Kid of Coney Island*, 80; *Buffalo Courier*, July 22, 24, 1901; *Buffalo Commercial*, July 26, 1901.

4. *Buffalo Commercial*, August 3, 1901.

5. *Buffalo Commercial*, August 3, 1901; *Buffalo Express*, August 4, 1901.

6. *Buffalo Commercial*, August 3, 1901; *Buffalo Express*, August 4, 1901; Register, *Kid of Coney Island*, 80–81.

7. *Buffalo Courier*, August 4, 5, 1901; *Buffalo Commercial*, August 5, 1901.

8. Peterson, *Diplomat of the Americas*, 172, 175; proceedings of the Board of Directors, August 12, 20, 1901, Box 1, Vol. 3, PAEC Records, BHM; *Buffalo Commercial*, August 2, 1901.

9. Proceedings of the Board of Directors, September 23, October 7, 1901, Box 1, Vol. 4, PAEC Records, BHM; WIB to executive committee, September 9, 21, 23, 24, 30, 1901, Box 6, Folders 7–8, WIB Papers, BHM.

10. Henry M. Nicholls, "Exposition Officials Outwitted Sheriff, Kept Big 1901 Show Going," *Buffalo Evening News Magazine*, April 28, 1951; Henry M. Nicholls, Recollections of the Pan-American Exposition, Henry M. Nicholls Papers, BHM; Roman, Impact on Buffalo, 37–41.

11. Report of the Commandant of Police Made to the Director-General, Pan-American Exposition, 1901, Box 3, Vol. 29, PAEC Records, BHM.

12. *Buffalo Commercial*, June 13, August 20, 22, 1901; *Buffalo Express*, August 3, 6, 18, 1901.

13. *Buffalo Courier*, August 18, 19, 20, 1901; *Buffalo Express*, August 18, 1901.

14. *Buffalo Commercial*, July 5, 6, 1901; *Buffalo Courier*, July 5, 6, 1901; W. V. Cox to J. H. Brigham, July 14, October 5, 1901, Letters Received Concerning Government Participation in the Expo, in General, RG 33, NA; Bamford, Behind the Scenes, Bamford Papers, BHM; entries for July 29, August 1, September 25, 1901, Theodore B. Sheldon Diary, James Sheldon Papers, BHM.

15. *Buffalo Courier*, August 24, 1901; *Buffalo Commercial*, August 24, 1901.

16. Report of the Commandant of Police, Box 3, Vol. 29, PAEC Records, BHM.

17. *Buffalo Express*, July 14, August 5, 1901; *Buffalo Courier*, July 14, 1901.

18. *Buffalo Courier*, July 15, 1901.

Chapter 19

1. Briggs interviews, CFP, MHS.

2. Briggs interviews, CFP, MHS.

3. Channing, "Mental Status of Czolgosz," 255; Johns, *The Man Who Shot McKinley*, 43; Fisher, *Stolen Glory*, 46.

4. Briggs interviews, CFP, MHS; Johns, *The Man Who Shot McKinley*, 13.

5. Johns, *The Man Who Shot McKinley*, 13–14, 30.

6. Briggs interviews, CFP, MHS; Johns, *The Man Who Shot McKinley*, 30–31.

7. Briggs interviews, CFP, MHS.

8. Johns, *The Man Who Shot McKinley*, 136–137.

9. Goldman, *Living My Life*, 290–292.

10. Fisher, *Stolen Glory*, 46; Johns, *The Man Who Shot McKinley*, 49.

Chapter 20

1. Mark Goldman, "McKinley in Buffalo, Part 1," *Buffalo Spree*, Summer 1983, 110; Joe Mitchell Chapple, "Affairs at Washington," *National Magazine* 15, no. 1 (October 1901), 9; Peterson, *Diplomat of the Americas*, 180–181; *Buffalo Express*, September 5, 1901.

2. *Buffalo Express*, September 5, 1901; *Buffalo Courier*, September 5, 1901.

3. Chapple, "Affairs at Washington," 9–10; *Buffalo Courier*, September 5, 1901; *Buffalo Express*, September 5, 1901.

4. *Buffalo Express*, September 5, 1901.

5. *Buffalo Express*, September 6, 1901; *Buffalo Commercial*, September 6, 1901; *Official Daily Program of the Pan American Exposition*, September 5, 1901; Peterson, *Diplomat of the Americas*, 182; Chapple, "Affairs at Washington," 10.

6. *Buffalo Express*, September 6, 1901; *Buffalo Commercial*, September 6, 1901.

7. *Buffalo Express*, September 6, 1901; *Buffalo Commercial*, September 6, 1901.

8. Richardson, *Messages and Papers of the Presidents*, IX, 6618.

9. *Ibid.*, 6619–6622.

10. Arrival of President, Memorandum in McKinley Papers, LC; *Buffalo Express*, September 6, 1901; *Buffalo Commercial*, September 5, 1901.

11. *Buffalo Express*, September 6, 1901; *Buffalo Commercial*, September 5, 1901.

12. *Buffalo Express*, September 6, 1901; *Buffalo Commercial*, September 5, 1901.

13. *Buffalo Express*, September 6, 1901.

14. *Ibid.*

15. Leech, *In the Days of McKinley*, 589; Walter Lord, *The Good Years: From 1900 to the First World War* (New York: Harper Brothers, 1960), 46; Stoddard, *As I Knew Them*, 231.

16. Arrangements for Trip of President McKinley and Party to Lewiston and Niagara Falls, Friday, September 6, 1901, Memorandum in McKinley Papers, LC; *Buffalo Commercial*, September 6, 1901; *Buffalo Express*, September 7, 1901.

17. *Buffalo Commercial*, September 6, 1901; *Buffalo Express*, September 7, 1901; Walter Wellman, "The Last Days of President M'Kinley," *The American Monthly Review of Reviews* 24, no. 4 (October 1901), 418.

18. *Buffalo Commercial*, September 6, 1901; *Buffalo Express*, September 7, 1901; Miller, *The President and the Assassin*, 300.

19. Louis L. Babcock, "The Assassination of President William McKinley," *Niagara Frontier Miscellany* 35 (1947), 18.

Chapter 21

1. *Buffalo Express*, September 7, 1901; Johns, *The Man Who Shot McKinley*, 88; Babcock, "Assassination of McKinley," 18.

2. Babcock, "Assassination of McKinley," 18, 30; Morgan, *McKinley*, 288.

3. Richard Sherman, "Presidential Protection during the Progressive Era: The Aftermath of the McKinley Assassination," *The Historian* 46 (1983), 2; Fisher, *Stolen Glory*, 46; Lord, *The Good Years*, 49.

4. Lord, *The Good Years*, 48–49; *Buffalo Courier*, September 7, 1901; John E. Wilkie to Samuel R. Ireland, September 19, 1901, Secret Service Papers Regarding the Assassination of President William McKinley, 1900–1910, BHM.

5. Lord, *The Good Years*, 42, 29; Babcock, "Assassination of McKinley," 18–20.

6. Babcock, "Assassination of McKinley," 19.

7. *Ibid.*, 20; Supreme Court, Erie County New York, *The People of New York vs. Leon Czolgosz* (hereafter *PNYVLC*), BHM, 252–253; Fisher *Stolen Glory*, 59; Johns, *The Man Who Shot McKinley*, 93; Statement of George F. Foster, Secret Service Papers Regarding the Assassination of President William McKinley, 1900–1910, BHM; *Buffalo Courier*, September 7, 1901; *Buffalo Evening News*, September 7, 1901. Exposition guard Homer James also described the man passed on as Italian. *The Noble County Leader* (Caldwell, OH), September 25, 1901.

8. Statement of S. R. Ireland, Secret Service Papers Regarding the Assassination of President William McKinley, 1900–1910, BHM; *Buffalo Evening News*, September 7, 1901.

9. Statement of S. R. Ireland, Secret Service Papers Regarding the Assassination of President William McKinley, 1900–1910, BHM; *PNYVLC*, BHM, 276; *Buffalo Courier*, September 7, 1901; *Buffalo Express*, September 7, 1901.

10. *Buffalo Evening News*, September 7, 1901.

11. *PNYVLC*, BHM, 214, 240–241, 247–248, 257, 270; statements of A. L. Gallaher, S. R. Ireland, and George F. Foster, Secret Service Papers Regarding the Assassination of President William McKinley, 1900–1910, BHM.

12. *Buffalo Evening News*, September 7, 1901; *Buffalo Express*, September 7, 1901; DeWitt Clinton Colegrove to Alice Elizabeth Colegrove, September 14, 1901, DeWitt Clinton Colegrove Letters, BHM.

13. Miller, *The President and the Assassin*, 302; Fisher, *Stolen Glory*, 60.

14. The quote used comes from the *Buffalo Courier*, September 7, 1901. Agent Foster also recalled the president asking Cortelyou "not to exaggerate things," Foster Statement, Secret Service Papers Regarding the Assassination of President William McKinley, 1900–1910, BHM. Other publications quoting McKinley as asking that the accounts not be exaggerated appear in the *New Orleans Picayune*, September 8, 1901; *Albany Journal*, September 7, 1901; and the magazine *Timely Topics*, September 13, 1901.

15. Statements of George F. Foster and S. R. Ireland, Secret Service Papers Regarding the Assassination of President William McKinley, 1900–1910, BHM; *PNYVLC*, 216,277; *Buffalo Courier*, September 7, 1901; *Buffalo Evening News*, September 7, 1901.

16. *Buffalo Express*, September 7, 1901; *Buffalo Courier*, September 7, 1901; *Buffalo Commercial*, September 7, 1901; *Jamestown (New York) Evening Journal*, September 7, 1901; *Noble County Leader* (Caldwell, OH), September 25, 1901.

17. Babcock, "Assassination of McKinley," 22; *Buffalo Courier*, September 7, 1901; *Buffalo Express*, September 7, 1901;

18. *Buffalo Courier*, September 7, 1901; *Buffalo Express*, September 7, 1901; *Noble County Leader* (Caldwell, OH), September 25, 1901; W. Bartlett Sumner, The Great Tragedy as Witnessed by a Chair Guide at the Pan-American Exposition, McCabe-Sumner Family Papers, 1885–1982, BHM; Babcock, "Assassination of McKinley," 22; statement of A. L. Gallaher, Secret Service Papers Regarding the Assassination of President William McKinley, 1900–1910, BHM.

19. Sumner, The Great Tragedy... McCabe-Sumner Family Papers, 1885–1982, BHM; Babcock, "Assassination of McKinley," 22–23.

20. *Annual Report of the Board of Police of the City of Buffalo for the Year Ending December 31, 1901* (Buffalo: Wenborne-Sumner, 1902), 18; *Buffalo Commercial*, September 7, 1901; *Buffalo Courier*, September 7, 1901; Irving R. Templeton, Reminiscences, BHM.

21. *PNYVLC*, BHM, 286–288.

22. Briggs interviews, CFP, MHS.

23. *Annual Report of the Board of Police*, 13–14; Briggs interviews, CFP, MHS; *PNYVLC*, 219–231, 289–294.

24. *PNYVLC*, 220–221, 290–292.

25. *PNYVLC*, 227–228; Leon F. Czolgosz, Statement, September 6, 1901, BHM.

26. *Buffalo Courier*, September 7, 1901; Walter Wellman, "The Last Days of President McKinley," *American Monthly Review of Reviews* 24, no. 4 (October 1901), 419–420; Johns, *The Man Who Shot McKinley*, 95.

27. *Buffalo Courier*, September 7, 1901; Statement of George Foster, Secret Service Papers Regarding the Assassination of President William McKinley, 1900–1910, BHM.

28. Nelson W. Wilson, "Details of President McKinley's Case," *Buffalo Medical Journal* 52 (1901), 207–208; P. M. Rixey, Matthew D. Mann, Herman Mynter, Roswell Park, Eugene Wasdin, Charles McBurney, and Charles G. Stockton, "The Official Report on the Case of President McKinley," *Buffalo Medical Journal* 52 (1901), 271; Wellman, "The Last Days of President McKinley," 420.

29. Nelson W. Wilson to Roswell Park, September 6, 1901, Box 4, Folder 1, PAEC Records, BHM; Adele Pillitteri, "OR Nursing 100 Years Ago: Nursing Care of President McKinley," *Today's O.R. Nurse* 13, no. 12 (December 1991), 20.

30. Selig Adler, "The Operation on President McKinley," *Scientific American* 208, no. 3 (March 1963), 121; Statement of George F. Foster, Secret Service Papers Regarding the Assassination of President William McKinley, 1900–1910, BHM; Pillitteri, "OR Nursing 100 Years Ago," 20; Fisher, *Stolen Glory*, 65.

31. Adler, "Operation on President McKinley," 121; Wellman, "The Last Days of President McKinley," 420; Rixey, et al., "Official Report," 271; Fisher, *Stolen Glory*, 64–66; Roswell Park, Reminiscences of McKinley Week, BHM.

32. Adler, "Operation on President McKinley," 121; Wellman, "The Last Days of President McKinley," 420.

33. Adler, "Operation on President McKin-ley," 122; Pillitteri, "OR Nursing 100 Years Ago," 21.

34. Fisher, *Stolen Glory*, 70; Adler, "The Operation on President McKinley," 122.

35. Fisher, *Stolen Glory*, 70–71; Wilson, "Details of President McKinley's Case," 209.

36. Fisher, *Stolen Glory*, 70, 72–73; Pillitteri, "OR Nursing 100 Years Ago," 21–22; Wilson, "Details of President McKinley's Case," 208.

37. Rixey, et al., "Official Report," 272–273; Wilson to Park, September 6, 1901, PAEC Records, Box 4, Folder 1, BHM.

38. Rixey, et al., "Official Report," 273.

39. *Ibid.*; Wilson to Park, September 6, 1901, Box 4, Folder 1, PAEC Records, BHM; Fisher, *Stolen Glory*, 75.

40. Fisher, *Stolen Glory*, 75–77; Wilson to Park, September 6, 1901, Box 4, Folder 1, PAEC Records, BHM; Rixey, et al., "Official Report on the Case of President McKinley," 273–275.

41. "Official Report on the Case of President McKinley," 274.

42. Wilson to Park, September 6, 1901, Box 4, Folder 1, PAEC Records, BHM; *The Cataract Journal* (Niagara Falls, NY), September 7, 1901; *The Niagara Falls Gazette*, September 7, 1901; Julian Park Notes, Roswell Park, Reminiscences of McKinley Week, BHM.

43. Park, Reminiscences of McKinley Week, BHM.

44. Fisher, *Stolen Glory*, 79; Rixey, et al., "Official Report on the Case of President McKinley," 276; Adler, "Operation on President McKinley," 124.

45. Park, Reminiscences of McKinley Week, BHM.

46. Wilson to Park, September 6, 1901, Box 4, Folder 1, PAEC Records, BHM; *Buffalo Commercial*, September 7, 1901; *Buffalo Express*, September 7, 1901.

Chapter 22

1. Fisher, *Stolen Glory*, 89.

2. Pillitteri, "OR Nursing 100 Years Ago," 23; Roswell Park, "Reminiscences of McKinley Week," *Selected Papers Surgical and Scientific* (Buffalo: Julian Park, 1914), 377; R. F. Mould, *A Century of X-Rays and Radioactivity in Medicine: With Emphasis on Photographic Records of the Early Years* (Philadelphia: Institute of Physics, 1993), 74–76.

3. Fisher, *Stolen Glory*, 87; *Buffalo Commercial*, September 7, 1901; *Buffalo Express*, September 8, 1901.

4. Fisher, *Stolen Glory*, 81–82; *Buffalo Com-

mercial, September 7, 1901; *Buffalo Express*, September 8, 1901.

5. Alice Sprague Reminiscencs, Pitts-Brayley-Keeting Family Papers, BHM.

6. DeWitt Clinton Colegrove to Alice Elizabeth Colegrove, September 14, 1901, DeWitt Clinton Colegrove Letter, BHM; "Eddy" to Libby Shumway, September 10, 1901, Mrs. E. C. Shumway Papers, BHM; *Buffalo Commercial*, September 7, 9, 1901; *Buffalo Express*, September 8, 1901.

7. Wexler, *Emma Goldman*, 104.

8. *Ibid.*, 105; Emma Goldman, "The Assassination of McKinley," *American Mercury*, 24 (1931), 53–54; Goldman, *Living My Life*, 295–297.

9. Wexler, *Emma Goldman*, 105–107; Goldman, "Assassination of McKinley," 55–62.

10. *Buffalo Express*, September 9, 1901; Adler, "Operation on President McKinley," 126; *Buffalo Commercial*, September 8, 1901.

11. Pillitteri, "Nursing Care," 23; Adler, "Operation on President McKinley," 126.

12. *Buffalo Express*, September 10, 1901.

13. Pillitteri, "Nursing Care," 23; *Buffalo Express*, September 10, 1901; *Buffalo Commercial*, September 9, 1901; Wellman, "The Last Days," 424.

14. John Taliaferro, *All the Great Prizes: The Life of John Hay from Lincoln to Roosevelt* (New York: Simon & Schuster, 2013), 407; Babcock, "Assassination of McKinley," 25.

15. *Buffalo Express*, September 11, 1901; *Buffalo Commercial*, September 11, 1901; Wellman, "The Last Days," 424; Palmer, Weiss, and Sentz, "Dr. Roswell Park and the McKinley Assassination," 186.

16. *Buffalo Express*, September 11, 1901; *Buffalo Commercial*, September 11, 1901; Wellman, "The Last Days," 424.

17. M. Ulrich to McKinley, September 12, 1901, August W. Noack to Cortelyou, September 12, 1901, J. W. McCulloch to John Milburn, September 10, 1901; Henry Rechter to McKinley, September 13, 1901, M. Brown to McKinley, September 10, 1901, William Farrand to Cortelyou, September 12, 1901, McKinley Papers, LC; *Buffalo Express*, September 12, 1901.

18. *Buffalo Express*, September 12, 1901; *Buffalo Commercial*, September 12, 1901.

19. Wellman, "The Last Days," 424; *Buffalo Commercial*, September 12, 1901.

20. Fisher, *Stolen Glory*, 107–108; Adler, "Operation on President McKinley," 127; "The Official Report on the Case of President McKinley," 282.

21. *Buffalo Commercial*, September 13, 1901.

22. *Canton Repository*, September 13, 1901; Fisher, *Stolen Glory*, 108–109; Wellman, "The Last Days," 424–435; Adler, "Operation on President McKinley," 127; John F. Courtney, "Doctors and the McKinley Assassination," *Resident Physician*, March 1968, 80; Jack Fisher, "McKinley's Assassination in Buffalo: Time to Put the Medical Controversy to Rest?" *Buffalo Physician*, Spring 2001, 15–16.

23. Proceedings of the Board of Directors, September 13, 1901, PAEC Papers, Box 1, vol. 4, BHM; Lord, *The Good Years*, 59; Wellman, "The Last Days," 425.

24. Wellman, "The Last Days," 425; Lord, *The Good Years*, 59.

25. Wellman, "The Last Days," 425; Lord, *The Good Years*, 59; Park, Reminiscences of McKinley Week, Park Papers, BHM.

26. Edmund Morris, *Theodore Rex* (New York: Random House, 2001), 1–7; Fisher, *Stolen Glory*, 109, 112.

27. Morris, *Theodore Rex*, 11–12.

28. *Ibid.*, 12–15; Babcock, "Assassination of McKinley," 25–26; Fisher, *Stolen Glory*, 116–118.

29. Fisher, *Stolen Glory*, 118–120.

30. *Ibid.*, 120–122; *Canton Repository*, September 14, 16, 1901.

31. *Canton Repository*, September 18, 19, 1901.

32. *Ibid.*, September 18, 19, 1901; Fisher, *Stolen Glory*, 121–122.

33. *Canton Repository*, September 20, 1901.

Chapter 23

1. Rauchway, *Murdering McKinley*, 20.

2. Briggs interviews, CFP, MHS.; Rauchway, *Murdering McKinley*, 27.

3. *Buffalo Express*, September 8, 1901; *Buffalo Commercial*, September 7, 1901; *PNYVLC*, BHM, 299–301.

4. *Buffalo Express*, September 8, 1901; *Buffalo Commercial*, September 17, 1901.

5. *Buffalo Commercial*, September 9, 1901.

6. Briggs interviews, CFP, MHS.

7. *Annual Report of the Board of Police of the City of Buffalo for the Year Ending December 31, 1901*, 15–16; Johns, *The Man Who Shot McKinley*, 190–191; *Buffalo Express*, September 14, 1901.

8. *Report of the Board of Police, 1901*, 17; *Buffalo Express*, September 14, 1901; *Buffalo Commercial*, September 14, 1901.

9. Thomas Penney to John D. Lawson, ND, quoted John D. Lawson (ed.), *American State Trials*, 17 vols. (St. Louis: Thomas Law Book, 1923), XIV, 161–162; Kenneth D. Ackerman, *Dark Horse: The Surprise Election and Political*

Murder of James A. Garfield (New York: Carroll & Graf, 2003), 443–444.

10. Lawson (ed.), *American State Trials*, XIV, 161–162, 165–167.

11. *Ibid.*, 166.

12. *Ibid.*, 164–165; Johns, *The Man Who Shot McKinley*, 194–195.

13. Lawson (ed.), *American State Trials*, XIV, 164–168.

14. Rauchway, *Murdering McKinley*, 39–42; MacDonald, "The Trial, Execution, Autopsy and Mental Status," 187.

15. MacDonald, "The Trail, Execution, Autopsy and Mental Status," 187–189.

16. *Buffalo Express*, September 22, 1901.

17. *Buffalo Commercial*, September 17, 1901; *Buffalo Express*, September 24, 1901; *Buffalo Evening News*, September 23, 1901.

18. *PNYVLC*, BHM, 5.

19. *PNYVLC*, BHM, 6–7.

20. *PNYVLC*, BHM, 12.

21. *PNYVLC*, BHM, 17–18, 26–28, 40–42, 56–57, 66–68, 121, 123.

22. PNYVLC, BHM, 25, 32, 46, 54, 73, 93, 102, 117, 120; *Buffalo Express*, September 24, 1901; *Buffalo Evening News*, September 23, 1901.

23. *PNYVLC*, BHM, 15, 157, 159, 162.

24. *PNYVLC*, BHM, 168.

25. *PNYVLC*, BHM, 196, 199–201.

26. *PNYVLC*, BHM, 302.

27. *PNYVLC*, BHM, 303.

28. *PNYVLC*, BHM, 303–305, 308.

29. *PNYVLC*, BHM, 309–310.

30. *PNYVLC*, BHM, 310–311.

31. *PNYVLC*, BHM, 311–313.

32. *PNYVLC*, BHM, 314.

33. Rauchway, *Murdering McKinley*, 48–49, offers a similar view.

34. *PNYVLC*, BHM, 317, 319–321.

35. *PNYVLC*, BHM, 334–336; Rauchway, *Murdering McKinley*, 50–51.

36. *PNYVLC*, BHM, 337; *Buffalo Express*, September 25, 1901; *Buffalo Evening News*, September 25, 1901; *Buffalo Commercial*, September 25, 1901.

37. *PNYVLC*, BHM, 339–346.

38. *Buffalo Commercial*, September 27, 1901; Briggs interviews, CFP, MHS.

39. Briggs, *Manner of Man*, 257; Briggs interviews, CFP, MHS.

40. Briggs interviews, CFP, MHS.

41. Briggs interviews, CFP, MHS.

42. Wexler, *Goldman*, 110; Goldman, "The Assassination of McKinley," 64.

43. Goldman, "The Assassination of McKinley," 64, 66–67; Wexler, *Goldman*, 108–110.

44. Briggs interviews, CFP, MHS.

45. *Buffalo Commercial*, October 29, 1901; MacDonald, "Trial, Execution, Autopsy and Mental Status," 185; Briggs interviews, CFP, MHS; Briggs, *Manner of Man*, 261.

46. Briggs, *Manner of Man*, 264.

47. MacDonald, "Trial, Execution, Autopsy and Mental Status," 185; *Buffalo Commercial*, October 29, 1901.

48. Rauchway, *Murdering McKinley*, 53, 55–56; Fisher, *Stolen Glory*, 135–136.

Chapter 24

1. Peterson, *Diplomat of the Americas*, 187; WIB to executive committee, September 20, 1901, WIB Papers, Box 6, Folder 7, BHM; Proceedings of the Board of Directors, October 7, 1901, PAEC Records, Box 1, Vol. 4, BHM.

2. Nicholls, Recollections, BHM.

3. Proceedings of the Board of Directors, October 15, 1901, PAEC Records, BHM; *Buffalo Express*, September 29, 1901; *Buffalo Commercial*, October 2, 21, 1901; *Buffalo Evening News*, November 2, 1901.

4. *Buffalo Express*, September 29, October 10, 20, 1901; *Buffalo Courier*, October 10, 20, 1901.

5. *Buffalo Commercial*, October 7, 1901; *Buffalo Express*, October 10, 1901; *Buffalo Evening News*, October 10, 1901.

6. *Buffalo Express*, October 6, 21, 1901; *Buffalo Courier*, July 21, October 19, 22, 1901.

7. *Buffalo Courier*, October 21, 1901; *Buffalo Express*, October 23, 1901; proceedings of the Board of Directors, October 22, 1901, Box 1, Vol. 4, PAEC Records, BHM.

8. Proceedings of the Board of Directors, October 22, 1901, Box 1, Vol. 4, PAEC Records, BHM; *Buffalo Courier*, October 24, 30, 1901; *Buffalo Express*, October 26, 30, 1901.

9. *Buffalo Express*, November 3, 1901.

10. *Ibid.*; *Buffalo Courier*, November 3, 1901.

11. *Buffalo Courier*, November 3, 4, 1901; *Buffalo Express*, November 3, 4, 1901.

12. *Buffalo Express*, November 4, 5, 1901; *Buffalo Commercial*, November 4, 1901; *Buffalo Courier*, November 4, 8, 1901.

13. *Buffalo Commercial*, November 4, 8, 1901; *Buffalo Express*, November 5, 1901; *Buffalo Courier*, November 4, 1901.

14. *Buffalo Express*, November 5, 1901; *Buffalo Courier*, November 18, 21, 1901; *Buffalo Commercial*, November 18, 1901; proceedings of the Board of Directors, October 29, November 19, 26, 1901, Box 1, Vol. 4, PAEC Records, BHM.

15. *Buffalo Courier*, November 7, 8, 10, 1901; *Buffalo Commercial*, November 8, 9, 11, 1901.

16. *Buffalo Courier*, October 21, November 4, 1901.

17. WIB, Report, 6–7, 62, 67, Box 8, Folder 13, WIB Papers, BHM; Roman, Impact of the Pan American, 41.

18. *Buffalo Courier*, November 26, December 3, 1901.

19. *Buffalo Courier*, December 7, 8, 1901; *Buffalo Express*, December 4, 1901.

20. *Buffalo Courier*, December 7, 8, 1901; *Buffalo Express*, July 1, 3, 1902; Roman, Impact of the Pan American, 41.

21. *Buffalo Express*, July 3, November 20, 1902; *Buffalo Commercial*, November 20, 1902, March 17, 1904.

22. *Buffalo News*, February 26, March 2, 1902; *Buffalo Courier*, March 5, 1902.

23. *Buffalo Courier*, March 16, 26, May 5, 10, 1902.

24. *Buffalo Courier*, March 16, 27, 1902, April 7, 1903; *Buffalo Courier*, April 27, May 5, 1902.

25. *Buffalo News*, March 14, 24, 1902; *Buffalo Express*, May 2, 1902, April 9, 1903; *Buffalo Commercial*, May 2, 1902.

26. *Buffalo Courier*, March 1, April 12, July 2, 13, 1902.

Appendix

1. *Buffalo Courier*, September 7, 1901.

2. Mitch Kachun, "'Big Jim' Parker and the Assassination of William McKinley: Patriotism, Nativism, Anarchism, and the Struggle for African American Citizenship," *Journal of the Gilded Age and Progressive Era* 9, Issue 1 (October 2010), 2; *Buffalo Express*, September 10, 1901.

3. John E. Wilkie to S. R. Ireland, September 19, 1901, Report of S. R. Ireland, Secret Service Papers Regarding the Assassination of President William McKinley, 1900–1910, BHM.

4. *Buffalo Courier*, September 25, 1901; Kachun, "'Big Jim' Parker," 9; *Buffalo Evening News*, September 28, 1901.

5. *Buffalo Express*, September 7, 1901; *Buffalo Evening News*, September 7, 1901; *Buffalo Commercial*, September 7, 1901; *Buffalo Courier*, September 7, 1901.

6. *Rochester Union and Advertiser*, September 9, 1901.

7. *PNYVLC*, 252–253, BHM.

8. *PNYVLC*, 204–205, 212–213, 276–277, 282–283, BHM.

9. *PNYVLC*, 239–240, 247, 253.

10. *PNYVLC*, 257.

11. *Noble County Leader* (Caldwell, OH), September 25, 1901.

12. *Buffalo Evening News*, September 7, 1901; "Assassination of President McKinley," *Timely Topics* 6, no. 2 (September 13, 1901), 20.

13. Kachun, "'Big Jim' Parker," 9; Carl Sferrazza Anthony, *Ida McKinley: The Turn-of-the-Century First Lady through War, Assassination, and Secret Disability* (Kent, OH: Kent State University Press, 2013), 291–292; *Washington Post*, March 23, 1907, March 27, 1908.

Bibliography

Manuscript material

Bamford, Heidi A., Papers, Buffalo History Museum.

Buchanan, William Inesco, Papers Buffalo History Museum.

Channing Family Papers, Massachusetts Historical Society.

Colegrove, DeWitt Clinton, Letter, Buffalo History Museum.

Cortelyou, George, Papers, Library of Congress.

Czolgosz, Leon F., Statement, September 6, 1901, Buffalo History Museum.

Letters Received Concerning Government Participation in the Exposition in General, 1899–1902, RG 33, National Archives and Records Administration.

Letters Sent by the Chairman, Board of Management, 1899–1902, RG 33, National Archives and Records Administration.

McCabe-Sumner Family Papers, Buffalo History Museum.

McKinley, William, Papers, Library of Congress.

Miscellaneous Records Relating to the Exposition, 1900–1901, RG 56, National Archives and Records Administration.

Nicholls, Henry M., Papers, Buffalo History Museum.

Pan American Exposition Company Records, Buffalo History Museum.

Park, Roswell, Reminiscences of McKinley Week, Buffalo History Museum.

Pitts-Brayley-Keeting Family Papers, Buffalo History Museum.

Report of Special Jury of Awards on United States Government Exhibits, RG 56, National Archives and Records Administration.

Report of the Board of Management, United States Government Exhibit, Pan-American Exposition, Buffalo, New York, 1901, RG 56, National Archives and Records Administration.

Secret Service Papers Regarding the Assassination of President William McKinley, 1900–1910, Buffalo History Museum.

Sheldon, James, Papers, Buffalo History Museum.

Shumway, Mrs. E. C., Papers, Buffalo History Museum.

Supreme Court, Erie County, New York, *The People of New York vs. Leon Czolgos*, Buffalo History Museum.

Templeton, Irving R., Reminiscences, Buffalo History Museum.

Newspapers

Albany Journal
Buffalo Commercial
Buffalo Courier
Buffalo Evening News
Buffalo Express
Canton (Ohio) Repository
The Cataract Journal (Niagara Falls, NY)
Columbus (Ohio) Dispatch
Jamestown (New York) Evening Journal
New Orleans Picayune
New York Times
Niagara Falls (New York) Gazette
Noble County Leader (Caldwell, OH)
Rochester Union and Advertiser
San Francisco Chronicle
San Francisco Examiner
Washington Post
Washington Star

Books, Articles and Theses

Adams, Edward Dean (ed.). *Niagara Power: History of the Niagara Falls Power Company, 1886–1918.* 2 vols. Niagara Falls, NY: privately printed, 1927.

Adler, Selig. "The Operations on President McKinley." *Scientific American*, March 22, 1963.

Aldrich, William S. "Mechanical and Electrical Features of the Pan-American Exposition." *The Engineering Magazine* 5, no. 21 (September 1901).

Allen, Lewis F. "The Cholera in Buffalo." *Publications of the Buffalo Historical Society* 4 (1896).

Anderson, Norman D. *Ferris Wheels: An Illustrated History.* Bowling Green, OH: Bowling Green University Popular Press, 1992.

Andrews, William C. "How the Niagara Has Been Harnessed." *The American Monthly Reviews of Reviews*, June 1901.

Annual Report of the Board of Police of the City of Buffalo for the Year Ending December 31, 1901. Buffalo: Wenborne-Sumner, 1902.

Armstrong, William H. *Major McKinley: William McKinley and the Civil War.* Kent, OH: Kent State University Press, 2000.

"Assassination of President McKinley." *Timely Topics* 6, no. 2 (September 13, 1901).

"Awards of Interest to Medical Men Made at the Pan-American Exposition." *Medical Record*, October 26, 1901.

Babcock, Louis L. "The Assassination of President William McKinley." *Niagara Frontier Miscellany* 35 (1947).

_____. *The War of 1812 on the Niagara Frontier.* Buffalo, NY: Buffalo Historical Society, 1927.

"Baby Incubators at the Pan-American Exposition." *Scientific American*, August 3, 1901.

Barry, Richard H. *Snap Shots on the Midway of the Pan-Am Expo.* Buffalo, NY: Robert Allan Reid, 1901.

Bartos, Virginia L. "'A Fine Exhibit by the Bureau of Ethnology': Dr. A. L. Benedict and the Presentation of Culture at the Pan-American Exposition." Ph.D. diss., State University of New York at Buffalo, 2004.

Becker, Sophie C. *Sketches of Early Buffalo and the Niagara Region.* Buffalo, NY: McLaughlin, 1904.

Beichman, Arnold. "The First Execution." *Commentary*, May 1963.

Belfield, Robert Blake. "The Niagara Frontier: The Evolution of Electric Power Systems in New York and Ontario, 1880–1935." Ph.D. diss., University of Pennsylvania, 1981.

Bennitt, Mark. *The Pan-American Exposition and How to See It....* Buffalo, NY: Goff, 1901.

Bigham, Matthew R. "'Savagery' in the Shadows of 'Civility': Africans on the Midway." MA thesis, University of North Carolina at Wilmington, 2000.

Blanchard, Frank L. "Niagara Power at Buffalo." *Harper's Weekly*, June 5, 1897.

Briggs, L. Vernon. *The Manner of Man That Kills.* New York: Da Capo, 1983, repr. of 1921 edition.

Buchanan, W. I. "The Organization of an Exposition." *The Cosmopolitan* 31, no. 5 (September 1901).

Burg, David F. *Chicago's White City of 1893.* Lexington: University Press of Kentucky, 1976.

Cappadonia, Keturah Beth. "Timekeeper of Progress: The Fight for Inclusion of the 'Negro Exhibit' at Buffalo's Pan American Exposition, 1901." MA thesis, University of Rochester, 2006.

Carlson, W. Bernard. *Tesla: Inventor of the Electrical Age.* Princeton, NJ: Princeton University Press, 2013.

Carrere, John M. "The Exhibition at Buffalo: Some of the Ideas Which Have Determined Its Artistic Character." *Scribner's Magazine* 29, no. 6 (June 1901).

Catalogue of the Exhibit of the U.S. Navy Department, Pan-American Exposition, Buffalo, N.Y. Washington, D.C.: Government Printing Office, 1901.

Channing, Walter. "The Mental Status of Czolgosz, the Assassin of President McKinley." *American Journal of Insanity*, October 1902.

Chapple, Joe Mitchell. "Affairs at Washington." *National Magazine*, October 1901.

_____. "Personal Impressions of the Pan-American Exposition." *The National* 14, no. 4 (July 1901).

Cheney, Margaret. *Tesla: Man Out of Time.* New York: Dell, 1981.

Clarke, F. W. "The Government Exhibit at Buffalo." *The Forum* 31, no. 6 (August 1901).

Clarke, James W. *American Assassins: The Darker Side of Politics*. Princeton, NJ: Princeton University Press, 1982.

Courtney, John F. "Doctors and the McKinley Assassination." *Resident Physician*, March 1968.

Dawes, Charles G. *A Journal of the McKinley Years*. Chicago: Lakeside, 1950.

"The Death of President McKinley." *Collier's Weekly*, September 21, 1901.

DeCroix, Douglas W. "A Legacy of Life and Hope: Dr. Rosewell Park." *Western New York Heritage* 13, no. 3 (Fall 2010).

Dickson, Jean. "When Mexico Came to Buffalo." *Western New York Heritage* 10, no. 1 (Spring 2007).

Diehl, Conrad. "Buffalo and the Pan-American." *Ev'ry Month*, April 1901.

Dobson, John. *Reticent Expansionism: The Foreign Policy of William McKinley*. Pittsburgh: Duquesne University Press, 1998.

Drimmer, Frederick. *Until You Are Dead: The Book of Executions in America*. New York: Citadel, 1990.

Dunlap, Orrin E. "The Wonderful Story of the Chaining of Niagara." *The World's Work* 2, no. 4 (August 1901).

"Edison at the Pan-American Exposition." *Western Electrician*, August 17, 1901.

"The Edison Storage Battery at Buffalo." *Western Electrician*, August 10, 1901.

Elliott, Robert G. *Agent of Death: The Memoirs of an Executioner*. New York: E. P. Dutton, 1940.

"Emergency Hospital at the Pan-American Exposition." *The Medical Standard*, April 1901.

"Exhibit of Infant Incubators at the Pan-American Exhibition." *Pediatrics* 12 (1901).

Fine, Edward J., et al. "The Contributions of Dr. Roswell Park to Epilepsy and Spinal Surgery." *Neurosurgery*, February 1998.

Fisher, Jack. "McKinley's Assassination in Buffalo: Time to Put the Medical Controversy to Rest?" *Buffalo Physician*, Spring 2001.

_____. *Stolen Glory: The McKinley Assassination*. La Jolla, CA: Alamar, 2001.

Foraker, Julia B. *I Would Live It Again: Memories of a Vivid Life*. New York: Harper & Brothers, 1932.

Foster, Abram John. *The Coming of the Electrical Age to the United States*. New York: Arno, 1979.

Freeberg, Ernest. *The Age of Edison: Electric Light and the Invention of Modern America*. New York: Penguin, 2013.

Freidel, Frank. *The Splendid Little War*. New York: Bramhill House, 1958.

Gage, Lyman J. *Memoirs of Lyman Gage*. New York: House of Field, 1937.

Gibson, Richard "The Pan-American Exposition." *Overland Monthly* 37, no. 1 (January 1901).

Glad, Paul W. *McKinley, Bryan and the People*. New York: J. B. Lippincott, 1964.

_____. *The Trumpet Soundeth: William Jennings Bryan and His Democracy, 1896–1912*. Lincoln: University of Nebraska Press, 1960.

Goldman, Emma. "The Assassination of McKinley." *American Mercury* 24 (1931).

_____. *Living My Life*. 2 vols. New York: Dover, 1970, repr. of 1931 edition.

Goldman, Mark. "McKinley in Buffalo." *Buffalo Spree*, Summer 1983, Fall 1983.

Goodrich, Arthur. "Short Stories of Interesting Exhibits." *The World's Work* 2, no. 4 (August 1901).

Gould, Lewis L. *The Presidency of William McKinley*. Lawrence: Regents Press of Kansas, 1980.

_____. *The Spanish-American War and President McKinley*. Lawrence: University Press of Kansas, 1982.

Gowronski, Brett, Jana Kasikova, Lynda H. Schneekloth, and Thomas Yots. *The Power Trail: History of Hydroelectricity at Niagara*. Buffalo: Western New York Wares, 2005.

Grant, Robert. "Notes on the Pan-American Exposition." *The Cosmopolitan* 31, no. 5 (September 1901).

Halstead, Murat. *The Illustrious Life of William McKinley, Our Martyred President*. Chicago: Author, 1901.

Harris, Mrs. L. O. "New Foods at the Pan-American Exposition." *Boston Cooking School Magazine*, October 1901.

Hart, Lavinia. "The Exhibit of Human Nature." *The Cosmopolitan*, September 1901.

Hartt, Mary Bronson. "The Play-Side of the Fair." *The World's Work* 2, no. 4 (August 1901).

Hartt, Rollin Lynde. "The New Niagara." *McClure's Magazine* 27, no. 1 (May 1901).

Hill, Henry Wayland. *Municipality of Buffalo, New York: A History, 1720–1923*. 2 vols. New York: Lewis Historical, 1923.

Hill, R. C. "One of the Marvels of the Rainbow City." *Success*, July 1901.

Holden, Edwin S. "The Pan-American Exposition Flag." *Our Record*, August 1901.

Horner, William T. *Ohio's Kingmaker: Mark Hanna, Man and Myth*. Athens: Ohio University Press, 2010.

Howe, Elizabeth M. "Some Educational Exhibits at the Pan-American." *Our Record* 33, no. 5 (August 1901).

Hughes, Thomas P. *Networks of Power: Electrification in Western Society, 1880–1930*. Baltimore: The Johns Hopkins University Press, 1983.

JAMA. "From Other Pages." March 30, April 6, 1963.

James, Isabel Vaughan. "The Pan-American Exposition." *Adventures in Western New York History*, September 1961.

Johns, Wesley. *The Man Who Shot McKinley*. South Brunswick, NJ: A. S. Barnes, 1970.

Joll, James. *The Anarchists*. Cambridge, MA: Harvard University Press, 1980, repr. of 1964 edition.

Jonnes, Jill. *Empires of Light: Edison, Tesla, Westinghouse, and the Race to Electrify the World*. New York: Random House, 2003.

The Journal of American Industries. Buffalo Edition, December 1900.

Jovich, John B. "The Last Smile of William McKinley." *Buffalo Spree*, Winter 1996.

Kachun, Mitch. "'Big Jim' Parker and the Assassination of William McKinley: Patriotism, Nativism, Anarchism, and the Struggle for African American Citizenship." *Journal of the Gilded Age and Progressive Era*, October 2010.

"Kellogg Telephone and Switchboard Exhibit at the Pan American Exposition." *Western Electrician*, October 19, 1901.

Ketchum, William. "The Origin of the Name of Buffalo." *Publications of the Buffalo Historical Society* 1 (1879).

Kilar, Jeremy W. "'I Am Not Sorry.'" *Michigan History Magazine*, November/December 1995.

Knauff, Ernest. "Artistic Effects of the Pan-American Exposition." *The American Monthly Review of Reviews* 23, No. 6 (June 1901).

Kohlsaat, H. H. *From McKinley to Harding: Personal Recollections of Our Presidents*. New York: Charles Scribner's Sons, 1923.

Larned, J. N. *A History of Buffalo Delineating the Evolution of the City*. New York: Progress of the Empire State, 1911.

Lawson, John W. (ed.). *American State Trials*. 17 vols. St. Louis: Thomas Law Book, 1923.

Leech, Margaret. *In the Days of McKinley*. New York: Harper & Brothers, 1959.

Loos, William H., Ami M. Savigny, and Robert M. Gurn. *The Forgotten "Negro Exhibit": African American Involvement in Buffalo's Pan-American Exposition, 1901*. Buffalo: Buffalo & Erie County Public Library, 2001.

Lord, Walter. *The Good Years: From 1900 to the First World War*. New York: Harper Brothers, 1960.

MacDonald, Carlos F. "The Infliction of the Death Penalty by Means of Electricity." *The New York Medical Journal*, May 5, 1892.

MacLaren, Malcom. *The Rise of the Electrical Industry During the Nineteenth Century*. Princeton, NJ: Princeton University Press, 1943.

McNichol, Tom. *AC/DC: The Savage Tale of the First Standards War*. San Francisco: Jossey-Bass, 2006.

Melosi, Martin M. *Thomas A. Edison and the Modernization of America*. New York: Pearson-Longman, 2008.

Meltzer, Milton. *The Terrorists*. New York: Harper & Row, 1983.

Millard, Andre. *Edison and the Business of Innovation*. Baltimore and London: The Johns Hopkins University Press, 1990.

Miller, Scott. *The President and the Assassin: McKinley, Terror, and Empire at the Dawn of the American Century*. New York: Random House, 2011.

"Models of Niagara Falls Power Houses." *Western Electrician*, July 13, 1901.

Modern Mexico. September 1901.

Moran, Richard. *Executioner's Current: Thomas Edison, George Westinghouse, and the Invention of the Electric Chair*. New York: Vintage, 2002.

Morgan, H. Wayne (ed.) "A Civil War Diary of William McKinley." *Ohio Historical Quarterly* 69, no. 3 (July 1960).

_____. "Governor McKinley's Misfortune: The Walker-McKinley Fund of 1893." *The Ohio Historical Quarterly* 69, no. 2 (April 1960).

_____. *William McKinley and His America*. Kent, OH: Kent State University Press, 2003, repr. of 1963 edition.

Morris, Edmund. *Theodore Rex*. New York: Random House, 2001.

Muccigrosso, Robert. *Celebrating the New World: Chicago's Columbian Exposition of 1893*. Chicago: Ivan R. Dee, 1993.

Murray, Donald. "The Automatic Age: Electrical Marvels and Mechanical Triumphs at the Pan-American Exposition." *Everybody's Magazine*, October 1901.

Musicant, Ivan. *Empire by Default: The Spanish-American War and the Dawn of the American Century*. New York: Henry Holt, 1998.

Muzzey, David Saville. *James G. Blaine: A Political Idol of Other Days*. New York: Dodd, Mead, 1935.

Nevergold, Barbara A. Seals. "'Doing the Pan': The African-American Experience at the Pan-American Exposition, 1901." *Afro-Americans in New York Life and History* 28, no. 1 (January 2004).

"The Newspapers and the Exposition." *Profitable Advertising*, June 1901.

Nicholls, Henry M. "Exposition Officials Outwitted Sheriff, Kept Big 1901 Show Going." *Buffalo Evening News Magazine*, April 28, 1951.

Official Catalogue and Guide Book to the Pan-American Exposition. Buffalo, NY: Charles Ahrhart, 1901.

Offner, John L. "McKinley and the Spanish-American War." *Presidential Studies Quarterly* 34, no. 1 (March 2004).

_____. *An Unwanted War: The Diplomacy of the United States and Spain Over Cuba, 1895–1898*. Chapel Hill: University of North Carolina Press, 1992.

Olcott, Charles S. *William McKinley*. 2 vols. Boston and New York: Houghton Mifflin, 1916.

O'Toole, G. J. A. *The Spanish War: An American Epic – 1898*. New York: W. W. Norton, 1984.

Page, Walter H. "The Pan-American Exposition." *The World's Work* 2, no. 4 (August 1901).

"Pan-American Exhibit of General Electric Company." *Western Electrician*, June 15, 1901.

"Pan-American Exposition Searchlight Signals to Toronto." *Western Electrician* 29, no. 8, (July 6, 1901).

The Pan-American Magazine, various issues.

Park, Roswell. "Reminiscences of McKinley Week." *Selected Papers Surgical and Scientific*, Buffalo, NY: Julian Park, 1914.

Percy, John W. *Buffalo-Niagara Connections: A New Regional History of the Niagara Link*. Buffalo: New York Regional Press, 2007.

Peterson, Harold F. *Diplomat of the Americas: A Biography of William I. Buchanan (1852–1909)*. Albany: State University of New York Press, 1977.

Pickenpaugh, Roger. "Front Porch Campaign." *Timeline*, October-December 2007.

Pillitteri, Adele. "OR Nursing 100 Years Ago: Nursing Care of President McKinley." *Today's O.R. Nurse* 13, no. 12 (December 1991).

"Police Signaling and Telephoning at Pan-American Exposition." *Western Electrician*, November 23, 1901.

Ponder, Stephen. *Managing the Press: Origins of the Media Presidency, 1897–1933*. New York: St. Martin's, 1999.

Potter, William Warren. "The Assassination of President McKinely." *Buffalo Medical Journal*, October 1901.

"The Power Plants of the Pan-American Exposition." *The Engineering Record*. May 25, 1901.

Pratt, J. Howard. *Memories of Life on the Ridge...* N.p.: Orleans County Historical Association, 1978.

Pritchett, Henry S. "Some Recollections of President McKinley and the Cuban Intervention." *The North American Review*, March 1909.

Profitable Advertising, June 1901.

Rauchway, Eric. *Murdering McKinley: The Making of Theodore Roosevelt's America*. New York: Hill and Wang, 2003.

Register, Woody. *The Kid of Coney Island: Fred Thompson and the Rise of American Amusements*. New York: Oxford University Press, 2001.

Richardson, James D. (ed.). *A Compilation of the Messages and Papers of the Presidents*. 10 vols. Washington, D.C.: Bureau of National Literature, 1913.

Rixey, P. M., et al. "The Case of President McKinley." *American Medicine*, October 19, 1901.

_____. "Official Report on the Case of President McKinley." *Buffalo Medical Journal* 52 (1901).

Roman, Karolina. "The Impact of the Pan American Exposition of 1901 on the City of Buffalo." MA thesis, Buffalo State College, 2003.

Russ, William Adam, Jr. *The Hawaiian Republic (1894–1898) and Its Struggle to Win Annexation*. Selisgrove, PA: Susquehana University Press, 1961.

"Searchlight Illumination at Niagara." *Western Electrician*, April 27, 1901.

Sever, George F. "Electricity and Electrical Exhibits." *Pan-Am Magazine*, January 1901.

Sharlin, Harold I. "The First Niagara Falls Power Project." *The Business History Review* 35, no. 1 (Spring 1961).

Sherman, Richard. "Presidential Protection during the Progressive Era: The Aftermath of the McKinley Assassination." *The Historian* 46 (1983).

Silbey, David J. *A War of Frontier and Empire: The Philippine-American War, 1899–1902*. New York: Hill and Wang, 2007.

Silverman, William A. "Incubator Baby Side Shows." *Pediatrics* 64, No. 2 (August 1979).

Skinner, Charles S. "Story of McKinley's Assassination." *State Service*, April 1919.

Smith, H. Perry. *History of the City of Buffalo and Erie County, with Illustrations and Biographical Sketches of Some of its Prominent Men and Pioneers*. 2 vols. Syracuse, NY: D. Mason & Co., 1884.

Smith, Jack H. "Buffalo's Pan-American Exposition." *Postcard Collector*, April 1993.

Snow, Richard F. "Martin Couney." *American Heritage*, June/July 1981.

"Some Medical Aspects of the Pan American Exposition: Infant Incubators." *Buffalo Medical Journal* 57, no. 1 (August 1901)

Spencer, David R. *The Yellow Journalism: The Press and America's Emergence as a World Power*. Evanston, IL: Northwestern University Press, 2007.

Stieringer, Luther "The Evolution of Exposition Lighting." *Western Electrician*, September 21, 1901.

Stoddard, Henry L. *As I Knew Them: Presidents and Politics from Grant to Coolidge*. New York: Harper & Brothers, 1927.

Sullivan, James E. "Athletics and the Stadium." *Cosmopolitan*, September 1901.

Taliaferro, John. *All the Great Prizes: The Life of John Hay, from Lincoln to Roosevelt*. New York: Simon & Schuster, 2013.

Taylor, Frederic W. "The Horticultural Exhibits at Buffalo." *Everybody's Magazine*, October 1900.

"Telephoning the Roar of Niagara." *Western Electrician* 28, no. 24.

Thomas, Evan. *The War Lovers: Roosevelt, Lodge, Hearst, and the Rush to Empire, 1898*. New York: Little, Brown, 2010.

Thompson, Joann Marie. "The Art and Architecture of the Pan-American Exposition, Buffalo, New York." Ph.D. diss., Rutgers, The State University of New Jersey, 1980.

Trask, David. *The War with Spain in 1898*. New York: Macmillan, 1981.

Travis, Miles Everett. "Mixed Messages: Thomas Calloway and the 'American Negro Exhibit' of 1900." MA thesis, Montana State University, 2004.

Tribe, Ivan M. *Sprinkled With Coal Dust: Life and Work in the Hocking Coal Region, 1870–1900*. Athens, OH: Athens County Historical Society, 1989.

Trump, Donald L., and Edwin A. Mirano. "Dr. Roswell Park, Physician with a Vision." *New York Archives*, Summer 2009.

Turner, C. Y. "Organization as Applied to Art." *The Cosmopolitan* 31, no. 5 (September 1901).

Tyler, Alice Felt. *The Foreign Policy of James G. Blaine*. Hamden, CT: Archon, 1965, repr. of 1927 edition.

Wachhorst, Wyn. *Thomas Alva Edison: An American Myth*. Cambridge, MA: MIT Press, 1981.

Walker, John Brisben. "The City of the Future." *The Cosmopolitan*, September 1901.

Walter, Francis Joseph. "A Social and Cultural History of Buffalo, New York, 1865–1901." Ph.D. diss., Western Reserve University, 1958.

Wellman, Walter. "The Last Days of President M'Kinley [sic]." *American Monthly Review of Reviews*, October 1901.

"Westinghouse Pan-American Exhibits." *Western Electrician* 29, no. 5.

Wexner, Alice. *Emma Goldman: An Intimate Life*. New York: Pantheon, 1984.

White, Eugene Richard. "Aspects of the Pan-American Exposition." *Atlantic Monthly* 88 (July 1901).

Williams, Lillian Serece. *Strangers in the Land of Paradise: The Creation of an African American Community, Buffalo, New York 1900–1940*. Bloomington and Indianapolis: Indiana University Press, 1999.

Williams, R. Hal. *Realigning America: McKin-*

ley, Bryan, and the Remarkable Election of 1896. Lawrence: University Press of Kansas, 2010.

_____. *Years of Decision: American Politics in the 1890s.* New York: John Wiley & Sons, 1978.

Williams, Talcott. "The Pan-American Exposition: Architecture and Sculpture." *The Churchman*, May 4, 1901.

Wilson, Nelson W. "Details of President McKinley's Case." *Buffalo Medical Journal* 52 (1901).

Winter, Frank H., and Randy Liebermann. "A Trip to the Moon." *Air & Space*, October/November 1995.

Yaeger, Alexis S. "Showcasing Electricity at the Pan-Am: The Development and Display of Electricity at the Pan-American Exposition of 1901." MA thesis, Buffalo State College, 2010.

Index